From Ignorance to Insanity

(Observations of an Old Man)

By: Robert D. Ohmes

From Ignorance to Insanity
(Observations of an Old Man)
All Rights Reserved.
Copyright © 2020 R. D. Ohmes
v3.0

The opinions expressed in this manuscript are solely the opinions of the author and do not represent the opinions or thoughts of the publisher. The author has represented and warranted full ownership and/or legal right to publish all the materials in this book.

This book may not be reproduced, transmitted, or stored in whole or in part by any means, including graphic, electronic, or mechanical without the express written consent of the publisher except in the case of brief quotations embodied in critical articles and reviews.

RDO Publications

ISBN: 978-0-578-23795-4

Cover Photo © 2020 www.gettyimages.com. All rights reserved - used with permission.

PRINTED IN THE UNITED STATES OF AMERICA

Table of Contents

About the Author i
1. Preface 1
2. Bias and Indoctrination in Our Colleges and Universities. 12
3. Indoctrination Displaces Education 31
4. The Destruction of Christianity and the Support of Islam in our Public Schools 37
5. Government, Media and Entertainment Industry Bias and Hatred. 41
6. What is Socialism? What is Fanaticism? 64
7. Sanctuary Cities, Violent Crimes and Homelessness. 70
8. Global Warming/Climate Change 78
9. Our Debt Crisis 89
10. National Health Care System and other free promises of the Democrats 93
11. The Supreme Court – Originalism vs. Living Constitution National Federation of Independent Business v. Sebelius (June 28, 2012) 99
12. The Green New Deal -The Democrat plan for America. 108
13. Overview of the Destruction of our economy wrought by the Environmental and Socialist changes proposed by Democrats. 121
14. Mass shootings, gun control and the Second Amendment 136
15. The Democrat Party and its Leadership; what have they done?. 140
16. Democrat Presidential Candidates and what they are proposing. 162
17. Food for Thought. 169
18. The Democrats and the Law 195
19. Patriotism. 202
20. Black Lives Matter versus All Live Matter. 212
21. President Trump's Accomplishments in his first Two Years. 227

22. Summary of My Observations 247
23. The Trump Impeachment 273
24. Conclusions 297
25. Encore – The Corona Virus (COVID – 19) 315

About the Author

I AM NOT without a background which gives me varied experience with peoples of almost all cultures and ethnicity. And my personal life in which I have faced tragedy and failures has helped me to better understand who I am and what I believe.

I have been engaged at the highest levels in businesses around the world and in the U.S. and hold a degree in Economics from Williams College; a JD degree from Fordham University Law School (retired member of the New York Bar); and an MBA degree in Corporate Finance and Economics from the Stern School of Business. Serving as Executive Vice President, Chief Financial Officer and General Counsel of Marine Management Systems, Inc. during my last 25 business years, I have done business in: Africa, Canada, Europe, Great Britain, Greece, Japan, The Netherlands, Norway, Peru and Sweden, as well as the U.S. I often had the opportunity to visit the homes and families of many I worked with in these countries particularly Canada, Great Britain, Japan, The Netherlands, Greece, Sweden, Peru and Liberia. I have negotiated contracts and worked under contract with the U.S. Federal Government, state governments and the United Nations. I've marketed, sold and installed industrial computerized maintenance management systems for such companies as Hershey Chocolate, Coca Cola Bottling of New York, Bristol Meyers (Clairol Division) and Poland Springs Water to name a few. I negotiated the acquisition of tankers in Japan for Mobil Oil and participated in the acquisitions of many companies for ITT including Hartford Insurance and Sheraton Corp. where I played a major role in the investment in Four Seasons Hotel's first major hotel property in downtown Toronto. I've taught Economics as a professor at U.S. Merchant Marine Academy and wrote the course text entitled "Economics and Planning in Marine Transportation". I've opened offices in Greece and England, started several businesses and experienced failures. I have been an Elder at West Side Presbyterian Church in Ridgewood, New Jersey, where I taught Sunday School and Adult Bible. In Weston, Ct. I was Deacon of the Norfield Congregational Church for 14 years where I also taught Sunday School. For 10 years I coached basketball and baseball for 7th and 8th graders in Weston Connecticut.

Prior to completing college, I worked in the textile industry as a member of the United Chemical Workers Union as a freight car loader of finished goods and I worked for Alcoa Aluminum as a member of the United Steel Workers Union as a mill hand on the night shift. I also served a summer as a tennis instructor at Pocono Manor Inn in Pennsylvania, having played varsity tennis and squash at Williams College and having played #1 singles for the Ridgewood High School Tennis team in New Jersey, where I went undefeated for two and ½ years, including winning the New Jersey State singles Championship in my junior year.

Before retiring, I served as Executive Vice President, CFO, General Counsel and Director for 25 years of a small company, Marine Management Systems, Inc. with offices in Stamford, London and Athens. Prior to that I held positions as a claim's investigator at Chubb and Son, Senior Analyst and Attorney at Mobil Oil; Director of Investments at ITT; Director of Business Development at Olin Corporation and Senior Vice President and Chief financial officer of Laird Enterprises an investment management group.

My sister and I grew up at the time of World War II. We experienced blackouts, air raid drills, gas and food rationing; and saving our money to buy U.S. bonds. We watched war movies, and Pathe News film reports at the movies on Saturdays. A neighbor donated a large plot for all his neighbors to develop victory gardens, where we would congregate with our neighbors on weekends, sharing our produce and talking about the issues of the day. Our neighbors were our best friends and we shared the responsibility of shopping for each other because of the gas rationing. We recycled tin cans, paper, and bottles. (There was no plastic). Friendship, trust, sharing, caring were the words that meant so much to us. We did not experience the hatred, vilification and deceit that is so prevalent today.

In school, we read from the Bible each morning, said the pledge of allegiance in the class room and we purchased stamps from the teacher to place in our War Bond redemption books, which we turned in when we had $18.75.

We had no TV; the radio, newspapers and the movie theaters were our sources for current events. And the reporters, gave us the news, honestly and without bias. We trusted them. We learned about the dangers of alcoholism from the 1945 movie: "Lost Weekend"; about the cruelties of anti-Judaism from the movie: "Gentlemen's Agreement"; We learned about how family, friends and honest toil make a wonderful life from the 1946 movie "It's a Wonderful Life" and we learned about the horrors of drug addiction from the 1955 movie: "The Man with the Golden Arm". We didn't have anyone extolling the virtues of marijuana and considering it a source of "joy" for the people.

At home our family ate dinner together and we had conversations about our day in school and sometimes about current events. Our parents were interested in us and what we did. I was very fortunate that my parents did not drink or smoke and I never heard a cuss word or foul language out of either of them. My sister and I went to Sunday school every Sunday. (There really wasn't anything else to do). There was no ball playing allowed until 1 o'clock on Sundays, the stores were all closed, there was no TV and cell phones and video games did not exist.

One Christmas when I was quite young, my dad gave me a statue of three monkeys sitting on a tree branch. One had its hands covering it eyes; one with its hands covering its ears and one with its hands covering its mouth. I said: "oh see no evil, hear no evil, speak no evil", pretty much the standard accepted meaning of the statue. But Dad taught me another meaning. He said: " take your hands from your eyes, not so that you can see , but so that you can perceive; take your hands from your ears not so that you can hear, but so that you can listen and take your hands from your mouth not so that you can speak but so you can discuss". How much more meaningful it is to think of the three monkeys in this way. And yet this meaning is lost on so many of us.

When I graduated from High School, our yearbook had individual pictures of each graduate. Underneath the pictures, along with a brief resume of what the classmate had done during his three years in high school, was a short saying that was to describe the classmate in some way. The student year book staff had provided this quote for me: "***Give me a man with a mind of his own***". I remember my mother wasn't sure whether this was a compliment. But I was proud of it.

One Sunday afternoon in the fall of 1955 or 1956, a group of my fraternity brothers gathered in the living room of our fraternity house. Sunday noon meals were always special. After the meal most of the fraternity brothers had returned to their rooms to study and some went to the Williams Inn to watch the Sunday NFL football game. We didn't have TV in the fraternity houses or anywhere on campus in the 1950's. There were about 10 or so of us and one brother asked all of us: "If you could go back to any time and meet one person who would that be and why? "There were typical answers that one might expect such as: Plato, Shakespeare, Abraham Lincoln and George Washington and others, all good choices and well deserved. When it came to be my turn I said: "Jesus Christ". I said regardless of one's faith or religion Jesus provided us with guidelines and understanding as to how we as human beings should live together in peace and harmony. He told us to "love one another"; "Do unto others as you would have them do unto you"; "love your neighbor" and to "judge not that you be not judged". At the time I did not understand the full significance of this last saying, documented in Matthew 7:1. It was only after reading Jesus' further explanation appearing in Matthew 7: 3-5 many years later that I fully understood what Jesus meant. This appears as one of the quotations I open with in Chapter 1. Jesus also taught the gatherings with parables like the story of the good Samaritan. The memory is vivid because the answer I gave that day has stayed with me all my life and I still, above all others, would like to meet and talk with Jesus.

I do not mean to portray that the period I grew up in was Idyllic. We had Pearl Harbor, World War II, the Holocaust; the use of the atom bombs against civilians in the cities of Hiroshima and Nagasaki; detainment camps for Japanese Americans; segregation in the South; the assassination of President Kennedy and his brother Attorney General Robert Kennedy; the Assassination of Martin Luther King; and the McCarthy witch-hunts against the entertainment industry and those who believed in Communism. But even with all that, the level of hatred and violence that exists today was not as prevalent in America in those early years of my life. There was much more bringing us together than tearing us apart.

In the mid and late 1960's I was fortunate to work closely with Harold Geneen, Chairman, President and CEO of ITT. He was probably the most renowned businessman of his time. He was best known for acquiring and managing in one corporation a wide variety of businesses. After one meeting in New York City Headquarters of his senior executives from all parts of the world, Geneen sent out the following memo entitled simply "FACTS" (excerpted here):

There is no word in the English language that more strongly conveys the intent of incontrovertibility (i.e. final and reliable reality) then the word FACT.

However, no word is more honored by its breach in actual usage. There are: "Accepted facts; "Apparent Facts"; "Assumed Facts"; "Reported Facts" and even "Hoped for Facts". In most cases these are not facts at all. What we must strive for are "Unshakeable Facts".

I have been married for 61 years, to my wonderful wife Lynne, my best friend and companion. We had three sons. Our oldest, Larry was killed in 1991 by a drunk driver, who ran off the road and slammed into Larry and my youngest son Scott, while they were changing a tire. It was around 9:30 P.M. on May 13, 1991, just outside Washington, D.C heading North in Maryland. My wife and I were there to witness this tragedy. My oldest son, Larry, died right before our eyes. After 10 days in a comma, our son Scott miraculously came back to life, although physical scars from the tragedy remain. The strong bond between Lynne and me, helped us endure this terrible, horrible night, although our lives would never be the same. This tragedy has helped me to become more introspective; more concerned with what I believe and seeking a better understanding of what is true. I also feel sorrow and anguish for all those mothers and fathers, sisters and brothers and families who have lost their loved ones due to some senseless horrible act of violence or some other horrible occurrence. Whether it is a shooting massacre, a drive-by shooting, a drug overdose, suicide or loss of life in service to the country, there is so much suffering for the survivors. My family and what have happened to them have been the most important motivators of my decision to write what I have observed and what I believe. There will be many who disagree with what I have written and some will even be upset and even angry with me. I can only hope that this challenges one to examine their own beliefs rather than think too unkindly of me.

I can only wish for the reader that you will always judge for yourself, making your decisions objectively and based on facts and you will do all right.

Robert Ohmes – July 4, 2020

CHAPTER 1

Preface

THE TITLE OF the Book "From Ignorance to Insanity" is silent about the two important ingredients or way-points that takes us along the path to insanity. We all start our lives in total ignorance. To the newborn baby, he or she has no knowledge, no understanding of the world about him. Certainly, the child has no knowledge of the world, economics, politics, or even a language with which to converse and dialogue. His or her ideas are formed over the years by indoctrination; first by parents, then maybe in church and also in the schools he or she will attend. Little if any opportunity is given to the child to formulate his or her own ideas. He or she is told what to believe, what to do and even what is right and wrong. The so-called formative years from birth to adulthood are the years where indoctrination prevails for most of us. The indoctrination can be good or bad, dependent upon whether the indoctrinators are truly compassionate, caring, loving, knowledgeable and wise or are they consumed by hate; refuse to dialogue and seek to continue to indoctrinate with hate and vitriol. Unfortunately, too many of the people not just in the U.S., but throughout the word have been so indoctrinated by hate that they refuse to even consider the possible value of treating everyone with love, respect and understanding. And they refuse to admit that they may be wrong. It is when hate becomes the catalyst for all of one's belief, that we finally arrive at insanity.

Insanity has been often defined as someone who keeps doing the same thing over and over again expecting different results. Look at the major cities in our country, all run by Democrats. Their policies have not changed in decades, but their cities just become more devastated. High crime rates, high murder rates, high homelessness, abuse of police, decriminalization of drugs, and even decriminalizing some crimes such as shop-lifting are the signatures of Democrat rule. Look at how New York City has deteriorated with the first Democrat mayor since David Dinkins. New York had become a safe, clean and desirable city to live in during the twenty years under Republican Mayors Giuliani and Bloomberg. But now citizens are leaving in droves to find less crime ridden and less dirty places to live. And the Mayor de Blasio says nothing about the riots, or hoodlums pouring pales of water on police, vandalizing police cars and carrying posters villifying police.

Ask yourself, what have the Democrat leaders done for you in the past 3 years? There is not one thing the Democrats have paid attention to, or tried to improve since Donald Trump has taken office. Three years and still their one and only focus has been their attempt to impeach President, with all the hatred and vitriol they can muster. Ask yourself, what exactly has President Trump done that is a crime or is deserving of impeachment? The Mueller investigation went on for 2.5 years at a cost of over $40 million and President Trump was found blameless of collusion. The Democrats had to find something else and they came up with a mundane July 2019 telephone conversation between President Trump and the Ukrainian President. This is now the Democrats sole focus. Why is that? The Democrats have nothing else to offer its constituents. Therefore, the only alternative is to drive President Trump from office, even though our country and our citizens have fared very well under his administration.

There are a number of observations or teachings that I have come across in my lifetime, which help me to form my beliefs. Here are a few of them:

"The unexamined life in not worth living" – Socrates, circa 400 B.C.E (I may modify this to say that an unexamined belief is not worth having).

"So, whatever you wish that man do to you, do so to them" Jesus - Matthew 7:12, Luke 6:31 – THE GOLDEN RULE

"You shall love your neighbor as yourself" Jesus - Matthew 22:39 (also see Old Testament, Leviticus 19:18)

"Why do you look at the speck of sawdust in your brother's eye and pay no attention to the plank in your own eye? You hypocrite, first take the plank out of your own eye and then you will see clearly to remove the speck from your brother's eye." - Jesus – Matthew 7:3-5

"He that is without sin among you, let him first cast a stone at her". – John 8: 7

"He that troubles his own house will inherit the wind and the fool will be the servant of the wise of heart". Old Testament, Proverb 11:29 Circa 1000 B.C.E.

"Pride (hubris) goeth before destruction and a haughty spirit before a fall" Proverbs 16:18

"Being in a minority does not make you mad. There is Truth and there is Untruth and if you cling to the Truth even against the whole world you are not mad." George Orwell, "1984"

"Power is in tearing human minds to pieces and putting them together in new shapes of your own choosing", George Orwell, "1984".

" My objective in life is to dethrone God and destroy capitalism" – Karl Marx

Whether one is Christian, Jew, Atheist, Agnostic or follower of some other religion, there are words of wisdom, truth and guidance and words of caution, that help direct us toward how we should live with each other as human beings. These words of wisdom are often found in the teachings of Jesus and

Preface

the philosophy of Socrates and Plato. In this work, I reflect on the stark reality of events that portray just how far we have strayed from wisdom and love to anger and hate. Even though there is so many encouraging accomplishments in our country that we should be genuinely proud of including the lowest unemployment levels in many years and the related improvement in the employment of minorities; outstanding economic growth in the GNP; vast improvement in the stock market; significant wage gains; significant tax reductions for most; a beginning of dialogue with nations unfriendly toward us; a growing independence from the need for foreign oil and the return of manufacturing to our country, nevertheless these are sad times.

We are living in some of the most discouraging times in my lifetime, which has spanned some very bad periods; the Depression, World War II, the Korean War, the Cuban/Russia nuclear threat, the Cold War, the assassinations of President Kennedy, Bobby Kennedy and Martin Luther King; Vietnam, Segregation and the associated racial tensions, 9/11/2001, and a number of serious economic downturns. There have been protests, anger, divisiveness but ultimately reason and justice seemed to have triumphed, though maybe not perfectly.

Today we face totally new challenges. Anger has turned to hatred and with hatred there is no chance for dialogue. Even where there is no hatred, good people, refuse to listen or discuss.

Liberty, Justice and Wisdom. They are portrayed on the cover of this book. These three are so essential to the way that we think and act and so necessary for us to live in peace and harmony with each other. Yet they exist in only small quantities, not just in the United States, but throughout the world. There is one further necessary ingredient and that is **Humility.** If we could come up with a potion to replace the hate and vindictiveness in the world, we would combine in a crucible the ingredients of liberty, justice and wisdom and also sprinkle in a large dose of humility. Hate would be gone; compromises would be forth-coming and we would have harmony among all people and the door to dialectics would be opened.

When we refuse to think for ourselves; when we listen and passively accept everything our educators, our government, our media, our entertainers tell us, when indoctrination takes precedence over education, we are doomed to exist in a continued state of fear, terror and violence. And that is what our leaders, educators, entertainers and media personalities seem to want in their unending quest for power. We are expected to listen to them and accept what they say, without question. And the more we allow ourselves to be indoctrinated, the more excessive will become the indoctrination and the less important will become education. And eventually, liberty, justice, and wisdom disappear altogether and the World as depicted in Orwell's "1984" will become a reality. And make no mistake, this has actually happened for a brief time in the 1930's and 1940's when Hitler and his Third Reich imposed his will with its accompanying horrors on the people of Germany, most particularly German Jews.

The rise to power of Hitler and the attending Holocaust was a perfect case study of what happens when people do not think for themselves. When collectively we do not examine our beliefs, we are subject to being led into chaos, tyranny and a state of existence well described in Orwell's "1984" and

From Ignorance to Insanity

Hitler's Germany.

One of the current popular conflicts exists between the "Pro-life" and "Pro-choice" advocates.

And the recently appointed Supreme Court Justices Neil Gorsuch and Brett Kavanaugh, had been under constant attack by the left who are predominately "pro-choice". Their outcry was that Gorsuch and Kavanaugh would be the votes necessary to overturn "Roe v Wade". How many of those who so vehemently oppose Kavanaugh because of his supposed threat to "Roe V. Wade" have actually read the case? And further, how many have read the very important companion case of Planned Parenthood v. Casey, that significantly modifies Roe V. Wade?

And for those defending Palestine against Israel, how many of you have read the Charter of Hamas, the majority and ruling party of Palestine that calls for the killing of all Jews? And how many have read the Qur'an before taking a position on Islam?

How many who support the "Black Lives Matter" movement have actually studied the history of slavery in Africa before, during and after slavery in America? How many have discovered that Black African tribes captured and enslaved their fellow blacks, placed them in yolks and chains, herded them across Africa, where millions died along the way and delivered them to Arab slave traders, who promptly castrated the men and raped the women. And this occurred in the 8th century, long before the slave trade to the new world. Or how many have noted the on-going slavery of blacks by blacks in the majority of countries in Africa and the atrocities that Africans still perform on their fellow Africans? Or how many have studied the history of slavery since the civil war and find that it has been consistently the Democrats who have mistreated blacks and forced them to live as second-class citizens. It is the Republican President, Abraham Lincoln who emancipated the slaves. It is the Supreme Court of the United States controlled by 7 Democrats who voted unanimously in the Dred Scott case, that the rule was to be "once a slave, always a slave" and the 2 dissenting opinions were Republicans. This was the decision that set the anti-slavery Republicans against the pro-slavery Democrats and would be the catalyst that led to the Civil War. And it was the Democrat South that fired on Fort Sumter to start the War to sustain their right to have slaves. And it was the predominately Republican North that volunteered to fight for the freedom of the slaves, 600,000 of whom were killed or wounded to attain freedom for those enslaved. And it was a radical Democrat, John Wilkes Booth who assassinated Abraham Lincoln. And it was the Democrats after the Civil War that introduced the Jim Crow laws, intending to keep Blacks forever segregated as to where they lived, worshipped, attended schools or limit the jobs they could have. And it was the Democrats that started the Ku Klux Klan that would hang thousands of blacks, destroy their homes, their churches and perform all sorts of atrocities against them. And it was a Democrat George Wallace who ran on a promise to keep blacks forever segregated. And it was President Woodrow Wilson, a vocal defender of the Ku Klux Klan, who purposely kept black Federal employees segregated.

From 650 Common Era (C.E.) to 1900, approximately 20 million Africans were enslaved by Arab traders and 8 million died on route, according to Dr. John Azumah in his book: "The Legacy of Arab-

Islam in Africa". Historians estimated that millions of abducted Africans never made it to the slave ships. Most died on the march to the sea, chained, yoked and shackled by their African captors long before they laid eyes on a white slave trader.

The atrocities of the Arabs toward the blacks after they had been delivered by the African slave traders to them included castrating male slaves and raping the women. About 6 out of every 10 boys bled to death from this practice on the way to the market, but the high price paid for eunuchs on the market made the practice profitable. The treatment of African women was no better as they were targeted for rape by Arab slave owners. A Muslim slaveholder was entitled by law to the sexual enjoyment of his slave women. The abuse of African women by Arabs would continue for nearly 1200 years.

In October 2013, the Los Angeles Times noted that African countries dominate a new global index of slavery with as many as 38 of 54 African nations still supporting slavery, most notably: Benin, Burundi, Central African Republic. Chad, Congo, Ethiopia, Eritrea, Ivory Coast, Gambia, Gabon, Madagascar, Mali, Mauritania, Niger, Senegal, South Sudan, Togo and West Africa.

We turn to what African leaders today have to say about the Atlantic slave trade. Ugandan President Yoweri Museveni said: "African chiefs were the ones waging war on each other, capturing their own people and selling them. If anyone should apologize it should be the African chiefs". King Kpoyo-Zoynme Hakpon IV of Benin to a black audience in Alabama in 2013: "I want to apologize for the role my ancestors played in the slave trade". At the Civil Rights Conference in Nigeria in 2009 the Congress concluded: "We cannot continue to blame the white men; as Africans, particularly the traditional rulers are not blameless…. It would be logical, reasonable and humbling, if African traditional rulers accept blame and formally apologize for their collaborative and exploitive slave trade". Former Ghana diplomat to the U.N., Kofi Awoonor, as early as 1994 said: "There is a shadow over Africa…dealing with our guilt and denial of our role in the slave trade. We too are blameworthy in what was essentially one of the most heinous crimes in human history". Finally, Senegal's President, Abdoulaye Wade urged Europeans, Americans and Africans to acknowledge publicly and teach openly about their (the blacks) shared responsibility for the Atlantic slave trade.

Yet the Democrats in their distortion of the truth would have us believe that the Republicans are the racists. The Democrats talk of reparations for the American ancestors of black slaves for past slavery, which they imply is the fault of Republicans. There are no Democrats that step to the plate telling the African Americans that for over 100 years from the time the Africans were freed, the Democrats have made life hell for the Africans. How can any African American believe that the Democratic party is the party of the African American, if he knows the truth?

How many of us claim to be Christians and fail to live by the most important of the teachings of Jesus? When we listen to the abusive rhetoric or immoral behavior of many of our political leaders; our media representatives; our entertainers, our educators, and even our clergy, where are Christ's guides to human behavior such as: "love thy neighbor as thyself"; "Do unto others as you would have done unto you", "judge not that you be not judged"; even "love your Enemies". To be a Christian is to follow the teachings of Christ and love not hate was a key focus of Jesus' teachings. Yet hatred is rampant in our country and the masses respond to it thoughtlessly and without questioning. Why do so many accept hate so readily?

How many of you have looked at the course catalogue of your College or University? Are you aware of the indoctrination that is taking place at your son's or daughter's college or university? Or how familiar are you with the curriculum in the elementary and high schools your children attend? Are you aware they are being taught to chant Muslim prayers, to dress as Muslims, view Pillars of Islam posters in their hallways, learn certain passages of Islam and have lessons on Islam even as early as 3rd grade, while at the same time any teaching or expression of Judeo/Christian theology is prohibited?

And while many may argue that we are experiencing global warming/climate change, how have you confirmed that it is attributable to CO_2? I'll review global warming from a factual basis in some detail.

Then there is the Federal income taxes the Liberal left will have you pay. The Democrats will repeal all the tax cuts that have been provided by the Republicans both personal and corporate and even double them in some instances. We must not forget how Nancy Pelosi informed all of us that the tax cuts were only "crumbs". Well most of us have just paid taxes for the first year under the new tax rates. The average family making $74,000 per year, has $2,300 more money to spend, thanks to the new tax rates and the average single taxpayer making $40,000 has $1,300 more to spend each year. These are the Nancy Pelosi "crumbs". And the reduction of the corporate tax rates has made the United States more competitive with the rest of the world, where before our country had the highest corporate tax rates in the world. The Democrats would not only take away these increases in "take-home" pay from the individuals and families, but they plan to pour on more taxes and we will show that the increases won't even begin to pay for the insane programs they wish to undertake. The increase in corporate taxes will not only see a massive exodus of jobs overseas, but it will also result in the increase in the cost of goods and services for both individuals and families. And, with jobs moving back overseas, there will be massive layoffs and unemployment will rise to new levels. This is what the Democrats hold in store for us.

How many of you have examined major socialist countries of the world to understand how poorly their economies are doing and how oppressed the people of those countries are? We find that where there is socialism there is a loss of freedom. Look at how China, Russia, North Korea, Cuba, Venezuela, Syria and Iran treat their people. Look at how Hitler and his socialist regime treated the German people during WWII. And right after World War II, compare the economic and social well-being of the people of East Germany under Russia's control with West Germany and its economic and social freedom. And how, did all these socialist regimes come into power? By purges of adversaries and submitting its people to a police state. The common denominator of all these countries is obtaining power through socialism. The socialist political system assigns all rights and powers to the state, including the right to life, the right to property ownership and the control over all means of production. The only way to obtain such power is to: 1) vilify and destroy your adversaries, 2) create unrest and riots within the country, 3) establish control over all media and use it to spread lies and falsehoods about your adversaries; 4) take control over education, 5) confiscate your weapons, 6) seize control over private property; 7) confront, flaunt and disregard existing laws; 8) attack, reinterpret and there-by render ineffective the U.S. Constitution; 9) create high levels of unemployment to help create a more dependent welfare state; 10) allow open borders so even more people will become dependent on the socialist welfare state; 11) denigrate Christianity and Judaism as part of program to defeat the rights assigned to every American by the First amendment, namely: Freedom of religion, speech, press and assembly and 12) Affirming the right to abortion at any time and even after birth as part of their Socialist manifesto, thereby taking the first step by the socialist state to determine the right of life and death for its citizens. This unlimited support for abortion, will make the creation of "death panels" under a socialist national health system, more acceptable and less morally repugnant to the people of this country.

The Electoral College - We have hatred and vitriol running rampant in our country since Hillary Clinton lost the election. Whether Democrat leaders, the media, the entertainers or our educators, so many, along with Hillary keep telling us that she won the popular vote and therefore should be President. It is a theme that has been pounded into us again and again over the past three years by the liberal left and they demand that specific provisions in Article II Section 1 of the Constitution should be removed.

Hillary Clinton and her fellow Democrats continuously emphasize that she won the popular vote by 2.9 million votes, yet conveniently ignore Article II of the Constitution that enumerates the procedure for voting, which includes the electoral college. Of course, the Democrats want to eliminate the Electoral College which has been part of our election procedures for over 225 years. Here are some observations regarding the electoral college, that may help the reader to better understand how vital the electoral college is to our method of electing Presidents.

There are 3,141 counties in the United States. President Trump won the majority vote in 3,084 counties. Hilary Clinton won the popular vote in only 57 counties. The State of New York has 62 counties. Trump won 46 of the counties and Hillary Clinton 16. New York City consists of five counties, namely Bronx, Brooklyn, Manhattan, Queens and Richmond. Trump won only Richmond. In these five counties alone, Hillary Clinton received 2 million more votes than President Trump. They accounted for her winning the popular vote for the entire country. These five counties of New York City comprise only 319 square miles of the total 3,797,000 square miles that makes up the United States. What an election by popular vote alone would mean for our country is up to the reader to decide, but as you read this book, you will hear some reasons and facts as to why doing away with the electoral college would lead to serious harm if not destruction of our country.

These are only a few of the observations that I will bring up in this book. We need to restore rational dialogue in our government chambers, in our public schools and in our colleges and universities in our media and in our entertainment industry. Just reacting to the diatribes from the left is not enough.

We must find a way to bring back serious objective discussion and debate. I do not know why our media, our entertainment industry, our educators and the liberal left have chosen hatred as their motivation for what they say or do. There is a lack of objectivity. A lack of civility.

Today, searching for the truth is not paramount and wisdom and justice are no longer goals. No one can deny the bias that we find in most of our media. Even a Harvard study tells us so. No one can argue there is not a lot of hatred in our liberal left entertainment industry. And no one can deny that our educators for the most part have become nothing more than left leaning indoctrinators.

The indoctrination is working. Whether liberal or conservative, neither side is all good or all bad. If we could all realize this, that would be a good place to start. How can one learn, if those with differing opinions are unwilling to discuss the differences objectively, logically and with the facts?

Whether our beliefs are spiritual or political, we better know what we believe, why we believe it and why it is worth defending. I will address many of my concerns that have arisen in my lifetime, many only recently. Our society and way of life will only get worse if we remain complacent and apathetic, and do not challenge our politicians, educators, the media and entertainers to start telling us the truth and stop their spreading of vitriol and hatred. I so wish and pray that all hatred disappears from Earth and that we can get along in peace and harmony with all mankind regardless of race, religion or political persuasion.

I am concerned over the status of our education in America. We see indoctrination at all levels revealing a strong liberal left bias and encouragement of censorship. We see violent demonstrations on many campuses by students. We see that 95% of our college educators advocating liberal left doctrines and virtually censoring any dialogue from the Right.

I am concerned with the hatred and bias in our media, entertainment industry and also among our government representatives who ignore their responsibility to serve all people, not just the group supporting their political agenda. "Multiculturism"; "Assimilation; and "Political Correctness" have become more than just catch words. They have become major themes of philosophical thought, imposed on us, under duress and in instances under threat of violence.

For three years we have witnessed the every-increasing hatred from our Democrat leaders, our media, our entertainment industry and our educators against President Donald Trump and Conservative Republicanism. If we examine what the Democrats have contributed to our society over the past three years it has been nothing but hatred. All the Democrats call for is impeach the president. For three years prominent Democrat congressmen have called for special investigations and hearings open to the public so that they can better spew their hatred and vitriol. And now, on the eve of the election they propose radical socialism to replace Democracy, just to get rid of our President even though this will destroy America.

Hatred is a terrible thing. You can't turn it on an off like a water spicket. You cannot immensely hate and at the same time truly love. And if you hate, you must indoctrinate your families, your children and your grandchildren to hate also. Because if you don't, they will sooner or later ask you why do you hate so much? This frenzy of hate has led our democrat leaders to propose policies that any rational human being, will tell you will destroy our country. And the same hatred has been embraced in our media, our entertainment industry and in our educational institutions. Once hatred has taken over our minds and hearts, it is very difficult to turn around. We saw how hatred was fostered by the Third Reich under Hitler. Hitler, with the help of the media led by the minister of propaganda was able to get the German people not only to hate Jews, but to look upon them as less than human and therefore it was all right to kill them. How many times have we heard emanating from the left that Trump should be impeached, that he is guilty of treason, which is punishable by death? How many times has the assassination of President Trump been called for by the Democrat socialist leaders and their supporters, either by cutting off his head; hanging him from the highest tree; blowing up the White House, knifing him to death, assassinating him like Lincoln, or destroying him and his family one way or another. So many have gravitated toward the hatred and vitriol of the liberal left. How is this hatred going to make your lives better? How are any of the polices proposed by the left going to help you? How in the world can any of these policies be implemented? They can't. The Democrats won't tell you that it is impossible to afford any of them. They know this so they are just lying to you to get your support. We will explore this hatred in depth and just how it will lead to the ruin of your lives.

Multiculturalism, Assimilation, Political Correctness

Multiculturalism on its face could be considered a good thing to the extent that it builds toleration of the beliefs of others. It becomes a terrible thing when the majority are forced to go beyond toleration and actually accept and condone the beliefs of others, even when they are at such odds with our own.

Assimilation is defined as the process of adopting or adjusting to the culture of a group or nation, or the state of being so adopted. (i.e. the assimilation of immigrants into American life). The definition has been expanded in practice, so that it no longer is the requirement of the immigrant to adapt to the culture of America, but rather, Americans must assimilate into the culture of the immigrants. Assimilation and Multiculturalism go hand in hand, requiring America to change its philosophical, religious and cultural beliefs to be equal to and no better nor worse than those of immigrants, who are welcomed to our shores and who are given refuge from the persecution in their own countries.

Political correctness has been defined as conforming to a belief that language and practices which could offend personal sensibilities should be eliminated. This certainly sounds "Orwellian" and strikes at the heart of the First Amendment to our Constitution. The idea behind political correctness, like multiculturalism and assimilation seems to be a good thing until we examine the extent to which it has been applied. No better example of political correctness then the Democrats, during the Obama Administration, refusing to use the term "Radical Islamic Terrorism" or to acknowledge that there was a "radical Islamic culture" bent on destroying all who refuse to accept Allah as their God. Some recent amazing examples of political correctness include:

1. Government workers in Seattle have been told that they should no longer use the words "citizen" and "brown bag" because they are potentially offensive to some.
2. A professor at Ball State University was banned from ever mentioning the concept of intelligent design because it would supposedly "violate the academic integrity" of the course he was teaching
3. An elementary school in North Carolina ordered a six-year-old to remove the word "God" from a tribute she wrote to her grandfather.
4. A Florida Atlantic University student that refused to stomp on the name of Jesus was banned from the class.
5. At a high school in California, five students were sent home from school for wearing shirts that displayed the American flag on the Mexican Holiday "Cinco de Mayo".
6. A school in Seattle renamed its Easter Eggs, "Spring spheres" to avoid causing offence to people who do not celebrate Easter.
7. Brown University – bans speech making people feel angry, impotent or disenfranchised.
8. Colby College – banned any speech leading to anyone losing his or her self-esteem
9. Bryn Mawr College – banned suggestive looks.
10. Haverford College – banned unwelcomed flirtation
11. University of Connecticut - banned inappropriate laughter

Political correctness is based on the non-existent right, not to be offended. It has become a form of censorship. If we think about it, it seems that only the statements or actions emanating from the conservative right are considered "politically incorrect".

The combination of multiculturalism, assimilation and political correctness is insidious. On the surface it would appear to have some merit. But when carried to an extreme, which includes: censorship; deprivation of freedom of religion; forcing one to subordinate his beliefs to those contrary to your own; the loss of rights; the elimination of certain privileges and the subjugation to violent attacks, they have gone too far. The combination has melded into a power force that is leading our country into secularization and away from traditional moral values. With it has come anger, hate and violence, that permeates our society today; not just here in the United States, but all over the Western World.

There will be some, who read this who have been so indoctrinated by radical socialism, maybe even for most of their lives, that they may stop reading here. This is where some humility and wisdom come in. Humility requires one to admit that they may be wrong. Humility requires one to read or listen to things they do not want to hear or do not want to understand. Wisdom requires that we seek to learn the facts, objectively determine what is true or false and with humility acknowledge that sometimes one may be wrong.

So do not take what is said here on face value. I may not have all the facts and in some instances I may be wrong. Challenge what I have said in this book, but do so objectively and without hatred and malice.

Preface

I too have bias and what I have stated herein, may not be totally objective. I can be faulted for this, but my fears are genuine. I am concerned for my country not from destruction from external sources, not from global warming, but from unmitigated power getting into the wrong hands and destroying our country from within. We are at historic cross-roads; unlike any we have ever experienced. We are facing the demise of our country and the very foundations that it has been built upon.

The Socialist Democrats are making many promises to you: 1) free education; 2) forgiveness of debt; 3) guaranteed income for life for every man, woman and child; 4) free medical; 5) a country with no CO_2 emissions; 6) reparations for blacks for the past sins of slavery; 7) freedom for everyone and anyone to come to the U.S. and receive a guranteed income and 8) defunding, if not abolishing our police departments across the country.

Well known author Andrew Watts, has written a series of interesting fictional books entitled "The War Planners" The five book series deals with how China has developed a scheme to take over America and it pits a beautiful but evil Chinese girl, who has gained citizenship in the U.S. and subsequently risen to a high level position in the CIA against a talented ex-Navy Seal, who is employed in special ops. The Plan is for China to take over the U.S. and establish its totalitarian government for the good of the people of America. State control would replace all freedom and private rights in the second book, entitled "The War Stage" the evil woman describes Democracy to the ex-Navy Seal. She is describing Democracy as it would be under socialism. "**Democracies let voters choose politicians that create unsupportable entitlement programs. These politicians** (Socialist Democrats, my words), **know better, but they promise their constituents the moon, because it gets them elected. By the time the programs fail or bury the nation in debt, the politicians who put us there are long gone…… the proper period of performance measurement does not fit within the same time frame as the voting cycle….They** (the voters) **do not have the wisdom to make the right choice.**

The ex-navy seal responds: "**I don't want to live in a world where a dictator tells me how many children I can have**"

Nor do I want to live in a country where I can't travel by air; where I can't own guns; where I can't eat meat; where I can't own a car; where I can't choose my own doctor; where the state dictates what I can read; where the state makes the decision whether I can live or die; where my grand-children are not educated but indoctrinated; where abortion is allowed at any stage for any reason; where my right to own a business is curtailed or totally eliminated; where I have to pay most of my income for taxes to support those who refuse to work and provide free college education to everyone; where I have to pay for the medical health, welfare, education, housing and even income for illegal immigrants. This is the legacy planned by the Socialist left and it is adhered to by all the Democrat candidates currently running for President.

President John F. Kennedy, in his inaugural address on January 20, 1961 said: "**And so my fellow Americans ask not what your country can do for you – ask what you can do for your country**" I hope the reader will keep this in mind as he reads this book.

CHAPTER 2

Bias and Indoctrination in Our Colleges and Universities.

A WASHINGTON TIMES Study published October 6, 2016, confirms what has long been known; that Conservative professors are vastly outnumbered by their liberal counterparts by a factor of 12 to 1. In September 2016, the Economic Journal Watch in a study of faculty voter registration at 40 leading universities, found Democrats outnumber Republicans 3,623 to 314 or a ratio of 11.5 to 1. The History Department is by far the least Conservative friendly department, where liberals outnumber conservatives by a 33.5 to 1 ratio. This stands in stark contrast to a 1968 study which put the Democrat to Republican ratio in the History department at 2.7 to 1.

When age is taken into consideration, the ratio of Democrats to Republicans among professors over 65 is 10 to 1, but this balloons to 22.7 to 1 among professors under the age of 36.

A further study by the Washington Times in October 2015 showed that 99% of the professors at the top 50 liberal arts colleges gave campaign donations to the Democratic party candidate.

Is there a correlation between left leaning liberal professors, along with their college and university administrators and the riots suppresing free speech on campuses? And is there a correlation between the growth of political correctness and the unsubstantiated attribution of racism, sexism, Islamaphobia and bigotry to Conservatives?

Professor Watchlist.org helps to demonstrate just how serious a problem is caused on our college and university campuses, when there is such an imbalance and bias in our education. Professor watchlist.org provides a database of College and University professors, which is intended to express and document radical professors across the country who have been engaged in anti-American and leftist behavior. While Professorwatchlist.org believes that professors have the right to say whatever they wish, students, alumni and parents should be made aware of the radicalism that has been institutionalized in our colleges and universities. So far, Professorwatchlist.org has identified over 200 professors at approximately 133 Colleges and universities throughout the country. I suggest the reader research

Professorwatchlist.org themselves, but here are some that are shared to help the reader understand just how serious a problem we have on the campuses of our schools of higher learning. Remember, most of these schools have been involved one way or another in stifling free speech where conservatism is concerned. But of more concern is how colleges and universities while quelling free speech and conservatism actually promote radical liberalism.

1. **Harvard University** – Danelle Allen "The rise of Trump is just like the rise of Hitler". And Mark Tushnet, Law Professor asked liberals "to begin treating Christians and Conservatives like Nazi". It is statements like this made so often by the liberal left that go unchallenged.

2. **Yale University** – Jason Kilhefner, Director of Academic Integrity Programs, called the Constitution, propaganda

3. **Princeton** – Peter Singer believes that children should be able to be aborted up to two years old.

4. **Cornell University** – Dr. Andrew Little said that while hiring more Republican professors would increase diversity of thought, it would lower the quality of professors on campus calling Republicans "anti-intellectual".

5. **Columbia University** – Kathy Boudin, despite having a lengthy criminal record, a convicted murderer and a member of Bill Ayer's far left radical and domestic terrorist group "The Weather Underground", had no trouble in finding a job, teaching at Columbia. Ms. Boudin had been sentenced to 20 years to life in prison after pleading guilty to second degree murder in association with the 1981 Brinks Armored Car robbery. She had assisted in ending the life of three people. Released in 2003, she landed the teaching position at Columbia in 2008.

6. **Boston University** – Dr. Saida Arundy, a professor at Brown stated – "Every week I commit myself to not spending a dime in white-owned businesses and every year I find it nearly impossible".

7. **Emory University** – Dr. George Yancy – Professor of Philosophy said: "Nothing says "Merry Christmas" like a letter to white Americans calling them racist. Make no mistake; if you are white, you are a racist." Yancy further called white America to examine the "racist poison that is inside you and he means all white Americans."

8. **Kent State University** – Dr. Julio Cesar Pinto, who faced investigation by the FBI for connections to ISIS, is strongly anti-Israel and calls Israel: "The spiritual heir to Nazism". A 2002 eulogy, written by Pinto praised Palestinian terrorist Ayer al-Akharas. (Ayer al-Akharas was the third and youngest Palestinian female suicide bomber, who, at the age of 18 killed herself and two Israeli civilians on March 29, 2002 by detonating explosives belted to her body).

9. **Brown University** – Matthew Guteri criticized University of Chicago for opposing "Safe Places" saying: "It is not our job to make intellectual noise -a raucous debate, a clashing set of ideas, a heartful back and forth, just because we can".

10. **Dartmouth** - Eng-Beng Lin teaches Gender and Queer theory classes. He blames Conservative

guns and Islamophobia for the Orlando massacre when Omar Mateen killed 49 people in a gay night club.

11. **University of California**- Berkeley is a bastion of Radical liberalism. "Professorwatch" has identified a number of radicals on this University campus, but we will only visit two. Nancy Hughes a professor at Berkeley blames the massacre at the gay night club in Orlando on the National Rifle Association. She also blamed the massacre in San Bernardino on "retrograde, orthodox conservatives who fear change, who lack self-discipline, courage and who suffer if it may be called that a "perversity of heart". Dr. Ronald Hendel in the beginning of his class "Jewish Civilization" tells his students not to take his class if they think the Bible is infallible. After one student started questioning and challenging the professor, Hendel told the student: "If you disagree with the approach we use, that's an F".

12. **Michigan State University** – William Penn teacher of creative writing in one of his classes complained about "dead white Republicans" who raped his country.

13. **New York University** – Professor Arthur Caplan compared Donald Trump to Hitler and that he used racism to gain political support. Dr. Mark Miller warned that President Bush was spreading propaganda in order to form a theocracy in America. He also compared Bush to Hitler.

14. **Northwestern University** - Dr. Arthur Butz, an engineering professor, wrote a book claiming the Holocaust to be "The Hoax of the 20th century". The book claims that not only were the Jews NOT virtually wiped out, but what's more no evidence exists to date that there was ever any attempt by Hitler to do so. Professor Butz also supported Iranian President Mahmoud Ahmadinejad, who also called the Holocaust a myth.

15. **Oberlin College** – Professor of History Carol Lasser shredded a copy of the U.S. Constitution because it was an "oppressive document" and caused students "pain".

16. **Oberlin College** – Joy Korega Professor of Rhetoric and Composition at Oberlin in February 2016 claimed that Jews or Israelis control much of the world and are responsible for 9/11. President of the College Marvin Krislov supported Korega's rights to free speech and no action was taken against her at the time. In November, 2016 even the Board of Trustees of this ultra-liberal school could not take Korega's comments any longer and terminated her. Korega's assertions that ISIS is really an arm of the Israeli and U.S. Intelligence agencies and that Israel was behind the Charlie Hebdo massacre in Paris were just too much. Charlie Hebdo is a French Weekly satirical magazine that in 2012 published cartoons depicting Muhammad. Twelve, mostly staff of French Weekly, were murdered by Muslim terrorists in the attack in 2015.

17. **Penn State** – Dr. Peter Hatem stated that Conservatives express more "Psychoticism", while on the other hand those on the left are more altruistic, well socialized, empathic and conventional.

18. **Washington State University** – Dr. John Streamas, in his class called "Introduction to multicultural literature', told his white students to defer to non-white students if they wanted to succeed in his class. He also said that WSU stands for White Supremacist University. Also, at Washington State University, Dr. Rebecca Fowler's "Introduction to Comparative Ethnic

Studies" informed her students that one grade would be taken off any time a student used the phrase "Illegal aliens" or "Illegals. And also, at WSU, Dr. Selena Lester in her "Woman and Popular culture" class threatened to give students a failing grade for using verbiage she considers "oppressive and hurtful language". Further, the punishment can include removal from class, failure of the assignment or in extreme cases, failure for the semester.

19. **Syracuse University** – Professor Dana Cloud professor in the Department of Communications and Rhetorical Studies and member of the International Socialist Organization is a leading proponent of the idea that America is the blame for 9/11 due to its interventionist foreign policy in the Middle East. She also wrote a new Pledge of Allegiance to the people of Iraq, Palestine and Afghanistan and to their struggle to survive and resist slavery to corporate greed, brutal wars against their families and the economic and environmental ruin wrought by global capitalism".

20. **University of Michigan** – Juan Cole, Professor of History believes right wing Jews and an "Islamophobic Network" were a "key influence" to the shooting that killed nine people at Emmanuel African Methodist Episcopal Church in Charleston, SC. He also argued that recognizing Israel as a state is racist. Also, at University of Michigan Susan Douglas, Professor of Communications published her hate for Republicans in an article from "In These Times" she says: "I hate Republicans. I can't stand the thought of having to spend the next two years watching Mitch McConnell, John Boehner, Ted Cruz or any of the legion of other blowhards thwarting immigration reform or championing "fetal personhood"

21. **University of North Carolina** - Professor Michael Waltman teaches a course in "Hate Speech" that openly blames the political right for its use. The course is designed to expose students to the nature of hate in American life sustained through racist and sexist ideologies promulgated by Republicans. (Unfortunately, there is no one on the North Carolina campus that can argue the sheer hypocrisy of this liberal claim).

22. **University of Pennsylvania** -Black professor, Dr. Author Butler states that God is a white racist.

23. **Drexel University** – Political Science professor George Ciccariello-Maher tweeted on Christmas Day 2016 that he wanted "White Genocide" for Christians and later tweeted: "To clarify, when the whites were massacred during the Haitian revolution that was a good thing indeed. In March, 2017, he tweeted that he wanted to "vomit" after seeing a uniformed soldier being given a first- class seat on an airplane by another passenger.

24. **Northern Arizona University** - Dr. Anne Scott and English professor lowered the grade of one of her students, Caitlin Jeffers for using the word "mankind" instead of a gender- neutral term. She said: I would be negligent as a professor who is running a class about the human condition and the assumption, we make about being human, if I did not also raise this issue of gendered language and ask my students to respect the need for gender neutral language.

25. **Washington University, Tacoma** – An "antiracist "poster in a college writing center written by the director, staff and tutors at the University of Washington which insists that American

grammar is "racist" and an "unjust language structure" declaring that it permeates rules, systems and expectations in courses, schools and societies. (Dos this not sound like it is right from George Orwell's book, "1984"?

26. **Ball State University, Muncie, Indiana** - Professor of Music, George Wolfe, Director of the School's "Peace Studies Program", without any academic credentials in the field, teaches a course using as his principle text Borash and Webel's "Peace and Conflict Studies". An excerpt from this text states: "the terrorists who killed three thousand innocent civilians from eighty countries in the heinous attacks of 9/11 can be viewed as "freedom fighters" striking at the oppressors because there is no other means available to them." The text also states that the attacks on American civilians were justified in precisely the same way that President George Bush made no distinction between terrorists and those states that harbor them". This was not presented to the students for discussion. It was presented as an irrefutable position dictated to the class by the professor. An unimaginable justification of 9/11. And "Peace and Conflict Studies" is the primary text used in more than 250 peace study programs at colleges and universities in America.

27. **Fresno State University, California** - Professor Lars Maischak, from Fresno's History department twittered in February 2017: "To save American Democracy Trump must be hanged; the sooner and the higher the better". He further tweeted: "Justice = The execution of two Republicans for each deported immigrant". And if there is any doubt of his hatred spewed against Christians there was this tweet: "If only Mary had had an abortion, we would have been spared the clerical – fascist crap. His glory, my Ass". And then as to his hatred of all those who voted for Trump: "You fascist Trump-voting white trash scum can wallow in your filthy hell-holes". The reaction of Fresno State was to launch an investigation to determine whether these statements were made as a civilian citizen or as a representative of the school; not whether these statements were horrible and not worthy of any professor whether stated in the class room or on his computer. Colleges and universities make it clear to student athletes that whether on the field, in the classroom or off campus social gatherings, they are representatives of their school and they should act accordingly. Fresno University apparently does not hold its professors to the same standard even when statements are so despicable and intolerable as to offend even the liberal left.

28. **Massachusetts Institute of Technology – Noam Chomsky,** currently Institute Professor Emeritus at MIT, a University he has been associated with since 1955, author of over 100 radical books and lecturer at Colleges and universities throughout the United States, deserves a special section in my book as maybe the ultimate radical to find support in our institutes of higher learning, as well as support from those who consider themselves radical or liberal socialists. Chomsky is a self-described "A Narcho Syndicalist", also referred to as Revolutionary Syndicalism, a political theory which views revolutionary industrial unionism as a method for workers to gain control of an economy and with that control influence society. No individual in our colleges and universities according to David Horowitz has done more to shape anti-American passions. On December 5, 2016, before an audience of 2,300 at Riverside Church

in Manhattan, Noam Chomsky would claim that with Trump's election "We are now facing threats to survival of the human species". He also argued that the Republican Party is the most dangerous organization in human history. In effect, he is saying the Republican Party of the United States is worse than the third Reich under Hitler.

A good example of the avoidance of dialogue and the application of logic in our government, was the passage of the Affordable Care Act, when it was presented for vote by the then Speaker of the House, Nancy Pelosi. She said: "We have to pass the bill so that you can find out what is in it away from the fog of controversy". There are approximately 2,300 pages to the bill. No one had read it, nor understood it, but the Democrats passed it, claiming things were in it that just weren't there. No Democrat seems to even mention much less discuss this travesty. By way of analogy, suppose you go to a lawyer to review a contract you are about to sign, say to purchase a home, a small business, or employment agreement and he tells you to sign it even though he has not read it and doesn't know what is in it, but assures you that it is for your benefit. And it turns out that the agreement is not what you wanted, nor to your benefit. What would you think of this lawyer that is supposed to have been representing you?

Safe Places - No better example of the avoidance of dialogue is the mounting number of "Safe Places" cropping up on our college campuses and universities around America. These so called "safe places" are intended to give students who might find some comments troubling a place to recuperate. Some safe places are rooms equipped with cookies, coloring books, play dough, soothing music, pillows and videos of frolicking puppies. A safe place is meant to protect people from speech they don't like and these places have arrived on such campuses as Duke Harvard, Brown, Michigan, West Virginia, Kent State, Kansas State, Loyola of Chicago, University of Chicago, University of South Carolina, Davidson, American University, University of San Diego, University of California, Berkeley and University of Maryland to name only a few. And as former President of Williams College and current President of Northwestern, Morton Shapiro states to his students: "We all deserve a safe place". But that has become symbolic of the total intolerance of dialectics and Socratic debate.

Another incredible example of the avoidance of dialogue is the refusal of our colleges and universities to allow intellectual inquiry on its campuses and smothering it students with political correctness. Who are some of the speakers that have been disinvited from speaking on campus?

Ben Carson - (Current Secretary of Housing) - Johns Hopkins
Condoleezza Rice - (Secretary of State under George Bush) - Rutgers
Christine Lagarde (Director of IMF) - Smith College
Robert Zoellick (Former President, World Bank) - Swarthmore
Ayam Hirsi Ali - (Author and outspoken critic of Islam) - Brandeis
Milo Yiannopoulos - (British far-right political commentator) -Univ. California, Berkeley
Robert Birgeneau (former Chancellor of University of Calif. - Haverford

Charles Murray – (Right-wing American political scientist and socialist) -Middlebury College

Ann Coulter – (far-right media pundit and syndicated columnist) - Univ. California, Berkeley

Let us look at some additional dis-invitees and the reasons for being dis-invited.

1. University of Chicago – disinvited Cook County State Attorney Anita Alvarez from speaking, because the protesters claimed that she was responsible for state violence against blacks in Chicago.
2. Trinity College - students advocating for the Palestinian cause shut down Bassem Eid, a human rights advocate (himself a Palestinian), because his comments seemed pro-Israel.
3. Hampshire College Emily Wong was disinvited from making the commencement speech because students did not believe that she directly addressed their concerns
4. Williams College – Cancelled the speech engagement of Journalist John Derbyshire, citing that some considered his writings to be racist.
5. University of Pennsylvania -cancelled the speech of the Director of the CIA John Brennan because of his involvement in drone strikes in the Middle East.
6. Virginia Tech - revoked the speaking engagement of Jason Riley a Wall Street Journal columnist, who is also black because he wrote a book entitled "Please Stop Helping Us; How Liberals make it harder for Blacks to succeed".
7. Williams College – revoked the lecture of Suzanne Venker because of her criticism of feminism
8. University of California Berkeley – scheduled to have a discussion of the value of higher education, Nicholas Dirks, Chancellor of the University of California Berkeley was shouted down at his own university by students claiming he wasn't doing enough to help blacks and his salary was too high.
9. California State University at LA – revoked Ben Shapiro's proposed lecture about "Black Lives Matter" and "Safe Places" claiming that it was not a debate but an attack.
10. Middlebury College – On March 2nd, 2017 at Middlebury College, a prestigious liberal arts school, American Enterprise Institute scholar Charles Murray was asked to speak and answer questions from faculty and students. As soon as Murray took the stage, students stood up and turned their backs on him and started various chants in unison, which were loud enough that he could not talk over them. All kinds of epithets were fired at him including "racist, sexist anti-gay, Charles Murray go away". The location was soon beset by an angry mob, banging on windows, pulling firearms and physically attacking Murray and Bill Burger, Middlebury's Vice president of Communications as they tried to leave. Professor Allison Stanger was grabbed by her hair and was later treated at a local hospital for neck injury. What should be a bastion of free speech and dialectic dialogue fell to a level of baseness that would even make George Orwell shudder. Is this a result of multiculturalism, political correctness and extreme liberalism? I'll let the reader decide for himself/herself.

11. University of California, Berkeley (Again) - On April 19, 2017, officials of the University of California, Berkeley announced that it was cancelling a speech by well-known author and speaker, Ann Coulter, because of previous violent student protests on the campus. They were referring to the cancellation of conservative Milo Giannopoulos speech, Giannopoulos had been asked to speak by a group of Republicans, which led to the violent protests by radical liberals, leading to the destruction of property and injuries to persons. The University was saying in effect they could not protect freedom of speech on their campus and they had done nothing to do so since the February violent outbreak. As a result of Ann Coulter's protest and her refusal to just walk away, the University apparently changed its mind on April 20, 2017 telling Coulter that they had found a venue where she could hold her speech, but it had to be on May 2 instead of April 27th. The proposed move to May 2 was a feeble attempt on the part of the University to show the world that it supports freedom of speech, since it was also a date selected to assure the least attendance of students. For May 2 was the beginning of the reading period before exams when there were no classes on campus and fewer students around. Even under threat that it was violating the First Amendment to the Constitution the University still found a way to frustrate Coulter's speech engagement.

Intellectual inquiry has been smothered on college campuses by "Political Correctness" and Conservative opinions are shunned, attacked or totally eliminated and students are even offered "safe places" to comfort one another and avoid hearing speakers with whom they disagree. Note that not one liberal advocate was disinvited or banned from speaking on a college campus. Quite the contrary. Recently, Cornell University was prepared to welcome ISIS terrorists to come to its campus and conduct terror "training camps" for students. Cornell's Assistant Dean Joseph Scaffido admitted to this on tape. He also told a prospective Moroccan student that Cornell would okay clubs that support "freedom fighters" in the Islamic states.

Case Study -Yale University renames Calhoun College, Grace Harper College.

While one may argue this is relatively unimportant and should not result in a lot of attention, nevertheless it led to Geraldo Rivera blasting Yale for overdoing political correctness and Rivera resigned from his position at Yale. But it is a good example of how debate may have led to a different conclusion. Calhoun College at Yale University was named after John C. Calhoun an 1804 graduate and Vice President of the United States under two presidents, John Quincy Adams and Andrew Jackson.

Calhoun was a strong advocate of States Rights and a strong advocate of slavery. When the subject of renaming the college first came up in 2016, the College Administration agreed to keep the name and apparently as the result of protest from the student body, the College Administration reversed itself and the college was renamed after Rear Admiral Grace Harper a graduate of Vassar and a recipient of a PhD. in Mathematics from Yale in 1934. Grace Harper was a highly decorated naval officer and received posthumously in 2016 the Presidential Medal of Freedom for her many contributions to computer programming. Her career was certainly meritorious and having a college at Yale named after her is understandable.

The issue regarding Calhoun was not that his service to our country lacked merit, but that he supported slavery. There are twelve colleges that make up Yale University. Timothy Dwight, Benjamin Silliman, Jonathan Edwards and Ezra Stiles all have colleges named for them at Yale and all were slave-owners along with Calhoun. But the worst of the eminent gentlemen associated with Yale, was Elihu Yale, himself, who not only owned slaves, but actually was a slave merchant, which substantially contributed to his wealth and most likely provided part of his financial contributions to the school giving rise to it being named after him. If the Yale student body seeks to remove the name of a college that has been in existence for over 80 years, then why do they not demand the change of the name of Yale, which honors a man who was far more supportive of slavery by actually conducting slave trade?

In a like manner, we know that George Washington owned over 300 slaves and Thomas Jefferson was not far behind him. Should the name of George Washington be removed from the Washington monument in Washington, DC? Should the stone carvings of Washington and Jefferson at Mount Rushmore be removed? Should the George Washington Bridge be renamed as well as our Nation's Capital?

Freedom of Speech on College Campuses

In the 1919 U.S. Supreme Court Case, Schenck v. United States, the Supreme Court held that the defendant's speech in opposition to the draft during WW I was not protected speech under the First Amendment of the United States Constitution. Oliver Wendall Holmes wrote the opinion for the unanimous court that ruled that it was a violation of the Espionage Act of 1917 (amended by the Sedition Act of 1919). Holmes argued this abridgement of free speech was permissible because it presented a "clear and present danger to the government's recruitment efforts for the war". Holmes wrote: "The most stringent protection of free speech would not protect a man from falsely shouting "fire" in a theater. The Schenck case was partially overturned by Brandenburg v. Ohio in 1969, which limited the scope of banned speech to that which would likely incite imminent lawless action such as a riot.

So, there is some limitation on freedom of speech in certain instances and falsely shouting fire in a crowded theater is still an exception to free speech. The question is whether the protests we see in cities and on college campuses fall within the recognized restriction on free speech since they are likely to incite imminent lawless action such as a riot. Where this fine line is drawn is certainly a subject for discussion and dialogue, but we must recognize that there is a threshold, beyond which the guaranty of freedom of speech may be abridged.

There isn't a week that goes by that there isn't some abridgement of free speech on the campuses of our colleges and universities. Each year the Foundation for Individual Rights in Education (FIRE) reviews and records the performance of our colleges and universities and their actions in abridging free speech and spotlights the 10 worst schools in violating 1st Amendment rights of their students. According to FIRE, 92 per cent of American Colleges and Universities maintain speech codes that clearly restrict free speech. Students are corralled into free speech zones and criticized even at times violently when they invite a speaker deemed "controversial" to speak on campus. The 10 worst colleges for 2017 include two of my Alma Maters, namely Fordham University and Williams College. Along with these two schools were such prestigious schools as Harvard, Georgetown, University of Oregon and California State. Using Williams College as an example of why it is on the list, I look to February 2016 when then College President Adam Falk, unilaterally disinvited author and conservative commentator John Derbyshire from the campus. John Derbyshire had been invited by student organizers as one of a series of speakers to address at their program entitled "Uncomfortable Learning". It didn't matter that the group's President, Zach Wood is an African American and that Derbyshire had been invited precisely so his writings and comments on race could be debated. President Falk claimed that "there is a line somewhere", where free speech is to be forbidden" and "Derbyshire in my opinion is on the other side of it". President Falk had declared that there were certain speakers and viewpoints the Williams students weren't to engage. Interestingly, this never applied to a speaker from the radical left.

In 2016 the Student Senate at Tufts University another prestigious New England School rejected a freedom of speech resolution drafted by a student organization calling themselves: Students Advocating for Students" (SAS). The resolution would ask the Tufts Administration to clarify its speech related policies. FIRE had given Tufts the lowest rating for policies that both clearly and substantially restricted freedom of speech. The Tufts Student Senate in keeping with the lowest rating of its school for not allowing freedom of speech, unanimously rejected the proposed resolution put forth by SAS with 26 of the 28 Senators voting against it and two abstaining. One student senator wrote that by voting against greater free speech protections in Tufts' policies, the Tufts' Senate has completed the important job of protecting restrictions Tufts has imposed on free speech. Tufts has a long history of censoring satirical articles and refusing to recognize certain religious groups on campus. (The student judiciary voted to officially ban Tufts Christian Fellowship from its campus). On November 28, 2016 Tufts University student leaders rejected a free speech measure calling it "unsafe". Tufts student Jake Goldberg's free speech resolution called for an end to campus anti-free speech rules at Tufts. In opposition, Tufts students held up a poster which read "We condemn freedom of speech that hurts other people's feelings". So free speech is officially dead at Tufts (unless of course it supports the radical left).

We have seen violence at Middlebury College, University of California, Berkeley, Auburn and many others; all the result of radical left protests, but they are acknowledged and protected under the hypocritical application of freedom of speech, where radical left speech is tolerated but conservative right speech is prohibited. The one place that freedom of speech should be the most protected is in the halls of education. What is the common thread behind all the suppression of freedom of speech? The liberal left. Every one of the colleges and universities that limit freedom of speech are run by Administrations and faculty that represent only the liberal left and often the most radical of the liberal left.

From Ignorance to Insanity

It may be time for all of us to re-read George Orwell's: "1984". Freedom of speech is now being curtailed in parts of America, notably California and Colorado so far as to require all language to be gender neutral. The words:" brother" and "sister" must be replaced with the word "siblings". The words "he" and "she" must be replaced with "they and "them". "Man-hole covers" must now be called "maintenance covers". A pregnant woman cannot be referred to as either "woman" or "female", but as a "person". Public bathrooms may not be referred to by gender. These are just a few examples of the insane directions our liberal left is taking us.

The Leadership Institute and Laura Ingraham - Recently, I became aware of the activities of **The Leadership Institute** from a letter written by Laura Ingraham. For those who may not know who she is, here is a short background. Laura Ingraham graduated from Dartmouth College and the University of Virginia Law School. She clerked for Supreme Court Justice Clarence Thomas and then worked as an attorney for the prestigious New York Law Firm, Skadden Arps, Slate Meagher and Flam. In the 1990's she became a CBS commentator and she hosted the MSNBC program "Watch It". In 2001, she launched the Laura Ingraham Show, which is heard on 306 stations and XM Satellite Radio. She is a visiting commentator on Fox News.

Laura Ingraham is affiliated with the Leadership Institute in Arlington Virginia. One of the major concerns and projects of the Leadership Institute is to make people aware (in Ingraham's words) that: "liberals enjoy a near stranglehold on American college campuses. Liberals control the textbooks, the course selection, the "official" student newspaper, the student government and of course what is taught in class. The Leadership Institute, located at 1101 North Highland Street, Arlington, Virginia 22201 is actively seeking support for a program headed by Morton Blackwell, to end the liberal monopoly on our college campuses. Thanks to Morton Blackwell and the Leadership Institute more than 1,885 Conservative student groups now exist on college campuses across the country. The objective of the Leadership Institute is not to eliminate liberalism on campus, but to achieve a fair and balanced dialogue on campuses. In short, to restore dialectics to or campuses and bring back **Socratic Dialogue.**

Case Study of Radical Left on Campus of Duke University – Remember the Tawana Brawley case of November 1987? This 15-year-old girl had been found missing from her home in Wappinger Falls, NY for four days. She was found lying in a garbage bag several feet from her apartment with racial slurs written on her body and covered in feces. After hearing the evidence, a grand jury concluded in October 1988 that Tawana Brawley's case was fraudulent. Brawley had accused New York Assistant District Attorney Steven Pagones of the alleged assault. The case got significant media attention and the press rushed to judgment because of the actions of her three advisors: Al Sharpton and attorneys Alton Maddox and Vernon Mason. Steven Pagones successfully sued the four for defamation for a total of $385,000. In 1990 Alton Maddox was indefinitely suspended from practice of law in New York by the New York Appellate division of the Supreme Court. Vernon Mason was also disbarred by the New York State Appellate Court in 1995 citing 66 instances of professional misconduct with 20 clients over a period of six years. Sharpton faced a 67-count indictment, alleging fraud and theft and was acquitted of all charges. However, Sharpton was found guilty in the civil case of defamation brought against him and the others by Pagones and instead of a unanimous decision and beyond a reasonable doubt threshold for a criminal action, Pagones only needed to show "preponderance of evidence" to win a verdict. Sharpton was required to pay Pagones $65,000 of the $385,000 verdict. The $65,000 was paid by his supporters. While this case does not involve college students and professors it is otherwise similar to the Duke University "Lacrosse case" in its fanatic use of the liberal theme of "racism" and the willingness to fraudulently accuse and incriminate "whites" under the guise of "social reform".

The Duke lacrosse case was a criminal case, brought in 2006 in Durham, North Carolina, the home of Duke University. Three members of the Duke University lacrosse team were falsely accused of raping a black woman, hired as a stripper. The issues for discussion of this case study concern "racism", "media bias" and "due process". The case started out as an issue of a racial crime of whites against a black woman, but it would end clearly as an example of black racism and media bias. There was a rush to judgment by the professors of Duke University, the media and the Assistant district attorney, representing the state of North Carolina. An apparent conviction was published in the local newspaper and covered nationally before any facts had been verified. Concepts of "equal protection under the law" and "due process" were flagrantly violated.

The alleged rape, which would turn out to be a false accusation by black stripper Crystal Gail Magnum, led to the University cancelling the remainder of Duke's lacrosse season, the firing of the lacrosse coach and the suspending the accused boys.

The prosecutor, Durham County district attorney Mike Nifong was more than zealous in his prosecution of the three lacrosse players. He stated that the alleged rape was a hate crime. On April 11, 2007 North Carolina Attorney General, Roy Cooper found the three Duke lacrosse players innocent of all charges and they were victims of a "tragic rush to accuse". (Sound familiar to the Brawley case?). District attorney Nifong was labeled by Cooper as a "rogue prosecutor". Nifong was disbarred for "dishonesty, fraud, deceit and misrepresentation."

Maybe the worst of the actions relating to this case was perpetrated by the so-called "Group of 88"; the 88 professors at Duke University who publicly condemned in an advertisement taken out in the local newspaper, the Duke lacrosse team for their alleged involvement in a rape that would later be declared a hoax. There were approximately 700 professors at Duke University at the time. So, the "Group of 88" represented approximately 12.5% of the professors on campus. These professors by their actions declared that the three lacrosse players did not deserve the presumption of innocence. After the alleged rape was proved to be a hoax, there were no apologies from the "Group of 88" and no incriminations. This is just another example of the liberal left believing they can say or do anything, even if it is illegal or fraudulent, if they perceive that it furthers their social agenda.

Other Cases of Indoctrination/Bias/Radicalism on College and University Campuses

University of Illinois, Chicago and William Ayers – William Ayers is a retired professor of Education at the Chicago campus of the University of Illinois. He holds the titles of Distinguished Professor of Education and Senior University Scholar. Ayers is best known for his radical activism. In 1969, he co-founded the Weather Underground, a self- described Communist Revolutionary group with the intent to overthrow "Imperialism". He was directly involved and participated in the campaign of bombing buildings in protest of the Vietnam War, including the New York Police Department Headquarters (1970); the U.S. Capitol building (1971) and the Pentagon (1972). Ayers confirmed this in his book: "Fugitive Days". He is a self-proclaimed "street fighting Communist" and expressed regret that on 9/11/2001 he and his fellow terrorists "didn't bomb enough".

University of Colorado and Professor Ward Churchill - In 2005 the University of Colorado made the headlines because of its Ethnic Studies Professor, Ward Churchill who described the victims of the World Trade Center attacks as "little Eichmann's", comparing all those victims to Adolf Eichmann, the leader of the barbarous genocide program under Hitler. He likened the United States to Nazi Germany as a "genocidal" nation. How such a radical professor could hold a teaching position in any College or University is hard to understand. But these statements were even too much for the liberal left. Churchill was fired, the University President resigned and the University lost more than $10 million in cancelled student applications.

Columbia University and Professor Nicholas DeGenova - In March 2003 at an anti-war "teach-in" on Columbia campus, Professor DeGenova publicly wished for a "million Mogadishu's" – the site where 18 U.S. Army Rangers were massacred by al Qaeda-trained Somali forces. He told Columbia students that "U.S. patriotism is inseparable from imperial warfare and white supremacy and that the only true heroes are those who find ways that help defeat the U.S. Military". He remained a professor of anthropology and Latino studies at Columbia University until 2009, leaving of his own accord to take up various teaching positions in European Universities, finally winding up as an instructor at King's College in London.

Columbia University and Jim Gilchrist and Mahmoud Ahmadinejad - Probably no better contrast of the bias treatment of opposing views than Columbia University's invitations to Jim Gilchrist in October 2006 and to Mahmoud Ahmadinejad in the fall of the following year (2007). Jim Gilchrist is a far-right political activist – co-founder and President of the Minuteman Project, whose aim is to prevent illegal immigration across the southern borders of the United States. He is a strong advocate of the 1st Amendment and conservatism. Mahmoud Ahmadinejad was the President of Iran, a self-proclaimed anti-Jew; a self-proclaimed enemy of the United States. He claimed that that the Holocaust was a hoax and called for the total destruction of Israel.

In October 2006, Gilchrist was invited by a group of Conservative leaning students to Columbia as a guest speaker. A group of liberal student activists shouted Gilchrist down when he tried to speak and expressed their view that anyone who shared Gilchrist's views "had no right to be able to speak here". Gilchrist was called a "racist"; he was threatened physically and driven off the stage. Now compare the treatment of Ahmadinejad. Invited by a group of Columbia faculty, Ahmadinejad is introduced by no less than the President of Columbia, Lee Bollinger who stated: "this is the right thing to do and indeed is required by existing norms of free speech the American University and Columbia University". (see page 62 – David Horowitz's book – "One Party Classroom". This statement by Bollinger rings a bit hollow after Jim Gilchrist is forced to leave the stage under threat of violence.

All the examples of radical liberalism and its denial of freedom of speech; its indoctrination of our youth and its hate mongering is rampant throughout our educational system. These are not anecdotal. They are the norms of our educational system and are alive and well in most of our educational institutions from k-12 and then through college.

What are the key elements of a Totalitarian state?

1. Control Education at all levels
2. Deny Freedom of speech
3. Eliminate, suppress and/or ridicule religion (particularly Judaism and Christianity)
4. Control the media
5. Develop effective propaganda programs to suppress conflicting ideas
6. Avoid/(disallow) Socratic Dialogue
7. Promote Hatred of those who disagree with or oppose you
8. Cause as many citizens as possible (by threat or otherwise) to be dependent on or beholden to the government (socialism)

This was at least for a time the ingredients successfully imposed by the leaders of the most horrific totalitarian states in my lifetime, namely: Hitler, Stalin, Mussolini and they seem to be the ingredients most closely associated with radical liberalism in the United States.

The U.S. news and World Report ranks the top universities and colleges each year. In order, the top 8 Universities are: Princeton, Harvard, University of Chicago, Yale, Columbia, Stanford, MIT and Duke. The top three liberal arts colleges in order are: Williams, Amherst, Wellesley. I have always been suspicious of how these Universities and Colleges reach such high ratings. Class size, education resources, number of professors/students, average SAT scores on admission, graduation rate, peer assessment and alumni giving are the principal factors going into the ratings. They all deal with quantitative factors, numbers and statistics. But none really tell us anything about the quality. Here are some factors, which I believe are important and not even considered. If they were, what would this do to the current ratings?

Here are some factors that I think should be considered:

1. Percentage of professors that are conservative as opposed too liberal
2. Evidence of student indoctrination
3. How often are controversial speakers excluded from campus
4. The prevalence of student rioting on campus
5. Level of rape on campus
6. The installation and support of safe places for students to avoid controversy
7. Number of cases of bias and restrictions to freedom of speech reported on campus

What about the epidemic of rape on our college campuses?

What seems to be closely associated with the liberal left indoctrination on our college campuses that so embodies hatred is rape on our campuses. One of the most intolerable of hate crimes and yet so prevalent on our liberal left campuses is rape. National rape statistics in the U.S. shows that there are 0.27 rapes per 1000 people. That number doesn't tell us much by itself until we look at it in comparison with the level of rape on our College and University campuses. Most know that there is a serious problem, but few realize that it has risen to epidemic proportions.

According to the Washington Post, in terms of total number of rapes, the 10 worst are:

College/University	Total Rapes	% Higher than the National Average
Brown	43	15,925%
University of Connecticut	43	15,925
Dartmouth	42	15,555
Wesleyan (Middletown, Ct)	37	13,704
University of Virginia	35	12,963
Harvard	33	12,222
University of North Carolina	32	11,852
Rutgers	32	11,852
University of Vermont	27	10,000
Stanford	26	9,629

Maybe another way to judge the seriousness of the college rape problem on campus is to look at the statistics based on how many rapes per 1000 students and here the worst offenders.

College	Rapes per 1000 students		
Reed College	12.9	Williams College	8.3
Wesleyan	11.5	Bowdoin	8.1
Swarthmore	11.0	Beloit	6.9
Knox College	10.0	Dartmouth	6.7
Pomona College	8.5	Davidson	6.2

What do these numbers tell us? Given the national average rapes per thousand is 0.27, then at Reed College a young lady is 48 times more likely to be raped than anywhere else in the United States and at Davidson, 23 times more likely. Let the reader do the math for the Colleges in between and by the way these are some of the most liberal schools in the United States.

To suggest a correlation between liberalism and college rape without any further analysis would represent an analytical bias. However, what if we looked at the 15 best Conservative schools in the country regarding campus rape. Would this be probative? Bestschools.org actually rates the Best Conservative Colleges and universities in the Country. We can then examine the rape experience on those campuses to see if there is a meaningful difference.

Here are the results, which are quite astounding in comparison to other Colleges and Universities. The 15 most conservative colleges and their reported rapes per 1000 students are as follows:

Conservative College	Rapes/1000 students
Hillsdale College (Michigan)	0.0
Biola University (California)	0.0
University of Dallas	0.0
Liberty University (Virginia)	0.0
College of the Ozarks (Missouri)	0.0
Houston Baptist University	0.0
Regent University (Virginia)	0.3
Brigham Young University (Utah)	0.0
The Kings College (New York City)	0.4
Ava Maria University (Florida)	0.0
Harding University (Arkansas)	0.1
Franciscan University Steubenville (Ohio)	0.4
Pepperdine University (California)	0.1
Thomas Moore College (New Hampshire)	0.1
Texas A&M University	0.1

According to "Rave" 55 colleges are under investigation for mishandling sexual assault cases.

Make your own conclusions, but there would seem to be strong support for believing rape is more prevalent where liberal indoctrination and radical liberal thought dominates the classroom. We will look at the subject of Indoctrination in education in more detail in the next chapter.

What Can We Do?

Recently, Kevin Allred, a Montclair State University Professor, who teaches a course on "Beyoncé" under the University's "Women's studies Program", called for the outright shooting of Donald Trump. When Allred taught at Rutgers University, campus police sent him to Manhattan for psychiatric evaluation after a number of students felt threatened by him following Trump's election. Yet this did not stop Montclair State's administration from hiring Allred to teach a course on Beyoncé. Just another example of a radical professor being hired to teach a useless course.

At Trinity College in Hartford, Connecticut, Professor Johnny Williams a 20-year teacher at the College, posted a number of racially charged comments against whites saying "let them {expletive} die" The American Association of University Professors immediately protested the suspension of the sociology professor by Trinity College for violating his academic freedom. The college, in anticipation of angry protests for the suspension, closed down the campus for a day. Specifically, less than one week after a gunman opened fire on more than a dozen Republican Congressmen on a Virginia baseball field, in which Republican Congressman, Steve Scalise was severely wounded, Williams made the assertion on social media that white people are inhuman assholes who should die. The liberal left deplores (as does the conservative right) white racist/supremacists, but where is the outcry against racism and bigotry from non-white professors?

Probably no worse example of left-wing racism and bigotry is espoused by California State University professor Mohammad Abed, a professor of ethics, social and political philosophy and classical Islamic philosophy. He believes that genocide of white racists is morally required. He claims that sometimes you just have to commit genocide to save the world from evil people like white racists. He has advanced his argument in a series of lectures in which he has said: "genocide is not in any sense distinctively heinous; nor is it necessarily immoral". Does California State University administration believe that it is all right for an ethics professor to teach that genocide under any circumstances is moral? Abed's statements are in keeping with his Muslim beliefs and as taught in the Qur'an that mass murder to achieve justice is acceptable.

The college student protests; the indoctrination of students of every age; the hate, vilification and condemnation of the right from the professors; the continued expansion of worthless courses on college campuses and the shutdown of debate by our college and university administrators is finally getting to the alumni and they are responding in the most poignant way they can; they are cutting back on their donations. A 1960 graduate from Amherst College has cut Amherst out of his will in response to protests on Amherst campus over cultural and racial sensitivities. He feels as an alumnus that he has been lied to, patronized, and basically dismissed as an old white bigot who is insensitive to the needs of the current college community. Another graduate of Amherst believes his college has lost its intellectual vigor and by erasing history from academia the school has only become more vulnerable to racism. He has confirmed his beliefs by talking with friends from Hamilton, Trinity, Williams, Bates, Middlebury and Hobart and none is pleased with what is happening on their college campus and their only recourse is refusing to write a check, hoping that this might make a difference.

Alumni across the country are finding these concerns:

1. Students are too wrapped up in racial identity politics
2. Students are being allowed to take too many frivolous courses.
3. Students are quick to repudiate the heroes and traditions of the past, judging them by today's standards rather than in the context of their times.
4. Freedom of speech is being curtailed if not outright prohibited. This is exemplified by the number of Conservative speakers that are either outright refused to speak on campus or are disinvited.
5. Students are being indoctrinated into only one way of thinking and that is the Liberal left
6. Safe rooms have been created so students cannot be confronted by different or disturbing ideas.
7. Colleges and Universities have become so wrapped up in their politically charged mission rather than an institution of higher learning

There is a terrible crisis on our college and university campuses. Alumni have been isolated from and ignored by their alma mater and college professors and college administrators have been allowed to run rampant over the substance of education on their campuses. The first thing alumni need to do is become more familiar with what is going on at their college and university. Start with the course catalog. Search the backgrounds of the college professors. Get reports on recent happenings and events on the college campus. Look into any protests or outbreaks of violence on their college campus. The second thing Alumni can do immediately is stop giving to their colleges and universities. There are many great charities one can give to where your contributions will really make a positive difference as opposed to a place which will continue to perpetuate biased indoctrination of their children. Finally, maybe there are a few of you that could actively seek to get a position on the Board of Trustees of their college or University or any College or University Board where a difference can be made. While you may not be able to change things overnight you would be able to provide a source for your fellow alumni as to what is really going on at your school.

As to our Churches, those who are active in their church, should demand that separation of church and state be a two-way street and that their church should not be making political statements or leading political causes. Political statements or political condemnations from the pulpit are not appropriate according to Christian theology. This is no more than we demand of the state that it stays separate from our churches.

We must get more involved with our public schools and learn exactly what is being taught to our kids. Demand information; establish open forums for discussion. Our educational system is a disaster that can only be turned around by active participation of the parents. This is so important that being too busy is not an excuse. Parents, you must find time to assure the well-being of your child's learning.

CHAPTER 3
Indoctrination Displaces Education

WE NEED TO look at some further examples of how our educational system from public schools through college and universities has been indoctrinated by the liberal left to the point that our children are no longer allowed to think for themselves or be challenged by those who may have differences of opinion, especially opinions from the Conservative right. There are many hundreds of examples of indoctrination across the United States, in almost every state, in almost every school system in almost every college and university. Here I use as my principal source **"Indoctrination Displaces Education – (parts 1 and 2)**. These two documents describe literally 100's of anecdotal evidence of how the public schools, colleges and universities are indoctrinating our children and young adults. Teachers and professors engage in a wild array of liberal left indoctrination and there is no one to refute them, since dialogue and conservative thought is not allowed. With well over 90% of all teachers and professors advocating the liberal left political philosophy, coupled with the strict censorship of the views of the Conservative Right, the indoctrination is almost Hitlerian. The reader can examine the indoctrination in more detail by going on the internet and searching on the above. Each anecdote is briefly summarized, but by clicking on the subject matter, the full article can be obtained including author and date. Here than are a few of the many, many examples of the indoctrination that our students of every age are undergoing throughout our nation. These are random and not in any order of significance.

1. St. Lawrence University – October 16, 2018, 1,500 alumni and faculty of St. Lawrence called for the school to rescind an honorary degree bestowed on Senator Susan Collins an alumnus of the school, (who had previously received an honorary doctorate of law degree from the school), because of her vote to confirm Supreme Court Justice Brett Kavanaugh. They signed a letter to the School saying that Susan Collins: "lacks the integrity and commitment to justice that we expect from the St. Lawrence body".

2. George Washington University – Nearly 200 students signed a petition for the University to adopt a new mascot and nickname because the name "Colonials" is extremely offensive.

3. High school History textbook "By the People", published by Pearson Education and authored by NYU Professor, James Fraser, teaches that Trump is mentally ill and most whites are racists.

4. Young Democratic Socialists of America (YDSA) urges socialists to take jobs as teachers in

order to exploit the supposed political, economic and social benefits of socialism.

5. University of Arizona recently hired radical left Norm Chomsky to teach at the University. Chomsky had previously expressed support of the radical Islamic group Hezbollah. One of Chomsky's claims is that Christianity is trying to destroy the world.

6. In May, 2018, the California Assembly discussed a bill that would replace Abraham Lincoln or George Washington's birthday with International Socialist Workers' day as a paid holiday. It was introduced as Bill AB-3042 after having made it through committees. The bill passed both assembly's Appropriations and Education Committees and lost by a narrow vote of 27 to 22.

7. A California State University – Fresno professor, Randa Jarrar, came under fire for cheering the death of Barbara Bush, calling her a "witch" and an "amazing racist". She gleefully claimed that she could not be fired because she had tenure.

8. Student leaders at a California High school in San Ramon have banned the National Anthem from school rallies because of a line in the third verse (which few people have ever heard). The third verse of the National Anthem included these words: "no refuge could save the hireling and slave from the terror of flight or the gloom of the grave". The school administration concurred saying: "It did not matter that the third verse is never played and very few Americans even know the lyric exists…. the entire song is tainted".

9. 200 students from Beacon High school in Manhattan were allowed to skip class to join protests in November 2016 at Trump Tower. They would chant: "No Trump, No KKK, No Racist USA. They obviously were unaware that the KKK along with the Jim Crow laws were created solely by Democrats in the 19th century.

10. Oberlin College – In November 2016 students and faculty marched in support of making Oberlin College a Sanctuary campus in response to the election of Donald Trump.

11. Stanford University in November 2016, 500 Stanford University students, faculty and staff members walked out of classrooms in protest of Donald Trump becoming President-elect.

12. In Brainerd High School in Minnesota, the 2017 edition of the Yearbook included a section on Trump asking the students: "How do you feel about Trump?" One student's response: "I would like to behead him". Apparently, the vision of Kathy Griffin holding up the severed head of Donald Trump was all the inspiration he needed for his comment.

13. Fresno State Professor in April 2017 tweeted that: President Trump must be hung to save American Democracy; the sooner and the higher the better".

14. At the Rancho Campano High School in California, an English teacher told her class that she lost a $100 bet because President Donald Trump had not been shot by Inauguration day.

15. In 2017, Duke University sponsored a workshop for the purpose of training students to engage in activism against the Trump Administration. The event was sponsored by the University program in gender, sexuality and feminist studies.

16. In Rutherford County Schools in Tennessee, a substitute teacher David Colin who was

supposed to be watching the students, posted on Facebook, his hatred of Trump saying: "The only good Trump supporter is a dead Trump supporter".

17. The principal of the Calhoun School in New York City, a private school, stated in an e-mail that the election of Trump was worse than September 11,2001 terrorist attack; more devastating than Vietnam or the Assassination of Martin Luther King.

18. In December, 2017, Fordham University investigated an incident on campus after a video showed that several members of the College Republican Club being kicked out of an on-campus coffee shop for wearing President Trump "Make America Great Again" hats. The self-identified president of the student run coffee house said: "I don't want people like you…..I am giving you five minutes to leave".

19. Stanford Associate Dean, Nanci Howe in November 2017 encouraged disruption and walkout of a Robert Spencer speech on Islam. In his coming of the Third Reich, historian Richard Evans explains how in the early days of National Socialist Germany, Storm Troopers (Brown Shirts) organized campaigns against unwanted professors in the local newspapers and staged mass disruptions of their lectures. And here we are again on the campus of Stanford University, a teacher encouraging violence and disruption as opposed to free dialogue.

20. At Princeton University in October, 2016 an op-ed in the Princeton University student newspaper attacks conservative's right to free speech, contending that "Conservatives don't deserve the right to free speech, because if Conservative arguments were strong…. they would not meet political opposition."

21. Wall Township High School Yearbook Advisor, Susan Parsons, a media teacher, edited photos removing images supporting President Trump. One student had his photo edited because he wore a T-shirt saying: "Trump, make America Great Again".

22. A recent Yale survey of 2000 students reported by the Yale Daily News revealed that Conservative views are "unwelcome" on the campus by a margin of 75% to 25%. One respondent said: "anyone who supported Trump or is a Republican is hated".

23. The nation's largest Catholic university, DePaul University in October 2016 prohibited: "Unborn lives matter" posters on Campus, lest it provoke the "Black Lives Matter" movement. The University President, Father Dennis Holtschneider said the poster contained bigotry. If the Catholic church isn't going to support pro-life then who is? The prohibition of Conservative speech is becoming routine at De Paul.

24. The University of Wisconsin in 2015 spent $2.7 million on guest speaker and lecturers, but not one was a conservative.

25. A Cedar High School, North Carolina English teacher, Amanda Harder, was recorded as saying: "basically the only people who seem safe from this guy "Trump" are white Christian males. She made her students compare speeches by Hitler and Trump. Once she discovered the students had secretly recorded her, she confiscated their cell phones.

26. Yale students (obviously already indoctrinated), who are English literature majors wish to

suspend the study of white male English poets such as John Milton, Alexander Pope and William Wordsworth, because they create a culture hostile to students of color.

27. Approximately 2,000 eighth grade students in Rialto, California School District were given an essay assignment asking the students whether the Holocaust "was an actual event in history" or whether it was "merely a political scheme created to influence public emotion and political gain?"

28. At Trinity College in Connecticut, professor John Eric Williams went on a tirade in August 2018 saying that all whites are inhuman and demanding that they should die.

29. Harvard Medical School removed portraits of prominent white male doctors in order to be more diverse and inclusive. (Couldn't they just add more portraits of deserving doctors of other races and ethnicities?)

30. Diablo Valley College professor Albert Ponce tells his class they must destroy the foundations of the United States because it was built on the laws created by white men.

31. Edina School district in Edina, Minnesota is teaching kindergarten children about the social injustices of white privilege.

32. A math professor at the University of Illinois wrote about some of the more racist aspects of math. Mathematics is generally viewed as "white" wrote professor Rochelle Gutierrez, because curricula emphasizes such terms as "Pythagorean" theorem and "pi", which perpetuate the perception that mathematics was developed by Greeks and other Europeans.

33. Georgetown University Law professor Preston Mitchum declared in July 2017 on social media that all white people are racist and all men are sexists.

34. The Spring Lake Park High School in Minnesota has stopped purchasing music composed by white guys, committing for one year to only buy music from composers of color.

35. A teacher at Norman Oklahoma's North High School declared to his class that to be white is to be racist.

36. White professor at Rutgers University decided that all white people are evil and some are only less bad than others.

37. Two more tax-payer funded universities, University of Wisconsin – Madison and University of Colorado-Denver began offering a course in 2017 on how "whiteness" is a serious social problem. At Wisconsin the course is simply entitled: "The Problem of Whiteness".

38. In 2016, a Sacramento California High School English teacher, Dana Dushiber said she avoids Hamlet and all the rest of Shakespeare's works because her minority students shouldn't be expected to study a long-dead British guy. Though Shakespeare has been long regarded as the premier writer of the English language, Dushiber says he is only regarded that way because "some white people ordained it and he can easily be replaced"

39. In July 2017, Professor Jerry Coyne a biologist at the University of Chicago stated that murdering infants is morally fine since newborn babies aren't aware of death and have no rational

faculties to make judgments.

40. A student at the University of Florida lost points on an essay assignment for using the word "men" instead of "humankind". His professor, Jack Davis wrote that the student, Martin Poirier had a thoughtful paper but the "writing mechanics" error reduced his grade to a B-.

41. Hunter College in New York City will offer students an "Abolition of Whiteness" course to discuss how "white supremacy and violence" influence individual identity. The course is taught by women and gender studies professor, Jennifer Gaboury.

42. Yale students in the English Department protest having to take a course entitled: "Major English Poets" because they are basically white male writers and therefore hostile to students of color.

43. Orange Coast Community College Professor Olga Perez Cox called Trump's election an act of terrorism.

44. Colorado State University found itself discriminating against pro-life students who sought a diversity grant to host pro-life speaker Josh Brahm from the Equal Rights Institute to discuss "Abortion and bodily rights". While they did not get the grant, in contrast the University funded a pro-choicer speech with mandatory student fees.

45. "Political Correctness" permeates vocabulary at Princeton University. Five words: actress, cameraman, freshman, mailman, mankind, along with many others are scrubbed from vocabulary by the Human Resource Department.

46. At University of Southern California, pro-life banners are removed from light poles and replaced by posters reading "women deserve the right to choose". The pro-life banners had gone through the proper channels to obtain approval only to be removed when the college administration reversed itself.

47. "Abortion is a gift from God" blares a poster at the University of Michigan and an art exhibit at the University honors abortion as an awesome life-sustaining act.

48. Students at Bonita High school in La Verne, California, published cartoons in their magazine depicting President Donald Trump as a Nazi and an officer wearing a KKK garb, while aiming a gun at a black child.

49. University of Pennsylvania Law School in 2018 removed Amy Wax from teaching required first year courses for publicly discussing the negative aspects of affirmative action. Her argument was that preferences may actually harm beneficiaries. Carrying it further, the leader of Black lives Matter in Pennsylvania plans to continue to disrupt things on the West Philadelphia campus. It is not a question of whether Amy Wax was right or wrong. It is a question of whether at a prestigious law school like Pennsylvania, where freedom of speech should be a focal point of American Jurisprudence, should blatantly censor such freedom of speech and literally prevent it from ever happening again.

50. University of Texas professor, so upset with the outcome of the 2016 Presidential election, publicly suggested that Texans deserved Hurricane Harvey because the state voted Republican.

51. In a June 16, 2017 Facebook post, Trinity College, Connecticut Professor Eric Williams suggested that the first responders to the shooting of Republican Congressmen at a softball team practice in Virginia, should have let them "f. ing die" because they were white. He labeled white people "inhuman assholes". Williams was placed on leave but was slated to return in 2018.

52. A University of Delaware Professor, Katherine Rettwyler claimed that Otto Warmbier, a young American who died after being held in a North Korean prison camp: "got exactly what he deserved". She claimed that he behaved like a spoiled, naive, arrogant U.S. college student, who never had to face the consequences of his actions, and he had the typical mindset of a lot of young, white rich clueless males that she teaches. Another white hating liberal left, that believes torture and killing are fitting punishment for those who do not believe as they do.

53. At Drexel University, assistant professor George Ciccariello-Maher called for "white genocide" in 2016 and again in 2017.

This is only a sampling of how left our education system has gone and the vitriol and hatred is rampant. The Conservative right is depicted as racists, white supremacists, that deserved to be hated and, in some instances, killed. The liberal left educators that dominate our public schools and colleges, give credence to our liberal Democratic leaders, who call Conservative Republicans "deplorable"; who state that there is "a special place in hell" for Conservative Republican Women and that Conservative Republicans should not be treated civilly, should be kicked when they are down and that the liberal left should "get in their face and disrupt their meetings and gatherings whenever possible'.

The liberal left has moved beyond just being liberal and calling for socialism to replace capitalism. Bernie Sanders, Governor of New York Cuomo, Elizabeth Warren, and other mainstream liberal Democrats are calling for free College and university education. They don't tell us how they plan to pay for this, but for certain it will be paid by an increase in taxes. How diabolical, how insidious, how clever. Now that the liberal left has control of education in the United States and is championing socialism on every campus, how simply wonderful it is to get the Conservative Right to pay for their own demise. Think of all the votes the Democrats will glean from the college graduates who have for four years been indoctrinated into socialism and now will be beholden to the liberal left for making free college and university education available to them.

CHAPTER 4

The Destruction of Christianity and the Support of Islam in our Public Schools

OUR COUNTRY RANKS very low in education compared to other countries, even though we spend so much more per student than any other country. We are so far behind in Math and Sciences that our overall ranking is around 17th in the world. During the last 8 years, under the Obama Administration what has our Department of Education (DOE) done for our children? Not only is the "Core Curriculum" under severe criticism, but its unbridled, focused indoctrination of our Public-School children into Islam, while disregarding all other religions is not only in violation of the First Amendment Rights under the Constitution, but also the teachings are biased and discriminatory. I have briefly discussed this before, but the danger to our children is so severe, I believe it warrants more detailed attention.

On March 28, 2017, the Christian Action Network sent a letter of demand to the U.S. Department of Education, mandating that it cease its Islamic Education program in our public schools, initiated under the Obama Administration, which includes sending instructional materials to all public schools throughout the U.S. The Program, "Access Islam" was funded by the Department of Education under the Democrat administration of President Obama. There were 10 lesson plans including:

1. Five Pillars of Islam
2. Salat: Prayer in Muslim Life
3. Ramadan Observance
4. Qur'an: Sacred scripture of Islam
5. The Haji – Journey to Mecca
6. Islam in America
7. Women in Islam

Students in public schools from grades 5-12 are taught these lessons. They are taught that Allah is God – they would never be taught that Jesus is God.

It is interesting that the Department of Education did not offer similar instructional materials for Christianity, Judaism, Buddhism or Hinduism. How this is not a violation of the Separation of Church and State provisions of our Constitution is beyond me. We know how the Christmas pageant, reading from the Bible, saying voluntary prayer, even referring to Christmas Vacation has been removed from our public schools. Then how can another religion have specific instructions, projects and assignments, exclusively dealing with that religion, namely Islam? In keeping with the notion of Islamic education in our public schools, Indiana Congressman Andre Carson, a Baptist convert to Islam stated that U.S. Public Schools should be modeled after Islamic Schools (Madrasa's) that are built on the foundations of the Qur'an.

Among the contentious material being presented through the DOE Islamic program are worksheets, questions, activities and media that steep children into the world of Islamic worship. Children are told to complete such assignments as:

1. Explore and understand the basic beliefs of Islam as well as the Five Pillars that guide Muslims in their daily life, belief, fasting, almsgiving and pilgrimage.
2. Focus about learning the core duties of Muslims
3. Read about what it means to proclaim faith or belief as a Muslim

In addition, students are expected to correctly understand and answer such questions as:

- Describe the process that Muslims go through to prepare for prayer
- What do prayers sound like?
- What are some of the things Muslims say during prayer?

The lesson plans are prepared for students in grades 5-12. Activities include having students create posters about the Five Pillars of Islam to be displayed in the hallways of the schools. Teachers are also asked to have their students meet with Muslims to learn about their beliefs and views. In short, our public schools are teaching our children to become Muslim through Federal Government sponsored programs with no similar education program for any other religion. Here are some specific examples of how our public schools are indoctrinating our children, much to the pleasure of the Islamic world.

- Seventh graders in California are subjected to an intense three-week course in Islam in which they are required to pray to Allah and memorize Qur'anic verses. They are taught to pray in the name of Allah the compassionate, the merciful and are instructed to chant: "Praise to Allah, Lord of Creation".
- In the Excelsior School in Buran, California, 7th graders dress up as Muslims and engage in Islamic role playing.

- In Jennison High school, Michigan, students were assigned to make a pamphlet about Islam that would be used to introduce Islam to 3rd graders. The pamphlet presented Allah as the same God of the Christians and Jews. No pamphlet was provided third graders on any other religion.
- In a Wichita, Kansas elementary school a poster of the Five Pillars of Islam is on display in the hallway.
- A world history class in an Olmstead Falls, Ohio middle school requires seventh graders to recite a Muslim conversion prayer called the Shahada. The Shahada profession of faith is: "There is no God but Allah, and Muhammad is the Messenger of Allah". The students were also required to watch a video on "How to pray as Muslims".
- In Alston Middle School in South Carolina, students must write on a worksheet that Islam is a religion of peace. The worksheet also teaches that: "There is no God but Allah".
- At Porter Ridge High School, North Carolina, ninth grade students were instructed to write: "Most Muslims have a stronger faith than the average Christian". Provocative and Biased to say the least, but what proof is offered for its validity?
- In Farmville Central School, North Carolina, seventh grade students had to learn vocabulary words by employing them in Islamic sentences.
- Eleventh grade students in La Plata High School, Maryland were told to write: "Allah is the same God that is worshipped in Christianity and Judaism".
- Seventh grade students at Manhattan Beach Middle School had to write: "All people must submit to Allah".
- In Canyon Lake Middle School, California, students were asked to make a group mural of the Five Pillars of Islam.
- In Pine Bush High School, New York, students listened to the morning pledge of allegiance being recited in Arabic.
- In Lyman High School, Florida, tenth grade students were given an assignment to design an Islamic prayer rug.
- In Revere Middle Schools, Massachusetts, students had to learn and say: "I bear witness that there is no god but Allah".
- In Wellesley Middle School, Massachusetts, students take a tour of a Mosque and instructed on how to pray as a Muslim. There was no similar tour of a Synagogue or Christian Church
- Students at Riverside High School, Virginia were asked to write: "There is no God but Allah".
- In Salem Junior High in Utah, 9th grade students were asked to draw a propaganda poster for an Islamic terrorist organization
- In Highland Hills Middle School, Indiana, seventh grade students were given a worksheet that praised Sharia law, polygamy, forced marriages and women wearing the burqa.
- Academic Freedom Conference held in Washington, DC in 2006 – The following is an excerpt

from David Horowitz's book "Indoctrination U (page 104). In April 2006 at the Academic Freedom Conference, an event supposedly designed to launch an Academic Freedom Campaign for k-12 schools, a sixteen year old high school student recorded his geography teacher, Jay Bennish, who in a 20 minute tirade, compared President Bush to Hitler and claimed that the victims of 9/11 were "not innocent people" but "military targets" because they worked for companies "that were directly involved in the military-industrial complex that supported military dictatorships in the Middle East, so in the minds of Al Qaeda they are not attacking innocent people".

Why do our schools fail to compare and contrast Islam with Judaism and Christianity and other religions such as Buddhism and Hinduism? For all who consider themselves Christians or Jews, do you want to continue Islamic Indoctrination and the exclusion of Christianity and Judaism from our schools? This has already been fostered by the Democrat Socialist left and will only be continued and expanded upon under a Democratic Administration. Freedom of Religion will be sorely tested if not abolished under a Democrat regime. The liberal left bias and hatred toward Republicans, those who are pro-life and those who are Christians and Jews is severe and mounting every day. This is just a small sample of what is in store for us, if the Liberal Democrats would have their way.

CHAPTER 5
Government, Media and Entertainment Industry Bias and Hatred.

IF THE LIBERAL left hatred and bias in our colleges and universities is not enough, here is a sampling of the hate, propaganda and bias spewed out daily by our liberal left political leaders, our media and our entertainment industry:

Nancy Pelosi – "I would eagerly back legislation requiring Trump to take a mental exam'. Pelosi would also say "With Trump in charge of America's nuclear arsenal – like a toddler playing with a loaded firearm." Yet every action Trump has taken refutes this, even his limited precision strike on the Syrian airfield from which Assad's chemical weapons were delivered against his own people; men, women and children. In fact, Nancy Pelosi supported this action. But more importantly, Trump has initiated talks and has sought personal relationships with the heads of China, Saudi Arabia, Palestine, North Korea and Russia and specifically he seeks to assist in any way that Palestine and Israel want in developing a lasting peace and peaceful co-existence between Palestine and Israel. Obama had ignored developing relationships with and understanding of our foreign adversaries, at least during the last two or three years of his presidency. Then there is her statement that she will give only $1 to build the wall and claiming that walls don't work. Then why does Pelosi have a wall surrounding her own home? I would expect that there are a number of other Democrats opposed to the border walls that are living in houses surrounded by a wall of their own.

Chuck Schumer - Senator from New York, Chuck Schumer went into a tirade at an upscale restaurant, Sette Mezzo, in the Upper East Side in NYC in late March, 20 17. Schumer encountered Joseph Califano, Jr., former U.S. Secretary of Health, Education and Welfare under President Jimmy Carter, and his wife Hillary. They were having a quiet dinner when Schumer became incensed that Hillary Califano had voted for Trump, even though her husband was a well-known Democrat. Schumer according to witnesses made a scene, yelling: "she voted for Trump". The Califanos left the restaurant, but Schumer followed them outside and continued his tirade, saying: "how could you vote for Trump?" "He's a liar" and he kept repeating that. Whether one is for or against Trump, one should not go off in an abusive rage in public and castigate someone for voting their conscience. Schumer is a very senior leader of the Democrats in the U.S. Senate. Yet his unbridled lack of control of his emotions and attack on the opposition certainly would call into question whether under any circumstances he could work with Republicans for the benefit of all citizens of the United States. Unfortunately, this attitude of destroying President Trump and the Republican Party at all costs and without regard to what is best for the country is all too prevalent among the liberal Democrat party leaders.

Maxine Waters – Maxine Waters tirades against Trump have been incessant and ongoing since the very day President Trump took office. She has vilified Trump and his administration with constant frenzied public attacks often with the aid of a bullhorn, such as: "Trump should be impeached." "I will fight night and day until he is impeached". Trump's Cabinet? – "This is a bunch of scumbags; that's what they are". Yet what is the impeachable offense that Waters is accusing Trump of? She never tells us. And what else is Maxine Waters noted for other than her constant tirade against President Trump. What has she accomplished for her district in California? She certainly does not represent her constituents very well as she has chosen to live apart from them in luxury in another district.

Tim Kaine – Democratic Senator from Virginia and former Vice- Presidential candidate with Hillary Clinton, Senator Kaine urged "Democrats must fight in the streets". If this were said by a Republican, he would be accused by the media of sedition, urging violent revolutionary action and bloodshed, yet the statement virtually goes unnoticed. Kaine would also claim that the Trump Administration denies the Holocaust. This is more than an irresponsible statement when in a recent televised meeting between Trump and Prime Minister of Israel, Benjamin Netanyahu; Netanyahu stated that Trump was the best friend Israel has had in many years. He would hardly say this, if the Trump administration really denied the Holocaust.

John Lewis – "Trump is an illegitimate President". This statement by Lewis and his boycott of the inauguration, demonstrated how hate dominates Democrat politics.

Elizabeth Warren - Arguably, one of the more irrational statements out of the mouth of Elizabeth Warren, Senator from Massachusetts: "America will never be ready for a male president after Trump". What possible purpose could this statement have? It is arbitrary, emotional, subjective, and clearly divisive. Elizabeth Warren is a candidate for president in 2020. She has consistently lied about her heritage fraudulently claiming to be a Native American and thereby gaining personal advantage for doing so. Now she wants to spend trillions of dollars, raise your taxes, and provide free college tuition that will bankrupt our country. She will destroy private ownership of property by placing higher taxes on estates. Farmers will lose their properties and small businesses will not be able to be passed on to their children and grandchildren. And the open borders and providing illegal immigrants with all the social benefits that she would create, will not only displace many workers who are citizens of our country, but the cost will bankrupt our country. And I have not as yet mentioned the Green New deal she supports, which will destroy America.

Beto O'Rourke - Former Congressman from Texas and now running for President, stated in October

2019, that he would end tax exemptions for Churches that only supported traditional marriages. This could not be a clearer violation of the 1st Amendment to the Constitution. O'Rourke would give the Federal Government the right to dictate to a church what it can and cannot believe.

Kamala Harris - Another candidate for Democrat President, Senator from California and former Attorney General of California was interviewed on October 18, 2019, by Anderson Cooper on "Anderson Cooper 360" show. She stated that former Mayor of NYC and current advisor to President Trump, Rudy Giuliani: "Has clearly broken many laws". When Anderson Cooper asked Harris what specific laws she believes Giuliani has broken, Senator Harris said: "Well I don't know, but we're going to find out". But I think the range includes abuse of power and perhaps miss-statement and miss-characterization of his role and responsibility, but I also really wonder just instinctively whether there is any bribery associated with Giuliani's conduct?" This so characterizes the thoughtlessness, abuse and vilification that is constant from the liberal left.

Gerald Sysnette – Field production supervisor for CNN. If there is any question about whether CNN has an extreme bias or hatred for Trump, the very words of Synette make this clear: "The only way this (Trump) will go away is when he dies. Hopefully soon." Was there any censure of these comments from the liberal left Democrats? Was there even a remark from CNN senior executives as to the inappropriateness of such a comment?

Leadership of the Democratic Party - The Democratic National Committee (DNC) after careful deliberation had selected to represent their party Tom Perez as chairman and Keith Ellison as Vice Chairman. These are the men chosen by the Democratic Party to represent their beliefs and objectives and hopefully represent the majority of the voters in coming elections. It would be anticipated that the objective of any party leadership would be to not only continue the support of existing Democrats, but also win over new recruits from the opposition.

1. **Tom Perez** - In a recent speech in Newark, New Jersey Perez ranted that Trump didn't win the election and Republicans don't give a sh*t about people. The response of the Democrats was to order T-shirts to sell that had emblazed on them: "Democrats do give a sh*t about people". In another instance Perez told the crowd that "Democrats can't be pro-life". You must be pro-abortion or don't bother to be a Democrat." There are a vast number of people who believe in the sanctity of life and that sanctity occurs well before the actual birth of the infant. Yet Democrat leadership would impose the belief in abortion as a requisite to being a Democrat. Does this sound like the Democrats seek to represent all the people of the United States? Isn't this in the same vain as Hillary Clinton's statements that half of the Republicans are "deplorable"; that Republicans are her enemies (Statement made to Anderson Cooper in an interview) and "there is a special place in hell for women who don't support women" (actually said by Madeline Albright when she introduced Hillary Clinton at a campaign rally. A video showed Hillary laughing and clapping with glee to this Albright remark)

2. **Keith Ellison – Deputy Chairman of the Democratic Party** - Ellison is a convert to Islam

from Roman Catholicism and was a Congressman from Minnesota's fifth district. His voting record is 100% pro-choice. He caused some consternation when he took the oath of office swearing on the Qur'an, making him supporter of Sharia law in opposition to our Constitution. In 1992 Ellison said that Black Americans do not have an obligation to obey the government because it considers them "less than human". He also wrote that the U.S. Constitution is evidence of a white racist conspiracy to subjugate other peoples. (Sounds like what any Muslim would say in support of the superiority of Sharia law). Ellison was known to be a strong supporter of Louis Farrakhan and the Nation of Islam and at one time was a spokesman for Louis Farrakhan leader, even publishing several articles in support of Farrakhan. Farrakhan loudly proclaims his hatred for the Jews, even to the point of saying that Hitler was a great man and that he refers to Jews as "termites". Farrakhan also has said that "Whites deserve to die" and "they (the whites) are going down". And yet in 1995 Ellison called Farrakhan a role model for black youth. Ellison also supported Farrakhan's statement: "since we cannot get along with them (the whites) in peace and equality we believe our contributions to this land and the sufferings forced upon us by white America justifies our demand for a complete separation in a state or territory of our own". Yet the Democrats have raised Ellison to the second most prominent position in the Democratic Party; a man who is actively anti-White and anti-Jew.

So, we see intolerance, hate, divisiveness, the support of anti-Christian values and the flaunting of our Constitution and the laws of our country all wrapped up in the Democratic Party and particularly its leaders. Is this the kind of democracy and leadership we want for our country?

Andre Carson – Congressman from Indiana and a convert to Islam would have: "our public schools should be modeled after Islamic schools that are built on the foundation of the Qur'an

Ilhan Omar and Rashida Tlaib - Newly elect Islamic Democratic Socialist Congresswomen Ilhan Omar from Minnesota and Rashida Tlaib from Michigan are welcomed by the Democratic party although they are both anti- Jew, anti-Christian and are opposed to the U.S. Federal Government. Just hours after being sworn into office Tlaib proclaimed that the American Democrat party would focus on ousting President from office and with all the hatred and vitriol she could muster was quoted as saying; "we are going to impeach the "motherf-----". Tlaib has also publicly suggested that Trump officials should be threatened with jail if they do not comply with the Democrats. She said: "They can hold all these people right here in Detroit". Rashida Tlaib recently visited the Detroit Police Department and told the chief of police, James Craig, an African-American, that all analysts working with recognition software in the police department should be African-Americans as non-African Americans think all African Americans look alike." The chief told Tlaib: "I trust the people that are trained, regardless of race or gender". Tlaib went further and told the chief to:" give some of our money back until they fix it".

Omar has made several anti-Jewish statements maybe the worst being: "Israel has hypnotized the world. May Allah awaken the people and help them to see the evil doings of Israel". And then recently,

Omar claimed that 9/11 was "some people did something", indicating that she is not just anti-Jew, she is also Anti-American. Ilhan Omar is also on record of saying that: "Our country should be more fearful of white men than Jihadists. Is that not racist comment? Do most Democrats fear white men because they are white?

So does a Democrat fear a white male Democrat or only white male Republicans. And no one on the liberal left takes exception to or criticizes these remarks. Hatred, racism and divisiveness is rampant in the Democrat party and it is time for the Democrat constituents to recognized this. And it is not just against white men. There is racism against Jews that is left unchallenged by fellow Democrats; there is hatred and bias expressed against all those who believe in the "right to life" and they would be banned from the Democratic party, according to the DNC chairman Tom Perez. And finally, Republicans are "deplorables" and there is a special place in hell "for women who don't vote for women".

Alexandria Ocasio- Cortez – This freshman member of the House Representative has stirred the Democrat party to new levels of radical Socialism and created a Green New Deal proposal, whose overwhelming cost will destroy our country. I cover this in detail, elsewhere. But besides her frivolous and insane ideas, which apparently are endorsed by the Democrat party, Ocasio-Cortez reveals her lack of patriotism and in fact hatred for our country. She has stated that America is "garbage". Specifically, she has stated: "but where we are is not a good thing. And this idea of like being 10% better than garbage, it shouldn't be what we should settle for". What Ocasio-Cortez wants for America is a Socialist regime like Venezuela. She claims that America's ideals of life, liberty and pursuit of happiness; of freedom and justice, shouldn't be what we should settle for as a country". Her hate for America even includes President Reagan, whom she also calls a racist. In the light of all the economic improvements that we have seen during the past two years, Cortez claims that America is in decline from its current state of garbage. And yet there is no rebuking of any of the statements made by Cortez. In fact, the House leader Nancy Pelosi seeks to accommodate Cortez in every way and endorses Cortez's vision of America. These angry, hateful statements are rampant throughout the Democratic party. Whether a Democrat or Republican, how can we expect our government to act in our best interests, when there is such rancor and such a do-nothing but impeach attitude among the Democrats along with their attitude to oppose Trump at any cost and without any concern for the outcome?

Leadership in our Cities - We have only to look at our cities across or country and to evaluate how well the Democrats have led our country. Start with Chicago and its Democrat Mayor for 7 years, Rohm Emmanuel. The incidence of black shootings and black murders is astonishing. The 10 cities in the U.S. with the highest crime rates are all run by Democrats and they include: Detroit, St. Louis, Oakland, Memphis, Birmingham, Atlanta, Baltimore, Stockton, Cleveland and Buffalo. Additional Democrat-run cities that could be added to the list because they have the highest murder rates include: New Orleans, Newark, Cincinnati, Miami and Baton Rouge. They are all run by liberal Democrats. Is this at least partially explained by the anti-police rhetoric and vitriol constantly emanating from the liberal left? And then there is the issue of homelessness most prevalent in liberal Democrat run cities, like Seattle, Portland, Oregon and San Francisco. More about this later

Sample of Media Hatred and Bias

MSNBC's Rachel Maddow in an interview with Rolling Stone stated that "Studying Hitler helped her understand Trump". In July, 2016, she reiterated that Adolf Hitler's rise to power helped her better understand Donald Trump's candidacy. Let's try to understand the illogic of Rachel Maddow's comparison of Trump to Hitler.

- Hitler hated Jews and even discussed their annihilation in his book "Mein Kompf, a book that Rachel Maddow claimed had led to her better understanding of Trump. In contrast, far from being anti-Jew, no less than the Prime Minister of Israel, Benjamin Netanyahu publicly claimed that Trump was the best friend Israel ever had.

- One of the first steps Hitler took in gaining control over Germany was to take control of education. It is the liberal left, not Trump that has been taking control of education in the United States, through its dominance with liberal left educators; through supporting national controlled education programs such as "Common Core" and through indoctrination of students to Islam through a nationally approved Islamic studies program for grades 3 through 12. Trump on the other hand seeks to return education to the local communities and Boards of Education and to increase freedom of educational choice; just the opposite of what Hitler established for the Germans and what the liberal left is establishing for American youth.

- Hitler took over control of all media and placed it under his propaganda minister Goebbels. Trump not only doesn't control the media; he is under constant attack by the far liberal left that dominates the media. The liberal left, and its supporting media are far more Hitler-like than the conservative right.

- Hitler was an active supporter and promoter of Islam, even to the point of envisioning it as the only religion for Germans. He would do away with Judaism and Christianity. It is the Democrats and the liberal left, through its control of education and the media that is pro-Palestine, Pro-Islam (refusing to use the term "radical Islam"), anti-Christian and anti-Jew. In contrast, Trump has said on a number of occasions he wants to bring Christmas back and is not afraid to use the term "radical Islamic Terrorists"

- Trump, unlike Hitler, does not support Islamic Sharia law". The Democrats and the liberal left on the other hand support Islam and Sharia law by placing at the top levels of their party, people who support Sharia law and oppose the U.S. Constitution.

- It is the liberal Left and the Democratic Party who like Hitler seeks to spread an agenda of hatred to gain support.

- In short, there is nothing in Trump's agenda or acts that would indicate that he is like Hitler. On the contrary, it is the words and actions of the liberal left, whether government, media, education or entertainment that wreaks of Hitlerism. And the liberal left has so far been very successful because so many people readily accept the hateful tirades that the liberal left unmercifully bombards us with.

MSNBC's Chris Matthews - Chris Matthews' disdain and hatred for President Donald Trump knows no bounds. One should be able to look to MSNBC for logical, honest reporting, but all we hear from Matthews is a constant diatribe against Trump. In March 2017, Matthews stated he had a hard time calling Trump President. In late March 2017, Matthews may have reached his lowest point in his hatred and bias against Trump when he compares Ivanka Trump and her husband Jared Kushner to Saddam Hussein's two oldest violent and murderous sons Uday and Qusay Hussein saying "You couldn't go to a restaurant and have eye contact with one of these guys without getting killed" In July 2015, Matthews had suggested that Ted Cruz feared Mr. Trump the same way Iraqi people feared Uday and Qusay Hussein. This is the kind of "objective" reporting we have come to expect from the so-called best of our commentators. Propaganda minister Goebbels would have welcomed Matthews and Maddow on his staff.

CNN's Wolf Blitzer – Just when you thought you heard the worst from Chris Matthews, CNN's Wolf Blitzer contemplates how the assassination of Trump could keep Obama's Administration in power. On Wednesday, January 18, 2017 Broadcast on CNN Wolf Blitzer introduces a segment: "What if an incoming president and his immediate successors were wiped out on day one?" Even to think this hypothetically, suggests the level of hatred spewed forth by our liberal left commentators and this sounds like just the kind of thought Hitler or Stalin would have had just before assassinating his enemies.

MSNBC's Joe Scarborough and Mika Brzezinski - These co-hosts of MSNBC's "Morning Joe" are not above spewing hatred and making irrational, unsupported comments about Trump, making you wonder if anything they say is believable, meaningful or newsworthy. On a recent "Morning Joe Show" the two hosts in an on-going effort to discredit President Trump spent a considerable segment questioning the President's sanity, saying that his mother had dementia for 10 years and that some of things said by Trump sound like his mother. Mika went on to say "I have lost hope completely". And in her avid support of suppressing any news from the Conservative right, suggested that "Everyone should ban Kellyanne Conway from their show". Kellyanne Conway is special Counselor to the U.S. President, someone that should be on the list of every news program as someone the public should be able to hear from and whose opinions, they should have access to. Mika is another person that Hitler and Goebbels would like to have on their propaganda staff.

In July 2019, Joe Scarborough on his MSNBC "Morning Joe" show went as far as to say that the Democrats should no longer fight by" the Marquis of Queensbury rules". He is suggesting fight dirty, insurrection, violence, anything to destroy the Trump Administration and his fellow Conservatives. This is the level of hate that Scarborough spews out to his audience on a daily basis. Does he represent what we all want for our country? Or do many of us just sit back and go along with the constant hatred of the liberal left. How easily we forget our history and think how Hitler through the spread of his hatred of Jews was able to convince so many that Jews were less than animals and should be exterminated. Hatred ruled in Nazi Germany and will rule gain; this time in the United States if the Democrats were to regain power.

Washington Post - editorial board in March 2016 warned voters that Trump could be another Hitler.

Palmer Report – Bill Palmer in one of his Palmer Reports, gave his opinion that "Vladimir Putin orchestrated a gas attack in Syria so Donald Trump could strike back in minimal fashion and that Putin told Trump ahead of time to go ahead and begin to build up troops in advance and Trump went along with this horrifying stunt. This may be a convoluted explanation, but it makes logical sense." Further, he claimed that Assad gassed his own people so that Trump could have an excuse for war" and Palmer goes on to say that: "Trump's attack on Syria was arranged by Putin" and that "Putin, Assad and Trump are betting on Assad's chemical attack motivating American people that it is okay with American intervention in Syria. The trio is gambling that most Americans won't notice they are entering war in favor of genocidal Assad instead of against him. Trump will either attack the rebels fighting against Assad or he'll copycat the Kremlin's playbook by pretending he's fighting against what little is left of ISIS in Syria, but actually targeting the rebels instead." The sheer absurdity, illogic and nonsense demonstrated here by the left should make it unworthy of being repeated, but it demonstrates just how far the left will go in its propaganda to vilify Trump.

Michiko Kakutani - In his review of Jason Stanley's book "How Propaganda Works", Kakutani begins his review with: "In "Mein Kompf" Hitler argued that effective propaganda appeals to the feelings of the public rather than to their reasoning ability; relies on stereotyped formulas repeated over and over again to drum ideas into the minds of the masses and uses simple "love or hate"; "right or wrong" formulations to assail the enemy while making intentionally biased and one-sided arguments. I was sure that Mr. Kakutani was talking about the Democrats and the far left until at a later date I learn that Kakutani sees Trump as Hitlerian in his thinking. Yet he has portrayed the activity of the Democrats, the media and the entertainment industry perfectly for the past three years.

Bill Maher –HBO political talk show host and representative of liberal left thinking recently reached a new low in liberal vitriol against Trump when he made on the air an incest joke about Donald Trump and his daughter Ivanka. Maher stated that: "when he (Trump) is about to nuke Finland or something, she's (Ivanka) is going to walk into Trump's bedroom and say: "Daddy don't do it Daddy" and lewdly makes gestures as if she is jerking her father off. Liberal left media made little or no mention of this and certainly did not criticize Maher. Could you imagine a Fox News Commentator making such a statement about Chelsea Clinton and her father? In the summer of 2019, Maher prayed that our country would suffer a recession, so that President Trump would be driven from office. Then in late August 2019, when David Koch one of the two billionaire Koch brothers died at the age of 79 from prostate cancer, Bill Maher applauded his death, even though the Koch Brothers have been great philanthropists. Bill Maher hated Koch because he did not support the contention that CO_2 caused global warming. Maher would say to his applauding liberal left audience: "I'm glad he is dead and I hope the end was painful. He further said: "as for his remains, he has asked to be cremated and have his ashes blown into a child's lungs".

Charles Pierce -Far left sportswriter, Charles Pierce suggested that Koch's corpse be dropped into the

Amazon Rain forest fire. There were a number of comments by others along these lines and they were cheered by their liberal left audience. The hatred spewing from the liberal left knows no limitations.

Stephen Colbert - Not to be outdone by Maher, CBS late Night Show host said this about Trump: "The only thing your mouth is good for, (Trump), is being Vladimir Putin's cock holster. Yet, again there was no critical fallout from the liberal left.

Jimmy Kimmel – Late night host and Executive producer of ABC's Jimmy Kimmel Live Show, has constantly vilified President Trump as a white supremacist and antifeminist. He constantly performs monologues for the benefit of his audience, which show his hatred for Trump and Republicans. One wonders how Kimmel can call anyone an anti-feminist when we need only look at his abhorrent background. Approximately 5 years ago, out in public on the street at night, Kimmel approached a number of women and asked them to "Guess what's in my pants". There is a five-year-old video clip, featuring him asking women to guess what's in his pants by using their hands to explore his crotch and even put their hands inside his pants. One "contestant" was aggressively groping around his penis and he commented "you're gonna be a fine wife". He suggested to another woman "use both hands" followed up by saying: "maybe it would be easier if you put your mouth on it". Kimmel asked another woman how old she was? When she said she was 18, Kimmel responded: "are you sure because Uncle Jimmie doesn't want to go to jail". How hypocritical can one get? Kimmel's offensive, distasteful actions speak louder than any words and they are about as anti-feminist as one can get. These women were being demeaned and were being used by Kimmel to demonstrate that women are subservient to men. At the end of the video, Kimmel shows one of the women, what was in his pants. It was a green zucchini, which he then told the woman could be used as a vibrator.

Boston Globe – Michael A. Cohen – On November 15, 2016, writer for the Boston Globe, Michael A. Cohen probably made the most clear and succinct statement of the attitude of the liberal left, whether they are politicians, media representatives, educators or entertainers. Michael A. Cohen spoke for them all when he said: I don't want Trump to succeed; I want him to fail spectacularly". He gives no reason for wishing this. How can anyone wish for their president to fail without identifying specific reasons why he wants him to fail? When you wish your President to fail, you are placing your personal hatred above the best interests of the people, certainly the interests of those that voted the president into office.

Washington Post – Washington Times - contrast report on Trump's Trip to Saudi Arabia – A historic trip was made to Saudi Arabia by Donald Trump, to see if a better relationship and level of understanding leading to peace and cooperation could be achieved between all nations, but specifically among the countries, with deep roots in different religions, namely Judaism, Christianity and Islam. The leaders of 50 Muslim nations, led by King Salman of Saudi Arabia were in attendance. Washington Post – Ann Applebaum characterized the Trump trip to Saudi Arabia as "President Trump's Trip to Saudi Arabia was bizarre, unseemly, unethical and Un-American".

Contrast this to Washington Times – S.A. Miller – "In a strong start to the journey, Mr. Trump chartered a new course for U.S. anti-terrorism and foreign policy with the leaders from 50 Muslim states". "It's a turning point in the relationship between the United States and the Arab and Islamic World" said Saudi Foreign Minister A del al-Juber. Trump received a hero's welcome when he arrived in Rihad and was greeted by King Salman on the tarmac, an honor denied Obama in 2009 and the King gave Trump a firm handshake, rather than the deep bow bestowed by Obama. Trump's message left no doubt the shift in U.S. Policy".

Trump's "new course" seeks peace between the Muslims, Jews and Christians; the eradication of terrorism; the respecting of each other's religions and the working together to achieve great things for the people of the Middle East, Israel and the U.S. There are 218 million Muslims in the Middle East; 323 million American citizens and 8.4 million Israelis. Force and violence will never bring these all together. We must find peace through negotiation, compromise and accepting our differences. That is exactly what Trump was trying to accomplish in this first step. Yet the liberal media will still find fault and seek to undermine any attempt to arrive at a just peace; preferring rather to condemn Trump's actions, whatever they may be even if those actions are for the benefit of not only the U.S. but the world community. This was a historical moment; the opportunity for a new beginning. Yet our media chooses to do what it can to make it fail. All because of its hatred and bias toward Trump. And for those on the liberal left that insist that Trump is anti-Semitic, tell that to the leaders of Israel and the Muslim world.

Now let us look at the last group to attack and vilify our President with vitriol, illogic, hatred and animosity; that is our Entertainment industry. Statements border on sedition and even are traitorous Yet no one from the liberal left even questions whether the statements are over the line. Let's mention a few of the shocking statements coming from our entertainment industry:

Michael Moore – Documentary film maker and author calls for Trump's arrest saying: Vacate you traitor". Describes Trump as: "wretched, ignorant, dangerous part-time clown and full-time sociopath". What does this irrational diatribe do for America? Where is the objectivity?

Madonna - Can anyone, even the most radical liberal actually support her seditious comment: "I thought an awful lot about blowing up the White House. God did not win the election". What hypocrisy for Madonna to invoke God? She certainly does not accept any of Jesus' teachings.

Whoopi Goldberg - Co-host on NBC's show "The View", American actress calls for the impeachment of Donald Trump stating that she "is more qualified to be president than Trump".

Joy Behar – Co-host with Whoopi Goldberg on "The View" "He needs to be impeached – He's as crazy as Kim Jong Yum" (referring to Kim Jong-un Supreme leader of the Democratic People's Republic of North Korea).

Cordozar Calvini Broadis - Better known as **SNOOP Dogg** the American rapper, shoots the likeness of Trump in his March 2017 musical video. Liberal Democrats need to ask themselves what would have been the outcry if Snoop Dogg had aimed and fired a toy gun at a likeness of President Obama?

Jennifer Lawrence - "His election might be the end of the world".

Chelsea Handler – "His (Trump's) win would mean the end of civilization" Neither Lawrence or Handler attempt to rationalize these statements with any kind of logic or rationale. These are two successful actresses, who like so many other entertainers, believe that anything they say has merit and that being in the entertainment industry, they are free to make outrageous statements, although specifically because of their notoriety, they should be more objective and careful in what they say. Fame and notoriety should bring with it a respect for objectivity and a caution in what one says as opposed to giving one more freedom to make outrageous remarks. After all, what the person of fame says is most likely because of their fame to be disseminated widely to the public. Here is another example of a thoughtless, irresponsible statement made by someone who because of his or her prominence can spew hatred to many millions of people.

Meryl Streep - One of the most emotionally outspoken people, whose demonstration of hatred against Trump is endless, Meryl Streep would publicly say about Trump: "If his catastrophic instinct to retaliate doesn't lead to nuclear war…." And "If you think people were mad when they thought the government as coming after their guns, wait to you see when they try to take away your happiness". President Trump has done more to open dialogue in the past two years with the leaders of the world, especially those with nuclear capability, than the Obama Administration did in his 8 years. Nuclear threats have subsided due to the leadership of Trump in contrast to the expansion of the nuclear threat under the Obama Administration.

Miley Cyrus - not the most exemplary character in the entertainment industry, nevertheless she is prominent in the eyes of the public and has been quoted as saying about Trump: "Wake me up from the nightmare – You will destroy everything we have overcome as women".

Susan Sarandon - "He reminds me of a drunk uncle at a wedding – I can't ever address him seriously". This is the best analogy that a once famous actress can come up with? To compare a sitting President to a drunken uncle at a wedding is not only silly. It has no foundation in reality like so many of the statements of our liberal left entertainers.

Johnny Depp – "If Trump is elected president, in a historical way it will be exciting because we will actually see the last President of the United States".

Johnny Depp – Once again, Johnny Depp speaks out in protest against our president. This time in June, 2017 before a large audience at the Glastonbury England film festival, he said "When was the last time an actor assassinated a president?" He then followed this comment with: "However, it's been a while and maybe it is time".

Kathy Griffin – By far the worst and most violent assault on the presidency was the photo shoot at the end of May that went virile showing Kathy Griffin wielding a severed and bloodied replica of President Donald Trump's head. There was virtually no outrage from the congressional left.

Barbara Streisand – On October 19, 2019, radical left-wing actress and singer, Barbara Streisand posted a photo on twitter depicting a bloodied President Trump being impaled by the spike heel of a women's shoe with the word "Pelosi" emblazoned on it. Again, no comment or outrage from the Socialist Democrat left.

Jim Carrey – In November, 2019, he released a gruesome political drawing of President Trump, depicting Nancy Pelosi banging a gavel down on President Trump's genitals. Is this something he should be proud of? Does this not help to inspire hatred in our country? This is the same hatred that has become the trademark of the Democrats toward police and all members of law enforcement. The Democrats refuse to condemn those on the far left who riot in the streets and destroy their own cities and constantly refer to police as "pigs", even screaming for their death. How can we forget the recent riot in New York City where hoodlums attacked police and through buckets of water on them? There was virtually no response from Mayor De Blasio's office other than to tell them to stand down and do nothing.

Debra Messing - A new experience of the hatred toward President Trump emanating from the liberal left raised its ugly head, when in early September, 2019 Debra Messing called for publicizing the list of entertainers attending a Beverly Hills fund raiser for President Trump. She wanted to publish the list so "the rest of us can be clear about who we wanna work with". This so called "black list" is so reminiscent of the Republican Senator from Wisconsin, Joe McCarthy's hearings and the "Red Scare" that occurred beginning in April 1954. This was a period of intense anti-communist suspicion in the United States that lasted from the late 1940's to the mid 1950's. This "witch hunt" resulted in hundreds of Americans being accused of being Communist. And the greatest to suffer were entertainers, specifically hundreds from Hollywood who were blacklisted and became ineligible for employment because of alleged communist ties. Many lost their careers for the rest of their lives. Messing would have that happen to any entertainer who supports the Republican party. Those of you who were born after World War II may not remember many of the outstanding writers and entertainers that were blacklisted, but here are some you may have heard about: Orson Beane, Leonard Bernstein, Abe Burrows, Charlie Chaplin, Ossie Davis, Jose Ferrer, John Garfield, Judy Holliday, Lena Horne, Burgess Meredith, Arthur Miller, Kenneth Roberts, Edward G. Robinson, Artie Shaw and Orson Welles, to name just a few. Messing's desire to blacklist the Conservative Right is no different from the "witch hunt of the 1940's and 1950's. Fortunately, in the mid and late 1950's the attitudes and institutions of McCarthyism slowly weakened and changing public sentiment contributed substantially to the decline.

David Simon – ABC producer of the Television show "Wire" the crime drama television series. came out with this statement right after Hurricane Dorian had totally decimated the Bahamas, and then threatened the south-eastern seaboard. He said: "After the last three years, the work of a just and righteous God cannot be considered credible evidence of his goodness, unless he picks all of Mare a

Logo (Trump's Florida Home) up by its roots, sails it cross half of Florida and heaves it atop of Doral". (Trump's Resort and Golf Course). Here is a far-left entertainer, willing that God kills 100's of people and destroys the property of innocents only because of his unquenched hatred for Donald Trump and the Conservative Right.

Central Park Re-enactment of Shakespeare's Julius Caesar in modern day dress – In this intolerable, promotion to violence against President Trump, the character of Julius Caesar is dressed and made up to look like Donald Trump and is assassinated on stage. Like Depp and, Griffin these words and deeds are meant to incite violence against the President of the United States. And these acts seemed to be accepted if not welcomed by the left including the liberal Democrats in Washington who supposedly are to represent all of us.

The Shooting of Republicans in Alexandria, Virginia – Early in the morning, on June 14, 2017, a 66 year old left wing zealot from Belleville, Illinois named James T. Hodgkinson, opened fire on the GOP Congressional baseball team, practicing on the field at Eugene Simpson Stadium Park for the annual game between Republican and Democrat Congressmen and their staffs. After confirming that the baseball players were Republicans, Hodgkinson went on the field with an automatic rifle with the intent of gunning them all down. House Majority Whip Steve Scalise was the only one seriously wounded of the four victims of the shooting. Many lives if not all would have been lost, if not for the heroic and immediate action of two Washington Capitol police officers, who shot and killed Hodgkinson. It was hatred of Republicans, particularly Trump and his administration that led Hodgkinson to take the liberal left hatred to the extreme. It is policemen like the two heroic cops, that many who are avowed liberal left, refer to as "pigs". Hatred is a breeding ground for violence and there is no better evidence of this then that day in June, when an angry, hateful Democrat was prepared to snuff out the lives of so many, just because they were Republican. Let us not forget that well known representatives of the Liberal left have: suggested bombing of the White House; called for the assassination of the President; held up a bloodied replica of the head of the President; pretended to shoot the president in the head, suggested mounting a military coups against the president and performed a mock killing of the president by a gang of knife wielding assassins.

Mayor Bill de Blasio - With crime rates in NYC growing and the number of homeless soaring, and the recent assassination of a police woman, Mayor De Blasio decides to skip the NYPD swearing in ceremony in early July, 2017 in order to prepare to jet to Hamburg, Germany to join the leftist protestors at the G-20 summit. He was the keynote speaker at the "Hamburg shows attitude" demonstration, that led to riots and violence in the streets of Hamburg. The New York City Mayor joined with the 8,000 or more taking part in the protest against the Summit titled: "G-20, welcome to hell". All the gains that New York City made under Mayors Giuliani and Bloomberg, in terms of reduction in crime and improvement of quality of life are being quickly dissipated under Mayor De Blasio. Ask the commuters about the status of the NYC subway system. Yet NYC Mayor finds time to fly to Hamburg and protest against the G-20 Summit. For those who may not be that familiar with G-20, it is an international forum of 19 countries plus the European Union representing the governments and central banks governors of the member countries. The countries include: Argentina, Australia, Brazil, Canada, China, France, Germany, India, Indonesia, Italy, Japan, Mexico, Russia, Saudi Arabia, South Africa, South Korea, Turkey, UK, U.S. and the European Union. These countries account for 85% of the world's GDP and 80% of the World Trade. The G-20 started in 2008, replacing the G-8 as the main economic council of wealthy nations. Since 2008 the summit has been a focus of major protests by left wing groups and anarchists. Why the mayor of a major U.S. city would protest the gathering of nations to seek ways to achieve international improvement in world economies makes no sense, yet there appears to be no criticism coming from the liberal left.

Rosie O'Donnell – Certainly a rather irrelevant person in the entertainment industry, nevertheless she has her following. She has come forward with a suggested "Trump Killing" game, where one can make Trump jump off a cliff again and again.

Bette Midler – Midler was recently challenged by Kirstie Alley, for being a "pure and real racist" for her comments concerning some blacks being Conservative and Republican. Midler apparently was surprised to see people of color backing POTUS and wondered if his campaign paid them to be "background". The implication could not be clearer. Midler is saying: 1) blacks have no right to think for themselves and 2) blacks can be bought. This is just another terrible example of white supremacism and racism imposed on black Americans not by Republicans but by Democrats over the centuries. When will blacks in America realize that it is the socialist left Democrats not the Republicans that not only are the racists, but also seek to use them to gain power and totalitarian authority over all Americans regardless of race, creed or color?

Let's not forget it was the 7 Democrat Supreme court justices who voted unanimously, that "once a slave always a slave" over-riding the two dissenting Republican Justices in the Dred Scott case. It was the Democrats, who started the Civil War to preserve slavery; it was the Democrats who assassinated Lincoln; It was the Republicans in the North who valiantly gave their lives in vast numbers so as the black slaves in the South could be free. It was the Democrat President, Woodrow Wilson, an avid supporter of the KKK, that imposed segregation on the Federal government; it was the Democrats that founded the KKK. It was the Democrats who established and enforced the "Jim Crow" laws in the South; It is the Democrats that control every major city in the United States where Blacks are under siege and it was the Democrat Alabama Governor Wallace who ran on a platform of" segregation forever"

Robert DeNiro – On June 10, 2018 before an audience for the 72nd Tony Awards, DeNiro who already had said publicly that he would like to punch President Trump in the face said to the standing ovation of our entertainment industry: "It's no longer down with Trump its "f.. k" Trump. This stalwart of our entertainment industry is now being sued for $12 million for bullying and harassment of an employee. Yet this is a guiding light of the Democrat party.

Democrats Embrace Socialism

Finally, I address my primary concerns in this book with the radical move towards socialism that is being sponsored by the liberal left. Democrats are proposing the following: 1) National Health System; 2) the elimination of all fossil fuels thereby putting all workers in the coal, oil and natural gas industries out of work including gas station operators and related convenience store operators; 3) the building of high speed rail systems to replace all air travel, thereby virtually destroying our airline and aerospace industries; 4) dictating what one can eat by abolishing all beef cattle; 5) Requiring the renovation or rebuilding of all buildings to eliminate the use of all fossil fuels; 6) free college education for all; 7) free child care for all; 8) replacing all motor cars and trucks with electric vehicles; 9) a minimum income for all including those who are unwilling to work; 10) abortion at all stages of pregnancy and beyond, which results in providing the government with the ability to control population; 11) prohibiting the building of border walls and even tearing down existing border walls and doing away with Immigration and Customs Enforcement (ICE) Agency, thereby telling undocumented and illegal immigrants that they can freely come to America, where they will be provided free medical, free education, free child care and 12) Nationalization of railways, schools, health, real property. (Think of how much property will have to be taken from private ownership by eminent domain to complete the 10's of thousands of miles of high-speed railways crisscrossing the country).

The Democrats are even saying that global warming will destroy us in 12 years. If that's the case we are already too late. Look at the fiasco of the high-speed California railway that was approved by California in 2008 and was to be completed by 2020. A revised time of completion was raised to 2032 and now it has been abandoned. That was only a 540-mile railway. And the billions of dollars already spent on the abandoned railway that could have been used to alleviate the homelessness and filth that pervades the major cities of California, have just gone to waste.

We are literally in a life and death struggle between Capitalism and Socialism. The most important concepts defining Capitalism are: "Free Society", "the right to life, liberty and the pursuit of happiness" and the right for indivudals to succeed based on merit. Production is driven by demand and prices are determined by the free interaction of supply and demand. These concepts are in direct conflict with Socialistic and Communistic doctrines, which seek to control human lives and human initiative Under Socialism the rights to private property are abolished particularly all means of production. All large-scale industries are government owned and/or controlled. Production decisions are driven by state rather than demand.

The Democrat Socialist Myth – The Democrats, particularly their confirmed socialist leader Bernie Sanders would have you believe that the thriving Nordic countries namely, Sweden, Norway, Finland and Denmark are all socialist. The myth that these countries are socialist is consistently and erroneously conveyed to the public by the liberal left. They confuse those who are willing to listen to them into believing that a government that provides some social welfare programs is the same as a government exerting control or ownership over business. These Nordic countries practice free market economics. None of these countries has a minimum wage and Sweden for example allows complete freedom of choice of education for each child. Families in Sweden receive vouchers and are left with the total freedom to choose regular public schools, government-chartered schools or private for-profit schools for their children.

The Economic Freedom Index - The Fraser Institute in Vancouver, Canada, a research based company, compiled a world-wide ranking of countries by an economic freedom index. This provided a comprehensive measure of Capitalism relative to Socialism. Its website explains that the ranking: "is an effort to identify how closely institutions and policies of a country correspond to a limited government ideal, where the government protects property rights and arranges for a limited set of "public goods" such as national defense and access to money of sound value, but little beyond these core functions. Clearly, a Socialist country should perform poorly in a ranking based on these principles and they do.

Now let us look at the Economic Freedom rankings of the world socialist countries. You will note that the countries that support capitalism not only have the highest economic freedom ranking, but also enjoy the highest GDP/Capita as we show later.

Country	Economic Freedom Ranking	Country	Economic Freedom Ranking
Capitalist Countries		**Socialist Countries**	
Hong Kong	1	Russia	98
Singapore	2	China	100
New Zealand	3	India	129
Switzerland	4	Pakistan	131
Australia	5	Egypt	144

Country	Economic Freedom Ranking	Country	Economic Freedom Ranking
Capitalist Countries		**Socialist Countries**	
Iceland	6	Afghanistan	152
United Kingdom	7	Iran	155
Canada	8	Ecuador	170
United Arab Emirates	9	Cuba	175
Taiwan	10	Venezuela	179
Iceland	11	North Korea	180
United States	12		(out of 180)

It is interesting to note that the one economy (Venezuela) that Bernie Sanders would have us emulate is the farthest left of all countries in the world other than North Korea. Yet 60 years ago Venezuela was 4th in the World Economic Freedom Index. What the Democrats have planned for our economy will lead us into the right-hand column with all of the other Socialist countries and our economic freedom and the corresponding well-being of our citizens will be gone forever.

But this doesn't tell the whole story. How do the capitalist nations compare with the Socialist/communist nations on the basis of GDP/Capita, which is the most accepted determination of how well a country is doing for its constituents? We can get a good idea how the socialist systems of the world have failed their countries by looking at the GDP/capita data provided by the International Monetary Fund for the year 2018. We break the countries down into Capitalist and Socialist/Communist Countries and in the following table show their world rankings and actual GDP/Capita in U.S. Dollars as follows:

Country	Rank	GDP/Capita ($')
CAPITALIST COUNTRIES		
Luxembourg	1	$114,234
Switzerland	2	82,950
Norway	3	81,695 (combined capitalist/state run)
Ireland	4	76,099
Iceland	5	74,278
Singapore	7	64,041
United States	8	62,606
Australia	10	56,352
Hong Kong	14	48,517
Germany	16	48,264
Israel	21	41,644
Japan	24	39,306
South Korea	28	30,025
Taiwan	34	24,971

Country	Rank	GDP/Capita
SOCIALIST/COMMUNIST		
Russia	60	11,327
China	67	9,603
Cuba	76	8,433

Iran	96	5,491
Venezuela	122	3,374 (78th and $7,977 in 2017)
Egypt	130	2,573
India	142	2,036
Syria	167	831
North Korea	176	685

What is intriguing about this table is the distinction between North and South Korea. They both exist on the same Peninsula. Their racial and ethnic backgrounds are the same. The only difference is that one country, South Korea is Capitalist and North Korea is Socialist/Communist.

Another insight into the failure of Socialism is what has happened to Venezuela and that in only the last year their GDP/Capita has fallen by almost 60% and is getting worse. Finally, the best of the Socialist/Communist countries (i.e. Russia) has a GDP/capita only 18% of the United States. With Democrats in power, we will move briskly into the column of Socialist/Communist countries and our GDP/Capita will erode by more than 80%. Is this what you Democrat voters really want for yourselves and your country?

Antifa

The claims that the conservative right are supremacists and racists persist from the liberal left and the reaction from the left includes the lawless tearing down of monuments and statues of our historical leaders that had participated in slavery. Regardless of the appropriateness of the statues, individuals should not be making their own decision as to what monuments or statues are allowed to exist. This should be the choice only of the majority. And the violence of the anti-white movement has been substantially expanded by a group calling themselves **Antifa** for "Antifascist". This violent movement in itself is not only racist, but ironically is built on ideas and ideals that are similar to the fascist movements in Germany under Hitler and Italy under Mussolini in the 1930's and 1940's.

The SA, Sturmabteilung, meaning "Assault Division", also known as the Brown Shirts and Storm Troopers was a violent paramilitary group attached to the Nazi Party in pre-WWII Germany. The Brown Shirts were instrumental in Hitler's and the Nazi's rise to power. The Brown Shirts were infamous for their operations outside the law, particularly in its intimidation of Germany's capitalist and Jewish population. There was a similar group in Italy under Mussolini known as the Black shirts. The Brown Shirts and Black Shirts functioned by using threats of violence to secure votes for Hitler and Mussolini to overcome their political enemies. Though they call themselves anti-fascist, the conduct of Antifa parallels the Brown Shirts and Black Shirts not just in terms of violence and brutality, but also in the wearing of black clothes from head to foot as a uniform.

The beliefs of Antifa lean to the far radical left. Antifa protests the amassing of wealth by individuals and corporations. And the radical ideas promoted by Antifa are being adopted by the liberal left, which have moved away from moderation to a conviction that hatred, vilification and brutality must play a role in reaching their socialist objectives for the country. There are no middle of the road Democrats anymore and Antifa seeks to show them the way to gain power.

The Antifa extremists consist primarily of Communists, Socialists and Anarchists all who believe that the Conservative Right represents White Supremacists. And even moderate Democrats support Antifa's attack on supposed White Supremacists, who Antifa defines as Conservative Capitalists. The Democrats need only to look back on their own history from before the Civil War to over 100 years after the war. They were the White Supremacists and claimed that "once a slave always a slave in their 7 to 2 Supreme Court Decision in the Dred Scott Case, (in which the only opposition was the 2 Republican Justice). The White Supremacist Democrats during those years started the Civil War, assassinated President Lincoln; established and enforced the infamous "Jim Crow" Laws to sustain segregation in the South. The Democrats founded the Ku Klux Klan to not only suppress the Blacks, but to harass them, destroy their property and even kill them. And even the Democrat President, Woodrow Wilson, sworn to uphold the laws, which provided freedom for all blacks, carried on a severe policy of segregation within his administration. When will the hypocrisies of the Democrats end? And more importantly when will our citizens wake up to the truth, that the Democrats over the years did everything they could to suppress the Blacks and maintain segregation in the South.

We need only to look at the recent Antifa violent outbreaks in Charlottesville, Virginia and on the University of California – Berkeley campus and the launching of a new Antifa cell in Philadelphia to recognize that this so-called antifascist liberal-socialist group is actually a terrorist organization. The new Antifa cell in Philadelphia is calling for property seizures, violence on police and an all-out revolution. The group hosts anti-police workshops called "Our Enemies in Blue" and calls for armed insurrection. In late August, CNN published a story calling ordinary supporters of President Trump, white supremacists and referred to the White House as the "Elite Supremacist house". History professor at Fordham University is cited in the CNN story for his comparison of Trump voters to nice people in the Holocaust and Rwanda who looked the other way while others performed horrific violence. Not a word is spoken against Antifa whose members perform violence against Conservative Republicans who they claim are all racists and white supremacists.

Antifa is by definition a terrorist organization. Terrorism is defined as the use of violence and intimidation in pursuit of political aims. A joint intelligence assessment by the Department of Homeland Security (DHS) and the FBI blamed the Antifa for attacks on a range of targets including police and government institutions and concluded that "anarchist extremists" were the main cause of violence at a number of public rallies.

The Antifa group first became noticed during the Trump campaign in 2016, when Antifa Terrorists "were showing up at Trump rallies with weapons, shields and bike helmets and just "beating the shit out of people…They're using Molotov cocktails, starting fires, throwing bombs and smashing windows. But the liberal left media, the entertainment industry and members of the Democratic Party remained remarkably silent. On August 30, 2017, Mark Theisen reported in the Washington Post, that in Berkeley, California, a group of thugs representing neo-Communist Antifa, attacked peaceful protestors at a "No to Marxism in America" rally. They wielded sticks and pepper spray and beat people with home-made shields that on them read, "No Hate". The post reported how one peaceful protester was attacked by five black-clad Antifa members, each wind milling kicks and punches into a man desperately trying to protect himself. Members of the Berkeley College Republicans were stalked by Antifa goons who followed them to a gas station and demanded they get out of the f…ing car, warning; "We are real hungry for supremacists and there is more of us".

Then there is the Dartmouth professor, Mark Bray, visiting professor at the Gender Research Institute at Dartmouth, who has defended Antifa's violent tactics. More than 100 Dartmouth faculty members rushed to the support of Mark Bray's repeated justification of Antifa's violence despite the Dartmouth President's condemnation of Bray's support for this so-called Antifascist group. Mark Bray, author of "Antifa – The Antifascist Handbook", has appeared in dozens of television interviews since the Antifa movement gained National recognition following the outbreak of violence in Charlottesville, Virginia. Bray supports Antifa's violence. describing it as "self-defense" and a "legitimate response" to what he termed white supremacism and neo-Nazi violence. He goes further and equates all Capitalists and Conservative Republicans to" White Supremacists" and therefore are Fascists and deserve to have valence used against them. Do all Democrats believe that all Right-Wing conservatives are fascists and should be destroyed? If not, why aren't Democrats speaking out against the violence of Antifa and censoring Bray for spreading terrorism and violence in our country?

In June, 2019 in Portland, Oregon a journalist, Andy Ngo was targeted by Antifa militants and was robbed and brutally assaulted. He was targeted, because he was developing a report that recorded the violence and brutality of Antifa. We heard no criticism of the violent conduct of Antifa coming from the left. The left must believe that the support of Antifa with its violence and brutality may be just what they need to gain power and successfully install socialism within our country.

It is interesting to note that a peaceful protest at Berkeley was organized not by a White Supremacist but by an anti-Marxist self-described "trans-sexual female who embraces diversity". The organizer, Amber Cummings announced on Facebook that Berkeley is at ground zero for the Marxist movement. It should be clear to the reader that the radical liberal left movement, seemingly embraced by the Democratic Party is a totalitarian movement. Its adherents are predominately communists, socialists and anarchists who believe that physical violence is ethically justifiable and effective. The members of Antifa are no different from the Nazis whose advocacy of violence led to the murder of over 25 million innocent men, women and children in the last century. And further, Antifa embraces the same murderous ideology that led to the killing of 85 to 100 million people under the Russian Communist regime, just prior to and during World War II. The Nazis and Communists practiced violence and preached hate. Antifa has the same ideology that gave us Hitler, Himmler, Goring and Stalin. I have well documented the hatred, which has become the focal point of the Democrats and the Liberal Left and now we see it being incorporated within the violence of Antifa and for the most part being ignored if not embraced by them.

We note that the media rightly demanded that the President and all Republicans condemn the neo-Nazis and the KKK and they did. So where are the calls for Democrats to condemn Antifa? Except for the House Minority Leader, Nancy Pelosi, the silence of the Democrats has been deafening.

Although the FBI and Department of Homeland Security (DHS) have officially classified Antifa activities as "Domestic Terrorist Violence", the Liberal Left, whether our government leaders, the media, our educators, or our entertainers have either embraced Antifa or at least endorsed it by their silence.

Recently Michael Isaacson, adjunct professor at John Jay College of Criminal Justice was suspended but not fired for saying; "It is a privilege to teach future dead cops". Isaacson is an avowed Antifa Leader. Here are the vitriolic words of a professor at a school specializing in the instruction of law and justice, indicating his support for the killing of policemen.

In January 2018, Democratic National Committee (DNC) Deputy Chair Keith Ellison, a convert to Islam, posted a picture of himself smiling and holding the Antifa Handbook and asserting that Antifa will strike fear in the heart of President Donald Trump. Keith Ellison is also known for his strong support of Louis Farrakhan and Farrakhan's overwhelming hatred of Jews. The Democrat party makes no attempt to condemn either Antifa for its radical and violent bias against Conservatism nor do they speak out about the anti-Jew sentiments of not only Keith Ellison, but also Ilhan Omar, Representative from Minnesota and Rashida Tlaib, Representative, both revealing their strong anti-Jew sentiments by seeking to introduce a resolution that would involve boycotting Israel products, disinvesting from certain American companies that supported Israel and. Imposing other sanctions on Israel. Ilhan Omar in sponsoring this resolution likened Israel to Nazi Germany in Isracl's treatment of Palestinians, a position echoed by Rashida Tlaib. While, the majority of the Democrat members of the House, rejected this resolution, there was no outcry among them regarding the anti-Jew sentiments of these two Muslim women.

Antifa attacks have been rampant throughout the United States resulting in property damage, attacks on police, injuries to by-standers and even the death to one woman run down by a vehicle driven by an antifa member. The most notable places of Antifa violence are Charlotte, North Carolina, Berkeley California (numerous times, Olympia Washington, Portland Oregon, and New York City. This is not an exhaustive list, just significant examples. But as Antifa tactics are praised by the left-wing mainstream progressives, these terrorist attacks will become more frequent and more aggressive.

We close our discussion of Antifa. with the condemnation of Antifa by the renowned legal scholar and Harvard Professor Alan Dershowitz. He is one of the few if not the only persons on the left to condemn Antifa. Dershowitz appeared on Fox and Friends in August, 2017 and stated: "Antifa is a radical, anti-American, anti-free market, communist, socialist, hard, hard left censorial organization that tries to stop speakers on campus from speaking. They use violence and just because they are opposed to fascism and to some of those monuments, shouldn't make them heroes of liberals". Dershowitz also commented on the sudden rush to destroy monuments throughout the country. He pointed out the most famous liberal Democrat of the 20th Century, Franklin D. Roosevelt, who placed 120,000 Japanese American Citizens into detention centers, certainly a form of slavery that should also be subject to Antifa's ideology. He commented that "once you start rewriting history of African-Americans in this country, you have to start rewriting history of discrimination against many other groups. He specifically referred to discrimination against Jews and women. He noted that we are both a nation of immigrants and a nation of discrimination against immigrants. That is an important history for us to remember. Also, we must not glorify the violent people who are now tearing down the statues".

The War on Monuments

In 1949, George Orwell wrote his novel "1984" a book on our high school reading list in the early 1950's. Here is a quote from his book that depicts a future that horrified us in the 1950's. But today it seems that Orwell's book has accurately portrayed the future. Only the events that were to have happened in 1984 really didn't happen until the new millennium and became accelerated in recent years. Here is the quote: "**Every record has been destroyed or falsified; every book rewritten; every picture has been repainted, every statue, street and building has been renamed, every date has been altered and the process is continuing day by day; minute by minute. History has stopped. Nothing exists except an endless present in which the party is always right."**

This is the legacy of the liberal left as it seeks to destroy statues, remove art work, rename sports teams, vilify founders of the country, remove history courses from our schools, remove Judaism and Christianity from public places and schools and substitute the teaching of Islam, prohibit dialogue and physically attack those who do not agree with the liberal left party line.

Robert E. Lee is one of several who have particularly come under fire by Antifa. Lee's statue has been removed from a Dallas, Texas Park named for the General. It had been dedicated by Franklin D. Roosevelt in 1936 as part of the Texas Centennial Celebration. Eric Fonner, a Civil War historian, author and professor of history at Columbia University speaking about Robert. E. Lee said: "He was not a pro-slavery ideologue, but I think it is equally important that he never spoke out against slavery. In 1856 Lee wrote a letter to his wife in which he said: "In this enlightened age there are few I believe, but what will acknowledge that slavery as an institution is a moral and political evil in any country". On September 13, 2017 the statue of Thomas Jefferson on the Campus of the University of Virginia is covered by a black shroud, because Jefferson owned slaves. In New York City the statue of Christopher Columbus in Central Park NYC is defaced with red paint. Mayor Bill de Blasio has created the "Advisory Commission on City Art, monuments and Markers" to seek out monuments that seem to be oppressive and inconsistent with the values of New York City. The mayor will have the final say and private property rights will be abandoned by a dictatorial, social Democrat Mayor. Goodbye to hundreds of years of history, tradition and respect for our past and hello to a communist/socialist imposition of cultural and martial law imposed on us by the liberal left. The statue of Christopher Columbus at Columbus Circle at the corner of Central Park is under investigation for removal. We may wonder where the destruction of monuments stops? Washington, Jefferson, Benjamin Franklin and many other signers of the Constitution owned slaves. Are they all subject to removal? There are the Washington and Jefferson Monuments in Washington, DC; there is the George Washington Bridge; There is Mt. Rushmore depicting among others Washington and Jefferson; There is the University Washington and Lee. There are state capitals, cities, roadways, schools all with names of slave owners as well as on our currency. Are they all to be changed or removed?

Al Sharpton targeted the Jefferson Memorial in Washington, DC, demanding the Federal Government shut down the historic monument because Jefferson owned slaves. Christopher Columbus is under attack in New York City for his treatment of Caribbean natives, even though he never set foot in this country. Benjamin Franklin is under attack for he too owned slaves. 41 of the 56 signers of the Declaration of Independence owned slaves at the time of the Constitutional Convention, six of the original thirteen colonies were slave-owning colonies, namely Delaware, Georgia, Maryland, North Carolina, South Carolina and Virginia. 25 of the 55 delegates to the Constitutional Convention owned slaves. Though the majority of the delegation didn't support slavery, it was not prohibited in the Constitution for fear that would deter the six slave-owning states from signing on. Slavery was wrong then and it is wrong now. And the outrage is well understood. However, isn't there a hypocrisy here, when the enslavement of blacks by blacks in Africa and the selling of the slaves first to Arabs and then to Western nations is not mentioned; nor the fact that there would have been little if any slavery except for the duplicity of black slave owners, selling their brothers for money? And where today is slavery still rampant? In most of the African nations.

CHAPTER 6

What is Socialism? What is Fanaticism?

BEFORE WE CAN critically discuss all the socialist programs that the Democratic left are proposing, we need to understand what is Socialism and how does it differ from Capitalism? We will examine the specifics and the dire consequences of a move by our country toward socialism.

Under a political/economic system of Socialism most means of production are owned by the state and the state provides or controls health, education and transportation. Private property is severely limited to home and personal property. Production decisions are driven by the state rather than by demand. Characteristics include: High taxes, price controls, elimination of private investment; elimination of profit incentive; and dependence on state to provide health, education and welfare. In a recent CBS/New York Times survey, only 16% of millennials could define Socialism accurately, yet 58% had a favorable view of it. Several years ago, in interviews of Debbie Wasserman Schultz then head of the Democratic National Party and Hillary Clinton, candidate for President, neither could explain the difference between a Democrat and a Socialist, nor could either define Socialism. You don't need to know what it is, but if your leaders say its good vote for it. Remember when Nancy Pelosi brought the Obamacare Heath Bill up to vote in the House? She said vote for it, then we can read what it says. This is exactly the mentality we see behind the **"Green New Deal",** which we will discuss in detail later.

By way of comparison, Capitalism is an economic system based on the private ownership of all means of production and their operation for profit. Characteristics of capitalism include: private property, capital accumulation, competition, pricing system based on supply and demand, lower taxes, freedom of choice of schools and medical services. Conservatism is committed to individual responsibility, hard work, personal initiative, traditional family values, free markets, less government control, less regulations and strict adherence to the Constitution.

The socialist ideas proposed by the new Socialist Democrat Movement, includes:

1. Eliminating car ownership – Democrat candidate Andrew Chang even suggests that the U.S. may have to eliminate private ownership of cars to combat climate change. He stated: "Privately owned cars would be replaced by a "constant roving fleet of electric cars". Who would then

control when and where you could travel? Travel would be rationed and the state would be your "Big Brother" knowing where you are at all times and even determining where and when you could travel.

2. Air travel would be eliminated and we would only be able to travel on the Nationalized rail system. Here again "Big Brother" would control your travel, ration it and determine when and where and even if you can travel.

3. A meat free diet will be mandated and to enforce this, the socialist state under Democrats would have to spy on your every move. The Democrats want complete control over our lives and eliminating car ownership and air travel and controlling what you eat goes a long way toward creating their totalitarian state.

4. The Democrats are proposing the confiscation of your guns. This is right out of Hitler's playbook. He sent his SS/Gestapo thugs door to door, to relieve every one of their guns. A key element in controlling the population and achieving their submission to a totalitarian state is to take away their guns so they cannot rebel.

5. The doing away with all fossil fuels and replacing it with solar and wind, is just another way to gain control over the people. The Democrat socialist government, would nationalize the energy industry, ration energy to suit its needs and even use their control of energy to obtain the submission of their adversaries. Those living in places where sunlight is available only 50% to 75% of the time, would have to rely on the State to provide them heat and light in an emergency. Here is just another way that the totalitarian state under the Democrats will control you.

6. The National Health Care Plan proposed by the Socialist Democrats, would remove the right of 120 million Americans to choose their own health plan. But more importantly, it would put these 180 million Americans under the control of the Government. Now medical care will be administered by the Democrat totalitarian state. There would be "Death Panels" that would be created to control costs, and they would decide who would live or die.

7. Abortion at any time is a primary goal of all the Democrat candidates for President. Once the murder of unborn children is acceptable, what is going to keep the "Death Panels" from determining who can live or who must die? Those elderly, who are on life support will immediately be candidates for death under the National health care system. And those who are just old, will be candidates to see little or no medical treatment. Cost containment will be necessary. Further, once abortion at any time becomes the law of the land, the State under the Socialist Democrats will be able to mandate abortions as they do in China under threat of severe penalty.

"It only stands to reason, that where there's sacrifice, there's someone collecting sacrificial offerings. Where there is service, there is someone being served. Those who speak to you of sacrifice are speaking of slaves and masters and intend to be the masters" – Ayn Rand

The Socialist Panacea – Printing More Money

Before launching into a review of all the socialist programs that are planned by the liberal left and how the costs thereof will destroy the United States, we need to look at the Socialist answer as to how enough money can be provided to cover the trillions of dollars of new costs and expenditures. It is a simple answer says the liberal left. Just print more money. Remember this when you read about the costs the liberal left would burden us with to achieve their goals.

An increase in the supply of money and credit relative to the available goods and services results in inflation and when left unchecked creates hyper-inflation. This is Economics 101. If the money supply is increased but the output stays the same, everything becomes more expensive and the currency will devalue against other currencies. When there is massive printing of money, this creates the worst inflation as the prices of commodities and services soar. It is hard for some to visualize that a loaf of bread could increase in price from $2 to $20 virtually overnight. But as in the case of Venezuela as this is being written, the price of a $2 loaf of bread in January 2018, would now be $25,000 and would be projected to cost $250,000 by the end of 2019. For the 40 million of U.S. citizens over 65 and on a fixed income, how do you think you would live if everything you purchase went up only 25 times in a year? So, let's say your groceries were $800 month for a family of four. What would you do if you now had to pay $20,000 for your groceries? Well, if you lived in Venezuela, you would either be dying of malnutrition, or eating scraps from the garbage trucks. More about Venezuela a bit later.

In 1922 in Germany, $1 was worth 90 marks. By November 1922, a $1 was worth $4.2 trillion marks. Yes, the currency inflated 42 million percent. In 1946, the Hungarian National Bank printed 100 Quintillion pingo banknotes, which resulted in a loss of value in their currency so fast that prices doubled every 13 hours. And now we turn to today's Venezuela and President Nicolas Maduro, the socialist leader so proudly endorsed by Bernie Sanders.

The Fall of Venezuela - Venezuela was once the envy of South America, blessed with the largest oil reserves in the world and a steady stream of U.S. dollar revenues and immense per capita wealth. By May 30th, 2018, Venezuela's inflation rate was 25,000% by the end of the year 2 million percent and forecast to be at a 10 million % rate by the end of 2019. It is very difficult to arrest hyperinflation. Even though the Venezuelan government raised the minimum wage 34 times, the average person could not afford to live. Tax receipts collected became essentially worthless when received by the government. **The solution was to print more money.** Today, Venezuela has run out of its foreign reserves and has lost its access to foreign debt markets. The average Venezuelan is beginning to starve to death and has lost 28 pounds in weight. By the end of 2018 prices were doubling every 19 days. A price of coffee during 2018 went from 190,000 Bolivars to 2 million bolivars. By way of comparison, if the U.S. had the same rate of hyper-inflation, a $2 cup of coffee would cost $21,000. **How did this happen?** The socialist policies of President Nicholas Maduro have resulted in the skyrocketing inflation in Venezuela. The forecasted rate of inflation for 2019 is 2 million percent. Venezuelans are now suffering from shortage of heat and electricity and severe shortages of food and medicine. President Maduro and his policies were avidly supported by Bernie Sanders. He was the socialist hero of Venezuela in Bernie Sanders eyes. In fact, Bernie seeks to emulate Maduro. Maduro almost single handedly orchestrated the demise of this once healthy vibrant economy. Three million Venezuelans, over 10% of the country's population have already left and these are some of the most productive people in the economy. Those that are left behind have been reduced to eating garbage. Videos of people grabbing garbage from garbage trucks to get their only food have been shown as well as the riots from angry, hungry mobs, who can no longer make a living, obtain food, keep their homes, or get medical treatment. Maduro sustains his regime through military force. Wages are now down to the equivalent of $5 per month. And Maduro will not even allow billions of dollars of food and medicine to be supplied to his constituents from foreign sources. Maduro has wrought destruction on Venezuela creating the worst economic collapse in Latin American history. He has trampled relentlessly on political rights and poverty has reached 94% and extreme poverty has risen to 65%. 80% of Venezuelan families lack food, are undernourished and famine is moving from a threat to reality. Remember, not too long ago, Venezuela was the bench mark of success in South America not America should be the dream of every American. Is this what we want to happen in America?

60 years ago, Venezuela was 4th on the World Freedom Index. Today, they are 179th and their citizens are dying of starvation. The Democrat Candidates for President of our country are proposing $100 trillion of new debt, five times the total debt that our country has accumulated in its history and 10 times the total debt of our country prior to the Obama presidency. This level of debt is unsupportable. But even worse, it will lead to high inflation loss of pension values, the massive plunge in the stock market, unemployment at levels never before experienced in the U.S. even at the heights of the great depression and the rendering of millions of American citizens homeless and starving. The Democrat leaders never discuss how they would fund their fantasy programs. They don't need to. They will convince many to believe that everything one wants can be provided totally free by the government and once they are in power, they can renege as they have done time and time again. They keep convincing America that they are the party of the people, but when you look at the state of our homelessness and the murder and crime rates in the cities and states they control, what exactly have they done for those unemployed, those living at poverty levels and the minorities who are suffering the most? Nothing. And what have the Democrat leaders done in the last three years for the American citizen? Nothing. All we have seen from the Democrats for three years is constant investigations, attempts to impeach the President, attacks on Supreme Court Justices, vilification of our nation's police, and consistent harassment and vilification of President Trump and his administration. And in foreign affairs, the Democrats have actually sought to sabotage President Trump's dealings with foreign heads of state. Even if we strongly disagree with the policies and activities of the leaders of countries like Russia, China and North Korea, it is imperative to keep the doors open to dialogue; to meet with our adversaries and get to know them face to face. For today the stakes are too high. Nuclear power changes everything and it is therefore more important, no absolutely essential, that we deal with and dialogue with our adversaries. The Democrats have done everything they can to unhinge this dialogue. They have offered no alternative to how best to interact with our nation's adversaries. Nor do any of the candidates have any background in dealing with foreign leaders. Do we really want inexperienced leaders, who will reduce military investment, refuse to deal with foreign leaders, leading our country?

The worst threat to our country is not Global Warming as the Democrats would have you believe. It is the threat of annihilation by a nuclear holocaust. The threat of this should be enough to raise the concern of all-American voters. The actions of the Democrats during the past 3 years should convince all Democrats that none of their candidates are prepared to be our leader on the international stage.

What is Fanaticism?

Fanatics, often Socialist dictators have waged war and murder throughout history. We look at the followers of Islam throughout the world. The vast majority are peace loving, family oriented and wish to live in peace and harmony with non-Muslims. They may not believe as a Christian, Jew, Hindu, Buddhist or atheist may, but they respect each person's right to be free to form their own beliefs. But this is not true of the fanatic Muslims, who unfortunately too often are the leaders and who dictate to their constituents through fear of reprisal, what they must believe. It is the fanatic Muslim that wages war and terrorism world-wide; who systematically slaughter Christians, Jews or tribal groups throughout Africa. It is the fanatic Muslims who bomb, behead, murder non-Muslims or even honor kill their own family members. It is the fanatic Muslim that teaches their young to kill and become suicide bombers. The overwhelming majority of Muslims wish to live in peace, but they don't matter because fanaticism, accompanied by hatred seems to always impose its will on the majority, and the majority almost always remains silent.

The people of Socialist Communist Russia wanted no more than to live in peace and friendship with their fellow man. But they were irrelevant. The Russian Communists/socialists under Stalin murdered over 20 million people and the lives of the Russian people under the Dictator Stalin were harsh and often inhuman.

The Chinese people were peaceful and loving until taken over by the rule of a Socialist dictator, Mao Tso Tung, who put to death over 70 million people who disagreed with him.

The Japanese people as a whole were friendly peaceful and family oriented but they too were led by a group of political dictators, who unilaterally started a war against China, slaughtering over 12 million Chinese Civilians. Their lust for war led them to a sneak and unprovoked attack on the United States on December 7, 1941, starting a war resulting in the loss of 100's of thousands of young American men and women.

And how can we forget the Socialist German Third Reich of the 1930's and 1940's and the Holocaust, in which over 6 million Jews, German citizens, all murdered by the Socialist Dictator regime under Hitler, just because they were Jewish. And the German Socialist Regime did not stop there as it declared war on Europe and the United States, which led to the death of millions of young men and women both military and civilians in Europe as well as American, Canadian and Australian military. Again, it was just a small group of German Socialist fanatics, filled with hate that dominated the vast majority of Germans, who only wanted to live in peace.

And we cannot forget the purges in Socialist Cuba and Socialist North Korea where 100's of thousands of dissidents were put to death, just because they opposed socialist dictatorships and just wanted the right to be free.

We are seeing here in the United States that a small group of fanatics, filled with hate, that are seeking to run our lives. Are we just going to stand by and allow this to happen as the people in Germany, Russia, China, Cuba, North Korea, Venezuela and many Middle Eastern and African Countries have?

Do not assure yourself that this cannot happen here in the United States. It is already underway.

CHAPTER 7

Sanctuary Cities, Violent Crimes and Homelessness.

A RELATED ISSUE to the controversy over the wall between the U.S. and Mexico, concerns sanctuary cities and states. The Illegal Immigration and Immigration Responsibility Act of 1996 was signed into law by President William Clinton after passing both houses of Congress. The act states that immigrants unlawfully present in the United States for over 180 days but less than 365 days must remain outside the U.S. for three years unless they obtain a pardon. If more than 365 days, they must stay outside the U.S. for 10 years unless they obtain a waiver. The bill is rather lengthy and has many provisions but it does call for mandated detainment of Illegal Immigrants that have been arrested for a crime followed by their deportation. The Federal Government has looked to the states, counties and cities to assist them in carrying out the provisions of the Immigration Law, by detaining a criminal illegal alien for up to an additional 48 hours. The law has been amended in the past and has been subject of numerous Federal cases. The law requires the mandatory detention and ultimate deportation of criminal aliens, national security risks and persons under orders of removal, who have committed aggravated felonies, are terrorist aliens or are illegally present in the country.

No doubt the law needs to be revisited and amended, and that some of the objections raised may be valid. But it is the law and has been the law for over 20 years. Anarchy and tyranny arise when people choose to disregard any laws that they don't like. And this is what we are facing with the conduct of some cities, counties and states in the United States which have come to be known as "Sanctuary cities". They are all liberal Democrat run cities.

A sanctuary city is one which not only permits residence by illegal immigrants (whether criminal or not), but also will help them avoid deportation. There are 300 U.S. jurisdictions that have chosen to disregard Federal law. Most of them are in California.

In response to these cities flaunting the Federal law, the then Attorney General Sessions ordered these jurisdictions to enforce Federal Immigration laws. Regrettably, Los Angeles Mayor Eric Garcetti, stated that his city will defy Federal law and continue offering a safe place for illegal aliens to stay. Likewise, Chicago Mayor Rohm Emanuel said his position of providing sanctuary to illegal immigrants will never change. And New York City Council spokesperson Melissa Mark-Vivirito said in continuing the City's opposition to Federal Law, "We are going to become the Administration's worst nightmare". The rape of a 14-year-old girl in Montgomery County, Maryland by an illegal immigrant apparently does not stop the State of Maryland seeking to become a sanctuary state.

The Federal Administration is most concerned about the estimated 820,000 criminals that have been reported among the 11 million illegal immigrants in the U.S. These too are protected by the sanctuary cities. To unilaterally flaunt Federal law is wrong. To help Illegal Immigrants who are also criminals to evade deportation is unlawful. The mayors of the sanctuary cities suggest no remedies, no compromises, no substitutes for the Illegal Immigration Act. This is where rational and logic break down and once again, we see the avoidance of discourse and dialogue, leading us to lawlessness and anarchy.

Violent Crime in our Cities

There are a number of lists of America's top Murder capitals which are easily researched on the Internet. Wall Street Journal's 2016 list of the Top 25 includes only 1 with a Republican Mayor.

Let's narrow it down to the top 10, all Democrat led governments.

City	Murder rate/100,000
St. Louis	59.3
Baltimore	51.2
Detroit	44.9
New Orleans	44.5
Cleveland	35.0
Newark (N.J.)	33.0
Memphis	31.9
Chicago	27.9
Kansas City (MO.)	26.4
Atlanta	23.9

Now compare New York City with the above cities. There were 335 homicides in New York City in 2016 or 3.9 murders per 100,000. What accounts for the difference? From January 1994 to December 2001, Rudy Giuliani was the Republican mayor and from January 2002 to December 2013 Michael Bloomberg was the Republican mayor. During their combined term in office, murders in New York City were down 81%. Since 2013, violent crime in NYC under Mayor Bill De Blasio has remained pretty constant with previous year's figures with the exception of rape, which during the years 2014 and 2015 was more than 100% higher than previous years, with rape levels at 2200 compared to approximately 1100 under Bloomberg.

In contrast to NYC look at Chicago under Democrat Rahm Emmanuel. In 2016 Chicago recorded 762 homicides up 57% from the previous year. Moreover, Chicago saw 1,100 more shooting incidents in 2016 then 2015. There were 4431 shooting incidents in Chicago compared to 995 for NYC. NYC has a population of 8.5 million compared to Chicago's 2.72 million, yet Chicago had 762 murders to NYC's 330 murders. The upward trend in violent crimes in Chicago is discouraging and in 2016, the 762 murders are the highest in Chicago in 19 years.

A City run by a Democrat Mayor whose statistics put it on some lists is Milwaukee Wisconsin. Milwaukee's murder rate is the second highest in the Midwest, trailing only Detroit. The city's murder rate has spiked 70.6% from five years ago. Then there is Minneapolis, Minnesota another crime infested city run by a Democrat Mayor and Council. As recent as September 16 2019, a gang ran rampant and beat and kicked unmercifully a peaceful citizen, putting him the hospital with a concussion. They wanted to steal his money and cell phone and even after they had obtained them and knocked him out, the continued to beat and kick him. No police came to his rescue. The police department has told the Mayor and the council that there is a desperate need for 400 more police. But the Mayor is only willing to authorize 17. It becomes more clear that the elderly will see less and less protection and more beatings on the streets as the Democrats have no desire to provide any protection. They are on record as seeking to abolish ICE, have open borders and provide sanctuary cities to protect illegal immigrants even if they are criminals. They would give citizenship to all illegals. The Democrats have fostered the "hate police" attitude in our country. Where are we going to get some of the money for the vast Green New Deal and National Health Care programs being sponsored by the Democrats? At least part will come from reducing expenditures on Safety and Security. Police forces around the country will be decimated and our Military Strength will be disabled and made obsolete in just a few years, returning us to the weakened state that existed under President Obama.

In contrast to the Democrat run cities of high crime and high murder rates, let us look at the 10 cities over 200,000 in population with the lowest violent crime rates in the country as rated by Areavibes. com. They are equally split five with Republican Mayors and five with Democrat as follows:

Cities with Lowest Violent Crime Rates

Republican Mayors	Democrat Mayors
Irvine, Calif.	Arlington, VA
Gilbert, Ariz.	Fremont, Calif.
Scottsdale, Ariz.	Henderson, NC
Virginia Beach, Va.	Plano, TX.
Chandler, Ariz.	Chula Vista, Calif

But this doesn't begin to tell the whole story. California is a wrecked state that owes its decimation to the policies and procedures of the liberal left. The state and most of the cities in California are run by the liberal left, who disrespect, police, flaunt the law and permit the once beautiful state to become a wasteland of garbage, feces, drug needles, and crime. Once the state that attracted so many has become the state where there is a massive exodus of its residents. San Francisco, San Diego and Los Angeles are examples of other Democrat run cities that now boast slums worse than many third world countries. Homelessness is up 35% in Los Angeles in the past two years. Crime rate has become so bad in LA and San Diego that residents are afraid to leave their homes.

San Francisco - Let us just look at the once beautiful city of San Francisco. The city now boasts the dirtiest slums in the world. In just one section of 153 blocks, 300 piles of feces and hundreds of drug needles were just lying on the sidewalks. San Francisco spends $30 million a year just to clean up the feces and needles. 12,000 needles are picked up in the streets every month. The city receives 60 calls a day from residents requesting human feces be removed from the front of their homes. Once thriving businesses, find themselves surrounded by tent cities and customers shy away from them.

San Francisco is the city not only with the highest number of property break-ins per day at 51, but also according to FBI date a total of 148 burglaries, larcenies, car thefts and arsons per day.

The State of California along with many of its cities are ordering their police not to arrest those who commit petty crimes and therefore these criminals can rob stores, commit vandalism, inflict minor assault or even sell small quantities of drugs with impunity. The attorney general of California even tells the police not to give aid to Federal authorities and therefore illegal immigrants are free to do whatever they want. Thousands convicted and imprisoned for lesser crimes are let out into the public and it is estimated that more than 10% of the homeless in California have been released from prison. In some instances, private business owners, along with local authorities are told they will be fined if they cooperate with ICE. In short, under liberal Democrat control, California has gone from the richest to the poorest state in the Union, burdened by high taxes, high debt, massive regulations and no incentive to encourage its constituents to get a job and/or get off drugs.

As a recent gesture of where liberalism can take us, San Francisco District Attorney, Chesa Baudin in November, 2019 stated that he will no longer prosecute so-called "quality of life crimes", which includes pubic urinating and defecating on the sidewalks of San Francisco; public camping, blocking of sidewalks and offering and soliciting of sex. Homelessness in San Francisco in 2019 is up 30% since 2017 and District Attorney Baudin has just assured the citizens of San Francisco that it is only going to get worse.

Seattle - One more example of the curse of liberal socialism is Seattle. A once beautiful city in the Northwest, it too is dying. Like San Francisco, it has become infested with drugs, filthy with human feces on its streets, rampant lawlessness and a local government which gives no support to its police force. Like San Francisco, San Diego and Los Angeles, the residents do not feel safe to go out on the streets.

Over the past five years, Seattle has seen an explosion of homelessness, crime and drug addiction. Seattle spends $1 billion a year fighting homelessness. Clean-up crews spread out through the city, picking up tens of thousands of dirty needles from the streets and parks each year. By any measure the city's efforts are not working and each year more and more crime, more addiction and more tents and cardboard boxes invade neighborhoods, providing shelter for the homeless. How can the government spend so much and accomplish so little? This is an endemic problem with socialism and we see the same problem in so many other cities run by Democrats, such as Portland, Oregon, Los Angeles and San Francisco. The Democrats have destroyed these cities with their socialism. Seattle has long been known as one of the most radical Socialist locals in the country. The city has been on a non-stop rampage to declare itself the most progressive society in the world and in doing so it has killed jobs and made life miserable for its residents. The city and the state have enacted so many rules and regulations that it is almost impossible to build housing there. The Seattle building code is 745 pages long and the residential building code is another 685 pages. With a crime rate of 61 per 1,000 Seattle has earned for itself the highest crime rate in the country. Seattle fails at its most important mission, which is to protect its citizens. That is one of the over-riding problems with Socialism and it will only get worse.

San Francisco and Seattle are only two examples of the conditions and disaster that is prevalent in so many Democrat run cities around the country.

I close with naming the three liberal Democrat run cities with the highest crime rates per 100,000 in 2017.

San Francisco - 6,168   Seattle - 5,258   San Antonio - 4,844

Homelessness - the curse from the Liberal Left

Along with the crime rates and incidence of drug abuse, there is the curse of homelessness brought upon so many people in the United States. Of the 10 cities with the worst homelessness in the United States, only one has a Republican Mayor, namely San Diego and there the City Council of nine members is dominated by 6 Democrats. And the two leading states for homelessness, namely California (121,000 homeless) and New York (92,000 homeless) are firmly entrenched as liberal Democrat strongholds. The 10 cities with the largest homeless problems included New York City, Los Angeles, Seattle, San Diego, Washington DC, San Francisco, San Jose, Boston, Philadelphia and Phoenix, all liberal Democrat run cities.

The Los Angeles Homeless Services Authority (LAHSA) estimates that there was a 12% increase in homelessness in LA County in 2019, but that doesn't begin to tell us about the problem of homelessness, which is exploding in California. The homelessness problem is growing even faster in other parts of the state. The increase in homelessness in California in 2019 compared to 2018 is as follows:

Sanctuary Cities, Violent Crimes and Homelessness.

County	2019	% homeless increase Over 2018
Orange		43%
San Bernardino		23
Riverside		22
Ventura		28
San Francisco		17
Alameda		43
Santa Clara		31
Kern		50
San Joaquin		69

While the State of California welcomes the influx of illegal immigrants and even protects them with "sanctuary cities" and while the State spent $3 billion on a failed attempt to establish a high-speed electric railway between LA and San Francisco, it has stood by as its California residents who are U.S. Citizens see their homeless numbers explode.

Who are these homeless people? Though the California politicians insist that the state's homeless crisis is caused by homeless people coming from other states, this is a typical falsehood perpetrated by the liberal left on its constituents. More than 2/3's of the homeless in California have lived in the state for over 10 years. The homeless on the streets of California are citizens and longtime residents of the state. Another falsehood that the politicians would have you believe is that most people on the street ended up there due to substance abuse or mental illness. The LAHSA statistics indicate that about 71% of people experiencing homelessness in California are neither mentally ill or suffering from drug abuse. Homelessness in California is a problem that has persisted and grown over the past decade under the auspices of the liberal left government. The failures of Democrats in California are only replicated in the states of Oregon and Washington.

While 10's of thousands of U.S. Citizens are being deprived of basic health and welfare and are deprived of human dignity and minimal comfort, the Liberal left is prepared to grant non- citizen illegal immigrants, the right not only to come and live in the United States but also to receive free food and shelter; free school and college education; free medical care and even a minimum monthly allowance, (suggested by one Democrat to be $1,000 per month per person even if the person doesn't want to work).

And there is no better example of how the Democrats are willing to put the rights of illegal immigrants ahead of their homeless citizens then the following. In a July 2019 report in the Washington Examiner by Anna Ciaritelli, regarding Democrat Congresswomen from El Paso, Texas, Veronica Escobar, Ciaritelli claims that Escobar has secretly sent staff members to Ciudad Juarez, Mexico to assist prospective illegal immigrants to obtain entry to the United States. The purpose of Escobar's staff was to coach illegal immigrants how to get into the United States by falsely claiming that they do not understand Spanish, thereby exploiting a loophole in the Migration Protection protocol existing between the United States and Mexico. Under this "Remain in Mexico" protocol, anyone returned to Mexico by U.S. Immigration must be fluent in Spanish and have no health issues. Those attempting to return have previously claimed they understood Spanish and had no health issues, now suddenly under the advices of Escobar's staff are trained to claim they suddenly no longer understand Spanish and now have health issues. In effect, the staff of Escobar, is perpetrating fraud and deceit against their own government, hardly what we should expect from our elected officials.

In a May 30, 2019 release in the Observer, written by Chris Roberts entitled: "Homeless Crisis; Obscenely out of Control" he reports "Anyone with eyes who has spent more than five minutes in San Francisco or Oakland was already aware that the region's homeless problem has devolved from international embarrassment to an ungodly humanitarian crisis. This is so similar to the crisis the Liberal Democrats have caused at our border with Mexico, where everyone but the liberal Democrats that have visited the border have verified that a crisis exists on our borders. As with homelessness, the Democrats refuse to acknowledge that there is one and they certainly refuse to take any blame for causing the crisis.

Back to the homelessness crisis in California. Roberts goes on to say "It is a Bay area thing but also a Los Angeles thing and Orange County thing and Bakersfield thing. Tents on streets; poor people living in RV's human misery filling in the landscape of fantastic human wealth. This is a California thing; the Liberal left thing that dominates our West Coast, and makes, free borders, unlimited immigration and sanctuary cities their primary concern rather than its own homeless citizens. This same scenario exists in the states of Oregon and Washington, which along with California were once states to be admired until the Liberal Left laid waste to these states.

How have the liberal left, Democrat run cities responded to the catastrophes within their borders? They literally fiddle with language change as the cities self-destruct from within. Let's take San Francisco as an example. This city in Orwellian fashion seeks to change in many instances our language putting "political correctness" above solving the problems of their decaying city. Forget the real problems facing San Francisco, a city run for many years by the liberal left. How do they respond to their failing city, rampant with feces, urine and drug needles inundating its streets? San Francisco has become the nation's leader in property crimes, under the watchful eye of the liberal Democrats. Here is what the city's Board of Supervisors are fiddling with while they watch their city decay. This is what has become paramount in their activity in recent months. They want to change the language used in relation to their city's criminals. Here are some of the examples:

Parolee – will now be referred to as a "person under supervision"

Juvenile Delinquent – Will now be referred to as a "young person with justice system involvement."

Drug Addict - Will now be a "person with a history of drug abuse

Felon - Will now be referred to as a "formerly incarcerated person" or "returning resident" or "justice involved person"

In schools across the country when a child is asked for his name, he must give his name and also identify his pronoun. A boy must say for example after his name that his pronouns are "he", "him" and "his. To further generate gender neutrality and obliterate any differences between boys and girls, the bathrooms are now gender neutral and young girls can watch young boys pissing in urinals. Why do the Democrats believe it is necessary that there be no distinction between men and women? If there is not a difference, why are male and female structured differently and have very different capabilities? The differences between men and women should be praised not condemned.

But the insanity of San Francisco doesn't end with language change. In September, 2019 the San Francisco Council formally labeled the National Rifle Association (NRA) as a Domestic Terrorist Organization. There are 5.5 million members of the NRA. How do you think they must feel being considered by the liberal left as terrorists? We all know members of the NRA. Do any of you consider that because they are members of the NRA, they must be terrorists? This is just a symptom of the disastrous road those on the liberal left will take us on, if they are capable of obtaining control of our government.

Yet this is only one example of a Democrat run city where denial, attempted shifting of blame, and creating a diversion are the subterfuges used to obscure the negligence and misconduct of its leaders in dealing with the terrible and ever-increasing problems of crime, homeless and street filth, pervading their once beautiful cities.

CHAPTER 8

Global Warming/Climate Change

WE HEAR SO much about global warming and how man's addition of CO_2 to the atmosphere is the major cause. Reflect on this after considering what our atmosphere consists of:

	Parts per 10,000	% of atmosphere
Nitrogen	7807	78.07
Oxygen	2094	20.94
Argon	92	0.92
Carbon Dioxide	4	.04
Other	<u>3</u>	<u>.03</u>
	10,000	100.00%

After reflecting a moment on the above break-down of our earth's atmosphere, it would seem that claiming global warming is directly the result of increase in CO_2 due to human causes is questionable considering that our atmosphere only has 4 parts per 10,000 of CO_2. The $100 trillion the Democrats will have us spend to reduce CO_2 admissions to zero will not begin to offset the increase in CO_2 emissions by the rest of the world. The U.S represents less than 5% of the earth's land mass and less than 5% of the world population and about 12% of the world's fossil fuel emissions. This makes our efforts to green America even more dubious since the rest of the world is expanding CO_2 emissions at a far faster rate than we are reducing them. But let's examine the subject a little further by discussing matter in general. The argument here is not that there is no global warming.

Dark matter Is a hypothetical type of matter, distinct from baryonic matter (ordinary matter) such as protons and neutrons and particle radiation (neutrinos). Dark matter has never been directly observed. However, its existence would explain a number of otherwise puzzling astronomical observations. Dark energy is an unknown force of energy which is hypothesized to permeate all of space tending to accelerate the expansion of the universe.

The best current measurement of the total mass-energy of the United States contains 4.9% ordinary matter (matter that we understand and have knowledge of), 26.8% dark matter and 68.7% dark energy. Thus, Dark Matter and Dark Energy constitutes 95.1% of total mass-energy content. So, of all matter, we hypothesize about 95.1% and only have direct knowledge of 4.9% of it. So, regarding global warming (or the lack thereof) our global-warming gurus are making their so-called scientific and unequivocal findings with knowledge of only 4.9% of the total matter and energy that comprises and/or affects our planet.

In a like manner to our knowledge of dark matter and dark energy, we have not been able to measurably tribute global warming to human impact on the environment. Scientists seem to have concluded that because global warming has occurred at the same time that humanly caused emissions of greenhouse gasses (such as CO_2) into the atmosphere has greatly increased, this must be the primary reason for global warming.

We know over the centuries and even millenniums the earth has experienced periods of global warming and periods of ice ages. And these have occurred long before there was any environmental impact caused by humanity. Regarding global warming, we still do not know what is the primary cause of global warming or even if human activities are a perceptible cause of global warming.

If we return to the 1970's, Dr. S. I. Rasool, a NASA scientist concluded that the emissions from fossil fuel burning would screen out so much sunlight that in 50 years the average temperature could drop by 6 degrees. In 1974 Reid A. Bryson of the University of Wisconsin theorized that fuel burning may block more and more sunlight and that after three quarters of a century of mild conditions, the earth's climate seemed to be cooling down. He further added, that meteorologists were almost unanimous that the trend on global cooling will reduce agricultural productivity by the end of the 20th century.

In 1974 the National Oceanic and Atmospheric Administration (NOAA) informed us that the average ground temperature in the Northern Hemisphere between 1945 and 1968 had dropped 0.5 degrees. When the almost unanimous opinion about man-made global cooling was deemed wrong, the liberal left environmentalists switched the other way, almost unanimously claiming that mankind was causing global warming.

The Heidelberg Appeal of 1992, published on June 1 of that year over the signatures of 46 prominent scientists and subsequently endorsed by some 4,000 scientists including 72 Nobel Prize winners stated that while they: "shared the objective of the Earth Summit, but advised the authorities in charge of our planet's destiny against their decisions which are supported by pseudo-scientific arguments or false non-relevant facts….The greatest evils which stalk our Earth are ignorance and oppression, not science, technology and industry. The Appeal went on to say; "We ae worried at the dawn of the 21st century at the emergence of an irrational ideology, which is opposed to scientific and industrial progress and impedes economic and social development."

There is also the Science & Environmental Policy Project (SEPP) founded in 1990 by atmospheric physicist S. Fred Singer. It disputed the prevailing views of climate change and ozone depletion. Its former president, Frederick Seitz was a former president of the National Academy of Sciences.

The Leipzig Declaration of 1996 issued in 1996 and updated in 1997 and revised in 2005 was signed by 80 scientists and 25 news meteorologists. The Declaration opposes the global warming hypothesis of the Kyoto Protocol. The Declaration asserts: "There does not exist a general scientific consensus about the importance of greenhouse warming from rising levels of carbon dioxide. On the contrary, most scientists now accept the fact that actual observations from earth satellites show no climate warming whatsoever.

The Global Warming Petition Project – 1998, (updated in 2007 by the Oregon Petition)

In response to the Kyoto, Japan convention in December 1997, which proposed to limit greenhouse gasses, 31,487 scientists and experts, including 9,029 PhD's came together and signed a petition strongly rejecting that global warming was caused by CO_2 emissions caused by humans. The signatories included individuals from the following disciplines:

Discipline	Count
Atmospheric, Environmental and Earth Sciences	3,805
Engineering and General Science	10,102
Biochemistry, Biology and Agriculture	2,965
Physics and Aerospace Sciences	5,812
Medicine	3,046
Computer and Mathematical Sciences	935

The petition urged the United States government to reject the global warming agreement written in Kyoto (Japan) in December 1997 and any other similar proposals. The petition stated that: "The Kyoto agreement proposes to limit greenhouse gases and this would hinder the advance of science and technology and damage the health and welfare of mankind". The petition went on to say: "There is no convincing evidence that human releases of CO2, methane or other greenhouse gasses is causing or will in the foreseeable future cause catastrophic heating of the earth's atmosphere and disruption of the earth's climate. Moreover, there is substantial scientific evidence that increase in atmospheric CO_2 produces many beneficial effects upon the natural plants and animal environments of the Earth".

Geologist Leighton Steward

Noted Geologist, Leighton Steward has observed that CO_2 levels are so low that more CO_2 is needed to expand and sustain plant growth. He points out that plants grown at higher CO_2 levels make larger fruits and vegetables and also use less water. Further, he states that higher levels of CO_2 are not harmful to humans. The study of our atmosphere within Navy submarines shows that the danger level for CO_2 is 8,000 parts per million, far higher than the current level of 400 parts per million.

Cato Institute Release of 2009

In 2009, 100 scientists submitted an advertisement to the public through the U.S. based CATO Institute which stated: "We the undersigned, maintain the cause for alarm regarding climate change is grossly over-stated. Surface temperature changes over the past century have been episodic and modest and there has been no global warming for over a decade now……The computer models forecasting rapid temperature changes, abjectly fail to explain recent climate change behavior. Mr. President, your characterization of the scientific facts regarding climate change and the degree of certainty informing the scientific debate is simply wrong".

Report to U.S. Senate 2010 Re Global Warming

In 2010 over 1,000 scientists prepared to be publicly named as opposing the proponents of fossil fuel induced global warming as presented to the United Nations Intergovernmental Panel on Climate Change. (IPCC). Their report to the U.S. Senate stated: "More than 1000 dissenting scientists from around the globe have now challenged man-made global warming claims made by the United Nations and former Vice President Al Gore. It should be noted that the over 1,000 dissenting scientists were more than 20 times the number of UN Scientists (52) who supported the theory that CO_2 emissions will cause catastrophic climate change.

In addition to the above specific initiative, a total of 31,487 American Scientists, including 9,029 with PhD's, signed a petition run by the Global Warming Petition Project, to publicly demonstrate that the scientific community in the U.S. rejected claims that the science around man-made global warming was either "settled" or that a "consensus" exists.

University of Alabama 2017 Global Warming Study

A recent (November 2017) study by the University of Alabama – Huntsville, presented by Anthony Watts in an article dated November 29, 2017, concluded that based on a review of the past 23 years there is no acceleration in global warming and that the claimed sensitivity to CO_2 is too high. In examining the warming trend in our atmosphere up to almost five miles, the warming trend per decade has been .096 C (.17F) per decade. Extrapolating this, it would take 100 years for the earth's temperature to rise 1 degree. Yet newly elected Congresswoman from New York, Alexandria Ocasio-Cortez claims that if we don't do something about fossil fuel emissions (CO_2) immediately, "the world is going to end in 12 years". And her statement has been endorsed by over 60 of her fellow-Democrat colleagues and not one Democrat has denied this outrageous statement. If this is so, we are already doomed, because none of her proposals could even be initiated let alone completed in 12 years.

A similar study was published by the University of Alabama's Earth System Science Center in 1994 based on 15 years of data, which showed a very similar warming trend of .09C per decade. Dr. John Christy, Director of the Earth System Science Center concluded that the climate models have the sensitivity to CO_2 much too high. The study also concluded that there is no accepted tool or technique for confidently estimating how much of global warming over the past 38 years is due to natural causes and not CO_2.

What is not factored into the global warming discussion, is the amount of CO_2 emissions from the breathing of humans and animals; nor the ever-growing destruction of plants and trees that supply food and building materials to support a growing world population; nor the massive CO_2 emissions resulting from volcanoes and forest fires; nor the removal of trees and vegetation, to make room for more buildings, shopping centers and industrial parks. Population growth directly or indirectly expands CO_2 emissions and so should we seek to control population growth as China has done until recently requiring the abortion of all unborn babies after the birth of the first child?

That the United States should go on the global warming frenzy, while the rest of the world is expanding CO_2 emissions doesn't make sense. Let's look at the numbers. How does the U.S. perform against the rest of the world, measured in terms of megatons/year of CO_2 emissions?

Discharge of CO_2 into Atmosphere
Thousands of megatons/year

	2005	2017	Percent Increase (Decrease)
Total World	30,049	37,077	23.4%
World (ex U.S.)	24,078	31,910	32.5
United States	5,971	5,107	(14.5)
European Union	4,250	3,548	(16.5)
China	6,263	10,877	73.7
India	1,211	2,455	102,7
Russia	1,734	1,765	1.8
Japan	1,277	1,322	3.5
Canada	581	617	6.2
South Korea	515	673	30.7
Brazil	381	493	29.4
Saudi Arabia	339	639	88.5
Australia	392	402	2.6
Turkey	150	246	64.0
Vietnam	99	219	121.2

While the rest of the world was increasing CO_2 emissions by 32.5% since 2005, the United States has cut its emissions by 14.5%. And the world's CO_2 emissions will continue to grow at a faster rate, far outpacing the CO_2 reductions in the United States. Yet the Democrat leaders and the Democrat Presidential candidates are all planning to spend trillions of dollars to reduce CO_2 emissions in the next 10 to 20 years to zero. They will in the process, destroy our country, render millions unemployed and homeless; deprive us of air travel, destroy our life savings and cause our pensions, IRA's and 401k's to evaporate. And we will be faced with inflation rates and interest closely matching what is currently being experienced in Venezuela, driving us from our homes. We will face homelessness, starvation, destitution and rising crime rates and for what? Because the liberal left has decided that the way to power, regardless of what it does to humanity can be accomplished by creating fear among Americans and the demise of life on our planet earth is the ultimate fear that they can create.

THERE IS A Flip side to lowering CO_2 emissions

CO_2 is not all bad. In fact, when CO_2 gets too low, large areas of living plants that need CO_2 will not survive. In fact, plants subject to higher levels of CO_2 actually thrive much better. Another benefit we receive from plant life, particularly forests and trees is that through photosynthesis, CO_2 is absorbed and oxygen is returned to the atmosphere. Fundamental activities such as farming; building new communities out of wood and providing paper products contribute to the reduction of our forests and the loss of natural elimination of CO_2. Think of all the timber that will be required to rebuild homes free of the use of fossil fuels? Think of all the railroad ties that will be needed. Think of all the millions of acres of trees that must be cut down to make way for the new high-speed railways crisscrossing our country. Think of the millions of acres of forests that will be decimated to build solar panel and wind farms. And think of all the trees that will be cut for firewood to heat the homes and shelters for those who are rendered homeless or are unable to afford switching to, solar or wind power. Most of these areas can never be reforested and America will become a great wasteland. Nor will there be plentiful forests to absorb CO_2 and replenish the atmosphere with Oxygen. Does the Green New Deal even help to achieve what it sets out to, or does its environmental impact cancel out what it proposes to accomplish?

A discussion of global warming could go on for pages but I pose nine questions:

1. Do most scientists believe that the only possible reason for global warming is environmental miss-management by humans? Do they have irrefutable proof? I have pointed out that that approximately 37,000 scientists confirming in 8 different petitions, appeals and studies, that CO_2 is not the cause of climate change. How many scientists have signed off that CO_2 is definitely the cause of climate change?

2. Since carbon dioxide (CO_2) represents only 4 parts per 10,000 in our atmosphere and it is the smallest volume of any major atmospheric gas, do man-made emissions really have such impact by themselves to change the level of temperature on this earth? It is claimed that CO_2 emissions have increased by one-third since the Industrial Revolution. This sounds significant,

but really this means the increase in emissions has gone from 3 parts per 10,000 to 4 parts per 10,000.

3. Since the beginning of this millennium, the United States has consistently reduced its emissions of CO_2. During the same time, the rest of the world has expanded its emissions of CO_2 at a faster rate than the United States has been reducing its emissions And given that the United States represents only 4.2% of the world population, 4.6% of the world's landmass, is it realistic or even rational to send our country back to the middle ages, create unemployment for millions of workers, expend 10's of trillions of dollars to eliminate air flight and refit or replace all buildings and replace all of our fossil fuel sources, increase our federal debt level from $25 trillion to $125 trillion, and suffer the consequences of hyper-inflation, when the rest of the world continues to develop and expand its use of fossil fuels at a faster rate than we reduce ours?

4. You will read in Chapter 12 just how costly the Green New Deal would be for our country. Can we afford to vote for people who will impose this insanity on us?

5. There are some unintended consequences associated with doing away with fossil fuel. Let us briefly look at the potential negative consequences of wind-power. First of all, it costs 20% more than natural gas even after Federal government subsidies of $4.7 billion a year. From an environmental prospective, 10 to 20 million, yes million birds per year are killed by existing wind farms, including endangered species such as eagles and condors. How many more will be killed if our landscape is littered with the massive expansion of windmills? Further, marine-life such as dolphins and whales are apparently harmed by the sound of the windmills, as they beach themselves as they are driven toward the sound of the windmills. Finally, when wind doesn't blow at a certain speed, there is no wind-power. So, like solar energy, it is an intermittent energy source.

6. Part of the solution to global warming offered by the Democrats is to eliminate cattle. It is unclear if that also includes dairy cattle. The Socialist Democrat government would actually mandate that everyone give up eating meat. However, cattle will just leave the United States and produce methane somewhere else. The result is the wealthy will still import meat at a cost that the average person will not be able to afford. A vegetarian died will be imposed on us by our government, meaning more lands will have to be turned into vegetable farms. Millions of more trees will be cut down, further eliminating a major sources of CO_2 absorption. Birds will be deprived of their nesting places and those animals that make their homes in trees and forests will lose their habitats.

7. As eating meat is mandated out of our diet, the eating of fish will become the new major source of our diet. We are already depleting our fish resources. What happens when the American consumer increase fish in their diets three or four-fold? Few already experience over-fishing. What happens to the world fish supply if the demand for fish increases three or four-fold? And where will the necessary fleet of new fishing vessels come from? There will not be any additions as existing diesel fueled fishing vessels must be rebuilt or replaced to run on batteries. Just when

we need more fishing vessels and fishermen, many will be abandoning the industry, because they cannot afford to convert their ships from fossil fuel powered vessels. Think also of all the steak houses, fast food chains, delicatessens, and other purveyors of meat that will go out of business, creating massive unemployment. Overnight we would see the demise of Subway, McDonalds, Burger King, Wendy's, Arby's, Hardee's, Sonic Drive in and Five Guys. Steak restaurant chains such as Outback, Longhorns, Texas Roadhouse, Ruth's Chris and Morton's just to name a few would be out of business.

8. What are the unintended consequences of building a rail system to replace airplanes and cars? The building of a high-speed rail system crisscrossing our country will require tens of millions of acres to provide railway corridors. More trees will be depleted, more birds and other animals will be deprived of their habitats and the natural source of CO_2 absorption and oxygen replenishment will be lost as our every increasing wastelands grow.

9. What are some of the other unintended consequences of wind, solar and water resources replacing fossil fuel? There is a final unintended consequence of the global warming insanity. The solution of wind, solar and water is imperfect to say the least. There will be the need for State control and power rationing. Further the cost of heat and electricity will be substantially greater. And there will be many who cannot afford to convert their homes to solar power. Where will the people turn to supply the heat and electricity that is now in short supply? They will cut down trees and create heat and light by burning wood. Millions if not billions of trees will be cut down. This very important resource of our country, our trees, which absorb CO_2 and give off oxygen will be decimated. This two-fold benefit will be decimated beyond belief to the point that the U.S. becomes a wasteland and the very goal of reducing CO_2 emissions can never be achieved. In fact, it is more likely that the loss of natural vegetation will result in such an imbalance that the CO_2 emissions by humans and animals can no longer be absorbed naturally.

It is a good thing to seek alternative sources of energy such as solar and wind. After all, fossil fuel sources are depletable. But to totally eliminate them in 10 to 12 years is insane. Our world objectives should be to clean up the environment from the waste that is poured into our rivers, lakes and oceans each year and to plant millions of more trees and require new building developments to include substantial plantings of vegetation that soaks up CO_2 and delivers oxygen to or planet.

In 1633, Galileo was put on trial for holding the belief that the earth revolves around the sun. This was considered heresy by the Catholic Church, much as the liberal Democrats believe that to deny that climate change is caused by CO_2 is heretical. The church had decided that the sun moved around the earth despite the fact that scientists had known for centuries that the Earth was not the center of the Universe. The Church declared that the idea that the earth moved around the sun is contrary to the Holy and Divine Scripture. Galileo, on the pain of death agreed not to teach the heresy anymore and he spent the rest of his life under house arrest. It took the Church 300 years to admit that Galileo was right and clear his name of heresy. In much the same way, the leaders of the liberal left, condemn those who believe CO_2 is not responsible for global warming, even in the face of 37,000 scientists including

70 Noble laureates who strongly deny that global warming is caused by CO_2. And the followers of these liberal Democrat leaders have been convinced that global warming is caused by CO_2 in the face of the strong evidence to the contrary.

Closely allied with any discussion of Global warming is a review of the incredible size of the ever-expanding universe and the corresponding insignificance of the earth. The global warming advocates, would have you believe that we can control our environment and that there are no factors outside our control that determine the future of Earth. Is there global warming? Yes. Is there climate change? Yes. But there is significant if not overwhelming scientific opinions by 10's of thousands of scientists that CO_2 is not the cause. Does that mean we should not develop alternative sources of energy? Absolutely Not. We need to develop alternative energy sources because fossil fuels are a depleting resource. But we don't need to destroy our country and way of life to do away with any and all CO_2 emissions.

We are one small planet in one Galaxy known as the Milky Way which has an estimated 400 billion stars and 100 billion planets. There are an estimated 100 billion galaxies each with another 100 billion planets and 400 billion stars. Our galaxy alone is 180,000 light years in diameter, one light year being 5.9 trillion miles. How can we be so precise about the causes of global warming when we know so little about our own planet, our own solar system, let alone the whole universe?

How many planets in the universe?

$$10,000,000,000,000,000,000,000 \text{ (approximately)}$$

A final thought. Instead of spending trillions of dollars; depriving everyone of air flight; forcing us to abandon eating beef; destroying whole industries; increasing our debt burden from $25 trillion to over $100 trillion; increasing unemployment from under 4% to over 15% or more; burdening our country with sky-rocketing inflation of 1000% or more and rendering a substantial portion of our population homeless and penniless, maybe there is something more positive, more productive that we could do. Why couldn't we spend $50 to $100 billion a year on reforestation of our lands and greening of our cities and suburbs? Not only would this create the natural absorption of CO_2, but there would be the extra bonus of adding more oxygen to our atmosphere, by the natural chemical process that takes in place known as photosynthesis. Why not spend another $50 to $100 billion to clean up our waste pollution?

Christmas Trees – A partial solution to reforestation

Plants and trees are a major source of improving our atmosphere. They remove CO_2 from the atmosphere and add back oxygen. Yet each year North America cuts down 40 million Christmas trees and Europe 50 million. The climate change zealots would have us stop air flights, eating beef, using gas fueled cars at costs to our economy that are off the charts. Yet they do not mention a program which could have instantaneous benefits to our atmosphere. Simply require that all Christmas trees be harvested alive and replanted after the Christmas holidays. The market for artificial trees already is greater than for real trees and the cost isn't that dissimilar. The average cost of a real tree is $78, while the average cost of an artificial tree is $104. That means the extra cost of an artificial tree is recovered in the second year. Tree farms could sell live trees year round and probably sell them at a higher prices; environmental groups, religious groups, boys and girls clubs, student bodies, could take on live tree harvesting and planting projects; builders would be required to provide more tree plantings at new developments; balconies on high rise buildings would be required to have small tree plantings. Unemployed workers could be hired by the government just to plant more trees; and efforts could be undertaken to make this a world-wide project.

Here are some interesting facts about the contribution an active program to plant trees.

1. 1 acre of trees provides the daily oxygen requirements for 18 people.
2. 5 billion additional mature trees world-wide, would absorb almost all the excess CO_2 in the atmosphere and replenish the air with all the oxygen consumed worldwide.
3. Two mature pine trees can provide oxygen for a family of four.
4. Trees clean air, absorbing pollutant gases and filtering particulates.
5. Trees cool cities by up to 10 degrees F. by shading our homes and streets; breaking up urban "heat islands" and releasing water.
6. Trees conserve energy. Three mature trees placed strategically around a single-family home can cut summer air-conditioning by 50% thus reducing CO_2 emissions from power plants.
7. Trees save water. Shade from trees slows down water evaporation from pools and lawns. They also increase atmospheric moisture.
8. Trees help prevent water pollution and soil erosion.
9. Trees provide food. An apple tree can yield up to 20 bushels of fruit per year and can be planted on a tiny urban plot. Trees also pride food for birds and wildlife.

Whether you support or oppose the theory that fossil fuels create CO_2, which in turn causes global warming, we can all agree that greening America through natural causes such as reforestation and cleaning up the waste we have spread on or land and in our waters would be a good thing. And we can also agree, the development of renewable energy sources and implementing them in conjunction with fossil fuels makes sense. But to plan to do away with all fossil fuel is insanity.

Solar Energy an intermittent energy Source. -There are 9 major cities in the United States that have solid overcast for more than 180 days per year, namely Seattle, Portland (Oregon) Buffalo, Pittsburgh, Cleveland, Rochester (New York), Columbus (Ohio), Cincinnati and Detroit Michigan. There are another 7 cities with substantial cloud cover for 75% of the year, namely: Miami, Hartford (Connecticut), Chicago, Indianapolis, Orlando, Milwaukee and Houston. The Metropolitan areas for these cities have a total population of 51.4 million. In addition, there are 10 states that have substantial cloud cover every year, namely Washington, Vermont, Alaska, New York, Oregon, West Virginia, Michigan, Ohio, Montana and Connecticut. The intermittent availability of sunlight, requires back-up from fossil fuel fired plants. Without fossil fuel plants most if not all people in the United States would face intermittent availability of electricity, heat, and air conditioning. Many if not most will from time to time face days if not weeks without heat, electricity and air conditioning. Where will they turn to provide heat, during down-times? They will cut down trees to provide fuel for man-made fires. Millions of trees will be cut down. The very trees that soak up CO_2 and release oxygen into our air.

Wind Energy an intermittent energy source - Similar to solar energy, wind energy is also an intermittent energy source and it too must rely on energy back-up from fossil fuel burning utilities. Like Solar Energy there is significant potential from this source and it is obviously like solar energy a renewable source. Also, like solar energy it is not suited to meet the base load energy demand for our country. There are three signficant negative attributes to wind energy, the first being that wind turbines are a major threat to wild-life, particularly birds. Secondly there is a noise problem for neighboring homes. And third, vast areas of trees would disappear to make room for the windmills. So, to summarize, many of us will lose our jobs; be rendered homeless, face extremely high costs for food clothing and shelter, the doubling and tripling of our taxes and those lucky to still have a home will face days of no heat, light or air-conditioning. And the global warming problem will still remain unanswered.

CHAPTER 9

Our Debt Crisis

WE HAVE HEARD from some of the Democrat leaders that global warming is our major concern. Yet terrorism, and the threat of nuclear power in the hands of radical Islamists willing to commit suicide in the name of Allah is clearly our most serious threat. Further, global warming is a worldwide problem and without the cooperation of countries like China, Russia and India, any program undertaken by the U.S. alone will be useless. Therefore, being realistic, our second most serious concern should be the crisis of our enormous debt. Under Obama's administration the United States lost its triple A credit rating for the first time. If any of the programs proposed by the Democrats were to come into fruition, our debt rating will go below investment grade and take us into "junk bond" status. And dovetailed with our debt problem is our costs of entitlements particularly Social Security and Medicare. The debt problem can only be fixed by increasing Federal Revenues and/or decreasing Federal government expenditures. This involves changing our entitlement programs and eliminating wasteful spending and undertaking only projects that are self-funding.

The United States is closing in on $25 trillion of debt with higher interest rates facing our government in the not too distant future. Over the past 50 years or so, interest rates on 10-year U.S. Government notes have ranged from about 1.5% to a high in the 1980's of 15.8%. Today the rate is just under 2%. Suppose the cost of borrowing by the U.S. went up to 6% or 7% a rate not inconsistent with what we have seen for many years in the past and considered a more typical rate than either of the extremes. Based on $25 trillion of debt, the increase in interest cost to the U.S. government each year would be $1.0 to $1.25 Trillion. Now our total U.S. annual government expenditures are around $4.0 trillion (fiscal 2019) and our receipts are only $3.4 trillion. Only $1.3 trillion of our budget is considered discretionary; that is funds that are not locked into Social security and welfare; Medical and Health and interest expenditures. If our interest rates only went up to 6%, we would see our interest expenditures almost quadruple from about $363 billion to $1.4 trillion and we would have only $300 billion left for discretionary spending. But the worst part of this is that we would be continually adding another $1 trillion to our deficit each year. That means, overhanging us in the future is an additional cost of debt equating to all of our discretionary spending. And the Democrats are only looking to spend more. Almost as much debt has been created since Obama took office then was created by all the

Presidents before him. When Obama took office in 2008 the total National Debt was $10.6 Trillion when he left office it was over $20 trillion. Now the liberal left is proposing $100 trillion of net new debt over the next 10 years or $10 trillion per year to fund its Green house and national health programs. Supposedly $20 to $25 trillion over 10 years can be eked out of our individual tax payers and corporations leaving $100 trillion to be covered by new debt. The Democrats propose $12.5 trillion of new expenditures each year, 4 times what our government is now spending per year. And this does not include the cost of a proposed minimum income for everyone; free education from pre- kindergarten through college. But more significantly there would be trillions of dollars increase in interest payments on the new debt required to fund these programs and billions of dollars of new welfare checks for the 15 to 20 million jobs lost by the elimination of the airline, fossil fuel industries, Health insurance and ranching industries. And none of this is included in the $12.5 trillion of new annual expenditures by the Federal government if the Democrats are successful and enacting their socialist programs.

When I hear of all the spending programs that are being offered by the liberal Democrats; that College should be free for everyone; that there should be free child care for the working woman; that a nationalized medical program should be instituted; that everyone should be guaranteed a minimum income even if they are unwilling to work; that eating beef should be banned and cattle ranching abolished to eliminate methane gas generated by cow flatulence; that airplanes should be replaced by high speed railroads and that the use of all fossil fuels should be eliminated in 10 to 12 years, I realize that our country is doomed if we proceed with these policies.

Remember the crises during the Jimmy Carter Administration in the United States in 1978-1980? Remember the energy shortages when motorists were forced to wait in long lines at gasoline stations. Crude oil prices doubled suddenly. This will happen long before we have successfully eliminated fossil fuel entirely, because the transfer to so-called clean energy doesn't happen overnight. Nor does the elimination of airplanes and gas driven cars end at a moment in time. Long before that occurs transportation will be affected as oil companies stop producing new oil and gas supplies; gas stations start to close and airlines cut back on-air travel and begin to scrap their planes. But much more apparent, even more insidious and destructive will be the rise in interest rates. Suddenly under Carter and the Democrats we saw interest rates soar to 22% and inflation rates to 16% and marginal tax rates to 70%. There were a series of failures of Savings and Loan associations and our banking industry was severely shaken. The Government under Jimmy Carter, was paying as high as 15% interest to obtain funds. In January 1977 when he became President, the 10-year Treasury notes were at an unsustainable 7.25%. They soared to almost 15% under his presidency. Imagine that our government interest rates returned only to 15%, which they would surely do and would probably go much higher if any loans to our Federal Government were even available. On $25 trillion of debt, we would be paying $3.75 trillion dollars, or as much as our total Federal budget is today for non-interest disbursements. What does that mean? That means there would be nothing left after just paying interest for Social Security, Unemployment, Medical and Health, Defense Education, Agriculture, Housing or Transportation. NOTHING. How can we even begin to pay for the $100 trillion Green New Deal, when we have nothing left to spend on any discretionary or no- discretionary existing programs. And God forbid our interest rates go higher than 15% or our debt goes higher than $25 trillion which it most surely will do. It is estimated that our debt would rise to over $100 trillion in 10 years if the Democrat plans were actually implemented. At that level, our interest rates would surely rise to 15% and our interest costs would be $15.0 trillion per year. Interest payments alone would be 4 times our current annual Federal budget. The ignorance of the socialist Democrats is clearly overshadowed by their insanity. And yet, there are still many who will vote for Democrats, even though they are signing their proverbial death warrant.

Before we even look at the cost and dangers associated with these wild proposals of the Democrats, before we even examine the merit or lack thereof of any of their ideas, we need to look at where we are in terms of our Federal government's sources and uses of funds and our exploding debt. We are already at a crisis level, even if we do not spend one more dollar than we receive. Our government is already spending well more than it takes in and the substantial costs of the liberal left proposals will destroy our country. Just look at what has happened to the once prosperous and leading economy of South America, namely, Venezuela.

Let us briefly look at the 2016 and 2019 Federal budget; where we are now: ($Billions):

Receipts			Disbursements		
Fiscal	2016	2019	Fiscal	2016	2019
Individual Income Tax	1,645	1,622	Social Security & Unemployment	1,369	1,455
Corporate Taxes	475	225	Medical and Health	1,106	1,225
Social Security	1,110	1,238	Interest	<u>283</u>	<u>363</u>
All other	<u>293</u>	<u>332</u>	**Total Non-Discretionary**	2,758	3,043
Total Receipts	**3,523**	**3,422**			
			Discretionary – Military	634	867
			Discretionary Veterans	166	83
			Discretionary Food & Agriculture	140	n.a.
			Discretionary Transportation	108	94
			Housing	83	29
			Education	79	113
			Energy	52	29
			All other	65	149
			Total Discretionary	**1,327**	**1,364**
			Total Disbursements	**4,085**	**4,407**
			Deficit	**(562)**	**(985)**

What we show here is that the government will spend about $1 trillion more than it takes in. But more importantly only 31% of disbursements are discretionary and those disbursements are totally funded by new debt. 69% of spending is not available for budgeting which explains why the proper funding of Military, Veterans and infrastructure is unachievable. But the amount of discretionary spending available to our country today is only possible because of the extremely low interest rates. For the period from January 1975 to January 1991 our Federal borrowing rates varied from 7.5% to 14.6%. Suppose our interest rates went from the current 2% to 7.5%? The result would be an additional $1.4 trillion of interest on the $25 trillion of indebtedness totally wiping out any funds for discretionary spending. Total non-discretionary disbursements would increase to $3.758 Trillion and our discretionary disbursements would have to decrease to 0 and we would still have an annual deficit of $235 Billion. Note our Federal Government only collects $1.2 trillion to cover Social Security, Unemployment and Medical and spends approximately $2.7 trillion to fund these entitlements. Only 44% of these activities are funded by taxes. Where do we get the $1.5 trillion to cover this shortfall? The Federal Government borrows money. What business, what enterprise can spend $1 and collect only $.44 and survive? And the liberal left insists that global warming is our major problem.

There is another serious concern relating to the expanding of the U.S. debt burden. At what point do foreign investors reduce or eliminate their investment in U.S. Government debt? We have already experienced a reduction in our government's credit rating under Obama. The lower the credit rating the higher the cost of debt. At the present. $6.2 Trillion of our $22 trillion debt (28%) is held by foreign entities up from 13% in 1988. China holds approximately $1.5 trillion and Japan about $1 trillion. In 2000 foreigners held only $1 trillion of our debt and in 2009 $2 trillion. As more debt is added to our Federal budget, the percentage held by foreigners will continue to rise. We have shown that just a change in our interest rate to 6% will increase our debt $1 trillion a year and another $1 trillion would be associated with our annual budget deficit. Thus, if we undertake no new government expenditure programs (such as, National Health Care, High Speed rail, free college tuition; free child care, minimum wage (for even the unemployed or unwilling to work); renovating and refitting all buildings to be free of fossil fuel utilization, implementing vast new programs for solar, wind, and hydroelectric energy (no nuclear), our deficit will double in the next 10 years. Now for sure, our interest rates will reach and even exceed 6%. At 10% interest and a $40 trillion debt level, our interest costs would be the size of our whole current budget and we wouldn't have been able to create one new spending program. We will be extremely fortunate if our country's credit is still investment grade and not junk bond status, but it will fall to the lowest level of investment grade. We can only hope that foreigners will be willing to increase their holdings of our debt and that at a 10% yield it may still be attractive. Let us assume that foreign holdings of U.S. debt increases to 50%. This would mean that $20 trillion of government debt would be held by foreigners earning $2 trillion per year. This is $2 trillion that would be leaving our country and unavailable to the U.S. to generate further investments and consumption in the U.S., which would be the case if it were held by U.S. investors. Our country is teetering and the Democrats through their ignorance and their insanity are ready to push it over the edge with the programs they are sponsoring.

Now let us look at some of the programs that the socialist left is now proposing.

CHAPTER 10

National Health Care System and other free promises of the Democrats

The non-partisan Urban Institute has estimated that a National Health Care system would raise government spending by $32 trillion over 10 years, or approximately $3.2 trillion/year. (Note this is lower than the $52 trillion that Elizabeth Warren is proposing as the cost of her Medicare for All Plan. These numbers are therefore much more conservative than the Warren projection). The government is currently spending $1.2 trillion on Medical, so there is a net new cost to the Federal Government of $2.0 trillion per year. It is estimated that additional taxes would be paid as premiums to the Federal Government in lieu of insurance premiums paid by taxpayers for private coverage. Still when this is netted out there would be about $550 billion a year of net new expenditures, uncovered by any additional receipts.

There are approximately 500,000 administrative employees in the medical health insurance field throughout the United States. Most if not all of these would lose their jobs. This does not include any indirect labor, (labor associated with providing goods and services attributed to the disposable income of displaced workers). An estimate of 1.4 jobs are lost for each 1 job, reflecting the multiplier affect associated with the jobs generated by the expenditures of disposable income of every worker. We also assume that the average worker supports an additional 2.5 people reflecting roughly the ratio between the population (330 million) and the total full-time employment (128.6 million). We will use these ratios throughout our analyses. Thus, the loss of 500,000 jobs in the Health Insurance industry, equates to the creation of a total of 4.2 million prospective additions to the welfare rolls.

Remember when the Affordable Care Act (ACA) was passed during the Obama Administration? Obama made three promises to the American citizens: 1) We could keep our doctor; 2) We could keep our plan; and 3) Our insurance costs would go down. These promises all turned out to be false. On top of that, under threat of penalty we were forced to buy insurance even if we wanted to self-insure. And when the 1,000-page bill was presented to the House by the then speaker of the house, Nancy Pelosi, she urged house members to approve it so they could then read it. As important and as great an impact this far-reaching, socialistic ACA law would be on the citizens of the United States, it was passed un-read and without critical review. We should all fear the Liberal and socialist Democrats if it were to obtain unfettered power in the legislative branch and implement their proposed radical socialist changes.

To underscore the concern with unfettered power, we need to understand how gullible and apathetic the average citizens of the United States are. How are the citizens of the United States so willing to accept socialism, when according to a Pew Survey only 16% of millennials could even define socialism?

The Veterans Administration – What better case study is there than the performance of the United States Government in administrating health for our 20 Million veterans? Remember the Veteran's Administration (VA) Scandal of 2014? In 2014 the VA scandal erupted with a reported pattern of negligence in the treatment of U.S. Military Veterans. 40 veterans died while waiting for care at the Phoenix, Arizona VA facility. The chronic failure and corrosive culture of the VA came under criminal investigation. The target for getting an appointment in a Veterans Hospital was 14 days. This was never achieved and staffs falsified appointment records so that it appeared the 14-day target was being met. Some patients died while they were on the list. An internal audit, released June 9, 2014, found that more than 120,000 veterans were left waiting or never got the care at all and the schedulers were pressured to use unofficial lists or engage in fraudulent practices to make the waiting times appear more appropriate. By June 2014 it was determined that VA hospitals around the country were identified as having the same problems as the Phoenix facility. At the Phoenix Hospital at least 1,700 veterans who wanted an appointment were never placed on an official wait list. The official report from the Phoenix hospital was that the average wait time was 24 days when in reality the average was 115 days. On April 30, 2014, CNN reported that at least 40 veterans died while waiting for care. Turning to the Virginia VA hospital, as of April, 2014, this hospital alone had paid out approximately $200 million for nearly 1,000 wrongful deaths. The audit further disclosed that staff bonuses were rampant. In one instance, Michael Moreland, Regional VA director of the region including the Pittsburgh VHA hospital received a performance bonus of $63,000 and a five-page performance evaluation which made no mention of the outbreak of legionnaires disease that led to the death of six veterans and illness for 21 others at the Pittsburgh Hospital. In 2010, 16,487 VA employees received a total of $110 million in bonuses. Based on a sample of 158 employees from this group, the Office of Inspector General concluded that at least 80% of these bonuses were questionable. According to the Government Audit Office the average wait time for veterans to receive treatment varied from a best case 21 days to 90 days and there were many instances where waiting times of up to a year occurred. The indifference toward the Veteran's Administration fraudulent and negligent operation was a travesty. How can we believe that our government, after its terrible and scandalous performance in running the Veterans Hospitals for many years, will be able to manage and keep free from corruption a system that will be ten times larger?

Triage – The term Triage means: "The assigning of priority order in allocating medical treatment on the basis of where limited funds and other resources can be best used or most needed on the most likely to achieve success. There are 40.3 million people in the United States over 65, representing 15.1% of the U.S. total population. And this segment is growing. This group of adults will all face the consequences of Triage and as resources become more limited and less available, there will be less and less funds available for treatment of those over 65; even many in good health but who will statistically have a shorter life to live. This has happened in Great Britain and Canada. Life expectancy in the U.S. will start going down as medical treatment for the elderly ls withdrawn. This will happen as there will just be too little money to cover all the programs that the Democrats wish to implement. Something has to give and the prime target will be the elderly. Not far behind will be the control of how many children one can have. As we see in China, abortion is mandated at any stage, sterilization of women after one or two births and/or serious financial penalties if the edicts of the state are not carried out.

Guaranteed minimum Income for everyone

The total unemployed under the proposed Socialist Democrat programs would be about 14% or 18 million of the 128 million in our labor force. Using the minimum wage of $15, the U.S. government would be funding $30,000/year for each unemployed (whether willing or unwilling to work). This would cost the federal Government $540 billion a year. Couple that with the loss of income taxes on 12.7 million jobs, (which for the most part would be high paying jobs such as airline pilots, air traffic controllers, oil nd gas related jobs, etc. Assume taxable income of $60,000 on average for these workers, there would be a loss of income tax of approximately $9,000 per year (15%) for those suddenly unemployed and $9,180 (15.3% social security employer/employee contributions for a total of $18,180 lost revenues per employee or a total of $327 Billion. So, the proposals of the Democrats would provide additional annual expenditures and loss of tax revenues of $867 Billion. This would be the lowest cost as the minimum acceptable income will continue to rise.

Free College Education –

The Socialist Democrats are also proposing free college education for everyone as well as pre-kindergarten schooling. We'll just look at free college education. There are approximately 30 million men and women between the age of 18 and 24. Assuming they would all be candidates of college and university because it is free and an average tuition, room and board of $25,000/student, this would cost the Federal government $750 billion a year. Democrat/Socialist presidential candidate, Bernie Sanders as part of his platform, would have the Federal government forgive all existing student debt at a cost of $1.6 trillion. This represents 1.3 times the Federal Government's total annual discretionary spending. The on-going expenditures of $750 billion of free college tuition would equate to 56% of our Federal Government's total annual discretionary spending and would require a 41% across the board increase in Personal and Corporate income taxes. Here are the costs associated with The National Health, The Green New Deal, Guaranteed income for everyone, free college and university education and lost Social Security and income taxes:

	Costs are in $trillions	
	Annual cost	10-year cost
The Green New Deal	$9.30	$93.00
National Health Care	3.20	32.00
Guaranteed Income	0.54	5.40
Free College Tuition	0.75	7.50
Lost income and S.S. taxes	<u>0.33</u>	<u>3.33</u>
Total	**$14.12**	**$141.23**

These expenditures (and loss of income tax receipts) of $14 trillion per year is 3.5 times our Federal governments current budget, which has already a built in $1 trillion deficit. Over the next 10 years we would be adding $15 trillion of debt each year. We are currently paying $363 billion interest on our debt. Our debt in the first year we start to implement the Democrat proposals would increase to approximately $40 trillion and within 10 years increase to $165 trillion. But after just the first year with our debt rising to $40 trillion and interest rates rising to 15%, our interest payments would be $6 trillion, which is in itself 1.5 times our current budget. And that is not included in the calculations above. And each following year our interest payments would be going up an additional $2.25 trillion a year. By the 10th year between the programs of the Democrats and the resulting increase in indebtedness, our country would have total debt of $544 trillion and be paying $82 trillion per year in interest based on the 15% rate experienced under Jimmy Carter. Our interest cost alone in 10 years will be 20 times our current total budget. There will be nothing left to spend for any program. There will be no Medicare for everyone; no social security, no defense program. Nothing. We will become a third world country overnight and probably invaded and taken over by China or Russia. There is even a Democrat presidential candidate that proposes $12,000 per year be paid by the Federal government to each man, woman and child in the United States. That would cost our Federal government another $3.84 trillion a year. Add that to the $14.12 trillion and we are looking at $18 trillion of annual costs being proposed by the Democrats. This is 4.5 times are present total annual Federal budget, which is already running a deficit. Where is $14 trillion going to come from? You could confiscate all the income of the top 25% of the taxpayers in the United States, and you would not have enough money to pay for any of the programs that the Democrats are proposing. This is insanity at the highest levels. Yet there are so many of you that, hate the President so much that you believe whatever the Socialist left tells you and you are so indoctrinated that you would allow your country to sink into oblivion, allow your family, your children and your grandchildren to become destitute and live on the streets gathering garbage for meals as we now see in the once proud and wealthy country of Venezuela.

Of course, well before we reach a level of debt which will exceed $100 trillion in very short order our country will be in a state of hyperinflation; our stock markets will have fallen to close to 0; we will emulate Venezuela in every way, with many of our citizens looking for garbage to eat and most of our population will be homeless. There will be violence everywhere, gangs will rule the streets and murders and suicides will be rampant. We will live in hell, thanks to the plans of the Democrats. If they are not ignorant; if they are not insane, then they are treasonous.

Today we have a level of prosperity that we have not seen in decades if ever. Our economy is at full employment, all ethnic groups are employed at a level never before attained, interest rates are low, prices are stable and the stock market has performed exceedingly well. Yet, the Democrats in search of complete power over us all is willing to destroy our country with falsehoods and many people still believe them. Where are the facts? Why aren't we all seeking the facts? The fault lies with us, if we allow the Democrats to impose their insanity on us.

Doubling our Taxes – Who and how much?

All of the Democrat candidates will tell their constituents that they are going to increase taxes, but they want you to believe that they are only going to raise the taxes on the very wealthy. The top 10% of income earners in the United States with threshold income of approximately $150,000 pay 70% of the individual income taxes. (The top 1% actually saw their taxes increase under the Trump Administration's new taxes.) A doubling of personal income taxes, without any leakage occurring would require new individual taxes of $1.6 trillion. $1.2 trillion would presumably come from those earnings $150,000 and more. Where will the additional $480 billion come from? Taxes would be doubled across the board for everyone. The Democrats would also, double the taxes on corporations. The doubling of personal and corporate income taxes, if we do nothing else; if we keep all other expenditures the same and there is no leakage, no rise in interest rates and no increase in the welfare rolls will provide us with a $1 trillion surplus, to cover Democrats proposed new spending of $14.1 trillion per year. But that will not happen. There will be leakages from four main sources. First, there will be many of the wealthy that will just leave our country and find a tax haven. And we will even lose citizens from middle income families, who find the tax rates and the massive cost of living increases too much of a burden to remain in our country. Secondly, there will be many corporations that will move out of our country to tax havens, leaving behind more unemployment and less tax revenues. Third there will be a massive number of companies that just will go out of business having been terminated by our government by the Medicare For All program and the New Green Deal, or just cannot afford the increase in tax burden and higher costs of doing business. There will be a massive increase in unemployment from the displacement of workers in the coal and oil industry; the airline industry; the restaurant and fast food industry, the cattle industry the aerospace industry and the automobile industry. This will not only reduce tax revenues but increase the number receiving entitlements under social welfare. Fourth, the interest cost on Federal debt will soar at least to 10%. The increase in interest rates from 2% to 10%, will increase the interest burden on the United States (assuming our debt burden stayed at only $25 trillion), by a cost of $2 trillion per year. That is the total amount of revenue the Government could expect to raise by doubling taxes. The tax increases will just offset the increase in the cost of interest and there will be nothing left to pay for the new socialist programs or infrastructure to replace airplanes. Finally, the cost of the socialist programs of free education, national health system, will soar beyond our ability to pay and our Federal government will not even be able to maintain a military and provide security for our country.

(The reader should note that different scenarios and different assumptions are used in different parts of this book. No matter what assumptions we use, the outlook for the U.S. always comes up as a disaster. Our country is facing destruction and each of us better wake up and carefully examine the facts. Your lives and the future of your families is dependent on it.

Is this the legacy we want to leave our families, our children, our grandchildren?

CHAPTER 11

The Supreme Court – Originalism vs. Living Constitution National Federation of Independent Business v. Sebelius (June 28, 2012)

THIS LANDMARK SUPREME Court Case in which the written opinion of Chief Justice John Roberts was upheld by a 5 to 4 vote found that the individual mandate in the Affordable Care Act to buy health insurance was a Constitutional exercise of Congress's taxing power.

The dissenting opinion expressed by Justices Scalia, Kennedy, Thomas and Alioto argued that the individual mandate was unconstitutional because it represented an attempt by Congress to regulate beyond its power under the Commerce Clause (Article I, Section 8), which grants Congress the right: "to regulate Commerce with foreign nations and among several states and with Indian Tribes". Chief Justice Roberts agreed that the mandate was not a proper use of the Commerce Clause, or the "Necessary and Proper" clause, which is the final clause of Article I Section 8, which grants Congress the right: "To make all laws which shall be necessary and proper for carrying into Execution of the forgoing powers and all other powers vested by the Constitution". However, the Chief Justice and the 4 supporting him, the so-called liberal wing of the Supreme Court, decided that the individual mandate was a tax and therefore fell within the purview of Article I Section 8, which opens: " The Congress shall have the power to lay and collect taxes, duties, imposts and excises to pay the debts and provide for the common defense and general welfare of the United States, but all duties, imposts and excises shall be uniform throughout the United States". In short, Chief Justice Roberts had to conclude that the mandate was a tax and not a penalty, even though President Obama and the proponents of the Affordable Care Act had vociferously claimed it was not a tax. So, we have the Supreme Court legislating what is or is not a tax in order to find it Constitutional. As the only people who had to pay the "fine" or "penalty" were those who chose not to buy insurance, it is hard to believe that 5 justices could declare it impartial and therefore a fair tax.

From Ignorance to Insanity

The 5-4 Supreme Court decision in the National Federation of Independent Business v. Sebelius, highlights the conflict between the two basic philosophies regarding American Jurisprudence; that is the interpretation of the Constitution based on either an "originalist" or "Living Constitution" philosophy. Originalism, as a way of interpreting the Constitution meant that the Constitution should be construed according to the time of its enactment, which can only be changed by Constitutional Amendments pursuant to Article 5 of the Constitution. Judicial adherence to a "living Constitution" meant that the Constitution is unrestrained by the original intent of the authors of the Constitution. The judges, who adhere to the "living Constitution" philosophy, believe that the Constitution changes in its meaning with time and therefore they are free to broadly interpret the Constitution in terms of today's society and environment. As a result these judges are free to make new interpretations of the Constitution and make new law without waiting for laws to be enacted by the legislature, which according to the Constitution is the sole body empowered to make law, The "living Constitutionalists" have even gone so far as to consult foreign law and have taken this right to the extreme by proclaiming that it was unconstitutional for the State of Oklahoma to prohibit its judges from consulting Islamic Sharia law in making their decisions, even though the vast majority of Oklahomans had voted to preclude judges from consulting Sharia law in rendering an opinion in their state.

Even if an argument can be raised by some as to the soundness of a "living Constitution" philosophy, it certainly raises a serious threat to abuse of power by the Supreme Court and potentially can cause serious damage to the checks and balances so carefully and appropriately constructed by our founding fathers in framing our Constitution.

Whether one is an Originalist or a Living Constitutionalist, this seems to be the basis of one's own political beliefs. Conservative Republicans are most likely to be Originalist and Liberal Democrats tend to favor the "living Constitution" philosophy. Why is that? The Originalist clearly seeks to preserve the separation of powers, certainly as far as the relationship of the Judiciary to the other two branches of government. The liberal Democrats, seek some form of socialism, big government and the power over people and resources. If the liberal Democrats can bring all these together, they will have the power and ability to turn our country into a socialist state, controlling our economy and dictating the way we live, and thereby limit our freedoms.

Taking control of the Supreme Court is just one of the objectives of the liberal left. There have been discussions among the liberal left legislators about "packing" the Supreme Court by increasing the number of justices from 9 to 12. They want a court that will do the wishes of a Democrat controlled Congress and not stand as a beacon of justice and a check and balance against improper, unconstitutional legislation. Just look at what has been accomplished by the liberal left to date and here is just one more piece they seek to control:

1. The liberal left Democrats control the media and use it to denigrate and vilify the Conservative Right. The veracity of claims or reports by the liberal left are irrelevant and yet they are treated as gospel by those who identify with the liberal left and believe that everything they stand for is

right and that everything the conservative right believes in is wrong. Does it really make sense to claim that the approximate 50% of the population that are on the conservative right are always wrong, while the 50% that are Democrats are always right? And do all those on the liberal left believe as Hillary Clinton believes that at least half of all those on the Conservative Right are "deplorable"? That is an irrational and divisive position, but it is just an example of how the liberal left characterizes those on the Conservative Right. How about Madeline Albright's statement that there is a special place in Hell for those women who would not support Hillary Clinton, which presumably would be any woman who supported the Conservative Right.

2. The Liberal left controls the entertainment community where hatred and vilification toward the Conservative Right is rampant. Well known entertainers have wanted to bomb the White House; suggest that it was time for another assassination of President; call for a military coup; hold up a replica of the severed head of the president; re-enact the murder of Julius Caesar, using the image of Trump as the victim. These are just a few of many examples of the tirades from the left against the Conservative Right.

3. The liberal left has taken over education at every level from elementary school through University, indoctrinating the children along the way with the greatness of socialism and the terrible nature of capitalism. Moreover, the educators have successfully prohibited any dialogue in their classrooms and on their campuses that is in any way contrary to liberal socialism. More about this later as I discuss: "Indoctrination Displaces Education".

4. And what about some of the leaders of the Democratic party like Cory Booker and Maxine Waters, who call upon the constituents to riot against the Conservative Right and to "get in the face" of Conservatives in restaurants, elevators and on the streets. And Eric Holder calls for kicking Republicans, when they go low. Remember Hillary Clinton saying that half of Republicans are deplorable? And she applauded Madeline Albright when Albright said "there was a special place in hell for all women" who didn't vote for Hilary Clinton. Well now she tells her liberal Democrats to throw civility toward Republicans out the window until the Democrats retake Congress. Does this sound like a party that would represent and treat fairly the 50% of the people in the United States who are Conservative Republicans? Or Tom Perez, elected by the Democrats as Chairman of the Democratic National Party, who stated on July 3, 2018 that Socialist political candidates like Alexandria Ocasio-Cortez, one of the most uniformed inexperienced, unknowledgeable candidates is the future of the party. He went on to say that along with Ocasio-Cortez, Ben Jealous a socialist running for governor of Maryland are examples of "spectacular candidates and represent the party's future. We are no longer a country where the differences in parties were simply along liberal and conservative lines. Now capitalism and our basic freedoms of life, liberty and pursuit of happiness are under attack. Socialism implies dictating to the constituents what they can have and what they can do. Freedom of choice will be abolished. Never has our way of life been so threatened and the irony is it is at a time when the United States is doing so well by almost every measure of economic well-being.

If Tom Perez as head of the DNC should have been enough of a concern, let's look at the former second in command who narrowly missed out on being the head of the DNC, Keith Ellison, Congressman from Minnesota. Ellison, born and raised a Roman Catholic, with strong Catholic roots, which included graduating from a Jesuit Academy, converted to Islam and took the oath of office swearing in on the Qur'an. Ellison was a strong supporter of Lois Farrakhan in the 1980's and 1990's and involved with and supported the Nations of Islam an anti- Jew group that actually called for a separate state for Black America, carved out of the United States and paid for by U.S. tax-payers. Farrakhan's hatred for Jews, which is apparently shared by Ellison recently came again into the news, when he referred to Jews as termites. And yet the Jews overwhelmingly support the Democrats even though bias if not hatred of the Jews is seen at the highest levels of the Democratic party. You would think that a selected leader of the Democratic party, who is a convert to Islam the most avowed enemy of Jews and a supporter of Farrakhan would be enough to turn a person of Jewish faith away from the Democratic party. Further, in the light of the vicious and unproven attacks on Brett Kavanaugh, by the liberal left, it is ironical and even hypocritical, that the Democrats have no problem in putting Ellison into a leadership position within their party, when he has been accused of abuse by an ex-girlfriend, Karen Monahan, who provides a medical report from her doctor, supporting her claim that she had been subject to physical and emotional abuse for 4 years at the hands of Ellison. So, there you have it. The Democratic party is represented by DNC leaders that are pro-socialism, anti-white, anti-Jew and anti-Christian. This is the fearful direction the Democratic Party wishes to take our nation.

5. Since the beginning of Trump's presidency, the Democrats has been calling for his impeachment without laying out the grounds for impeachment. For two years the Leaders of the Democratic Party and the entertainment industry has made unfounded accusations that President Trump has somehow colluded with Russia and yet, the collusion seems to be within the Democratic Party. Even after the Mueller investigation found that there was no collusion or conspiracy, the Democrats continue to harass President Trump with their hatred vitriol and unrelenting attempt to get him out of office.

6. The Liberal left has tried at any cost to prevent an originalist from becoming a Justice of the Supreme Court, condemning him and vilifying him and his family with uncorroborated accusations and false witnesses in the confirmation hearings of Bret Kavanaugh. We have seen the breakdown of all-American Jurisprudence. Where was the presumption of innocence, so fundamental to our jurisprudence? And why didn't it matter that there was no corroborating evidence? And why when the accuser could not identify the year, month or day of the supposed assault, nor how she got to and from the supposed party, nor could she provide a witness to corroborate, she is still considered credible. Yet when the accused presented a detailed calendar of where he was during the supposed time of the assault, that did not matter to the 10 Democrats conducting the questions at the hearing. The statements by Christine Ford on their face were slanderous and her documented accusations were libelous. She would be guilty of slander and libel actionable against her in a civil court of law. She would be the defendant

and would then have the burden of proof to prove the truth of her slanderous statements and libelous writings. Truth is the only defense and she would have to cross the threshold of the "preponderance of evidence" that her statements and accusations were true. As the accuser, it was up to Christine Ford to prove the veracity of her accusations. Yet from the beginning it was Brett Kavanaugh that had to prove his innocence. Whether one liked Christine Ford better than Brett Kavanaugh; whether you believed she was a credible witness, or more credible than Brett Kavanaugh, the law requires that the facts of a case be reviewed fairly, objectively and without personal subjective opinions based on factors that have nothing to do with the case.

In the hearings on the qualifications of Kavanaugh by the Senate Judiciary Committee, underlying the position of the Democratic members of the Committee, was Judge Kavanaugh's philosophy as an Originalist and his perceived position on Roe v. Wade, a case that the Democrat leaders would have women believe that Kavanaugh would seek to reverse, much to the violent opposition of those who support "pro-choice". Brett Kavanaugh had made it clear that he strongly supported "legal precedent" also referred to as "stare decisis". He could not opine on how he would vote regarding Roe V. Wade, because no Jurist can state how he or she would vote, until the facts of a case are adjudicated. Almost all the Democrats on the committee were lawyers and they well knew Kavanaugh could not give an opinion on Roe v. Wade, but they pursued this to raise an outcry among "pro-choice" women to gain their support in seeking to deny Kavanaugh a seat on the Supreme Court bench. Pro-choice advocates need to ask themselves is there any time that an unborn child has an independent right to live or be considered a human being?

I have had conversations with some who believe that right up to the day of birth, the woman has a right to abort. There are even far left pro-choicers, who believe in sex-selection abortion, where they find out that they are pregnant with a boy or girl and do not want a child of that sex. But sex selection abortion isn't the worst of the pro-choice believers. Extreme pro-choicers even support killing babies after they are born if they believe it benefits them or their family. More college students today according to an article in the College Fix, dated October 29, 2014 are showing a growing acceptance of post-birth abortion. Mark Harrington, Director of "Created Equal" reports that staff members have encountered acceptance of fratricide on such campuses as: Purdue, University of Minnesota, Ohio State and Central Florida.

In an article appearing in Volume 23 Number 3 of the Christian Research Journal, Peter Singer, Professor of Bioethics at Princeton University, suggested that no newborn should be considered a person until at least 30 days after birth and the attending physician should kill any disabled babies on the spot. As early as 1979 he wrote: "Human babies are not self-aware. They are not persons, therefore. The life of a newborn is of less value than the life of pig, dog or chimpanzee". Then there is the American University philosophy professor Jeffrey Reiman who asserted that infants do not: "possess in their own right a property that makes it wrong to kill them". He expressly holds that infants are not persons with a right to life and that: "there will be permissible exceptions to the rule against killing infants that will not apply to the rule against killing adults and children". It is the beliefs and statements by these liberal left educators that fuel the doctrine of the "pro-life" advocates, for certainly if it is all right to take the life of a newborn child, it certainly is acceptable to take the life while in the mother's womb. When in the mind of the advocates of post-birth abortion, does the infant gain the right to live?

How close are we getting to advocating genocide? Hitler justified the annihilation of a whole race based on claiming that Jews were not human. A point in favor of life beginning at conception is that it is definitive, there is no question of a subjective determination of some hypothetical time. At least the viability test as pronounced in the Planned Parenthood v, Casey case provides some protection for the unborn child. Although imperfect it does protect the unborn child against any purely arbitrary decision as to when he or she can be killed.

The "pro-choice" advocates loudly protest that the "pro-lifers" are against women's rights. And they believe this, because the liberal left has told them so. It is a tactic from the Liberal Left to get a certain sector of the populaton to vote Democrat. The underlying and fundamental argument by "pro-life" advocate is not making a statement against women; their focus is whether the unborn baby has any rights as a human being that ought to be protected. It's hard to believe that "pro-choice" advocates cannot at least acknowledge that the "pro-life" stand is not unreasonable or without some merit. There would seem to be a reasonable moderate stand that could be acceptable to both "pro-choice" and "pro-life" advocates. In fact, we have this with Roe v. Wade as modified by Planned Parenthood v. Casey.

7. The liberal left has sought to obtain amnesty for all illegal aliens and in California even allowing them to vote although they are illegal let alone citizens. Open borders, no wall, amnesty for all illegal aliens is the cry of the liberal left and they have raised the fury and anger of the masses to protest any denial of an immigrant's right to be in America. The liberal left has even gone as far as to not only ignore the laws of the United States, but also to actively confront and oppose the laws through the creation of "sanctuary cities".

The liberal left are strong proponents of the ends justifying the means and they advocate only to achieve the objective of getting more votes to put them in the place of power. The Roe v. Wade arguments; the attending attempt to block Brett Kavanaugh from becoming a Supreme Court Judge, is all about gaining more votes for the liberal left. Look how the liberal left has changed its stance about immigration over the years. In the mid-1970's, Governor Jerry Brown of California opposed the admission of hundreds of thousands of Vietnamese "boat people" after the fall of Saigon. Governor Brown would be quoted in the Los Angeles Times: "There is something a little strange about saying: 'Let's bring in 500,000 more people' when we can't take care of the one million Californians out of work." Senator Joe Biden of Delaware would introduce legislation to restrict the arrival of Vietnamese. Senator Robert Byrd of West Virginia, would demand extreme vetting of Vietnamese refugees, in order to cull the "barmaids, prostitutes and criminals". But the most telling comment came approximately 20 years later, when President William Clinton addressed Congress in his State of the Union address. He said: "All Americans, not only in the states most heavily affected but in every place in the country, are rightly disturbed by the large numbers of illegal aliens entering our country. The jobs they hold might otherwise be held by U.S. citizens or immigrants. The public services these impose burdens on our taxpayers". In 1994, the Chair of the U.S. Commission on Immigration Reform, Barbara Jordon a Democrat Congresswomen from Texas, in a statement to the New York Times said: Those who choose to come here must embrace the common core of American civic culture – We must assist them in learning our common language: American English. We move to the Democrat platform of 2000. Less than 20 years ago, the Democrats "believe in an effective immigration system that balances a strong enforcement of our laws with fair and even-handed treatment of immigrants and their families". The Democrats at the time also condemned illegal immigration for over-burdening government services, harming local communities and hurting American workers. Finally, as recently as 2006, Hillary Clinton, Barack Obama, Chuck Schumer and twenty-three other Democrat Senators voted in support of a fence on the Mexican border. So much for the liberal left supporting unlimited immigration, open borders and multiculturalism. Why the drastic change in the liberal lefts position on immigration? It has only to do with votes. They do not care about the damage to our country, that uncontrolled immigration will cause, although they readily admitted to this in the past. The hypocrisy, the deception, the willingness to sacrifice the well-being of its constituents just to gain power, is so clearly demonstrated here by the liberal left. (This section has been gleaned primarily from Tucker Carlson's recent book "Ship of Fools").

8. The liberal left consistently opposes any reduction in taxes. On the contrary, they wish to increase taxes of every kind and nature. Even in the light of the substantial improvement of almost every aspect of our economy as a result of lowering taxes especially on business, the tax reductions are still opposed by Democrats and Nancy Pelosi, even refers to them as "crumbs". The Democrats are not talking about tax increases for the rich. Everyone will see higher taxes and even doubling them will not pay even a minute fraction of the programs the Democrats are promoting

9. The Democrats seek open borders, no walls, amnesty for illegal immigrants and the elimination of ICE (Immigration and Customs Enforcement). Elizabeth Warren a potential contender for President in 2020, believes no borders, no walls no ICE with freedom for those to immigrate and if illegal be granted immediate amnesty. ICE is not only our only defense against illegal immigration, but more importantly, it is the organization that seeks to keep illegal drugs from crossing our borders as well as violent gangs. We all know that the drug problem in the United States has never been so bad. So many lives are destroyed each year in the U.S.A. from drugs. There were 72,000 deaths from drug overdose in the U.S. in 2017 up 12.5% over 2016. This was after an increase of 21% in 2016 over 2015. In two years, that's a 33% increase. In the face of this statistic, the Democrats want to make it even easier for drugs to come across our borders. No ICE, no wall, no immigration control, how much better can it get for the drug

lords of Mexico and South America and this is what the liberal left is supporting.

10. The Socialist Democrats time and again have encouraged "in your face" protests against the supporters of the Conservative Right, in restaurants, in their homes, in public buildings and on public the streets. No one is worse than Maxine Waters who time again has told her fellow Democrats to "get in their face" or Hillary Clinton "don't be civil to them" or Eric Holder: kick them when they are down". The Liberal Left Democrats have denied the Conservative Right freedom of speech in public schools, and on college and university campuses throughout the country (more on this follows in a separate section entitled:" Indoctrination Displaces Education").

11. The Socialist left has supported the defamation of our flag and National Anthem and belittled our Judeo/Christian faith. while supporting the teaching of Islam in our public schools, in violation of separation of church and state in accordance with Amendment I of the Constitution as interpreted by the Supreme Court Case of Murray v. Curlett (1963). This case effectively terminated reading from the Bible in school and would lead to the elimination of any Judeo/Christian theology no matter how limited, from our public schools. At the same time the liberal left would embrace the teaching of Islam and reading from the Qur'an and actually learning some Islamic prayers.

12. Nowhere is the hate and vitriol emanating from the liberal left, more evident than in the extreme efforts they made to derail the selection of Bret Kavanaugh as a Justice of the Supreme Court. He was accused by Christine Ford of molesting her while drunk, when she was 15 years old over 35 years ago. She wanted to keep her charges anonymous, but the Democrats decided to exploit her claims as the last-ditch effort to prevent Bret Kavanaugh from becoming a Justice and thereby providing a conservative "originalist" interpretation of the Constitution. They leaked her claims to the press; they obtained a lawyer for her that was particularly sympathetic to the liberal Democrat agenda; they apparently paid for her legal fees and lie detector test, and although this was not conclusively determined, the fact that Christine Ford was unable to say who paid these fees would indicate that at least she did not. We learned that Christine Ford had once coached a person how to take a lie detector test. Although as a witness for herself, Christine Ford appeared quite credible. However, she could not confirm, what year the attack by Kavanaugh took place, exactly what month or what day; or how did she get to and from the party. Yet she was sure that it was Kavanaugh and that she had only one drink. Not one of her supposed witnesses corroborated her testimony. Kavanaugh claimed, unequivocally that he was not even at the claimed party and that he had never molested any women or girl. By way of evidence he submitted a detailed calendar, which was like a diary that stated where he was and with whom during the summer when the supposed molestation took place. The veracity of the accusations did not even come close to the threshold for a civil action of "preponderance of evidence". In fact, no evidence at all was provided other than the accusation by Christine Ford. The Democrats claimed that the rules of law do not apply and the presumption of guilt is acceptable, since this was only a job interview to become a Supreme Court Justice. I ask all the readers, when were you ever on an interview, where you were interrogated by 21 people

and had to defend yourself against an accuser of a crime, which could not be corroborated? This was not a job interview.

The underlying motive for this relentless attack on Bret Kavanaugh is the Liberal Democrats position on abortion being "pro-choice" and the perception that Bret Kavanaugh would seek to overrule Roe V. Wade because he is a "pro-life" advocate. Of course, he couldn't say to the Judicial Committee, what his stand is on this issue. The judge cannot render an opinion without first hearing and understanding the facts. It is even quite unclear what Brett Kavanaugh's position is on Roe v. Wade or for that matter any Conservative judge in the light of Planned Parenthood v, Casey. As it stands now, the state has a right to protect the unborn child against the rights of the mother, if and when the unborn infant is viable, that is, can live outside the mother's womb by artificial means or otherwise. Recognizing that there are almost always two sides to a moral issue, it would seem that the existing viability test should be acceptable to both pro-life advocates and pro-choice advocates and the concern of the pro-choice advocates is much to do about nothing. It could even be argued that the Roe v. Wade case coupled with Planned Parenthood v. Casey seems to favor the pro-life advocates and yet the pro-choice advocates are violently opposed to its repeal.

We know that a Supreme Court Judge is appointed for life. There are nine of them and it is the position of the liberal Democrats that when they come into power, they will "pack" the Supreme Court, by increasing the number of judges so that a living, revisionist interpretation of the Constitution will prevail. Now we see clearly the goal of the Democratic party. Its inexorable goal is to achieve power over all branches of the Federal Government. Their craze for power is so clearly evident in its actions against Brett Kavanaugh. They betrayed Christine Ford, she had asked for and supposedly obtained an understanding of anonymity from the Democrats, only to have that anonymity leaked out to the public. Their hatred and incessant vilification of Bret Kavanaugh and his family almost succeeded in destroying him. The level of betrayal, anger and willingness to dispense with any sense of decency by the Democrats has never been matched in my lifetime. Yet many applauded the actions of the Democrats in the Judiciary Committee's confirmation hearings. We can just imagine how the liberal Democrats will react if they come to power in the legislative branch of the government. They will seek to impeach the President; impeach Kavanaugh, expand and stack the supreme Court and our country will become more divisive and the Democrats will have the power to dictate the political, social, religious and economic lives of all Americans.

CHAPTER 12

The Green New Deal - The Democrat plan for America.

NEVER MIND THAT there is still significant evidence that global warming is not caused by CO_2 as I have previously discussed. Never mind that even if we were to reduce our CO_2 emissions to 0, it would not begin to offset the ever-increasing CO_2 emissions by the 96% of the rest of the word, most notably China and India that represent almost 40% of the world population compared to the U.S. 4%. Yet here is the plan that is being introduced by the Liberal left; also known as the Democrat Socialists.

The hypocrisy of the Democrat leaders, the entertainers and those that are so outspoken about the Green New Deal, is that many if not most emit CO_2 at levels 10,000 times the rate of the average person. They are the ones that fly around the world in their private jets, emit vast quantities of CO_2 in heating their homes and run their gas guzzling cars. In a climate change summit in Italy some time ago featuring Barack Obama and other elites, 114 private jets descended on the airport where the meeting was hosted. Both Al Gore the patriarch of the global warming movement and the outspoken and influential supporter of a global warming crisis and former President Barack Obama have bought multi-million-dollar beach front homes and yet they insist that sea levels are about to reach cataclysmic levels. Al Gore's 10,000 square foot estate in Nashville uses an average of close to 20,000 kilowatt hours of fossil fuel generated energy per month which is 21 times the average American family.

Coming from virtually out of no-where is a freshman Congress woman from the Bronx, Alexandria Ocasio-Cortes that has released a sweeping package of environmental measures crafted in conjunction with Democrat Senator Ed Markey of Massachusetts and 60 Democrat co-sponsors in the House. It is known as **"The Green New Deal"** The plan is technologically impossible but would cost approximately $100 trillion dollars or $10 trillion/year; 2.5 times our total current Federal Government budge. We can't even meet our current $4 trillion and a doubling of our personal and corporate income taxes (on everyone) would raise an additional $1.9 trillion, which with no new programs would leave us with a $900 billion surplus. So where is the missing $9.1 trillion per year going to come from?

The Green New Deal -The Democrat plan for America.

The plan calls for a drastic and rapid shifting away from all fossil fuels and other sources of CO_2 emissions that supposedly cause global warming. It also calls for moving away from nuclear power. This leaves us with sun, wind, thermal and water as our only energy sources. Cortes and her 60 colleagues would have this all accomplished in the next 10 to 12 years.

Some of the specific provisions of the plan include:

1. A dramatic expansion of renewable energy and water efficiency upgrade for all existing buildings throughout the United States. Every building in the United States would either be rebuilt or renovated to achieve state of the art energy efficiency.
2. An overhaul of the countries transportation system to eliminate pollution and CO_2 emissions from that sector, by expansion of investment in zero-emission vehicles, public transit and high-speed rail. The objective would be to eliminate all air travel. High-speed rail travel would be built at a scale where air travel would become unnecessary
3. Ban nuclear energy and fossil fuels within 10 years.
4. To accomplish this elimination of all nuclear and fossil fuel usage, all new jobs will be required to be unionized.

An addition to the program described above, was the proposal of New Jersey Senator and Presidential candidate Cory Booker, to eliminate all cattle and prohibit the eating of beef, in order to eliminate the methane gas produced by the flatulence of cows. Remember Hilary Clinton's proud proclamation that she was going to put all coal miners out of work? Now another Democrat is calling for putting all the cattle ranchers, their workers and their families out of work. The liberal left Democrats, keep telling us they are the party of the people. Yet they are the ones who are planning the demise of many jobs and making workers and families destitute.

Separate from the Green New Deal are Democrat proposals of: Medicare for all; Jobs guarantee (Federal Government is the employer of last resort); family leave; abolishment of Immigration and Customs Enforcement (ICE); free public college and trade schools; marginal tax rate of 70% for incomes over $10 million and a host of infrastructure projects for renewable energy. (The increase in the marginal tax rate to 70% even if it is on incomes over $150,000, won't even begin to pay for the costs of the insane proposals by the socialist left).

We will look at the cost and the impact on jobs for each of the suggested objectives of the Democrat plan to abolish fossil fuels and other gas emissions. The plan includes the elimination of the production of all fossil fuels (coal, oil and natural gas); the replacing of all airline travel with high speed rail transportation and the prohibiting the consumption of beef.

Elimination of all oil, natural gas, and coal production, distribution and sales.

These industries account for the following jobs: Oil Drilling 90,000; Oil Extraction 53,000; Oil Support 282,000; natural gas 1,000,000; retail gas delivery 700,000 (175,000 stations with 125,000 having associated convenience stores and we are assuming 4 employees on the average for service, facility maintenance and store sales; coal industry 60,000 That's a total of 2,125,000. Add the indirect employees of 2,975,0000 that would provide a total of 5,244,000 jobs lost just associated with the elimination of fossil fuels. Associated with each of these jobs are the families of the workers and assuming 2.5 dependents for each job this would add an additional 13,110,000 family members, providing a total of 18,354,000 that otherwise could provide for themselves, now added to the welfare rolls.

(Note another estimate in 2009 suggested that 4 million jobs both direct and indirect are attributable to the Natural Gas Industry, as opposed to the 2.4 million estimated above. Using the formula of 2.5 dependents for each job, the total would be 14 million for the natural gas industry as opposed to 8.4 million) and the total workers and families displaced by the elimination of the fossil fuel industry would be 33,600,000.

Elimination of Air-flight and replacing with High speed rail

The airline industry provides 9 million Domestic flights each year and transports 890 million passengers per year or 2,440,000 per day. It directly employs 1.2 million people and 1.68 million of indirect workers would also lose their jobs, providing a total increase in unemployment of 2.880,000. Using the 2.5 additional family members for each employed worker the displacement of the airline industry would increase the welfare rolls by 10,080,000.

It is the objective of the Green New Deal to replace airplanes with high-speed rail crisscrossing the country, adding 10's of thousands if not 100's of thousands of miles of rail and taking by eminent domain millions of acres of property, including forests, farms and areas of natural beauty that should be preserved. Railroads today handle 550 million passengers per year, so our rail system would have to increase its capacity by 162% in 10 years. We can point to their insanity of the proposed network of high-speed railways in the U.S., to be built in 10 years by looking at California's failed attempt to build a high-speed railway between Los Angeles and San Francisco. In 2008, California voters approved a 520-mile-high speed rail link between Los Angeles and San Francisco. It was initially estimated to cost $33 Billion and be completed in 2020. Subsequently the cost was increased to $77 Billion and the new estimated completion date was changed to 2033. The time for completion changed from approximately 10 to 12 years to 25 years. Yet the total nation-wide system being proposed by the Green New Deal group will be completed in 10 to 12 years. Now, just this year, California Governor Newsome has abandoned the project on the grounds that it would cost too much and take too long. The cost had burgeoned to $148 million per mile. The U.S. government cancelled the remaining $929 million it agreed to pay California and is seeking to recover the unspent $2.5 billion it has already advanced. It was noted that the development of the railway was bogged down by environmental studies. Assuming that 100,000 miles of additional rails would have had to be built at a cost of $148 million per mile (or total cost of $14.8 trillion) and estimating that 2.5 million acres would have to be acquired by eminent domain, it is rather disingenuous that the Democrats find a $5.8 billion wall requiring approximately an additional 1,000 miles and maybe requiring 25,000 acres to be acquired by eminent domain too costly and too unfair to landowners along the route of the wall.

So, the Democrats are proposing to spend $100 trillion dollars to build a network of high-speed railways crisscrossing the country to replace our airlines and also to do away with gas fueled autos and fossil fueled buildings. And they propose to do this in 12 years, even though the only experience the Democrat run Federal Government and Democrat run State government of California have in high speed rail, is a failed rail system in California which would only serve the relatively short corridor between Los Angeles and San Francisco. That system cost Billions of dollars, was supported by the Federal government and was supposed to be completed in 12 years and then rescheduled for completion in 25 years and finally abandoned. The same people who would have the U.S. spend 100 trillion dollars to replace our airlines and gas-powered vehicles, have only their experience of a failed system, which was already 12 years late in completion when it was finally abandoned.

The other major component of the Green New Deal is solar energy. And what has been the experience of our Federal Government in introducing solar energy? Remember Solyndra? This $500 million spectacular failure of the U.S. Government during the Obama Administration. Solyndra is a stunning example of the Federal Government's failure to administer a relatively small environmental project. Solyndra developed, manufactured and sold solar energy panels, which they claimed to be unlike any other products ever tried in the industry. In September, 2011 the company closed all business activity and filed for bankruptcy. Solyndra successfully misled the Department of Energy, costing the U.S. Taxpayer $500 million. The Inspector General's Office found several shortcomings with the DOE's management and approval of the loan guarantee for Solyndra. The Democrats would have the taxpayers of the United States, fund $100 trillion, or $10 trillion per year which is 3 times our total current annual Federal Budget, based on their failed railway and solar panel energy ventures.

What would happen to our Aerospace industry as companies like Lockheed and Boeing would be forced out of business? The loss of these employees is not included in the above. What would happen to our military that counts on the Civilian aerospace industry for much of its aeronautical research and development and also to build military aircraft? And just think of the loss of productivity associated with having to travel a day or two to cross the country instead of a 4-hour flight? And by eliminating a flight alternative, what happens when the sole means of transportation between cities around the country is the railroad and it breaks down? And what happens to the ability to crop dust or fight forest fires from the air? How will people from Hawaii, Puerto Rico, the Virgin Islands and Alaska get to mainland U.S? And will people be able to travel on demand, or will they have their travel scheduled months in advance, restricted in number of times someone can travel each year, or even have travel rationed on a need basis, virtually eliminating any vacation travel? We cannot look to solve global warming concerns, by returning us to the 1800's and eliminating all the advances we have made in travel. The folly and insanity of the New Green Deal is already apparent, but let's go on.

Elimination of gas fueled cars, trucks and busses

There are 275 million vehicles in the United States, which includes Cars, Trucks, Busses and motorcycles. These vehicles account for 75% of all passenger miles in the U.S; the rest being rail and air travel. There are 6 to 7 million new cars and trucks sold each year. There are 17.6 million used cars and trucks sold each year. The used car market is a $350 Billion per year industry and the vehicles are sold through approximately 138,000 dealers, which employ an estimated 500,000. The used vehicle market would evaporate long before the change over from diesel and gas fueled vehicles, since no one will buy a vehicle which will be prohibited in just a few years. New Car dealers will also see their business come to an end, way before the changeover to total electric vehicles as buyers will stop buying gas driven vehicles and await the availability of the new mandated clean air vehicles. Many new car dealers will go out of business before they can transition to the new mandated cars. Some, however will find a way to survive, so we won't count the impact on new car dealerships of the Green New Deal mandate, but it will be substantial. There are approximately 21,000 New Car dealers employing a total of 1.2 million and there is another 800,000 associated with parts supply and service. This is a $700 billion industry, with 3.9 million used cars sold annually at an average price of $18,000. Some of these 2 million employees will be able to transition to the new mandated vehicles but many jobs will be lost in the transition, but we cannot accurately estimate the job survival rate so we will just stick with the used car dealerships that will be totally abolished by the displacement of fossil fuel vehicles. Using our formula of 1.4 indirect jobs for every direct job and the average employee supporting a family of an additional 2.5, there will be a loss of 1.2 million jobs, associated with the elimination of the used car market and a total of 4.2 million added to the welfare rolls.

Now look at the irrational aspect of merely implementing a plan to do away with fossil fuels within 10 to 12 years, even regardless of cost. By 2040 there will be 1.8 billion cars, light trucks and SUV's on the road world-wide up from the 1 billion today. That in a short span of 10 to 12 years we can even begin to implement a program to do away with all fossil fuel vehicles is absurd. Recently, the International Energy Agency (IEA) forecasted that more than 50% of the world's energy consumption would still be fossil fuels, yet according to Forbes (March 2017) and contributing writer Jude Clemente, given that wind and solar compete only in the electricity sector and don't compete in the majority of the world's energy market, the displacement of even close to 50% by renewable energy sources is unrealistic. 6 out of 7 humans today live in underdeveloped nations and oil consumption is just getting started. For most of the world, solar and wind energy are not competitive. Yet research is constantly being undertaken to make vehicles more efficient in burning fossil fuels and the focal point is the use of turbochargers and the use of the engine's exhaust gas and feeding it back into the engine when the driver accelerates. If the Democrats only stopped to examine reality, their goals of the elimination of CO_2 levels to zero in 12 years is more than a fantasy. It is insane. The reduction of CO_2 (regardless of whether it actually causes global warming) to a more environmentally friendly level can be obtained over a much longer period of time, without destroying our economy. We all can agree that it is very much to everyone's interest to develop renewable alternatives to fossil fuels, which are depletable fuel sources.

The Democrats have even proposed doing away with ownership of cars all together, and have everyone depend on a Federally run car service. How can we allow the Federal government to take away our right to own cars along with our right to own guns, chose our doctors or even eat meat?

Elimination of Cattle

As part of the Green New Deal, it has been suggested by some Democratic Congressmen, led by Cory Booker, that the Federal Government should ban the eating of beef because of cow flatulence. Lamb and pig farming cannot be far behind in needing to be banned. They too cause flatulence but not to the levels of cows. It is true that the methane gas generated by cows is more toxic than CO_2 and the quantities of Methane generated is quite substantial. But the American Cattle Industry Generates 25 Billion pounds of beef for consumption each year, which works out to about 80 pounds of beef consumed each year per person. Fish consumption is approximately ½ of beef consumption. Approximately 32 million cattle are needed to produce the 25 billion pounds of meat.

There are approximately 725,000 beef farms and ranches in the U.S. employing about 775,000 and another 26,000 employees engaged in feedlot operations. There is also another 530,000 engaged in processing packaging and distributing beef. This provides a total of 1,331,000 direct employees, who would lose their jobs of cattle production, processing, packaging and distribution if eating beef were to be banned. Adding indirect employees of 1,863,000, there would be a total loss of direct and indirect jobs or 3,194,000. Adding the families that these former wage earners support, there would be a total of 11,179,000 people added to the welfare rolls of the United States, just from the elimination of the production of cattle and the consumption of beef.

Although Cory Booker and the rest of his cohorts do not specifically mention Dairy Cows, how do they differ from any other cow in creating methane gas? Are Dairy cows to be spared? Shouldn't the Dairy cow be eliminated for the same reason as the beef cow, because it flatulates the same way? There are approximately 40,000 dairy farms in the United states with an average of 235 milk producing cows per farm, providing a total of 9.4 million dairy cows in the United States. The dairy cows produce 100 million metric tons of milk per year. The leading dairy states in our country include: California, Wisconsin, Idaho, Pennsylvania, New York, Texas and Minnesota. Milk is a major source of calcium, very essential for the development of the bones in our children. Also, it is the principal ingredient in cheese and yogurt. Are we prepared to have all milk, cheese and yogurt eliminated from the diet of Americans? That of course won't happen, because our Dairy production will just move to Mexico and Canada and our price of dairy products will double, triple or even more. The same cows will be producing the same methane in foreign countries and we will of course be sustaining the production of methane by dairy cows; only it will be in other countries. The suspending of dairy cows, like meat cows, does nothing for global warming but it would certainly create higher costs for the consumer and would seriously increase our trade imbalance. This is just another example of the insanity that will be imposed upon us by the liberal left.

Elimination of Used Car dealers

There are approximately 138,000 used car dealers in the United States. Once we no longer have gasoline available for cars, who is going to buy them? They become totally useless. In fact, years before electric cars are available, used car dealers will go out of business. The used car business will begin to wind down long before the electric car can fully replace them No one will buy a used car that will shortly become obsolete. We estimate that the average dealer consists of the owner and two employees. So, there is an additional 400,000 workers whose jobs will be eliminated. In addition, there would be 560,000 indirect jobs and 2.4 million family members, providing an additional 3,360,000 on the welfare rolls

Elimination of gas and diesel driven fishing vessels

Just when the creative Democrats who support a Green New Deal calling for their constituents to give up beef and presumably switch to fish, they would render every American fishing vessel inoperable because there can be no gas or diesel driven vessels. The Democrats would say that they would give the commercial fishermen an exemption, but where are the fishermen going to get fuel that is no longer available? And of course, all pleasure craft, will be rendered worthless because they no longer can be used and the owners of pleasure craft won't even be able to give their boats away.

The Fishing industry produces only 40% as much food for consumption as does the cattle industry. 10 Billion pounds were provided in 2016 compared to the 25 billion pounds of beef. Just when the U.S. fishing industry would need to triple to replace the beef no longer consumed, it is totally destroyed, as no commercial fishing operation no matter how large could afford to replace its vessels with new electric engines. And long before that transition would occur, the price of diesel fuel will have spiraled out of control, or even worse become unavailable. Then too, what would happen to our marine environment, if the fishing industry actually tripled its production overnight to replace the loss of meat from our diets? There are already limits and controls on the amount of fish that can be harvested, to protect our marine environment. How can we increase fishing production three or four times without seriously impacting the future supply of fish?

There are 1. 2 million employed in the fishing industry, 71,500 of which are involved with the actual catching of the fish. We will only use the employees that are actually engaged in the catching of fish in our analysis. Using our 1.4 indirect jobs for each direct job, we estimate that the mandating of environment friendly vessels will cause the loss of 173,000 jobs and 606,000 addition to the U.S. welfare rolls.

The Green New Deal -The Democrat plan for America.

Let's summarize the loss of jobs and related numbers that will go on welfare in the United States as the result of the insane proposals of our Democratic party, which has shifted so far to the radical left.

Lost Jobs and New Welfare Recipients Due to the Green New Deal

Industry	Direct Jobs	Indirect Jobs	Total Jobs	Family Members	Total New Welfare Recipients
Oil Drilling	90,000	126,000	216,000	540,000	756.000
Oil Extraction	53,000	74,000	127,000	318,000	445,000
Oil Support	282,000	395,000	677,000	1,692,000	2,369,000
Coal	60,000	84,000	144,000	360,000	504,000
Gas stations/ Convenience stores	700,000	980,000	1,680,000	4,200,000	5,880,000
Natural Gas Delivery	1,000,000	1,400,000	2,400,000	6,000,000	8,400,000
Sub-total	2,185,000	3,059,000	5,244,000	13,110,000	18,354,000
Airline Industry	1,200,000	1,680,000	2,880,000	7,200,000	10,080,000
Cattle Ranching	775,000	1,085,000	1,860,000	4,650,000	6,510,000
Feed lot operations	26,000	36,000	62,000	156,000	218,000
Beef processing/ Distribution	530,000	742,000	1,272,000	3,180,000	4,452,000
Commercial fishing	72,000	101,000	173,000	433,000	606,000
Used car dealers	400,000	560,000	960,000	2,400,000	3,360,000
Total lost jobs and new Welfare recipients	5,188,000	7,263000	12,451,000	31,129,000	43,580,000

The above are the jobs that would be lost and welfare claims generated as a result of the Green New Deal and the elimination of fossil fuels. There are 128 million full time employees in the U.S. This would lead to an increase in our country's unemployment rate from 3.5% to 14%. In addition to these job losses, we must also include the job loss in the Health Insurance industry resulting from nationalization of medical coverage and also those lost from cutbacks in services in our hospitals such as nurses, janitors, clerical workers, technicians, etc.

Health Insurance	500,000	700,000	1,200,000	3,000,000	4,200,000
Hospital Support	1,500,000	2,100,00	3,700,000	7,500,000	11,200,000

This would bring the total job loss due to the Socialist plans of the Democrats to 17,351,000 and would result in our unemployment rate climbing almost immediately to 17% and 58,980,000 more men, women and children being added to the welfare rolls of our country. Using an average income of only $50,000/yr. and an average tax rate of 20%, the 17.351 million jobs lost will result in a loss of Federal tax revenue of approximately $174 Billion/year. And it will only get worse from here as unemployment will skyrocket beyond 25%. Look at Venezuela today. Is that what you want for America tomorrow?

Federal Income taxes yield a total of $2.1 Trillion/year If taxes were doubled on everyone, corporate and individuals alike, our Federal Government would have $4.2 trillion of income tax receipts. But not so fast. The 13.65 million jobs lost averaging $60,000 taxable income, would pay 60.6% in taxes (income and social security) or approximately $500 Billion. There would also be the lost receipts from the displaced oil, gas, natural gas, coal airline aerospace and health insurance industries, which is not quantified here.

Also not quantified here is the loss of manufacturing jobs associated with American business moving production abroad to avoid not only rising taxes, but higher production costs associated with retrofitting plants, paying higher cost utilities, paying of higher wages and falling demand for their products as inflation spirals out of control.

Let's for a moment, just look at one industry, the cattle industry. The banning of beef planned by the Democrats is lunacy right from the start. Americans will not stop eating meat. They will import it, albeit at a much higher cost (two or three times or more than what they pay now). And the cow will take its flatulence to another country. The same 1.5 billion cows that are grazing on this planet will still be grazing on our planet except they will have been relocated and the same amount of methane gas will still be spewed into our atmosphere. So, the Democrats have achieved no benefit for the environment of our planet. All they have accomplished is to create unemployment for approximately 775,000 cattle ranchers and feed lot operators, unemployment for an additional 1.1 million indirect workers and placed a total of 6.5 million on welfare; all due to the elimination of cattle ranching.

The Impact on the Car Manufacturing and Steel Industries

We have not even factored in the impact of the Green New Deal on the Car Manufacturing and Steel industries, because one might assume that there would be no loss of jobs or loss of need for steel when we transition to electric from fossil fuel cars. But there would be a terrible impact on these industries from the transition.

Eliminating gas fueled vehicles and replacing with electric vehicles is not like switching a light on and off. Passing the law is the first step. There will be studies of the economic impact and environmental impact and studies from these industries that will demonstrate the irrationality of such a switch out of fossil fuels. Let's say at best this will take two to three years to accomplish and actually have the Green New Deal Law passed. So, given two years until the New Socialist Congress passes the Green New Deal and three more years until the law is implemented, the Green New Deal will not even be ready to start for five years. Remember, the Socialist Democrats are saying we only have 12 years from now, before our atmosphere is doomed and we will have a wasteland and no food. Now we have the implementation of a Democrat plan that will replace our airlines and create high speed trains crisscrossing the United States. We have already discussed a timeline to accomplish at the very earliest of more than 25 years and that the first attempt at a high speed rail-way has already failed in California. Now let us look at an equally irrational idea to replace all fossil fuel vehicles in not 25 years but 7 years.

The Big three auto manufacturers Ford, GM and Fiat/Chrysler generate about $450 billion in revenues each year and employ approximately 600,000. The number of these jobs that are domestic would be significantly less because the three companies are also engaged in foreign manufacturing and sales. It would be safe to assume that over half of these jobs would leave the United States to a more corporate friendly foreign environment. Nevertheless, we are not including them in our loss of jobs calculations.

There are approximately 260 million vehicles registered in the United States. 113 million of these are passenger cars and 133 million are light trucks including SUVs. The balance are heavy trucks busses, motorcycles, etc. Motor Vehicle production in the United States over the past 5 years has been between 11 million and 12 million per year. Thus, it would take approximately 22 years to replace all the existing gas fueled vehicles. About 5.3 million passenger vehicles are produced each year. Therefore, to replace 113 million passenger cars would take 21 years. What are people to do in the interim? At current production levels, it will take some people 21 years to get an electric car, but they will not be able to use their gas fueled car in the interim. Prices of cars will skyrocket based on the simple laws of supply and demand. Can you even contemplate the cost when there is a demand for 113 million cars and there are only 5.3 million produced per year?

Once the Green New Deal was enacted, there would be a number of immediate responses. Oil companies would stop drilling for oil, refineries would begin to slow down production and pipelines would reduce shipments. Oil inventories would drop, gas stations would begin to close and imports of oil would increase to cover shortfalls from downward spiraling domestic production. Prices at the gas pump would increase, just because of foreign sourcing of oil. The balance of trade would turn further negative, domestic oil company revenues would erode substantially as well as the income taxes associated with the reduction of income. And all this would happen long before the Green New Deal can be implemented.

But worst of all, people will stop buying new gas fueled cars. They will make existing cars last longer. Sales of Ford, GM and Fiat/Chrysler will drop precipitously as all of a sudden no one would be buying new cars and trucks. As the sales of existing cars and trucks are virtually eliminated, where will the car industry find the funds for re-tooling to build new electric powered vehicles?

What about the steel industry? About 80% of a car's weight is steel. The underlying chassis that forms the car's skeleton, door beams, roofs and body panels are all made of steel. There is 2,400 pounds of steel in a car, and much more in trucks but let's say roughly 1.5 tons per vehicle times 12 million vehicles per year equals 18 million tons of steel needed each year for car and truck manufacturing. The total U.S. production of steel is approximately 85 million tons per year, which means over 20% of steel production in our steel mills is for automobiles and trucks. This will be drastically reduced because the typical car owner will delay the purchase of new cars.

Post-Script - The Recent Vote on the Green New Deal Plan - On March 26, 2019 the Senate voted to block consideration of the **Green New Deal.** Not one Democrat supported the Green New Deal in this test vote, although they are the ones that have initiated it and almost unanimously supported it. How can that be? What kind of representatives put forth an idea for a new plan for our country to reduce global warming and then don't even vote in favor of it? Is this the kind of leadership we should have in our country and are we to rely on the promises of Democrats, when they won't even vote for their own plan? Yet, Democrat Senate Leader Chuck Schumer claimed that the Democrats are "on the offense" about climate change. The vote was 57-0 against the Green New Deal with 54 Republicans and three Democrats and one Independent voting with the Republicans. What did the rest of the Democrats do? They all, including Chuck Schumer and the Senator Ed Markey from Massachusetts who co- sponsored the bill all voted "present". This is very telling. The Democrats showed their true colors when they refused to even take a stand for a plan they proposed. The Republicans took a stand and voted down the Green New Deal, dismissing it as a government takeover of the economy that would bankrupt our nation. I have provided details on how insane the Democrat Green New Deal proposal is and when called upon to support their radical plan for our economy, all the Democrats can say is we are "present". The only conclusion that one can take away from the Senate vote, was that the Democrats will make broad promises to its constituents to get their votes knowing full well that they cannot or will not fulfill their promises. There will be no free college, there will be no free medical, there will be no guaranteed income, there will be no free child care, there will be no high-speed rails crisscrossing our country, there will be no doing away with meat and fish, there will be no doing away with air travel. The Democrats will try to convince its constituents that the Republicans are grandstanding by bringing the Green New Deal plan to a vote. How can the Democrats accuse the Republicans of grandstanding for bringing to a vote the very plan that the Democrats have proposed? They do not like being caught in a lie. They do not like being exposed to their insanity. They couldn't vote yes for the Green New Deal, because that would open them to ridicule for the stupidity of their plan. They cannot vote "no "and side with the Republicans, because than they would truly look unfit for office. How do you vote "no" for your own plan? And somehow, they think that their constituents won't see that a vote "present" is the most ludicrous, inept, stupid position one can take. Is this going to garner them respect from their constituents? Challenged to support their plans, the Democrats can't even vote in favor of it. Is that what Democrat voters can expect from their leaders in the future?

As to the House of Representatives, speaker Nancy Pelosi recognized the precariousness of bringing the Green New Deal to a vote in the House. She just won't allow it. The Republicans have challenged the Democrats to show some political courage and initiative and agree to a recorded vote on the Green

New Deal. Pelosi recognizes that if the Green New Deal were brought to a vote in the House, her fellow Democrats would face the same problem of portraying themselves as a "feckless, wishy-washy, arrogant group of non-doers who are unwilling to make a decision or at least support their plans and promises.

The Squad - Nothing in our history is more indicative of the hatred and radical socialism that has crept into the Democrat party, than the group of first year Congresswomen, who have gained the support and endorsement of most Democrats. This is the name given to the four new members in the House of Representatives namely: Alexandria Ocasio-Cortez (New York); Ilhan Omar (Minnesota); Rashida Tlaib (Michigan) and Ayanna Presley (Massachusetts). A squad is defined as a small group engaged in a common effort. It is also defined as a gang. So, the Squad within the Democratic party is a gang that has been raised to a level of importance, beyond all other members. The Squad an anti-Jew, radical socialist group condemn all Conservative White Republicans as racist and white supremacists. They have come together to attack our country with a brand of hatred and vilification we have not heard before. And yet, their fellow Democrats standby and allow them to do so without any criticism or censure. The Squad members are the most outspoken supporters of the Green New Deal and Alexandria Ocasio-Cortez was a co-sponsor of the Green New Deal.

Alexandria Ocasio Cortez is best known as one of the sponsors of the Green New Deal Resolution which called for the U.S. to reach net-zero greenhouse gas emissions within 12 years. This would cost the government $10 trillion a year for the next 10 years. To put that kind of expenditure in perspective, $10 trillion represents 2.5 times the total annual budget of our Federal government, which already is operating at a yearly deficit of $1 Trillion. We already discussed the 10's of millions of jobs that would be lost, the uncontrolled inflation that this would cause quickly matching the inflation experienced in Venezuela; millions of families would be rendered homeless and our economy would soon emulate Venezuela where 65% of its population are in abject poverty and forced to forage for food from garbage trucks. Those who were lucky, would see the demise of their country and move out early, just like the mass exodus from Venezuela where over 10% of the population has already left. For most it will be too late as they will have no IRA or pension or Social Security to provide the wherewithal to leave the United States. The values of homes will go to virtually zero and IRA's and investment accounts will be wiped out. There even will be no money left in our Federal Government to pay social security benefits, let alone Medicare. Every single dollar that the Federal government could raise through taxes and borrowing will have gone to fund the Green New Deal. Ocasio-Cortez doesn't stop there. She wants open borders and guaranteed income and free medical and education for everyone, including illegal immigrants. Just where is this money coming from after the government spends $10 trillion each year on the Green New Deal? Yet no Democrat speaks out against the illogic and insanity of the Green New Deal. On the contrary, they vilify Trump for creating jobs in the energy and manufacturing sector that contributes to some additional CO_2 being launched into our atmosphere.

Ilhan Omar – focuses her Muslim hatred of Jews. Her rhetoric is abundant with anti-Jew remarks.

Omar introduced a resolution to support the anti-Jew Boycott, Divestiture, Sanction (BDS) movement, which seeks to cripple Israel financially because of supposed mistreatment of Palestinians. (Remember that the Palestinian HAMAS charter specifically calls for the murder of all Jews and the removal of every last Jew from Israel).

In a poll in July 2019 by Patriot Pulse, 99% of those responding to the poll, consider Ilhan Omar racist; 86% believe that the Democrats were the blame for the hostile environment and 92% believe she should be expelled from the House of Representatives.

Rashib Tlaib – born in Detroit, to Palestinian Immigrant parents, she stirred controversy soon after arriving in Washington using the expletive "mother….f" to describe the President. She has publicly expressed her hatred for Jews, saying in one instance that the Holocaust gave her a calming feeling and noted that it was her ancestors that provided the Jews a safe haven at terrible cost to the Palestinians. Tlaib will not tell you that during the Nazi regime under Hitler, the Arab Muslims supported and contributed to Hitler's "final solution" even providing two Muslim divisions in Hitler's Army. Hitler himself envisioned Islam to be the only religion (which he would head) after he conquered the world and there would be no Jews allowed to live in it.

Ayanna Presley- not to be outdone in her hatred of the Conservative right, showed her hypocrisy when she stated: "we don't need any more black faces (or brown faces) that don't want to be a black voice (or brown voice)". She is stating you can't be a Black and a Republican. She is saying that blacks should dissociate themselves from any black that doesn't believe as a Democrat.

Two other examples of the attitude of Democrat leaders that hate and vilify those who do not go along with the party line. The Chairman of the DNC, Tom Perez stated that you can't be a Democrat and be pro-life. So as far as the Democrats are concerned, if you believe in the sanctity of life, and that aborting an unborn baby is murder, you cannot be a Democrat. It is difficult to argue that one that believes in abortion at any time is on the moral high ground but to ostracize anyone from the party because he or she believes in the right to life, is just another indication of the hatred pervading the Democrat party.

These are the people who would bring you the New Green Deal that would destroy us all.

CHAPTER 13

Overview of the Destruction of our economy wrought by the Environmental and Socialist changes proposed by Democrats.

SO FAR, WE haven't begun to explain all the damage that will be wrought on our country, if these insane programs of the Democrats were ever to be implemented. We need to discuss the impact on our stock market, on our financial institutions, our pensions and our social security distributions. We need to discuss the impact on our charitable foundations, our college and university endowments, and our personal 401 k's and IRA's. We need to discuss where $128 trillion is going to come from to fund all the insane projects suggested by the Democrats and how are we going to pay for it. We need to revisit the impact of soaring interest rates and soaring inflation. We need to discuss how companies will be driven out of business and there will be far more serious unemployment then we have outlined above. We need to discuss what are the implications of mass exodus of Americans to other countries. We need to discuss the impact of the unwillingness of the private sector to invest in the United States, not just the unwillingness of foreigners to invest in the U.S. We need to discuss how our balance of payments deficit is going to explode, first from the elimination of any future exports of oil and gas and secondly because our higher prices for our goods will render us non-competitive in the world. Our Balance of payments deficits will explode into trillions of dollars instead of billions and just when our country needs our money the most, it will be going abroad. We need to discuss that while our demand for fish will go up, we will have no domestic fishermen and we will have to rely solely on imports of fish from foreign markets.

First we need to explain what we mean by the 'Trade Multiplier Effect" and the "Marginal Propensity to Consume", both of which can provide substantial benefits to our economy, when the goals of increasing the production of goods in the U.S.; Increasing exports and decreasing imports; obtaining and maintaining full employment and maintaining a level of taxes and regulations that do not impair our competition with foreign sources. Conversely, the damage to our economy is accelerated by these two "multiplier affects", when we raise taxes, regulate businesses out of existence and remove economic incentive for private investment. We need to find out how exactly the Democrats expect for Americans to travel to and from foreign countries? Where will planes land in the U.S.? Where can they refuel? Will we be relegated to travel to Mexico or Canada by rail and then fly from there to the foreign country of our choice? We have already described the terrible impact on employment in the United States and; the incredible cost and the rapid decline into a welfare state that the Democrat's proposed New Green Deal will cause. What about the insane travel restrictions the Green New Deal will impose on us?

The "Trade multiplier Effect" and its impact of the Trade Deficit, our Economy, and Employment.

In 2016 our Country suffered a trade imbalance of over $503 Billion. Three countries, namely China ($347 billion) Japan ($68.9 billion) and Mexico ($63.2 billion) accounted for $479.1 Billion representing 95% of our trade deficit. Whereas an increase in exports has an expansionary effect on National Income the increase in imports will bring a retraction of National Income. Further, the effect of an increase in imports will have significantly larger impact on National income because of the "trade multiplier effect" (economics 101). A reduction in National income results in a loss of jobs and higher unemployment. The trade multiplier reflects the generation of additional income (from exports) and conversely the additional loss of income (from imports), beyond the actual surplus/(deficit) in the balance of trade. Think of $1.00 of exports. To produce that sale of goods requires American labor and American materials. The amount paid to labor (employees) is in turn used for the most part to purchase more goods and services, creating additional labor demand. This cycle can be produced a number of times, with some leakages along the way in the form of savings and purchases of foreign goods. When imports exceed exports, the reverse occurs and the impact of the import/export imbalance is far greater than the imbalance itself. And this can be quantified by the "foreign trade multiplier" (M). The foreign trade multiplier is theoretically the reciprocal of the marginal propensity to save (s) plus the marginal propensity to import (i) which can be expressed by the formula:

$$M = \frac{1}{s + i}$$

Let us say hypothetically that the marginal propensity to save (s) is 10% and the marginal propensity to import is 20% then M = 1/.1+.2 or M = 3.33. One may argue that the propensity to save is less than 10% and the propensity to import is less than 20%, or there are other leakages, but this is presented as an example of the real cost of foreign trade deficits. Thus, a trade deficit of $503 billion is really impacting our economy in the amount of $1.67 trillion.

The trade deficit also impacts our national debt. Let us look just at the loss of manufacturing jobs to offshore. Our economy lost 5.8 million manufacturing jobs and the closure of 57,000 manufacturing firms under Obama. These American workers and companies provided revenues for the Government in the form of taxes. Along with the loss of revenues, the cost to the Government is compounded as a result of the increase in government expenditures on unemployment, health and welfare. The difficulty is how to quantify the cost of the loss of 5.8 million jobs and 57,000 businesses. The 5.8 million direct loss of manufacturing jobs leads to the loss of additional jobs associated with providing goods and services to the 5.8 million who have lost their jobs and their families. The average cost per year for an unemployed person is $8,500 according to 2/1/2011 report by Business Insider entitled: "Income, Energy and the Cost of Unemployment". $8,500 x 5.8 million = $49.3 Billion. This does not include the loss in tax revenues from the manufacturing jobs and businesses or the loss of additional jobs and additional welfare costs associated with the jobs lost as a result of loss of manufacturing jobs. And most importantly it does not take into consideration any of the non-manufacturing jobs that are lost to foreign countries not the least of which are maintenance and service jobs associated with computers maintenance and software technology. Today, if we set the cost of the lost jobs at $50,000, the cost would be $50,000 times the 5.8 million jobs lost for a total of $290 billion of lost income and at a tax rate of 25% (combined income and social security), there would be a loss of $73 billion of tax revenues directly attributable to the jobs we lose to other countries.

The Marginal Propensity to Consume and the Multiplier Effect

A companion to the "**trade multiplier**" is another Economics 101 concept, namely the Marginal **Propensity to Consume.** The underlying concept of the "Marginal Propensity to Consume" is that an increase in personal spending (consumption) occurs with an increase in disposable income (income after taxes, savings and other transfers). The importance of the Marginal Propensity to Consume is the resulting multiplier effect. Let us assume that out of every $1 of income, $.33 is unavailable because it is either paid in taxes or saved. This means that $.66 is available for spending, which in turn becomes disposable income for someone else. This will continue based on the multiplier effect. The multiplier is determined by the following simple equation:

$$\text{Multiplier (M)} = \text{I(income)}/1 - \text{MPC (Marginal propensity to Consume)}$$

In our case above the Multiplier would be 1/1.00-.66) or 1/.33, meaning that each $1 of spending actually generates a total of $3 new spending. If taxes and transfers were reduced to 25% the MPC would increase to 4 and conversely if taxes and transfers were increased to 50% the multiplier would decrease to 2. So, you can see how higher taxes have an impact substantially greater than just decreasing disposable income. A doubling of our income taxes would result in an additional $1.6 trillion of personal income taxes, which at a multiplier of 3 would impact our economy annually by a massive $4.8 trillion.

The Financial Impact on Our Economy

I have saved the worst to last. The loss of jobs; the increase in welfare recipients, the incredible increase in our debt and the rising of interest rates to above 15%; the doubling of taxes and inflation rates well in excess of 100% if not 1,000%, the loss of jobs to foreign countries and the increase of the balance of payments deficit doesn't tell the whole story. Almost every business in the United States will suffer including the Aerospace Industry; the Oil Industry, the Auto Industry; Retail businesses, Restaurants, Hotels, Resorts, Fast food, Health Insurance; Consumer manufactured goods, the electronics industry, the agriculture industry (particularly fish and cattle), Apparel Industry and the financial industry. I may have missed a few, but the reader should get the picture. The Green New Deal; and The National Health Programs will circulate through our economy and damage every part of it. We can't go through all the stocks in the S&P 500, but it is probably safe to say that many of the companies will experience massive erosion of their businesses, if not total liquidation very similarly to the Dow Jones 30 stocks. Of the 30 stocks in the Dow Jones, group, 18 or 60% will suffer dire consequences (including in many instances bankruptcy) if the Green New Deal ever became the law.

Let us list the companies that will certainly be doomed from the enactment of the Green New Deal (or anything coming close to it):

Apple – Market for computers dries up as unemployment increases and the availability of discretionary funds decreases, as a result of higher taxes high inflation, higher consumer interest rates and severe unemployment.

Boeing - With the elimination of air travel, there will be no need to build new airplanes. Our country's security will also be severely eroded as Boeing's military aerospace research and the building of military equipment will be severely limited if not destroyed.

Chevron – No more fossil fuels no more Chevron

Exxon – As above

Home Depot - Discretionary income drops to levels where home improvements are postponed if not eliminated due to inflation, higher taxes and unemployment.

J P Morgan/Chase; (Wells Fargo, Bank of America, Citibank) – as foreclosures explode, as the unemployed walk away from their homes where the underlying mortgage exceeds the depressed value of their homes and credit cards become delinquent and major companies go bankrupt; banks like JP Morgan, Wells Fargo, Citibank and Bank of America will become bankrupt as will all other banks. The only remaining source of funds in the United States will be the Federal Government and the only answer the Federal Government will have is to print more money. Inflation sky-rockets well beyond 1,000%. What has happened to Venezuela begins to happen in the United States and the skyrocketing price of goods and services will have disastrous effects on the population, particularly those who are on fixed incomes. Those retired will see their pensions, 401K's, IRA's, Annuities erode to levels where $.10 on the dollar will not be hypothetical, it will be a reality. The Banking industry will be gone.

Goldman Sachs – similar to what will befall the banking industry, the investment banking industry will also fail. There will be no investments to make, no portfolios to manage and the investment banks will be stuck with a lot of worthless paper representing stocks of companies that have failed and bonds representing debt of bankrupt corporations.

Walt Disney - Airplane Travel no longer available; disposable income way down, vacations at Disneyworld and Disneyland will virtually cease.

Coca Cola - Water becomes substitute for soda and other soft drinks. Disposable income down, unemployment at highest rate since the crash of 1929, the demand for Coca Cola products will diminish to almost 0.

McDonald's – What happens to this franchise along with others such as Berger King, and Arby's, when beef can no longer be produced in the United States?

Microsoft - Who will be able to afford new apps, games or software upgrades?

Visa – Delinquencies soar as credit card holders cannot pay; credit cards are cancelled as credit ratings of individuals slide precipitously; and credit card holders' liability increases between time of purchase and time of payment as prices inflate daily.

Nike – Purchase of new sneakers will be postponed as sneakers become a luxury item that can be deferred.

United Health - Health Insurance companies will disappear as they will be replaced by a Federal Government National Health single payer system.

Traveler's Insurance - A broad array of property and casualty insurance will disappear. Homeowner's insurance will be down as mortgage foreclosures sky-rocket and people walk away from their homes or just stop paying for insurance. People losing jobs will not be able to afford insurance as they struggle just to provide food clothing and shelter for their families.

Caterpillar – this provider of construction and mining equipment will see its business suffer dramatically as there will be no oil or coal mining activities after the government bans fossil fuels.

United Technologies – Manufacturer of Aircraft engines and heating and ventilating equipment; its business will be severely curtailed and they may not survive.

Walmart - With the disastrous reduction in discretionary funds as a result of sky-rocketing unemployment, higher taxes, inflation and consumer interest rates, there will be a catastrophic loss of business for Walmart and other consumer products wholesalers and retailers. Shoes, clothing and consumer hard goods such as water heaters, refrigerators, ovens, TV's air-conditioning unit will be postponed or more than likely eliminated.

Ford, GM, Fiat Chrysler, U.S. Steel – none of these companies is in the Dow Jones Industrials, but they are very significant companies and as we discussed above, would be significantly damaged by abolishing gas fueled vehicles as we previously pointed out.

What does this all mean for the investment portfolios of Pension funds, 401K's IRA's, Annuities, Mutual Funds, Investment Portfolios, Charitable Foundations and College and University Endowments?

There are a number of factors that affect the valuation of stock. These are:

1. the earnings of a company;
2. the dividends paid;
3. the interest rate generally reflected by the Federal 10-year Treasury Bond rate;
4. funds available to invest and
5. Investors' confidence in the market.

All of these can be affected by the Federal Government. Higher taxes reduce the earnings of a company. Higher spending by the government, leads to more debt and raises interest rates. During President Jimmy Carter's presidency, the interest rates went from 8% to 15% and the stock and the Dow Industrial's Price/Earnings (P/E) ratio hovered between 7 and 10.

Why are interest rates so important in determining the valuation of the stock market? When interest rates rise (10-year Treasury notes are used as basis), the P/E ratio will fall to reflect the higher yields available for the alternative investment into bonds. The P/E is a function of expected growth and dividend yields in competition with bond yields. If yields and expectations go down as interest rates go up, the P/E will dramatically erode and so will the price of stocks.

The price of stocks is also a function of earnings and if taxes are doubled, earnings after taxes would be halved and this would have a further impact on stock prices. The double whammy on stock prices caused by higher taxes and higher interest rates both the direct result of the spending plans of the Socialist Democrats, would cause erosion of the stock market by 50% to 80%, if nothing else happened. (The stock market would go down 60% by the soaring interest rates bringing it to 40% of previous values and another 50% from higher taxes, bringing the stock prices down a total of 80%.) This erosion would be the direct impact of: The Green New Deal, free college; National Health Plan; and guaranteed income for all even those unwilling to work. But this doesn't tell the whole story. We have shown that over half of the Dow Stocks would be directly affected by the insane proposals of the Democrats. Many will go bankrupt and others will be so damaged that pre-tax earnings will erode dramatically. There will be a drastic rush by stockholders to sell their stocks in companies about to go out of business. People, who have lost their jobs will cash in what little they have to meet the higher costs of living. And the investment losses of pensions, 401k's annuities, etc., will result in reduction of the investment and annuity income that so many retired people depend upon. Finally, there will be massive margin calls by lending institutions as the underlying security for stock purchases erodes. We will be fortunate if there will be $.10 on the $1.00 still remaining of value in the stock market. You will look back and remember that it was your fault in supporting Socialist Democrats and their crazy plans to bring down our nation.

Today the Dow and Standard & Poor's 500 P/E's are about 16. The Dow Jones Price hovers around 27,000. And with a 72% erosion will fall to 7,560 and at the more likely 80% erosion to 5,400. This is probably the best-case scenario. Let's provide a hypothetical case, how do we get there. For the purpose of our discussion, let us assume that representative company A is selling at $100 per share. It is selling at 16 times earnings; is paying a combined Federal and state income tax of 30%, and pays out a 2.2% yield in dividends on its stock. What happens when corporate tax rates double from 30% to 60%. And then, what happens when there is a run on the market, margin calls, and earnings and dividends start eroding at an accelerating pace. Also, as interest on debt goes higher, bond investments become more attractive and a substantial amount of investment will move from the stock market into more secured and higher yielding bond investments. The 16x earnings multiple will quickly drop to 8x. Here then are the results:

	Current @ 30% tax	Adjustment for 60% tax	Adjustment for above factors
Stock Price	$100.00	$57.12	$28.56
P/E Ratio	16X	16X	8X
EPS Pre-tax	$8.93	$8.93	$8.93
EPS after tax	$6.25	$3.57	$3.57
Dividends at 2.2%	$2.20	$1.26	$0.63

Note, we have not taken into consideration all the companies that will go out of business and there are many major ones that are in most IRA and 401K portfolios and are part of pension and annuity portfolios. Note also I have not taken into consideration that the typical company will see an increase in cost of goods due to inflation, higher mandated worker benefits, greater federal regulations and the costs to switch to wind and solar for its energy supply. These will certainly erode earnings even further and therefore this may very well be the best-case scenario.

Who suffers? All, who rely on annuities, pension funds, 401k's and IRA's to provide some or most of their income, especially the retirees; they will see these sources of income in many cases disappear. Suppose you were relying on $25,000/year pension and you receive a letter that you will be paid only $5,000 from now on?

Suppose you purchased a guaranteed for life annuity, that would pay you $5,000 a year and you receive in the mail notice that you will now get only $1000 per year. Suppose you have a 401k or IRA that you have built up over the years by carefully putting aside money for your later years only to find the value of IRA or 401K has eroded by 80% and where you thought you had $250,000 put aside, it now only has a value of $50,000? And to make matters worse, you cannot re-finance your home unless you are willing to pay 15% or more interest instead of the 4% you are now paying. Even worse, your home value has eroded so much, your equity is gone and you can't get any refinancing. You can't move away to a lower state tax jurisdiction because you can't sell your home.

And you note that a dozen eggs you use to pay $2 for now costs you $10 or more? There are 40 million of us over 65. Be prepared to suffer beyond anything you have ever dreamed, if the Socialist Democrats get into power, because they will make your life Hell.

The Loss of Value of American Assets

The total value of U.S. Houses is estimated at $33.3 trillion and the U.S. Stock Market has a value of $32 trillion. We have discussed how the stock market is likely to lose 90% of its value as interest rates sky-rocket, unemployment explodes above 15%; taxes double, foreign investment drops off; millions flee our country and soaring inflation hits our country, forcing private investors to sell their assets to meet the spiraling cost of living. In a similar manner, home valuation will deteriorate dramatically for many of the same reasons. As prices for the essentials of food, clothing and shelter escalate five or ten times (far less than the Million percent inflation experience in Venezuela), home owners will be forced to skip mortgage payments and banks will be forced to foreclose on homes and in many instances, homeowners will just abandon their homes since there will be no equity left in them. Using the 10% of the population leaving Venezuela as a yardstick, that would mean 32 million Americans will be leaving the United States to live abroad. This will put further pressure on the price of homes as the supply of homes available for sale keeps increasing while at the same time the demand keeps falling. The total value of all homes in the United States will easily fall by 75% or $25 trillion and thanks to the programs of the Socialist Democrats specifically, the Green New Deal, The National Health Care, program and the free college tuition, the $$32 Trillion of stock market investments will fall to $8 trillion. The combined stock investments and home investments will fall from a total of $65.3 trillion to $16.3 trillion And the $137.5 Trillion of the programs planned by the Socialistic Democrats will have been barely started and will never be completed.

The American will no longer have airplane transportation, no gas-fueled cars, no beef to eat and many will be unemployed, unable to pay for food, clothing and shelter, forced to live on the streets or in abandoned decrepit gas stations that pock mark the U.S. landscape and scavenge for food as we have seen in Venezuela.

There is a rule in Economics that we learn in our first day in Economics 101: "There is no such thing as a free lunch". Nothing is ever given away free. Somewhere, someone in the economic chain is paying. There is no free college tuition; there is no free income for those unwilling to work; there is no free medical care, there is no free child care. You never get something for nothing. Any benefit received must be paid for, by somebody. The Socialist Democrats would have you believe that they can provide everything for everyone for free. They would even have you believe that they can spend $14 trillion a year for the next 10 years which is 3.5 times our current budget and 4.5 times our Federal Governments current total receipts. The Socialist Democrats don't mention to the Millennials and young people that crave free education that it will be their parents and grandparents who will pay for these irrationally excessive programs, through higher taxes, higher interest rates, higher costs for the necessities of life and a deterioration (even loss) of their pensions, annuities, 401K's and IRA's. The 40 million over 65 will for the most part be destitute and there is nothing planned by the Socialist Democrats to help those unfortunate to be over 65, to survive. They will just wither away, or triaged out of existence when they become sick.

The plans of the Socialist Democrats will create virtual control over our lives and we will be under a dictatorship which will tell us what we can eat, when, where and how we can travel, ration our medical care favoring the young and healthy, dictate even further what we can learn and deprive us of our right to own private property. And true of any dictatorship, there will no longer be any freedom of press, speech or religion, as any criticism of the programs of the Socialist Democrats, will be swiftly met with prison or worse. We already have freedom of speech repressed by Democrats at all levels of education and by our Social Democrat run states and cities. It will only become worse if the Democrats take full control of our governments at the Federal, State and city levels. For those who don't believe this can happen, look at what Hitler did in the 1930's that led his small minority to take over control of Germany and put to death 6 million Jews including women and children. He gained his position by taking control over education; taking control over media and promulgating hatred against the Jews through propaganda; burning all literature written by Jews; destroying all criticism of his regime; and succeeding in gaining the support of the majority of Germans by a constant barrage of the propaganda of hatred against the Jews. These are exactly the same tactics that the Socialist Democrats are using against President Trump and Republicans.

A Brief Look at the Democrat Presidential Debate of October 15, 2019

For three hours 12 candidates for the Presidency of the United States debated as to why they should become the next president. The moderators Anderson Cooper and Erin Burnett from CNN and Marc Lacey from the New York Times were all from the liberal socialist left. They all avoided questioning the candidates on the Green New Deal, which is unquestionably the biggest proposal that the liberal left wishes to put forth at a cost of $100 trillion over the next 10 years. The biased moderators made no attempt to bring up the obvious; how are they going to pay for their over $130 trillion of new expenditures during the next 10 years or an average of $13 trillion a year, which is 4 times our Federal Government's total annual budget. In three hours, there were no questions on international affairs, how the candidates will create jobs, what did they think about expanding or government debt levels by 4 items the current level and incurring indebtedness each year that will be 10 to 12 times higher each year than in any previous year in American history. Nor did they question how the U.S. government is going to provide health care for 320 million people when tit cannot even provide quality and safe health care for 20 million veterans. Nor did they question how a massive high speed electric railroad system could be created to crisscross the U.S at a cost of $ trillions and accomplish that in 10 to 15 years, when the U.S. and California State governments could not even build a high speed railway between San Francisco and Los Angeles in 20 years and after spending $3 billion had to abandon the project. Nor did they ask the candidates whether they had any limitation on immigrants, or was it to be open borders, everyone welcome and the U.S. taxpayer will be called upon to pay more taxes to fund the health, education and welfare of these millions of non-taxpaying immigrants that flood into our country and take the jobs of our hard-working taxpaying citizens.

The debate, if you want to call it that, took place at Atterbein University in Westerville, Ohio. For three hours we listened to:

Senator Elizabeth Warren – Massachusetts
Senator Bernie Sanders – Vermont
Mayor Peter Buttigieg – South Bend, Indiana
Congresswomen – Tulsi Gabbard – Hawaii
Former Congressmen Beto O'Rourke Texas
Tom Steyer – Businessman

Former Vice President Joe Biden
Senator Corey Booker – New Jersey
Julian Castro – Former HUD Secretary
Senator Amy Klobycher – Minnesota
Senator Kamala Harris - California
Andrew Yang – Businessman

Impeachment, Hatred and Vitriol

The debate opened with an expression of hatred and vitriol towards President Trump by all 12 candidates, each trying to outdo the other in their expression of hatred. This was not a debate; it was a tirade and it was the single most significant and time-consuming effort of the 12 candidates lasting almost 30 minutes.

The candidates charged Trump with criminal misconduct, but not one specific alleged crime was identified. In fact, the candidates falsely stated that the Mueller investigation found that President Trump had obstructed justice, when he had clearly not. What the Mueller report had determined was that neither the President or his campaign staff had colluded with Russia to tamper with the 2016 election. If there were no collusion, then what justice was Trump obstructing?

The Trump-Ukraine controversy was unnanimously and solely given by the Democrats as a reason for seeking the impeachment of Trump, even though the transcript of Trump's call to the Ukranian President showed no "quid pro quo" and the President of Ukraine confirmed this. This apparently did not satisfy the 12 Democrat presidential candidates. Yet the fact that Democrat candidate Joe Biden threatened to hold back $1 billion of loan guarantees to Ukraine unless it removed its Prosecuting General, who was actively investigating a company his son Hunter Biden was a director of and receiving $50,000 per month for doing nothing was considered totally acceptable by the Democrats.

The Warren Medicare for All Plan

Elizabeth Warren stated that she would raise taxes only on the rich. When asked by Marc Lacey for a simple yes or no answer, would she be raising taxes on the middle class to help fund her $30 trillion health plan, she refused to answer, saying only that middle-income families will pay less for their National Health under her plan. Joe Biden pointed out that doubling everyone's taxes would not begin to pay for her National Health Plan and she was proposing something that never could be done.

Even economists from the far-left institute, University of California Berkeley are saying there is no way to pay for Warren's "Medicare for All Plan" without substantially raising taxes for everyone.

Mike Bloomberg has issued a report that has shown that her planned tax on the rich and big corporations will provide her" Medicare for All Plan" a staggering $30 trillion shortfall in covering costs.

Finally, Elizabeth Warren came out with her own estimate of the costs of her Medicare for All Plan. It will cost $52 trillion or a net new $20.5 trillion over the next 10 years to be spent at the rate of approximately $2 trillion per year. Warren admitted that it would result in the loss of 2 million direct jobs, but doesn't include the 1.4 million of indirect jobs that would be lost. She plans to raise $9 trillion in new Medicare taxes on employers over the next 10 years, or $900 billion per year. Corporations currently pay $621 billion in payroll taxes and $216 billion in income taxes for a total of $837 billion. Elizabeth Warrens is suggesting more than doubling the taxes on corporations. Warren has also not factored in the cost of providing Medicare for the wave of illegal or undocumented immigrants that the Democrats will allow in over open borders. Let me point out the reasons why this Medicare for all plan is more than a disaster, it is insane:

1. With the doubling of corporate taxes, corporate earnings will be halved. What does that mean? The very best outcome will be that corporate income will only be cut in half, with the result that the stock market will drop by 50% and Corporate dividends will drop by 50%. Everyone with a pension, IRA, 401K, annuity or dividend paying portfolio will at the very least see his dividend income cut in half and the value of his investment assets cut in half. This does not take into account the impact on investments from panic, margin calls, higher interest rates and companies going out of business, particularly in the Health insurance and Health care industries. The losses in investment value and dividends could well reach over 80%.

2. Even with $900 billion a year addition from doubling corporate payroll taxes and corporate income taxes, there still is a $1.1 trillion funding shortfall to be covered. Elizabeth Warren proposes to tax only the wealthy. Even if you increased the taxes by 50% on those earning over $150,000 (i.e. the top 10%) this would raise only another $550 billion. The top 10% pay 70% of all individual income taxes or approximately $1.1 trillion of the $1.6 trillion a year personal income taxes. We would still need another $550 billion. Elizabeth Warren proposes to cut back spending in undetermined areas, but they would have to included; infrastructure, defense spending and homeland security, with resulting additional job losses.

3. Elizabeth Warren does not consider the substantial "leakage" in our economy. All those businesses that have moved back to the United States, creating 500,000 new manufacturing jobs and a total of 6 million new jobs since President Trump took office will disappear and many tax-paying individuals will just leave our country. High income tax payers will leave, will invest more abroad and the percent unemployed will continue to rise as more of those employed find other countries to live and work in.

4. Elizabeth Warren proposes to increase inheritance and estate taxes, making it much harder for farmers and the owners of small business to pass them on to the next generation. Just another reason for many to leave our country to preserve their wealth and assets from the onerous taxation proposed by the Warren, Medicare For All plan. Many Americans will not just sit back and watch their assets disappear to fund medical for illegal immigrants. Their only alternative will be to leave our country.

5. Warren plans to move 180 million people from private plans to the Socialist government program in 4 years. No longer will those covered by insurance plans have a choice of doctors or facilities. Remember how Obama promised that under Obamacare you could keep your doctors and that turned out to be a lie? Now there is no question, that the doctor patient relationships that many have developed over the years will be taken from them. Also, those concerned about doctor-patient privacy, will now know that all their medical treatments will become available to the bureaucracy that will determine whether or not you can receive treatment.

6. The Warren Plan calls for a transition in 4 years to a federally controlled and monitored health system. The Federal Government could not even run a medical system for 20 million veterans, without fraud and many dying from lack of timely medical service. What makes you think that the Federal Government can effectively run Medicare for 330 million people?

7. The proponents of Medicare for All reference Canada as the panacea of nationalized health plans. But the population of Canada is only 38 million not 320 million and the wait times and the rationing of organs has led to many unnecessary deaths.

8. Part of the Elizabeth Warren, Medicare for All Plan, calls for massive cost reductions and one of the main ones is a massive reduction in what doctors can earn, (some suggest as much as 40%). Doctors across the board will be treated the same whether a general practitioner or a specialist. What will be the incentive to spend two or three extra years to become a heart surgeon or neurosurgeon, if there is no financial benefit? There are approximately 1 million doctors in the U.S. roughly 50% are primary care and the other 50% are specialists. It is estimated that we will be facing a shortage of 122,000 physicians by 2032. This shortfall doesn't take into consideration that the shortage will be significantly greater as fewer and fewer young people turn to medicine, because it will no longer be a high-income profession, where you can achieve recognition and gratitude from your patients. The doctor in the future will be just some salaried employee, unknown by his patient, paid to perform no better than mediocre on some unknown body, identified only as a human.

9. Those over 65 will likely suffer the most under the Warren Medicare for All Plan. Costs will

have to be held down. The new Medicare for All autocracy will need to find ways to cut costs. One way often described are "death panels" to determine life and death decisions for the elderly. "Save the taxpayer, but not the retiree, because the taxpayer pays us money and the retiree costs us money". Many of the over 65 will be triaged out of existence.

10. The millennials are overwhelmingly for socialism and a National Health Plan. 70% supposedly support socialism and would support the Elizabeth Warren Plan or any other similar one. It doesn't make sense. The Millennials are characterized as wishing a better life for themselves, their children and their family. They believe they need to work hard to get ahead and earn their own better quality of life. Yet, they are ready to support a plan that would be absolutely destructive of that. Apparently, the idea of free medical health is so appealing to them, that they do not even think of its cost. Do millennials really want to destroy their parents and their grandparents, to get something for themselves that is free? Are 70% of them that thoughtless and uncaring?

Socialism at its highest

Bernie Sanders, appeared recently after recovering from a heart attack. He appeared of sound health, but it was a bit disconcerting that he is all out for total socialism for our country and he has received the endorsement of the most radical socialist Democrats in our country, namely: Congresswoman Alexandria Ocasio Cortez, Jew-hater Rashida Tlaib and Jew Hater Ilhan Omar. It is interesting how those that are anti Jew support a Jewish candidate and gravitate to the Democrat party.

Abortion

When the abortion issue came up, Kamala Harris made it clear that it is the woman's right to have abortion at any time for any reason. Apparently killing an unborn child is acceptable to Harris. Her statement: people need to keep their hands-off women's bodies and let women make the decisions about their own lives" This sounds like a fair and reasonable comment, but what about the lives of the unborn child? The lives of all women including pregnant women should be respected and protected. But that should not mean that the unborn child has no rights and in fact the Constitution protects the unborn child and considers the unborn child a person, modified to some extent by Roe V. Wade and the later case Planned Parenthood v. Casey, which prohibits abortion after the unborn child is considered to be viable. The Democrat led by Kamala Harris slams the Republicans for being prolife. Harris would nullify state-passed pro-life laws, even though that is the will of the majority of people in the state.

Elizabeth Warren and Joe Biden seem to think that Roe V. Wade and accompanying decisions legalized abortion through all nine months. Both should know better, particularly Elizabeth Warren, who is supposedly an attorney. Neither Roe V. Wade nor the later case Planned Parenthood v. Casey support abortion at any time. On the contrary, Roe v. Wade limited abortion to the first and second trimester and Planned Parenthood v. Casey further limited abortion based on the test of the viability of the baby, including if its life outside the womb can be sustained by artificial means.

Elizabeth Warren who is known for telling untruths and uses that for her personal economic and political advantage, misleads the public if not outright lies to them as to where the public stands on abortion. She claims that 75% interpret Roe v. Wade to mean abortion is acceptable at any time during the pregnancy. A Gallup poll shows only 60% of the public supports Roe V. Wade, but also back major restrictions on abortion. According to the Gallup poll only 25% of Americans say abortion should be legal anytime. Most Americans according to Gallup oppose abortion in the second and third trimester. No candidate on the stage acknowledged the reality that a child in the womb at some stage is a human being and as such has a right to life. Each of them apparently supports the murder of unborn children.

The Chinese Socialist state controls birth and even demands abortion after the 1st child (now 2nd child) and failure to do so will result in a severe penalty as much as three or four times the annual salary of the violator or the confiscation of all the family's personal property

The Chairman of the Democrat party, Tom Perez has even said there is no place for you in the Democrat party if you do not believe in abortion. Under Democrat leadership it will be the woman's right to murder an unborn child at any time. It should be anticipated if that is the position of our government it is not a very large step for the Democrat government to order abortion for any reason that they deem appropriate.

The Democrats are even suggesting that Roe V. Wade should be codified so that it cannot be overturned by the Supreme Court

Climate Change

There is probably no more extensive and more threatening to our existence than the proposed Democrat plan entitled the Green New Deal. Yet there were no questions raised by the moderators, nor was there any discussion. The Green New Deal Plan is the single most expensive and economically devastating plan ever to be created by mankind. It will cause massive unemployment, inflation rates that have never before been experienced in our country and a resulting expansion of our Federal Debt level by a factor of 4 or 5 times. And it will achieve absolutely nothing. No wonder the moderators stayed away from the Green New Deal. How can we propose spending $100 trillion that will bankrupt our country, put 10's of millions of people out of work, cause inflation rates of 1000% and more, destroy our air transportation and automobile industries and many others, when the CO_2 emissions of 88% of the world will continue to expand at a rate far greater than the reduction of CO_2 emissions by our country?

Legalization of opioids, cocaine and heroin

Andrew Yong and Beto O'Rourke endorsed decriminalizing of opioids and heroin as a way to control the drug epidemic that is ravaging our communities all across the country. "We need to open up safe consumption and injection sites around the country to save lives", said Yong. Just look at what has happened in the states of Washington, Oregon and California where marijuana has been legalized. Drug addiction has steadily become worse and is now uncontrollable in these states, all Democrat led states. And now the Democrats are suggesting we legalize all drugs?

CHAPTER 14

Mass shootings, gun control and the Second Amendment

OVER THE WEEKEND of August 3, 2019, thirty-one people were killed in less than 13 hours. The first shooting was at a Walmart store in El Paso, Texas resulting in 22 innocent people being killed and 26 injured. Then on early Sunday morning, August 4th, at the entrance to Ned Pepper's bar in Dayton, Ohio, 9 innocent people were killed and 27 injured. The murderer in the El Paso, Texas shooting, Patrick Crusius, was a Republican and a Trump supporter and that was enough for Democrats to seek to use the tragedy for personal gain. The first comments regarding these two unrelated shootings came from two Democrat presidential candidates Beto O'Rourke from Texas and Peter Buttigieg, mayor of South Bend, Indiana. Beto O'Rourke claimed that President Trump's rhetoric was directly responsible for the El Paso killings. Peter Buttigieg blamed an ideology of white nationalist terrorism condoned by the Trump Administration. There was no showing of sorrow or sympathy by these two. They both seized on this horrible tragedy for personal political gain. In times of tragedy, the true colors of a person oft times come out. This was a heartless, compassionless attempt to condemn Trump and his administration. But these were not the only Democrat candidates who chose political gain over condolences for those who had died and the grieving families. Joe Biden, Cory Booker, Elizabeth Warren and Bernie Sanders all candidates for President, chose this terrible tragedy to attack and blame President Trump for causing it.

The Liberal press immediately took up the cry of a mass killing being caused by President Trump; but what about the Dayton Ohio shooting? The press was conspicuously silent. Because the shooter in Dayton, a Connor Betts, was a proud leftist and supporter of Elizabeth Warren and Bernie Sanders as well as ANTIFA and communism.

While the Democrats would have you believe that mass killings are due to the rhetoric of President Trump and white nationalist terrorism supported by the Trump Administration, they would ignore the 31 mass killings that occurred during President Obama's administration. The media and the entertainment industry would never seek to blame Obama for these tragedies, nor would the

Republican leaders. Because it just wasn't the case. For those who do not remember, or never even heard about the mass killings during Obama's Presidency, here is just a few:

1. February 14, 2008 Dekalb, Illinois - 5 killed on campus of Northern Illinois University
2. June 25, 2008 Herdson, Kentucky – 5 killed at plastic factory
3. March 29, 2009 Tucson, Arizona - 6 killed and 13 injured at Safeway market
4. April 3, 2009 Binghamton, NY – 14 killed at the American Civic Association
5. November 5, 2009 – Fort Hood, Texas 13 killed and 29 wounded
6. August 3, 2010 – Omar Thornton enters warehouse and kills 9
7. July 20, 2012 - James Holmes shoots and kills 12 and wounds 58 at midnight theater massacre
8. December 14, 2012 Newtown Connecticut, Adam Lanza kills 26 inside Sandy Hook Elementary school
9. April 15, 2013 – Boston Marathon 3 killed and several hundred wounded, including 16 who lost limbs
10. June 7, 2013 - John Zawahiri kills 5 on the campus of Santa Monica College
11. May 17, 2015 – Waco, Texas 9 killed at a restaurant.
12. June 17, 2015 – Charleston, South Carolina- 9 killed in Historic Black church
13. October 1, 2015 – Roseburg, Oregon 9 killed and 7 wounded at Umpqua Community College
14. December 5, 2015 – 14 killed and 17 wounded at San Bernadine, California
15. June 12, 2016 – Orlando, Florida. Omar Siddique Mateo kills 49 and injures 53 at a gay night club

And there were at least 15 more massacres during Obama's watch. Bu it would never occur to me or any other reasonable person to lay blame on Obama for these mass murders.

In June 2017, Bernie Sanders wasn't held responsible when a shooter targeted a Republican Congressional softball team, practicing in Virginia, just outside Washington. He very nearly killed House Minority Leader, Steve Scalise and would have killed many more, but for the heroic efforts and quick response of the police. The shooter an avid Democrat had participated in Bernie Sanders' presidential campaign.

In July, 2019 Alexandria Ocasio-Cortez wasn't held responsible when an ANTIFA sympathizer attempted to detonate an incendiary device at an ICE detention facility in Oregon. The bomber echoed many of Ocasio-Cortez's points, comparing ICE detention facilities to Nazi concentration camps and he proudly announced his intentions to free imprisoned immigrants by any means necessary.

This is just another example of the massive hypocrisy of the liberal left. The media and Democrat politicians have stirred up a frenzy of hate toward President Trump, claiming that both El Paso and

Dayton mass murders were Trump's fault, while ignoring any similar claims that could be made against the Democrats.

The Constitution and Gun Control - The regulation of gun ownership starts with our Constitution, specifically the second amendment. Amendment II starts with the reason for allowing unfettered gun ownership with the words: "A well-regulated militia being necessary to the security of a free state". At the time of the issuance of this amendment, there was no standing army. The soldiers had returned to their farms and would be called upon to return to the Federal militia, in time of peril. The government would not supply the arms; each soldier would be required to bring his own firearms. Thus, the second part of the amendment reads as follows: "the right of people to keep and bear arms shall not be infringed".

Article V of the Constitution addresses how amendments are to be made to the Constitution. It starts: "The Congress, whenever 2/3's of both houses deems it necessary, shall propose amendments to the Constitution, or on the application of the legislatures of 2/3's of the several states, shall call a convention for proposing Amendments….". Article V then goes on to say how an amendment becomes part of the Constitution: "when ratified by the legislatures of ¾'s of the several states, or by the conventions in ¾'s of the states. "

This is an arduous threshold, but instead of bickering over the appropriateness or inappropriateness of the 2nd Amendment, bi-partisan efforts should be made to permit the people and their respective states to amend or replace Amendment II.

The latest in the radical vitriol of the Liberal left is their claim that anyone belonging to the NRA must be a "domestic terrorist". Statements like that gives rise to members of the radical left who are fanatic and may think that any terrorist is open game for assassination. The Democrats understand this and it is just one more example of Democrats countenancing violence and murder to attain power. We've have heard and seen the cry for assassination of the President from the Left; we've seen the willingness of the left to kill an unborn baby for any reason at any time; we've seen them spawn hatred and condemnation towards Jews, we see them refusing to condemn radical Islamic terrorism against Jews and Christians; we've seen ANTIFA thrive under their wing and now we see them calling anyone who is a member of NRA a domestic terrorist and in addition suggesting that they would go door to door and take away the guns of all law-abiding citizens. This is what is in store for us as a nation if the Liberal Democrats were ever to come into power and control our destiny.

Mass Shootings, murder by guns and gun suicides – the facts

There is probably no issue that the Trump Administration and the NRA get blamed more for than mass shootings in America. It makes no matter that these mass shootings have consistently occurred through the years including during the 8 years of the Obama Administration, yet the lack of gun control was never blamed on Obama. Moreover, the Liberal left is totally silent about the murders and the violence that occurs every year in the major cities around the country that they control. Nor does the Socialist left talk about the growing deaths occurring from overdoses on drugs principally trafficked into the United States, from Mexico. On the contrary, the Socialist left want to make drug trafficking easier from Mexico. They would tear down the border walls that already exist; do away with ICE; eliminate border patrols and provide sanctuary cities and states for illegal immigrants including drug traffickers and murderous gangs such as MS13. Mass shootings alone is the sole focus of the socialist left. It is for sure problem. It is a terrible way for families to be deprived of their loved ones. But it is just as serious a problem in deaths due to murders in general, deaths by suicide and deaths by drug overdoses and yet the Democrats do not mention any of these, let alone focus on these problems. Let's look at the statistics:

Year	Deaths By Mass Shootings	Gun Deaths Excluding Suicides	Gun Deaths Including Suicides	Gun Deaths City of Chicago
2019*	283	9,932	31,932 (est.)	363
2018	340	14,623	36,623 (est.)	530
2017	346	15,658	39,773	660
2016	382	14,415	38,658	770

* Through September, 2019

What sticks out about these statistics are that more murders are committed each year in Chicago alone then are killed in mass murder shootings. The statistics all tell us that 2/3's of those dying from guns are suicides and that 2% of all deaths excluding suicides and less than 1% of all deaths from guns including suicides are from mass shootings. Mass shootings are a terrible tragedy and they need to be addressed and a way to stop them must be found. But 98% of gun homicides are not from assault weapons or mass killings, and the massive deaths from suicide remains a consistent and terrible problem. Yet the Democrat leaders never mention the terrible job their city mayors and city council members are doing to contain and reduce the deaths in the cities they run. Nor do they even mention the suicide problem in the United States where 2/3's of all the gun deaths are self-inflicted suicides. You will note a reduction in murders in Chicago over the past few years. This improvement is mainly due to the addition of 1,000 police, yet the Democrats consistently criticize and vilify police, claiming that they are brutal and often referring to them as pigs. The Democrat disdain for police even includes eliminating ICE and all border patrol agents along the Mexican/U.S. border.

CHAPTER 15

The Democrat Party and its Leadership; what have they done?

WHERE IS A good place to start? Let's look back briefly on the history of the Democratic Party and their leaders in relation to African Americans, Jews and the Working Class; those the leaders so loudly proclaim they support.

Starting with the 1850's, it was the Democrats that solely supported slavery. I have previously recounted in the Preface about the Dred Scott Case where the decision that "Once a slave always a slave" was unanimously decided by the 7 sitting Democrat Justices on the Supreme Court and it was the two Republican justices that dissented. It was a radical pro-slavery Democrat, John Wilkes Booth, who assassinated the Republican President, Abraham Lincoln, for being anti-slavery and it was President Lincoln who placed the freeing of slaves above the lives of the Northern (mostly Republican) men and 600,000 would be killed or wounded, fighting for the freedom of blacks. And it would be the Democrats who would fire on Fort Sumpter to start the Civil War. As we moved into the 20th Century, it would be the Democrat President, Woodrow Wilson, a strong advocate of the Ku Klux Klan, that would keep blacks segregated. And it would be the Democrats who founded the Ku Klux Klan that would stain America forever, for its murder of thousands of blacks by hanging or burning to death. And it would be the Democrats, who would pass and enforce the infamous "Jim Crow Laws", which were state and local anti-black laws in the South that codified a system that dominated the South's treatment of blacks until the 1960's. These laws mandated segregation of schools, parks, libraries, drinking fountains, restrooms, busses trains and restaurants. "Whites only" and "colored" signs were a constant reminder of forced segregation. The Jim Crow laws were upheld by the state and local Democrat government officials and reinforced by acts of terror perpetuated by the Democrat vigilantes. How can anyone forget Democrat George Wallace who would become governor of Alabama and in his inaugural speech would say: "I draw the line in the dust and toss the gauntlet before the feet of tyranny and I say segregation now, segregation tomorrow, segregation forever". In 1970 Wallace successfully ran again for governor, running on a slogan: "Do you want the black bloc electing your governor". It was the hatred emanating from the Democrats, the segregation and brutality against the blacks imposed by the Democrats that spurred Martin Luther King to come forth and champion the rights of blacks to freedom and equality, but he too would be assassinated by a Democrat just because King was a champion for human rights, rights that the Democrats had strived so hard to suppress for 150 years.

U.N. Security Council Vote Against Israel December 23, 2016 and other Anti-Jew actions of the Democratic Left.

On December 23, 2016, the United States rebuked Israel when it abstained on a UN Security Council Resolution demanding an end of Israeli Settlements in Gaza and on the West Bank, allowing the Resolution to pass 14-0. The U.S. was one of five members of the Security Council with a veto and for the first time in over 40 years refused to exercise it to support Israel.

The Resolution demanded that Israel immediately and completely cease all settlement activities in the occupied Palestinian territories including East Jerusalem. It declared that the establishment of settlements by Israel has: "No legal validity and constitutes a flagrant violation under International Law". Never mind the flagrant violations of International and Natural Moral law by the Palestinians and the Arab nations surrounding Israel. It had been a long standing American Foreign policy of vetoing one-sided resolutions against Israel at the United Nations.

By failing to veto this Resolution, the U.S. had in effect served to isolate and delegitimize Israel and at the same time legitimize Palestine. This high-profile rebuke of the Israeli government will hamper Israel's negotiating position in future peace talks with Palestine. Israel's right to exist has as a result of this Resolution, been severely impaired. The magnitude of this anti-Jew decision by the Democrats and the Obama administration can only be realized when one reads the Charter of Hamas, the beliefs and objectives of the ruling party and the majority of the Palestinians.

The Charter of Hamas, leading party of Palestine as well as its Military arm. - Imbedded in the Charter of Hamas, section 13 are the following words: "The time will not come until the Muslims will fight the Jews and kill them, until Jews hide behind rocks and trees that will cry 'O Muslim, there is Jew hiding behind me; come and kill him." But this does not tell the reader the whole story about Palestine, Hamas and its resolute unwavering objective to kill all Jews or at least drive them out of Israel. Make no mistake, for Palestine there cannot be a two-state solution. Here are some of the statements directly taken from the Charter of Hamas:

1. Peace initiatives, the so-called peaceful solutions and the international conferences to resolve the Palestinian problem are all contrary to the beliefs of the Islamic Resistance Movement. For renouncing any part of Palestine means renouncing part of the religion.
2. There is no solution to the Palestinian problem except by Jihad. The initiatives, proposals and international conferences are but a waste of time; an exercise in futility.

3. When our enemies usurp some Islamic lands, Jihad becomes a duty binding all Muslims. In order to face the usurpation of Palestine by Jews we have no escape from raising the barrier of Jihad. We must spread the spirit of Jihad among Islam, clash with the enemies and join the ranks of the Jihad fighters.

4. There is no escape from introducing fundamental changes in educational curricula in order to cleanse them from all vestiges of the ideological invasion which has been brought about by Orientalists and Missionaries.

5. The path of Allah is better than the entire world and everything that exists in it. It indeed wills us to go to war for the sake of Allah. It will assault and kill, assault and kill, assault and kill.

6. The enemies of Islam…realize that if they can guide and educate the Muslim women in a way that could distance themselves from Islam, they would win the war. Therefore, you can see them making consistent efforts in that direction by way of publicity and movies, curriculum of education and through the various Zionist organizations such as: Freemasons, Rotary Club, gangs and spies and the like. All of them are nests of saboteurs and sabotage. When Islam will re-take possession of the means to guide the life of Muslims, it will wipe out those organizations which are the enemy of humanity and Islam.

7. The Nazism of the Jews does not skip women and children, it scares everyone. In their horrible actions, they mistreat people like the most horrendous war criminals.

8. Oh, ye who believe, take not for intimate others than your own folk, who would spare no pain to ruin you (Surah III verse 118).

9. The Zion invasion relies to a great extent for its meddling and spying activities on clandestine organizations which it has established such as: Freemasons, Rotary Club, Lions and other spying organizations. They stand behind the diffusion of drugs and toxics of all kinds in order to facilitate its control and expansion

10. Jihad means not only carrying arms and denigrating the enemies. Uttering positive words, writing good articles and useful books and lending support and assistance, all that too is Jihad in the path of Allah, so long as intentions are sincere to make Allah's banner supreme.

11. Under the shadow of Islam, it is possible for the members of all three religions, Islam, Christianity and Judaism to co-exist in safety and security. Safety and security can only prevail under the shadow if Islam. The members of other religions must desist from struggling against Islam over sovereignty in this region.

12. Egypt has left the conflict with Israel through the treacherous Camp David Accords. This is a major act of treason and will bring a curse upon its perpetrators.

So, the Democrats would have you believe that the Jews are totally at fault in the disputes with Palestine. That they alone are to be rebuked. Can anyone accept this after reading the Charter of Hamas? While the Democrats keep telling us that the Republicans are the party of anti-Jew, the hypocrisy and lies belie this. We have already discussed Ilhan Omar, Rashida Tlaib and Andre Carlson members of Congress and one Keith Ellison former Congressman and Deputy Chief of the Democrat Party. They have all expressed radical anti-Jew sentiments and even recently verbally attacked Jews. The Democrat party leaders, refused to sanction or criticize their fellow Democrats even though they have raised such hatred toward Jews. Even the most radical Jew-hater Louis Farrakhan is welcomed by the Democrats into their political community.

- **Keystone Pipeline**

Hillary Clinton opposed the Keystone Pipeline stating: "I think it is imperative that we look at the Keystone Pipeline as what I believe it is, a distraction from the important work we have to do to combat climate change. I oppose it because I don't think it's in the best interest of what we need to do to combat climate change". This was the consensus of Democrats. Yet, the environmental risks were minimal, especially in comparison to a number of train accidents over the past few years carrying oil. The pipeline would create an estimated 4,000 construction jobs for the pipeline alone and according to the State Department report it would support more than 42,000 ongoing jobs. This is just the beginning of the Democratic tirade against fossil fuel and would lead directly to the Green New Deal.

- **Coal Mining**

Going even further than just the attack on Keystone Pipeline how can we forget Hillary Clinton's attack on the Coal Mining industry? During CNN's Democratic Town Hall Meeting in Ohio on Sunday March 13, 2016 Hillary Clinton promised that in her administration she would: "We're gonna put a lot of coal miners and coal companies out of business". This was not a slip of the tongue; it was Hillary carrying on the "legacy" of Barack Obama as she had repeatedly promised to do. The coal industry since 1970 has reduced emissions from coal-fueled power plants by 92%. If she had her way, the approximate 75,000 coal workers in 25 states would be out of work and they, along with their families would be impoverished. Where are coal miners going to find other jobs? Assuming a family of four for each of these workers, there would be 300,000 people placed on welfare and Medicaid, with no hope of ever getting off the welfare rolls. This does not include the ancillary workers, who provide goods and services to the coal miners, who would also be put out of work. Coal is an abundant cheap form of energy and technology is making it cleaner every year. This callous willingness to destroy the lives of all workers and their families in the coal industry, is just the beginning of the Democrat onslaught on the lives of so many workers and their families as we have previously detailed. The Democrats keep telling us that they are the party of the common man; the blue-collar worker and their families. Yet the Democrats by their plans and actions time and again show that they care little for those they profess to represent especially if it interferes with their gaining of power. For the Democrats, what is the best road to gaining power? Make people have to rely on the Federal Government, and promise them that under Democrat leadership, the Federal Government will give instant prosperity to everyone; free health; free education; free child care; and all the income they need even if they are unwilling to work. And how much more appealing will this be, if the Democrats by putting millions of people out of work and thus forcing these millions to turn to the Democrat Federal government for their very existence?

The Legacy left by the Democrats under the Obama Administration

How soon we forget the terrible state our country was placed in as a result of the 8 years under the Democratic Administration of Obama.

- **Status of our Military** - The overall spending on National Security had dropped every year since 2011, for an accumulated reduction of 15%. These cuts occurred during the Obama Administration. We only need to look to the Heritage Foundation's Assessment of U.S. Military power and readiness, to see the serious plight of our armed forces.

  1. The U.S. Army's Capacity Score rated weak, capability score, marginal readiness scores weak, overall score weak. Only 12 of the 32 Brigade combat teams (BCT's) are ready. Of the 12, 9 are support of ongoing operations and 3 are fully trained for "decisive action operations". "Unrelenting budget constraints have degraded Army readiness to historically low levels ", stated Army Chief of Staff General Ray Odiemo to a Senate panel on March 15, 2015.

  2. The U.S. Navy Capacity score was marginal; capability score weak and readiness marginal. Degradations in training and maintenance were key issues.

  3. The U.S. Air Force Capacity is weak, capability marginal and readiness marginal. Less than ½ of its combat air force meets readiness requirements. America's air force is the smallest and oldest since its inception in 1947. Of its roughly 5,000 aircraft, the average age is 25 years old. The curtailed modernization due to defense budget cuts has resulted in procuring 175 fewer aircraft per year than 25 years ago. The F-16 Fighter is the backbone of our air force. Its 1623 aircraft represents 32% of our total fleet of 5,000 aircraft. The F-16 will be between 36 and 40 years old at their predicted retirement in 2026.

On top of the aging problem of our Air Force fleet of aircraft, there is a corresponding severe maintenance problem. Airmen responsible for maintenance are leaving in droves, requiring the Air force to pay re-enlistment bonuses worth up to $90,000. Fox News published in May 2016 that the U.S. Air Force is short 4,000 airmen to maintain the fleet and short 700 pilots to fly them and the Air Force is short the vital parts to keep the Jets in the air. The shortage is so dire that some have been forced to scrounge for parts in a remote desert scrap-heap known as "The Boneyard". At South Dakota's Ellsworth Air Force Base, where there are only 20 aircraft to maintain, only 9 are flyable. This is typical. Only about 1 of 3 aircraft is capable of flying throughout the U.S. Air Force. How could our government be so inattentive to the needs of our military, especially the U.S. Air force? How could we be cutting our defense budget in the light of these catastrophic conditions existing in our military?

This was the legacy left to us by the Democrats and yet the Democrats and the media will give the Trump administration no credit for turning this grave situation around.

- **International Policy Concerns and Disasters Under Obama Administration**

1. **Syria's use of Chemical Weapons** - In August 2012, President Obama issued his "red line" warning to Syria, when he stated that any attempt to move or use its chemical weapons would evoke the possibility of more direct U.S. intervention. He reiterated this again at a news conference in Stockholm, Sweden on September 4, 2013. When in August 2013, Syrian President Assad's army killed more than 1,400 people including 400 children with Saran gas, Obama decided not to bomb Syria. Through Russian intervention, the Assad regime admitted having a massive chemical weapons program and supposedly removed 1,300 tons of chemical weapons, which was also supposedly all of it. On October 31, 2014 Secretary of State Kerry assured the citizens of the United States that 100% of Syria's chemical weapons were removed. Obama in turn was very proud of his actions in delegating the chemical weapons issue to Russia, feeling naively confident that Russia had seen to it that the chemical weapons had indeed been removed. A decline in courage and conviction may be the most striking feature of the Obama Administration, a feature that Hillary Clinton had indicated she would adhere to in her repeated assertion that she would carry on the legacy of Obama. In Obama's state of the Union address in 2014, he declared that "American diplomacy backed by the threat of force is why Syria's chemical weapons are being eliminated". In July, 2014 Secretary of State John Kerry declared: "We struck a deal where we got 100% of the weapons out".

    But the lie associated with Kerry's and the Obama Administration's claim that all of the Chemical weapons of mass destruction were removed begins to unfold. Susan Rice, the Benghazi storyteller, in January 2017 made a knowingly untrue statement that: "we were able to get the Syrian government to voluntarily and verifiably give up their chemical weapons stockpile". The Washington Post fact checker gave Rice four Pinocchio's, its worst rating for veracity for this statement, as the reality was that there were continued chemical weapons attacks by Syria after they had supposedly rid themselves of all their chemical weapons. Further, chlorine attacks have been documented in Syria throughout 2014 and 2015 that surely Obama and Kerry must have known about. Therefore, while President Obama, Secretary of State Kerry and Susan Rice have been bragging to America that their wonderful negotiations worked and all of Syria's chemical weapons had been destroyed, James Clapper's testimony and documented chlorine attacks proved they were lying to America. Yet journalist Jeffrey Goldberg in the August 2016 issue of the Atlantic wrote an article praising Obama's decision to ignore his "red line" to punish Assad regime if he ever used chemical weapons. What chance do we have for truth when not only do our top Democrat officials lie to us, but those lies are regularly supported by the liberal media? The Saran gas used by Assad against his own people was a modification of the gas that Hitler and his socialist government used to murder 6 million Jews

2. **Benghazi** - Another international fiasco under the Obama administration and another failure of the Liberal press to adequately report the intolerable conduct of the State Department under Hillary Clinton that led to the death of four Americans. On September 11, 2012 attacks on

our embassy in Benghazi led to the death of our Ambassador and three soldiers, who provided the only and woefully inadequate security for the embassy. The Secretary of State and other administrative officials tried valiantly to cover up their negligence even trying to hide their neglect and incompetence by falsely claiming that it was not a terrorist uprising but an unanticipated response to some video that blasphemed, Allah. Those engaged in the cover-up, well knew that their subterfuges were lies. Repeated requests for additional security in Benghazi were routinely denied by Secretary Clinton's State Department. During 2012, from January through the time of the terrorist attack there were 569 requests/concerns about the level of security in Benghazi e-mailed or sent by cable to the State Department. The actual number of requests may be in dispute, but even if there were only 200 requests ignored, this would be outrageous. Many were sent by the ambassador himself. And remember Hillary Clinton's claim that none ever reached her desk? Either this made her a liar or extremely incompetent, because how can the Secretary of State claim that not one of the requests from her direct subordinate ever reached her?

3. **The Nuclear Arms Deal with Iran** – It was a big win for Iran to be allowed to continue to enrich Uranium for peaceful purposes. It was also allowed to have 6104 centrifuges instead of 20,000 for the enrichment of uranium, essential to acquire a nuclear weapon. And while Iran agreed to reduce its stockpile of Uranium by 98%, Iran is not prohibited from shipping it and stockpiling it somewhere else (i.e. Russia).

Some of the terms of the deal expire in 10 to 15 years, at which time the breakout time (the time it would take to make enough enriched material for a nuclear bomb) would be zero.

How sure are we that the inspectors from the International Atomic Energy Agency truly have "extraordinary and robust" access to Iranian nuclear facilities? Remember Obama and Kerry had assured us that 100% of Syria's chemical weapons of mass destruction had been removed and this represented a far easier verification process than policing the development of nuclear capability throughout Iran.

What has Iran received for agreeing to this non-binding treaty? First it received over $150 billion from the release of frozen assets. Second, Russia has commenced delivering S300 anti-aircraft missile systems to Iran. Third, China is now building five more nuclear reactors in Iran and finally $400 million was paid out to Iran for the release of five Americans. And fourth, and most importantly the pledge that Iran would never be allowed to have a nuclear weapon pursuant to the 1970 Nuclear non-proliferation Treaty, signed by 191 nations and pledged by the Clinton and Bush administrations, had now been abrogated. Iran in a relatively short time would now be free to produce nuclear arms and they have indicated that they would not hesitate to use them.

On January 17, 2016, the same day five American hostages were released from custody by Iran, a jetliner dispatched from the U.S. delivered $400 million in cash to Tehran's Mehrabad

Airport. Actually, the pallets unloaded from the airplane contained Swiss francs, Euros and other foreign currencies. The shipment was secret until the Wall Street Journal broke the story on August 2, 2016. The $400 million amounted on its face to a gigantic ransom, which is barred under U.S. law. But of more concern was that the details were hidden from the public, because the payment of $400 million in foreign currency, coupled with its secret delivery on the same day that 5 hostages are released surely raises suspicions, especially since a wire transfer between banks would be the normal way to transfer money.

But most importantly is the burgeoning relationship of co-operation between North Korea and Iran, which blossomed under the Obama Administration. A seven-member delegation from North Korea, comprised of experts in nuclear warhead design and ballistic missile guidance systems spent a week in April 2015 in Iran. This was the third such nuclear and missile team visit to Iran in 2015. In addition to the joint development and exchange of nuclear technology, North Korea has been engaged in training Iranian operators in advanced infiltration techniques. So much for the Obama Nuclear treaty with Iran as progress toward nuclear capabilities for both countries continue right under our noses. Nothing prohibits Iran from developing guidance systems and now thanks to the Obama Administration and particularly John Kerry, Barrack Obama and Hilary Clinton, they have $150 billion to buy missile technology from North Korea.

And now, the Democrats in their hatred of Trump and the Republican Administration seek to frustrate and thwart any attempt by the Trump Administration to find peace and cooperation between North Korea and the United States and remove the North Korean Nuclear threat through peaceful negotiation and offering assistance and aid to North Korea is establishing a healthy productive society.

North Korea (officially, Democratic People's Republic of Korea) is a country of about 25 million with a nominal per capital GDP of $1,700 ranking it 179th out of 183 countries. By contrast, South Korea has a per capita GDP of $39,000 ranking it 29th among all countries. North Korea maintains one of the most closed and centralized governments in the world. In the 1980's South Korea surpassed North Korea in GDP per capita and look where they are now? By this measure, the GDP of South Korea is 2300% higher than North Korea. Nowhere in the world is there a greater contrast to demonstrate the success of capitalism over socialism. We also can look to the contrast between Socialist China and the capitalist region, Hong Kong and the neighboring country Taiwan. Today, Hong Kong with a $61,000 GDP per capita ranks 10th in the world and Taiwan with a $52,000 per capita GDP ranks 19th. China and its socialist policies can only achieve a 78th ranking with a GDP per capita of $16,600. We can look back in history to the dramatic contrast between East and West Germany. East Germany with its socialist economy and control over the lives of its people made life so miserable for them that they sought to leave in droves. East Germany put up walls to keep the people from leaving and as an alternative to providing a strong economy and prosperity, the leaders chose to shoot anyone that tried to leave. When an economy fails, when socialistic reforms lead to misery, the answer from the leaders is to: take away all freedoms, including freedom of speech and freedom of religion and if necessary, murder any who protest. We have seen this in Russia, China, Cuba, North Korea and now Venezuela. And yet so many believe that socialism and the Democrat party is the best for them.

The economy of North Korea is heavily subsidized. Food and housing are sustained by government subsidies and education and health care are free. North Korea has already implemented what the Socialist Democrats are planning for the United States And what benefit has socialism been for the people of North Korea?

Former President Barack Obama adopted a policy of "strategic patience" resisting any attempt to negotiate with North Korea. Obama ignored North Korea, while North Korea continued to develop a nuclear arsenal, possibly including a hydrogen bomb capable of reaching the United States. North Korea continued tests of its missile capability even causing missiles to fly over parts of Japan. With the election of Trump, negotiations with North Korea immediately began to eliminate the nuclear threat and offer assistance to Kim Jong-un in building a stronger, economically competitive economy, that would bring prosperity to his country.

On April 27, 2018 an inter-Korean summit took place between South Korea President Moon Jae-un and North Korea's Kim Jong-Un. It was the first time a North Korea leader had entered South Korea territory since the Korean War. On June 12, 2018, President Trump met with Kim Jong -Un in Singapore. This was the first step toward dialogue and negotiations between the U.S. and North Korea. And the nuclear tests by North Korea stopped. In February 2019 another meeting between the leaders was held, this time in Hanoi, but the two leaders failed to reach any agreement.

But look at the active steps the Democrats took to assure that this meeting would be unsuccessful.

On Wednesday February 27, 2019 the House Oversight Committee chaired by Democrat Elijah Cummings held a seven hour nationally televised hearing to interrogate convicted felon and liar, Michael Cohen, for the sole purpose to vilify and discredit President Trump. The interrogation of Cohen by the Democrats focused solely on the eliciting of disparaging remarks from Cohen about President Trump. It was a degrading display of scandal mongering by the Democrats, yet there are those on the left who will say that it was justified.

But why in the world would Elijah Cummings and the Democratic majority on the committee schedule the hearing on the exact date that President Trump was meeting with North Korean President Kim Jong-Un? Why couldn't the Committee schedule the hearing the following week? The discrediting of the President just before President Trump's meeting with Kim Jong-Un, severely impacted President Trump's ability to negotiate with the North Korean leader. if you were the leader of North Korea, wouldn't you believe your bargaining position was substantially strengthened by the severe weakening of the President caused by the leaders of the majority party in their vitriolic condemnation of the President? So, the Democrats, almost treasonous in their actions at this hearing, were willing to undermine President Trump's attempt to achieve peace and safety for the American people; they were willing to demolish any hope of reaching an accord with Kin Jong-Un and thereby keep the threat of a nuclear attack on the United States alive. All this because of their hatred for President Trump.

But the effort on the Democrat's part did not stop there. Democrat representative Adam Schiff had mysteriously and abruptly around February 7th postponed the hearing scheduled for February 7th to February 28th and that the closed-door hearing, scheduled for February 7 would now be an open hearing, coinciding perfectly with President Trump's meeting with Kim Jong-un. Schiff would give no reason other than: "In the interest of the investigation". Elijah Cummings would meet with Michael Cohen in the interim, but more importantly Adam Schiff and his staff, unbeknownst to the Republican members of the committee, held 4 private meetings with Michael Cohen for a total of over 10 hours to help put Michael Cohen's testimony together. Michael Cohen would admit that he met with Elijah Cummings, Adam Schiff and Schiff's staff. What a travesty.

4. **The Obama Legacy – The Raging Drug Problem.** Robert King wrote on 9/12/2016 in the Washington Examiner an article entitled "The Obama Legacy – A Raging problem with Heroin and opioids". He stated that the crisis of drugs had been building for the last 5 years and some claimed that the government even contributed to the crisis by approving pain killers, liable to be abused in their use. He pointed out that according to the Center for Disease Control and Prevention (CDC) from 2009 to 2014, the rate of overdose deaths from heroin abuse increased by 240% from 1 per 100,000 people to 3.4 per 100,000. John P. Walters of the Hudson Institute on April 13, 2016 noted that Heroin use and overdose has soared including a 440% increase in heroin deaths during the 7 years of the Obama Administration. It was also noted that most of the Heroin coming into our country came through Mexico and Opium production in Mexico increased in 2014 alone by 50%; obviously because there was a rapidly expanding market in the U.S. And the failure of the Obama Administration to do anything about this is evidenced by the fact that only 1.8% of the drugs coming into the U.S. are detected. And today the Democrats, particularly the ones that are running for president in 2020, want to make sure that the raging drug problem will even get worse, by openly opposing the building of a Wall along our Mexican Border; calling for open border and even suggesting the disbanding of the Immigration and Customs Enforcement Agency, which is responsible for providing security at our borders. And further, it is the Democrat controlled cities and states where the drug traffickers are actually harbored and protected by the "sanctuary city" regulations that curtail and render ineffective the activities of ICE. Our country faces far more addictions and deaths from overdoses, if the Democrats can gain control of our country.

In 2017, there were 70,237 drug overdose deaths in the United States. From 1999 to 2017,

207,700 Americans died from drug overdose. This is roughly twice the number of all the deaths by homicide or suicide that occur in America, yet not only do the Democrat leaders ignore it, they actively seek to destroy any efforts to reduce the interdiction of drugs into our society. Their policies of no wall between the U.S. and Mexico; tearing down existing walls; doing away with ICE; doing away with border patrol agents and providing sanctuary cities for all illegal immigrants will just open the gateway for even more drugs to destroy our young men and women and also our children.

And the problem is getting much worse for our citizens as the new synthetic drugs like Fentanyl are just so much stronger. Fentanyl is 50 to 100 times more potent than morphine and 30 to 50 times more potent than heroin. Most Fentanyl is manufactured in China and shipped to Mexico and then smuggled into the U.S. by the drug cartels. The drugs that are taking the lives of our people, namely cocaine, heroin and fentanyl almost universally come over the Mexican/U.S. border. Over 90% of all drugs coming into the United States are carried on the backs or in body cavities of so-called "mules" crossing the Mexican Border with the United States. The plans of the Democrats will provide an easier pathway for illegal immigrants; some of which most assuredly will be carrying drugs into or country. To exacerbate the problem, the Democrats plan to provide all illegal immigrants with free income; free medical; free education through college and university. Some propose paying every individual $1,000 per month, which means that an immigrant family of four will receive $48,000/year. Illegal immigrants will descend on our country in massive numbers. Where else in the world can they get $48,000 free income, free medical and free education. The insidious fact is that the U.S. citizen will pay higher taxes so that the immigrants whether legal or illegal can take some of our jobs. Make no mistake, among the illegal immigrants pouring into our country will be not only the "mules" delivering the high-powered drugs to kill more of our young people, but gang members from such criminal and terrorist organizations as MS13 who will perpetrate murder and violence on our citizens. This is part of the legacy our socialist left wishes to build for our country.

5. **Operation Fast and Furious - The** reader may remember "Operation Fast and Furious", the feeble if not ludicrous attempt by the Justice Department to get to the top officials in the Mexican drug cartels between 2009 and 2011. Under the Phoenix office of the Bureau of Alcohol, Tobacco, Firearms and Explosives, an agency of the Justice Department, a "sting" operation was authorized. In the operation, agents actually permitted weapons to be illegally purchased and circulated on both sides of the border by Mexican drug dealers and their agents in the United States. The intent was to send guns to Mexican cartels to help build cases against the Mexican drug lords. The plan did not succeed. All the Department of Justice had to show for their operation was that it had supplied guns to the Mexican drug traffickers. Whether or not Obama knew about the operation or approved it, it occurred on his watch. The failure of the Democrat administration was so complete and the drug problem has become so bad under the Democrat administration; yet the Democrats have the hubris to criticize and ridicule Trumps strategy to build a wall and significantly expand the number of borders guards.

Wouldn't it be nice if just once the Democrats would become a bit more introspective, examine their own failures before ridiculing and condemning those who offer different ideas and solutions?

6. **What is the impact of legalizing marijuana-** 8 states and Washington, DC have legalized Marijuana, namely: Alaska, California Colorado, Maine, Massachusetts, Nevada, Oregon and Washington? Only Alaska is a so-called "red state", the others qualifying as liberal democratic states. A consequence of the legalizing of marijuana in a number of states is that Mexican drug trafficking is now flooding the U.S. with cheap heroin. While the amount of marijuana coming from Mexico has fallen by 37% since 2011, this has been more than offset by the growth in Heroin. From 2007 through 2015 heroin users in the United States has shown a four-fold increase from 145,000 to 600,000 according to the U.S. Drug Enforcement Agency. U.S. law enforcement agents seized 2,181 kilograms of heroin in 2014 coming in from Mexico nearly three times the amount confiscated in 2009.

We learned that criminal organizations in Mexico are no longer marketing bulk marijuana. Now that marijuana is freely available in the legalized states in the U.S., hard drugs have become the growing trend. Heroin is far easier to transport and the U.S. border officials see a growing trend of more border-crossing pedestrians carrying drugs strapped under their clothing or in body cavities. While the legalizing of marijuana in itself may be acceptable, it should not be looked at in a vacuum and must be examined in the light of terrible consequences such as the raging expansion of the trade in and use of hard drugs.

On the average, 130 Americans die every day from opioid overdoses. The rampant drug problem in the United States has escalated at an alarming rate. Th first wave began in the 1990's with overdose deaths involving prescription opioids. The second wave during the Obama Administration began in 2010 involving heroin. And the third wave began in 2013, also during the Obama Administration involving synthetic opioids, particularly Fentanyl. It has become a health epidemic in the United States and has reached crisis proportions.

How have the Democrats responded to this epidemic? By far the greatest source (over 90%) of all illegal drugs is coming across the Mexican border. Yet without exception, the Democrat leaders; the 2020 Presidential candidates do not want border walls; they want to take down existing walls and they want to do away with ICE. In short, they want open borders, that will assure the continuation and expansion of the drug trafficking into our country. And more of our sons and daughters will die. The Obama Administration kept reassuring Americans that our southern border was secure, yet the overwhelming majority of addictive drugs coming into the United States, continued to come from Mexico and Mexican traffickers remain the greatest criminal threat to the United States.

Not only do the Democrats want open borders, they want to federally legalize marijuana. The legalization of marijuana has become a mainstream consensus of the socialist Democrats and Presidential candidate Kamala Harris is outspokenly in favor of its legalization because it would bring "joy" to a lot of people. Other candidates endorsing Federal legalization of marijuana include: Cory Booker (D-New Jersey); Kirsten Gillibrand (D-NY); Bernie Sanders (D- VT), Elizabeth Warren(D-MA) and Beto O'Rourke (D- TX).

It is true that there are conflicting views as to whether or not Marijuana is a "Gateway Drug" to more addictive drugs. It is true that marijuana has some medical benefits when properly used. However, research has established that early exposure to marijuana increases the vulnerability to move on to more addictive drugs. Research has also concluded that from 9% to 30% of those who use marijuana may develop some degree of marijuana disorders. Known effects of marijuana use include: impedes brain development and impairs, thinking, memory and learning functions. The use of marijuana has also been linked to a higher likelihood of dropping out of school, more job absences and accidents

Observations About Hillary Clinton

We cannot talk about what the Democratic party has done, without a look at Hillary Clinton. After all, her loss of the presidency gave rise to much of the hate and vitriol we hear from the liberal left, including not only U.S. Senators and members of the House of Representatives, but also our universities, media and entertainment industry. She was the heroine of the far left and she left behind her a legacy of hatred that has been unmatched in the history of our country. She was the focal point of the Democrat party, a socialist at heart that would provide the initial thrust to the radical socialism that pervades the Democrat party.

On Tuesday night, October 13, 2015 at a Democratic debate, Anderson Cooper asked Hillary Clinton "which enemy that you made during your political career are you most proud of?" Hillary Clinton responded "probably the Republicans". To declare approximately half the country your enemy certainly should concern us all, whether Democrat or Republican. Then on Saturday, February 6, 2016, Hillary Clinton had former Secretary of State Madeline Albright introduce her at a campaign rally in New Hampshire. To the smiles and cheers from Hillary Clinton (with the support of many around her) Madeline Albright said: "and just remember, there's a special place in hell for all women who don't help each other". Hillary Clinton went absolutely ecstatic with Madeline Albright's comments, thanking her profusely.

So, let's be clear on this. Hillary declares half the people of our country her enemy because they are Republicans and condemns all women to hell if they vote for someone other than a woman. Let's do the math. Say 50% of Americans are Democrat's and 50% of Democrats are women, thus representing 25% of the population. Now of the 25% say one-half (or 12.5%) support a woman for president just because she is a woman. Therefore, according to Hillary, she would doom to hell 12.5% of the population, just for voting for a man. This means that approximately 62.5% of the potential voters in the U.S are either hated Republicans or doomed to Hell.

We are known by the company we keep

- **Jorge Cabrera** – a convicted felon from Florida, Cabrera was invited by the Clinton's to a pre-Christmas party at the White House in December 1995, where he was photographed with Hillary Clinton. In January 1996 Cabrera was arrested with three tons of Columbian cocaine. He had been previously arrested twice on drug charges. Cabrera was given a 19-year prison sentence.

- **Yah Lin Trie** - long-time friend of Bill and Hillary and Democratic fund raiser, he pleaded guilty in a 1999 trial in Arkansas to two charges; a felony charge for false statements and a misdemeanor count for making political contributions in the name of others. Trie arranged for Chinese weapons dealers Wang Jun, Chairman of CITIC the chief investment arm of the People's Republic of China, to meet with President Clinton at a Democratic Party event at the White House on February 6, 1996. At the same time Clinton was meeting with Wong, the Bureau of Alcohol, Tobacco and Firearms and the Customs Service were completing an investigation, which caught Wang's company smuggling at least $4 million worth of 2,000 AK-47 assault weapons destined for gangs in California. Bill Clinton would later admit that Wong's attendance at his party was "clearly inappropriate".

- **Jeffrey Epstein** - We have previously mentioned this unsavory character. He is a convicted felon having served 13 months for soliciting prostitution and he remains a registered sex offender. Since then approximately 40 women have accused him of sexual misconduct. Bill Clinton was very close to Epstein. Court records show the convicted billionaire, pedophile, pimped out underage girls to powerful men. He had 21 contact phone numbers for Bill Clinton in his computerized phone directory. Epstein organized orgies on his private island in the Virgin Islands. Clinton flew on Epstein's private plane with Epstein on multiple occasions to his private island between 2002 and 2003. Court documents also claimed that Clinton was friends with an unnamed woman who kept images of naked under-aged children on her computer and helped recruit under-aged children for Epstein. While Clinton cut off his ties with Epstein around the time of Epstein's arrest, the woman's abuses apparently did not end the relationship as she was reportedly one of the 400 guests at Chelsea Clinton's 2010 wedding.

- **Grigori Loutchansky** - He was linked by Interpol to the Russian Mafia and involved in money laundering and nuclear smuggling across the Baltics and international illegal arms trading, Loutchansky at a private meeting with Mr. Clinton at a Democratic White House dinner in October 1993 and he was invited back to a second DNC dinner in July 1995. Clinton's CIA directors James Woolsey and John Deutch had informed Clinton that Loutchansky's Nordex Company was an organization associated with Russian criminal activities.

- **Eric Wynn** - A twice convicted securities promotor who pleaded guilty to stock manipulation that benefited the Bonnano organized crime family and who served two years in prison for theft and tax fraud, attended a December 1995 White House coffee with Clinton and in 1996 attended four DNC fund-raising events for Clinton.

- **Roger Tamraz** - An international fugitive from Interpol, he donated $177,000 to Democrats and attended several White House dinners and coffees in 1995-1996. Tamraz went on to attend four more White House events with Clinton, which included receptions, dinners and the premier of the Movie "Independence Day". Tamraz would also meet with Clinton for coffee on April 1, 2006.

- **Norman Hsu - former** Democratic fund raiser, Hsu was sentenced to more than 24 years in prison in 2009 for fraud and breaking campaign finance laws. Hsu contributed an undisclosed amount of money for Hillary Clinton's 2008 campaign. In his sentencing, the Judge accused Hsu of funding his fraud by manipulating the political process in such a way that it "strikes at the very core of our Democracy".

- **Chung Lo** - Another friend of the Clinton's contributed $10,300 to the DNC. In July 1996, Ms. Lo was arrested on 15 counts of bank and mortgage fraud. Lo's arrest came just four days before she was to host a $400,000 Asian-American fund raiser for Bill Clinton. The event was cancelled

- **Marc Rich** was an international commodities trader and hedge fund manager. He had been indicted by the U.S. government for illegally making oil deals with Iran during the hostage crisis and for tax evasion. He was indicted on 65 counts. He was on the FBI's list of the 10 most wanted fugitives. At the time of the sudden and unexpected pardon, Rich's wife Denise gave $1 million to Clinton's political party; $100,000 to Hillary's campaign for Senator and $450,000 to Clinton's foundation. Donations continued from Marc Rich until his death, but the Rich pardon would pay dividends to the Clinton's even after his death in 2013.

- **Sergei Kurzin,** a Russian investor who worked for Marc Rich in the past, arranged a speech for Bill Clinton in Russia for which he received $500,000. He also donated $1 million to the Clinton Foundation. This occurred while Hillary Clinton was Secretary of State. But these gratuities to the Clinton's were not without getting something in return. Kurzin arranged the purchase by Russian interests of 20% of all the Uranium production capacity in the United States. This deal had to be signed off by Hillary Clinton as Secretary of State and as a result a substantial amount of control of U.S. Uranium is now in the hands of a Russian consortium. It should be noted that the Clinton's made $57 million alone during the four years Hillary Clinton was Secretary of State, with deals like this Uranium one contributing significantly to their haul. On January 20, 2001, Clinton's last day in office, he pardons Marc Rich one of the 100 last minute pardons he would make.

Hillary Clinton's years as Secretary of State 2008-2012

Examples of Proclivity to lie

Remember when Brian Williams lied about being aboard a helicopter that was shot down by an RPG in 2003? For that he was fired and most believed that the firing was justified. Well, Hillary Clinton did the same thing. She claimed in 2008 that she "remembered landing under sniper fire in Bosnia in 1996 and she went into details as to how she had to avoid the sniper fire. 12 years later she would claim that she misspoke. Actual video showed that this just didn't happen. She is actually greeted by a child on the Tarmac, with no signs of any stress. What is the difference? Are we saying that we lower the bar for integrity for someone running for president than we do for an TV commentator? And why would she lie about this in the first place, unless she is a compulsive liar?

Hillary claimed that her daughter Chelsea was jogging around the World Trade Center on 9/11. Later she would admit that Chelsea was actually safely at home in her Union Square apartment at the time of the attack.

Hillary claimed that she was named after Sir Edmund Hillary, one of the first two men to climb Mt. Everest. Sir Hillary actually didn't climb Mt. Everest until Hillary was six years old.

Hillary claimed to be instrumental in the Northern Ireland peace process yet she was nowhere to be seen at the actual negotiations.

Hillary claimed that her family was dead broke when they left the White House. The Clintons only made $12 million in the first year after leaving the White House and Bill's pension as a former president amounted to close to $250,000 a year, plus certain continuing perks.

Regarding the Benghazi attack, Hillary claimed that it was in response to a disgusting anti-Muslim video and it was not a terrorist attack. Not only did Hillary lie about Benghazi, she failed to respond to the pleas for help and as a result, four American lives were lost. Her classic comment during the investigation of Benghazi tragedy as to what happened, she flippantly and callously answered "what difference does it make?". More about Benghazi later.

Hillary's Claim to be Champion of Women

In 1992 Hillary Clinton made an obviously demeaning remark concerning stay-at-home women, where in an interview, she flippantly said "I obviously could have stayed home and baked cookies" as if this was the major if not the only thing a stay-at-home mother does.

During Hillary Clinton's four years as Secretary of State, according to data from the office of Personnel Management, men in her Department were paid $16,000 more a year than women with the same degree and qualifications. And finally, even more telling of Hillary's hypocrisy, men working for her Clinton Foundation were paid 38% more than women.

Hillary Clinton's e-mail Scandal

1. "I thought it would be easier to carry one device for my work", claimed Hillary Clinton in reference to why she used her personal e-mail address for official business as Secretary of State. (March 10, 2015). A couple of weeks later a Freedom of Information Request by Associated Press discovered that Hillary Clinton used multiple devices to send e-mails including an I-Pad

and a Blackberry. Another Hillary lie: "I've never had a subpoena". Confronted by CNN Brian Keller on July 8, 2015, why she deleted 33,000 e-mails, while under investigation, Hillary Clinton claimed it was a common practice. Keller pressed, "even if you are under subpoena?" Hillary Clinton was under subpoena after Trey Gowdy requesting Clinton's e-mails in December 2014 got nowhere and sent her a subpoena in March 2008. Another Hillary Clinton lie.

2. Hillary Clinton claimed that her server contained personal communications from her husband. If that is true, it is a surprise to Bill Clinton. Spokesman for Bill Clinton, Matt McKenna stated that Bill Clinton had sent a total of two e-mails to his wife during his life and those were as president. Another Hillary lie.

3. In March 2015 Hillary Clinton asserted that: "there is no classified material on her server". This was another flagrant lie. In fact, her rule breaking arrangement using her personal unsecured server resulted in over 1000 classified e-mails passing through it from five or more U.S. Intelligence agencies.

4. Next, Hillary Clinton claimed she hadn't personally sent or received any classified information via her server. Government officials stated that at least six e-mails were written and sent by Hillary Clinton that contained classified information.

5. Then Hillary Clinton looking about for another excuse claimed that she hadn't trafficked in any materials that were classified at the time; only information that was retroactively deemed classified. Not only is this argument irrelevant, two inspectors general flagged e-mails that contained highly classified information from the time they were generated. These messages pertained to such sensitive subjects as the North Korean Nuclear program and Iranian nuclear talks.

6. The talking point that Hillary Clinton settled on is that she didn't exchange information that was marked classified at the time of the exchange. This is irrelevant and she knew it. Hillary Clinton received and signed an agreement acknowledging her duty to properly protect classified material **whether marked or unmarked.** Briefly, the statement she signed reads as follows: "I intend to be legally bound; I hereby accept the obligation in this agreement in consideration of my being granted access to classified material. As used in this agreement, classified information is marked or unmarked information. And pursuant to Executive order 12976, or under any other Executive Order or Statute that requires protection for such information in the interest of National Security, I understand and accept that being granted access to classified information, special confidence and trust shall be placed in me by the United States Government.

7. Missing from Hillary Clinton's 30,000 returned e-mails were at least 15 e-mails with Sydney Blumenthal that Blumenthal provided Congressional investigators. Sidney Blumenthal was a special advisor to Hillary Clinton, who had been banned from the Obama Administration because of his corruption. Hillary Clinton lied about her claim that Blumenthal wasn't her advisor. She claimed that Blumenthal's e-mails were unsolicited, yet Trey Gowdy presented to her an e-mail she had sent to Blumenthal: "Greetings from Kabul and thanks for keeping

this stuff coming. Any other information about it? What are you hearing now?" Hillary never explained this discrepancy. Another tranche of previously unidentified e-mails consisted of a series of exchanges with David Petraeus then head Central Command between January and February 2009.

8. Hillary further relied on a defense that the Federal Records Act puts the obligation on the government official (in this case Hillary Clinton) to determine what is and what is not a Federal Record. After months of consistently relying on this as one of her defenses, Hillary Clinton, under questioning admitted that she never exercised any judgment to determine what is a Federal Record. Hillary Clinton did not review a single e-mail to determine what she had to preserve and what she could delete. When asked whether she could say with certainty that she didn't delete anything she was supposed to preserve, Hillary Clinton responded: "All I can tell you is that when my attorneys conducted their exhaustive process, I did not participate…I didn't look at them". Under what authority do Hillary Clinton's attorneys have the right to review the former Secretary of State's e-mails, that may in all probability contain classified material? More importantly, under what authority do Hillary Clinton's attorneys unilaterally determine what is or is not classified and therefore what may or may not be wiped off the server?

- **The Travesty of Benghazi**

Of all the issues concerning the travesty of Benghazi and the numerous and sustained lying on the part of Hillary Clinton to cover up her ineptness and downright dereliction of duty, nothing strikes me as more significant than the fact that the State Department team in Libya asked for more security over 600 times and Hillary Clinton claims she never received any of them. She is either lying or she is the most negligent, incompetent Secretary of State we have ever had. Ambassador to Libya, Chris Stevens reported directly to Hillary Clinton. That was the chain of command. How could 600 communications be kept from her. How could she not know? Benghazi never should have happened. 4 men died needlessly and the fault lies squarely with Hillary Clinton. If there truly was ignorance, that is inexcusable and it certainly reflects a level of incompetence and lack of leadership that we cannot permit in the White House. It is far more likely that Hillary Clinton must have known that there was a serious cry for help from the Embassy and she ignored it. This is much more than incompetence. This is a dereliction of duty. It is a serious level of malfeasance, misfeasance and nonfeasance all wrapped into one. And Hillary Clinton seeks to cover up her dereliction of duty with a stream of lies and deceit.

Apparently, Chris Stevens wrote Hilary Clinton, asking whether the Benghazi compound would be closed. Her answer was that Chris Stevens was just being a jokester and wasn't serious. You don't think 600 communications from Benghazi asking for more security wasn't serious enough?

We know from her e-mails that Hillary informed her daughter Chelsea and the Prime Minister of Egypt within 12 hours after the murder of Christopher Stevens, that he had been killed in Benghazi by al Qaeda terrorists. At the same time, the public record from the Obama Administration blamed the killings of the Ambassador and his guards on an anonymous crowd's spontaneous reaction to an anti- Muhammad video. Hillary had to cover-up for her dereliction of duty and one way was to make it look spontaneous and unplanned, rather than a well-conceived terrorist attack, which had been the unheeded concern of the Libyan Embassy. Hillary had received e-mails from the CIA within 24 hours of the Ambassador's murder that it had been planned by Al Qaeda 12 days before the actual killing. When Hillary Clinton received the bodies of Ambassador Stevens and his three body-guards at Andrews Air Force Base three days after their murder, she still told the media and all the families of the deceased that the four had been killed by a spontaneous mob reacting to a cheap 15-minute anti-Muhammad video. It should be noted that later on when she was questioned about the facts surrounding the murder of the four men, her glib uncaring response was: "What difference does it make?"

Hillary Clinton's incompetence, dereliction of duty and negligence led directly to the four victims of the terrorist action in Benghazi. Is this the type of cover-up we should continue to expect from the liberal left, if they get into power?

- **Keystone Pipeline**

Hillary Clinton opposed the Keystone Pipeline stating: I think it is imperative that we look at the Keystone Pipeline as what I believe it is, a distraction from the important work we have to do to combat climate change. The pipeline would create an estimated 4,000 construction jobs for the pipeline alone and according to the State Department report it would support more than 42,000 ongoing jobs.

- **Coal Mining**

During CNN's Democratic Town Hall Meeting in Ohio on Sunday March 13, 2016 Hillary Clinton promised that in her administration she would: "We're gonna put a lot of coal miners and coal companies out of business". The coal industry since 1970 has reduced emissions from coal-fueled power plants by 92%. If she had her way, the approximate 75,000 coal workers in 25 states would be out of work and they along with their families would be impoverished. Where are coal miners going to find other jobs? Let's not forget CO_2 emissions in the rest of the world is expanding at a greater rate than we are reducing our CO_2 emissions and even if we were to bring CO_2 emissions down to zero, CO emissions throughout the world would continue to expand.

- **The Hillary Clinton - Supported Iranian Nuclear Treaty and its aftermath**

The New York Times reported on Friday May 6, 2016 that the Obama administration misled Americans about supposed "moderates" that officials were dealing with in the Iranian theocracy to forge a nuclear proliferation deal – all to make the deal more palatable to the American public. On January 12, 2016, two United States Navy Riverine Command boats drifted into Iranian waters and were seized by the Iranian Islamic Revolutionary Guard. 10 Navy sailors were held captive for approximately 16 hours and Iranian videos of the captives were used as propaganda to ridicule and deride Americans. In a speech on Wednesday January 13, 2016, Secretary of State John Kerry would thank the Iranians for releasing the sailors saying: "I want to express my gratitude to Iranian authorities for their cooperation in swiftly resolving this matter. So much for better relationships with the "so-called" moderate Iranians that we were supposedly dealing with.

Ben Rhodes, Deputy National Security Adviser for Strategic Communications even boasted how he helped create the false narrative to mask that Iranian hard-liners were really calling the shots. Leon Panetta, former Secretary of Defense told the Times that the hard-liner regime and its military arm were still in charge at the time of the Iranian deal negotiations despite what Obama's administration said. Iran has escalated tension since the deal that Obama claimed would "make the world safer". It has turned out to be anything but what Obama has claimed. On March 30, 2016, just one day before the Nuclear Summit Meeting hosted by Obama, Iran's Supreme leader, Ayatollah Ali Khamenei said: "Those who say the future is in negotiations, not in missiles are either ignorant or traitors". Further, Tehran used the special occasion during Vice President Biden's March trip to Israel to demonstrate a blatant contempt for Israel and the West in a message proclaiming that: "Israel must be wiped off the face of the earth".

Iranian Revolutionary Guard Aerospace Division Commander Brig. General Amir Ali Hajizadeh described the display on Iranian State television a video showing underground tunnels over 500 yards deep within mountains spread all over the country as only samples. He stated that Iran would begin deploying a new "advanced generation" of long-range missiles that will "erupt like a volcano from the depth of the earth".

In a separate deal with Russia, the Iranians purchased $8 billion of Russian fighter jets and helicopters. With $150 billion of money recently released by the U.S. as part of the Nuclear Treaty, Iran now can well afford to purchase more military equipment.

Of more concern is that Iran has been financing North Korea's nuclear military program in return for missile technology. Kim Jong Un's regime is even supplying missile components to Iran in violation of UN sanctions on both countries. Although details of those shipments were included in Obama's daily intelligence briefings, they were kept secret from the UN.

Iran's access to North Korea's nuclear warheads along with delivery systems and its alliance with North Korea against the U.S. is frightening. Yet Hillary Clinton suggests that global warming is her number one concern. Last month a photo was released by North Korea of Kim Jong Un posing with a miniaturized nuclear warhead and boasting that he could wipe out Manhattan with a hydrogen bomb much larger than the one developed by Russia.

Remember, Hillary Clinton embraced the Nuclear Treaty with Iran in a statement in July 2015 when she said: "I support the agreement because I believe it is the most effective path of all the alternatives available to the US to prevent Iran from acquiring nuclear weapon". She gave Obama and Kerry unequivocal praise for getting the deal done. Hillary Clinton's stated goal had consistently been to carry on the "legacy" of Barack Obama, a legacy that most assuredly advances the threat of nuclear destruction in our future.

The Totalitarian State under Socialist Democrats.

It is so hypocritical and crass for the Democrats to call President Trump a dictator who seeks a totalitarian state, when this so aptly defines the direction that the Democrats wish to take our country. Socialism is certainly a step toward totalitarianism and every Socialist state sooner or later leads us into a dictatorship, simply because the government keeps controlling more and more.

All the examples of radical liberalism and its denial of freedom of speech; its indoctrination of our youth and its hate mongering is rampant throughout our educational system and are key elements of a totalitarian state. Further, the liberal Democrats are actively seeking to establish socialism in the United States, to supposedly provide us for free all our medical, health and even income needs and at the same time control all our businesses with excessive regulations and higher taxes needed to support a socialist state. It seeks to control each and every one of us. The examples I have given are far more than anecdotal. They are the norms of our educational system and are alive and well in most of our educational institutions from k-12 and then through college.

What are the key elements of a Totalitarian state?

1. Control Education at all levels
2. Deny Freedom of speech
3. Eliminate, suppress and/or ridicule religion (particularly Judaism and Christianity)
4. Control all forms of media -TV, radio, newspapers, entertainment industry.
5. Develop effective propaganda programs to suppress conflicting ideas
6. Avoid/(disallow) Dialogue
7. Promote Hatred of those who disagree with or oppose you
8. Cause as many citizens as possible (by threat or otherwise) to be dependent on or beholden to the government (socialism)
9. Discourage if not outright ban independent wealth and income security, (for to allow this, surely interferes with the creation of the totalitarian state.

This was at least for a time the ingredients successfully imposed by the leaders of the most horrific totalitarian states in my lifetime, namely: Hitler, Stalin, Mussolini, Castro and they seem to be the ingredients most closely associated with radical liberalism in the United States.

The U.S. news and World Report ranks the top universities and colleges each year. In order, the top 8 Universities are: Princeton, Harvard, University of Chicago, Yale, Columbia, Stanford, MIT and Duke. The top three liberal arts colleges in order are: Williams, Amherst, Wellesley. I have always been suspicious of how these Universities and Colleges reach such high ratings. Class size, education resources, number of professors/students, average SAT scores on admission, graduation rate, peer assessment and alumni giving are the principal factors going into the ratings. They all deal with quantitative factors, numbers and statistics. But none really tell us anything about the quality. Here are some factors, which I believe are important and not even considered. If they were, what would this do to the current ratings? Here are some factors that I think should be considered:

1. Percentage of professors that are conservative as opposed too liberal
2. Evidence of student indoctrination
3. How often are controversial speakers excluded from campus?
4. The prevalence of student rioting on campus
5. Level of rape on campus
6. The installation and support of safe places for students to avoid controversy
7. Number of cases of bias and restrictions on freedom of speech reported on campus

We need to look not only at our own Alma Maters to review and understand the policies they are endorsing and the curriculum they are providing, but also at what our public schools are teaching and what propaganda are they spreading?

The Liberal Socialist Democrats want to impose on our society a totally new radical government, which if examined objectively in the light of history, would show that similar governments have always failed. A definition of insanity is where one does the same thing he has done in the past again and again, and each time expects a different result. Look at Venezuela, Cuba, North Korea, East Germany (before the wall came down). Don't let this happen to our country. The socialist left is surely seeking to take us there.

CHAPTER 16

Democrat Presidential Candidates and what they are proposing.

THE RADICALIZATION OF the Democrat party has gone so far, that everyone in our country is at risk. The radical platform of the Democrats include uncontrolled spending, promises of all sorts of free services that cannot be attained because they would bankrupt our country; abortion at will; free and open borders; sanctuaries for illegal immigrants; the massive destruction of jobs and the government control of health and education. These irrational and insane programs will lead to spiraling inflation; unsustainable debt burden five to 10 times higher than we have now; huge increases in interest rates, unprecedent inflation rates of 1,000% or more; vast unemployment placing millions on welfare, rationing of medical services, triaging senior citizens right out of medical care; rationing of travel, massive foreclosures of homes and property with the home values like the stock market closing in on 0;, the bankruptcy of thousands of corporations; the failure of our banking system; the disenfranchising of all who are on fixed incomes; an unprecedent loss in the stock market, virtually destroying all pensions, annuities, IRA's and 401K's and an increase in crime and violence. Ultimately our country will have fallen to an economic level far worse than Venezuela or North Korea. The Democrat's plans will create a hell on earth. Every one of their programs that they are proposing will lead to the destruction of the United States. The reader must take the time to read or re-read George Orwell's "1984" to get a better understanding of exactly what the plans and platforms of the Democrat party will lead us to.

There are already 20 Democrats offering themselves as candidates for President of the United States in 2020 and there will probably be more. Without exception they all are for (or at least have not spoken out against) the following disastrous programs:

1. **The New Green Deal** – banning of all fossil fuel. The result would be no gas, oil or coal; no airplanes; no cattle; major job layoffs resulting in rampant unemployment; rebuilding or refitting all buildings to eliminate the use of fossil fuel; astronomical expenditures on new high-speed trains; the abolishing of all gas and diesel fueled vehicles; unimaginable increase in the Federal debt levels accompanied by astronomical increases in interest rates; and budget

deficits 5 to 10 times higher each year than we are currently experiencing. We have seen how the Federal Government has already failed in trying to develop inexpensive solar energy in the infamous $550 million fiasco of Solyndra Systems and the failure of the high-speed railway between San Francisco and Los Angeles. The planned New Green Deal is based on the two failed attempts to replace fossil fuels and the Democrats would have you believe that they can do this in 10 years. We have already covered the insanity of this in detail.

2. **Free education from K-12 and then through college and university for everyone.** There is no need to strive for excellence in school, since grades are rarely given anymore and no-one has to perform well to get into college. This is just an extension of the Democratic policy, which we can refer to as" the dumbing of America'. That the far-left entertainment industry is well on board with this has been recently demonstrated by the fraudulent efforts some have taken to get their dumb, lazy children into the college of their choice. We have learned that some of the wealthy "Hollywood" people have spent upwards of $25 million to get their children into the college of their choice, by bribing college administrations; by falsifying their child's SAT tests, by committing fraud to have scores actually changed or having someone take the exam for the child. In some instances, the so-called Hollywood elite have spent as much as $500,000 to buy their child's way into college. And the children are participating in the fraud. What is motivating them to go to college? They want another 4 years of partying and drinking and spring break. These "Hollywood" types are some of the people who verbally champion young people, but are so willing to deny the hard-working ambitious child the opportunities that he or she should have been entitled to based on merit. What do the Democrats expect to achieve by granting everyone free college education? This will spawn a new generation of lazy, selfish, unmotivated ignorant young men and women. Who is going to strive for excellence if no-one is challenged to earn a degree rather than being given a degree? At the same time the Democrats are advocating the extending the life of irresponsibility and frivolity for our young. The Democrats are calling for children as young as 16 years old to be given the right to vote. Give a youth free education; extend his time for frivolity and irresponsibility and you gain a vote. This is not good for the nation but it is good for the Democrats and therefore it is a plan they will pursue. Further, the Democrats by seeking to establish free college education are attempting to extend its control over our educational system from kindergarten through college and thus further stifle individualism and independent thought.

This may be the time to discuss the hypocrisy of the Hollywood Democrats that so perfectly represent the entertainment industry. Those of us who watched the Oscar show this year, saw the hundreds if not thousands of attendees wearing their $10,000 and up dresses; displaying their $50,000 and up jewels, arriving in their limousines after coming from their $10 million mansions. These are the people who talk of assassinating the President, holding up an effigy of his severed head; calling for the bombing of the White House and even wishing for an assassination of the President as John Booth assassinated Lincoln or re-enacting the assassination of Julius Caesar in Central Park, only substituting President Trump as the victim. Here are the people who demonstrate only hatred when it comes to public displays and claim to be for the working people, although they do not want to live in their districts. They want to live behind walls surrounding their luxurious mansions, and they want to spend lavishly on themselves for jewels, yachts, limousines, private airplanes and vacations and live a life of luxury and gluttony.

3. **Free Income for everyone** – The Democrats propose guaranteed income for everyone even for those unwilling to work. Where is this money coming from? This is an obvious "robbing Peter to pay Paul" plan. All it does is makes a lot of people worse off to make a few people better off. And giving money to people who do not work, should be offensive to all the hardworking people in the United States.

4. **Massive tax increases for everyone** - Doubling the taxes on individuals making over a certain amount and also on corporations is not nearly enough to stave off insolvency of our government. We have already shown how even doubling the taxes on all households, would not even fund the increases in interest costs that government would have to pay. The tax cuts under the Trump Administration provided the average American family with an income of $74,000, with an additional $2,300 of disposable income, each year and the average single taxpayer making $40,000 saw his "take-home" pay increase by $1,300 a year. This is the tax relief to our taxpaying citizens that Nancy Pelosi called "crumbs". For Pelosi, who is worth 100's of $millions, it probably would be considered a crumb. How out of touch with the common man and woman, can Pelosi be and this is indicative of the Socialist Democrats as demonstrated by the insane programs designed to hurt every single person the Democrats say they are representing. The tax cuts for corporations from 35% to 21%, just made our country competitive with the rest of the world. Prior to these cuts, the United States Corporate taxes were the highest in the world.

5. **National Health Care** - The Democrats would have our government spend $32 trillion over 10 years (Elizabeth Warren claims it will be $51 trillion over 10 years and cost at least 2 million jobs). Where does this money come from? It will be partially funded by higher taxes; partially by more debt, partly by less benefits and Government mandating choices of doctors and facilities, but most importantly by triaging benefits and denying people medical care based on age as we see in Canada. We have seen how well the Federal Government performs based on the travesty of its operation of the Veterans' Administration. We saw the extent of the fraud and deceit practiced by the Veterans Administration in running the Veteran's Hospitals in order to cover up their failures. It was the Trump Administration that took a major step on behalf of Veteran's to alleviate the horrible medical treatment they were getting. Now thanks to the Trump Administration, the Veterans have access to private medical care, if there is a delay in the medical services available through VA hospitals. We have an administration that cares for our soldiers and veterans.

6. **Abortion at any time**. The Democrats are proposing the murder of a baby any time, even after birth. The Democrats will permit the termination of a baby, even with a rigorous heartbeat, right into the labor room and beyond. They do not accept that at any time during pregnancy is an unborn child a human. This is a giant step toward having the government make life and

death decisions for every mother and father. Whether you are "pro-life" or "pro-choice", the Democrats will make the decision for you. They will move us one step closer to the Chinese position on abortion. The Chinese government encourages abortion at any time and mandates that after 2 children. Chinese women are even forced to be sterilized whether they want to or not. And if all else fails, the parents will be fined as much as 4 times their annual disposable income and failing that, they will have their property taken away from them. This is just another dark way the Democrats are seeking to control our lives. This may even be too far for the "pro-choice" advocates.

7. **Open Borders, No Walls; No ICE** - The Democrats not only refuse to support the building of new walls along our Mexican border, they even advocate tearing down existing walls; having completely open borders and doing away with Immigration and Customs Enforcement (ICE) along our borders. What possible reason would a sane person or persons have to allow 100's of thousands if not millions of illegal immigrants (along with massive amounts of drugs that are killing our people) to cross our borders? Since most will immediately be placed on some form of welfare and therefore under control of the government, they more than likely will vote for the Democrat socialist party that gives them free income, free education ad free health care. Open borders and no walls and no ICE is a ridiculously simple scheme to enhance the power of the Democrats, and more quickly lead to the destruction and demise of our once wonderful country.

8. **Destroy Jobs and families** -The Democrats and their propaganda media would have you believe that they are for the common workers. Remember the famous comment, that was part of Hillary Clinton's campaign "We are going to put a lot of coal miners out of work". Think of the 60,000 coal miners, the 84,000 indirect jobs lost and the related family members totaling 504,000 that will be left destitute, with welfare the only hope for survival. But this only opened the door to the cold heartless plans that Democrats have put forth for the workers and their families. 13.65 million jobs will be lost and a total of 53 million new additions to our welfare system, will result from the insane plans of the Democrats if they are ever implemented.

9. **Reparations for the Black Community-** In the preface, I briefly discussed "Black lives Matter" vs." All Lives Matter". The Democrats are now actively considering that reparations should be paid to the Black community. And some, particularly the followers of Louis Farrakhan, and especially Keith Ellison the former Deputy head of the Democrat National Party are even suggesting that a part of the South be carved out and given to the Blacks as a new nation. Who should pay for these reparations? Should it be those of us whose ancestors never owned any slaves (which is by far the majority of the population)? Should it be those whose ancestors fought and died on the battlefields of the civil war and were killed or severely injured as they fought so bravely to free the slaves? Or should it just be the individuals whose southern Democrat ancestors actually owned slaves; started the civil war, founded the Ku Klux Klan, established the Jim Crow Laws that kept blacks in a state of slavery until the 1960's? And what about the African Americans whose African ancestors first enslaved their fellow blacks and sold them into slavery, first to the Arabs as early as the 7th century? And what about the many

African nations today that still support enslavement of their fellow blacks? Is there historical justification for reparations to the Black community in the United States or is it just another Democrat hype to gain votes and try to blame Republicans as white supremacists and racists?

Trans-Atlantic slavery between 1525 and 1861 - During this period 12.5 million black Slaves were shipped to the New world. Only 10.7 million survived the passage, disembarking in North America, the Caribbean and South America. Only 388,000 were shipped to North America. The overwhelming number were shipped to the Caribbean and South America with Brazil receiving 4.86 million Africans alone. Almost every slave bought to America was purchased from a black slave owner. It has been estimated that between 60,000 and 70,000 Africans ended up in the United States after first landing in the Caribbean. Thus the 42 million members of today's African-American Community descended from a relatively small group of about 500,000 Africans, almost all of which had first been owned by black slave owners in Africa.

An 1830 U.S Census found there were 3,775 free blacks who owned 12,740 black slaves. Free blacks had a real economic interest in the institution of slavery and held fellow blacks as slaves in order to improve their economic condition. In 1860 the total number of slave owners in the United States was 385,000, almost all southern families and almost all Democrats.

Let's summarize some facts about slavery that most people do not know:

1. At the peak of slavery in 1860 only 1.4% of Americans owned slaves.
2. From 1525 to 1866, 12.5 million Africans were shipped to the New World. 10.6 million survived the passage. Only 388,000 were transported to North America. The balance were brought to the Caribbean and South America.
3. At the height of slavery in America, there were 3.9 million African slaves and 500,000 African freemen. By way of contrast, Nazi Germany forced 20 million people into slave labor, eventually murdering 8 million of them, 6 million of whom were Jews. By 1944, a quarter of the German workforce were slave laborers (13.5 million). To better understand the slavery in Germany and occupied territories such as Poland, it may be worth-while to read: "Life in a Jar" by Jack Mayer, or any of the many books about Irene Sandler and her heroism in saving the lives of 2,500 children destined for the German death camps.
4. In 1860 over 75% of white families did not own slaves. The 25% who were slave owners were predominately Southern Democrats.
5. Over a million white Europeans were held as slaves in Africa from the 1530's until the 1780's. There were more white slaves in Africa than African slaves in North America.
6. The first six states that seceded from the Union were all Southern Democrat States, namely; South Carolina, Mississippi, Louisiana, Alabama, Florida and Georgia. In Mississippi and South Carolina, over 55% of the population was African American. In the other four states the

African American population was over 45%.

7. Almost all slaves brought to America from Africa were purchased from black slave owners.
8. According to the census of 1830, 3,375 blacks owned 12,740 black slaves.
9. The first legal slave owner in American History was a black tobacco farmer named Anthony Johnson.

- North Carolina's largest slave owner in 1860 was a black plantation owner named William Ellison.

- American Indians owned thousands of black slaves.

- Brutal black on black slavery was common in Africa for thousands of years.

- The Census of 1860, at the height of slavery in America there were a total of 394,000 white slave owners out of a total population of 27,233,000, representing 1.4% of the total population. Of that 1.4% the vast majority were Democrats, not Republicans. On the contrary, it would be the Republicans who would gain freedom for the blacks and it would be the Southern Democrats who would sustain slavery as best they could first with the Dred Scott Supreme Court decision. This was soon followed by Assassination of President Lincoln, by radical Democrat, John Wilkes Booth; the creation of the Ku Klux Klan and the implementation and vigorous and brutal enforcement of the "Jim Crow" laws in the South. The cry of the Democrats for over 100 years has been:" once a slave always a slave" or "Segregation forever". And the indifference towards blacks by the Democratic party is shown year after year in the 25 major cities of the United States, where the murder of young blacks, including women and children occurs without abatement. These crimes ridden and murder ridden cities in the United State are all run by Democrats. Yet the majority of black voters seem to gravitate to the Democratic party, which has never been their friend, never supported them and has even shown an indifference to their plight, which has left thousands each year dead and tens of thousands of black family members bereft of their loved ones.

- Slavery has been historically widespread in Africa and still continues today in many African Countries. In fact, Africa has the highest rate of modern-day enslavement in the world. About 9.2 million blacks still live in servitude in Africa. And of the 10 countries that have the highest prevalence of slavery in the world, 5 are African nations including Mauritania, South Sudan, The Central African Republic, Burundi and Eritrea. The non- African nations with the highest incidence of slavery in the world include: North Korea, Afghanistan, Pakistan Cambodia and Iran.

- Other African nations that still enslave their fellow Africans include: Benin, Chad; Congo, Ethiopia, Ghana, Madagascar, Mali, Niger and Togo.

- In many African countries, children are sold into labor by their parents, sent to Muslim schools where they are forced to beg on the streets by Muslim Imams. They are also recruited as unpaid porters or child soldiers by armed militias. Girls are often married young, denied education or forced to be sex slaves.

It should be of interest to everyone how hypocritical Democrats blame the Republicans as racists, when their history shows they were the racists and white supremacists that not only engaged in slavery but continued to suppress blacks long after the Emancipation Proclamation. And blacks blame whites as racist and white supremacists, when their ancestors were the ones to inaugurate black slavery and actively participate in slavery before during and way after the slavery of blacks by whites had ceased.

Legalization of Drugs – Adding to the many disasters that will befall our country under Democrat rule is the Democrat proposal to legalize opioids and heroin and making them available at clinics across the country. We have seen how legalizing marijuana has virtually destroyed cities like Seattle, Portland, San Francisco and Los Angeles as the opioid and heroine usage has expanded along with marijuana. We will see not just the 70,000 deaths we now experience each year from drug overdoses, but multiples of that. Look at California, now the leading producer of marijuana for U.S. consumption in the world. So much is being produced in California that the supply has outrun demand and prices have fallen. The legal marijuana growers in California are now exporting their drugs to other states where marijuana still remains illegal. But there still remains opportunities for unlicensed growth and sale of marijuana in California and the illegal market can compete successfully against the licensed market. A terrible consequence of legalizing marijuana is that the drug cartels in Mexico have rapidly expanded the marketing of the much more profitable opioids, heroin and cocaine and, the deaths from overdoses keeps rising as the drugs being sold become more potent. At the same time, the Democrats would open our borders and remove walls and border patrols, just to make it easier for the drugs to make their way into the hands of our young people including children.

Forgiveness of Student Loans - The Democrats want to forgive $1.5 trillion of student loans. This sounds on its face to be a great idea, but where is the money going to come from, when there is nothing left after the Green New Deal and the Medicare for All programs? This $1.5 trillion would immediately require a family making $50,00 a year to pay off the debts of doctors, lawyers and engineers. And how about those who had previously gone to college and paid off their loans? They would now be obligated to pay off the loans of someone else. The elimination of tuition at all colleges and universities would cost about $80 billion a year. That doesn't sound like much, when compared with the $13 trillion a year for other planned programs of the Democrats. But the $80 billion would soar as many more will choose to enter college and not join the workplace for an extra 4 or more years.

CHAPTER 17

Food for Thought

George Orwell's 1984

GEORGE ORWELL'S BOOK, "1984" was published in 1949. Its setting is 35 years in the future. We are introduced to the new state, Oceania, one of the three existing states in the world. Great Britain has been annexed to Oceania. The United States no longer exists. Oceania is ruled by the "Party", that employs thought police to persecute individualism and independent thinking. The Party (which seems to have come into reality today in the form of the Socialist Democratic Party), no longer identifies its leader as the President. He is now called "Big Brother". Beto O'Rourke, John Hickenlooper, Bernie Sanders, Cory Booker, Jay Inslee, Julian Castro, Andrew Yang, John Delaney or Joe Biden would become the United States first "Big Brother" (If Elizabeth Warren, Kamala Harris, Kirsten Gillibrand, Amy Klobuchar or Marianne Williamson were elected, she would probably be called "Big Sister").

Oceania has come into existence by civil conflict. We see that today in the constant vilification and vitriol used by the Democrat Congressional leaders, the entertainment industry, the media and our educators against President Trump. The civil conflict is between Conservatism and radical liberalism. Oceania has become one of the three totalitarian states that rule the world. The people of Oceania are ruled by constant surveillance and propaganda. (We see these constantly in evidence in the Democratic party.

The principle character in the book is Winston Smith who works for the Ministry of truth, where he re-writes historical records to conform to the state's ever-changing version of history. We see the beginning of this as various Democrat groups seek to remove any statues of historical significance, because they had been slaveowners. Statues of Columbus are also targets for removal and even Yale University changed the name of one of its colleges from Calhoun (a slave owner in the early 19th century). And why not the name of Yale University; since Eli Yale was actually a slave trader?

Winston even re-writes past editions of the Times, while the original documents are mysteriously destroyed by fire. A quote from the book explains just how far the Party will go to fabricate, falsify and lie: "**Every record has been destroyed or falsified; every book rewritten; every picture has been repainted, every statue, street and building has been renamed, every date has been altered and the process is continuing day by day; minute by minute. History has stopped. Nothing exists except an endless present in which the party is always right**"

Those people who fall out of disfavor with the party become "un-persons" disappearing with all evidence of their existence removed.

In "1984", George Orwell describes the "two-minute hate program" as a daily ritual in his totalitarian state, Oceania. The "two-minute hate" is a daily period in which party members of the Society of Oceania must watch a film depicting the Party's enemies and express their hatred for them for exactly two minutes. The Party's enemies are most notably Emmanuel Goldstein and his followers. Within 30 seconds of the start of the film, any pretense of hate was unnecessary because a hideous ecstasy of fear and vindictiveness, a desire to kill, to torture to smash faces with a sledge hammer seems to flow through the whole group turning one even against one's will into a screaming lunatic. Within the novel we are introduced to "hate week", an extrapolation of the "two minute" period into a week-long festival. And in "1984" we learn that Big Brother presents three slogans of the party:

> War is Peace
>
> Freedom is Slavery
>
> Ignorance is Strength

This is very similar to the "political correctness" language changes, we already discussed occurring in the United States, as exemplified by San Francisco.

Anyone who looks at the two-minute video from the movie "1984" can well see the same hateful protests by the liberal left student bodies on campuses across our nation and such protests are being encouraged by our college and university professors.

George Orwell further explains in "1984" that in order to create a revolutionary future it is necessary to mobilize hatred against the existing order to destroy it. This was the goal of the Third Reich. This seems to be the goal of Chomsky and the radical liberal left. As Horowitz points out, Chomsky uses certain words over and over again like murder, genocide atrocities, rape, and massacre. It is obvious that he seeks to promote hatred; hatred against those labeled Republicans or Conservatives. This hatred is fostered not only by our professors in colleges and universities but even in our public schools, our media and our Democrat politicians.

The bitterness, the vitriol, the anger and hatred displayed by so many liberal Democrat Congressmen, the media, entertainers and the Democratic constituents as a result of Trump's election is unlike anything I have witnessed in my lifetime. Logic, objectivity, reason, rational dialogue is nowhere to be found. As our country's debt soars, as the Affordable Care Act has turned into a disaster, as our trade imbalance grows, as the nuclear threat from those who would destroy us proliferates, and terrorism expands throughout the world, and our roads and bridges deteriorate before our eyes; as our drug abuse runs rampant and the education of our children falters, Democrats choose to make, filibustering Gorsuch; the release of Trump's tax return, impeachment of Trump; and Trump's failure to shake hands with Angela Merkel their major priorities. There has never in my lifetime been a better example of "Nero Fiddling as Rome Burns", than the inaction and irrational and illogical set of priorities that the Democrats have chosen. No attempt to work with the government is being made by the Democrats and this is evidenced right at the start by the boycott by 70 Democratic Congressmen of Trump's inauguration. Those who have played competitive sports, more specifically, football, basketball, hockey, and other contact sports know that when the game is over it is time to shake hands and be friends, even though on the fields of athletic battle, you consider them your enemy and you wish to attack them fiercely and aggressively. Would that our politicians could understand that; that it is in the best interest of their Government and their constituents to seek to work together. Unfortunately, the Democrats would rather bring down our Government than to seek success through reconciliation and compromise. And for this striving for anarchy, I find serious fault with the Democrats. And the "herd mentality" of the Democrats exacerbates the problem. Republicans on the other hand disagree among themselves and enter into open dialogue to try to find answers. This is a blessing and a curse, because along with the vigorous debate there is often an un-willingness to compromise and this can be as damaging as to agreeing to anything for the sake of the Party. There is a cure for the recalcitrance in the Republican Party, just find a way to compromise. The Democrats have a significantly higher hurdle. The only thing I see the Democratic Party doing during the first half of Trump's Presidency is to criticize with ridicule, hate and anger, Trump, his family, his actions and plans for the country, without offering one single forward-looking proposal. The Democrats have nothing to compromise on since no ideas have been put forth for them to debate among themselves. And the Democratic political leaders are aided and abetted by the radicalized media, the far-left entertainment industry and the educators in our public schools, colleges and universities. You would think that at least some of those who voted for and supported Democratic representatives would take a hard look at what they accomplished during the last 8 years under a Democratic President and during the first three years of the Trump presidency other than to divide our country with hatred and vilification. And yet the Democrat leadership would get so many to believe that they were not only guiltless in generating hatred and divisiveness within our country, but that they truly had the best interests of Americans at heart. Tell that to all those on the Conservative Right, who have been referred to as "deplorables" or told that there was special place in hell for them, or that their jobs were going to be taken away from them.

This is the legacy of the liberal left as it seeks to destroy statues, remove art work, rename sports teams, vilify founders of the country, remove history courses from our schools, remove Judaism and Christianity from public places and schools and substitute the teaching of Islam, prohibit dialogue and physically attack those who do not agree with the liberal left party line.

Robert E. Lee is one of several who have particularly come under fire by Antifa. Lee's statue has been removed from a Dallas, Texas Park named for the General. It had been dedicated by Franklin D. Roosevelt in 1936 as part of the Texas Centennial Celebration. Eric Fonner, a Civil War historian, author and professor of history at Columbia University speaking about Robert. E. Lee said: "He was not a pro-slavery ideologue, but I think it is equally important that he never spoke out against slavery. In 1856 Lee wrote a letter to his wife in which he said: "In this enlightened age there are few I believe, but what will acknowledge that slavery as an institution is a moral and political evil in any country". On September 13, 2017 the statue of Thomas Jefferson on the Campus of the University of Virginia is covered by a black shroud, because Jefferson owned slaves. In New York City the statue of Christopher Columbus in Central Park NYC is defaced with red paint. Mayor Bill de Blasio has created the "Advisory Commission on City Art, Monuments and Markers", to seek out monuments that seem to be oppressive and inconsistent with the values of New York City. The mayor will have the final say and private property rights will be abandoned by a dictatorial, social Democrat Mayor. Goodbye to hundreds of years of history, tradition and knowledge of our past and hello to a communist/socialist imposition of cultural martial law imposed on us by the liberal left. The statue of Christopher Columbus at Columbus Circle at the corner of Central Park is under investigation for removal. We may wonder where the destruction of monuments stops? Washington, Jefferson, Benjamin Franklin and many other signers of the Constitution owned slaves. All statues and monuments to them are subject to removal. There are the Washington and Jefferson Monuments in Washington, DC; there is the George Washington Bridge; There is Mt. Rushmore depicting among others Washington and Jefferson; There is the University Washington and Lee. There are state capitals, cities, roadways, schools all with names of slave owners as well as on our currency. Are they all to be changed or removed?

Al Sharpton targeted the Jefferson Memorial in Washington, DC, demanding the Federal Government shut down the historic monument because Jefferson owned slaves. Christopher Columbus is under attack in New York City for his treatment of Caribbean natives, even though he never set foot in this country. Benjamin Franklin is under attack for he too owned slaves. 41 of the 56 signers of the Declaration of Independence owned slaves at the time of the Constitutional Convention, six of the original thirteen colonies were slave-owning colonies, namely Delaware, Georgia, Maryland, North Carolina, South Carolina and Virginia. 25 of the 55 delegates to the Constitutional Convention owned slaves. Though the majority of the delegation didn't support slavery, it was not prohibited in the Constitution for fear that would deter the six slave-owning states from signing on. Slavery was wrong then and it is wrong now. And the outrage is well understood. However, isn't there a hypocrisy here, when the enslavement of blacks by blacks in Africa and the selling of the slaves first to Arabs and then to Western nations is never mentioned; nor the fact that there would have been little if any slavery except for the duplicity of black slave owners, selling their brothers for money? And where today is slavery still rampant? In many of the African nations.

Harvey Weinstein and the Hollywood Crowd

What is so shocking about the lurid sex scandal out of Hollywood, involving Harvey Weinstein, is how his behavior was shrugged off as an "open secret" and deemed a normal institutional practice of the "Hollywood Casting Couch". The level of sexual depravity in Liberal Left Hollywood was not just limited to the raping and sexually assaulting women. It goes beyond that according to former child star, Corey Feldman who has long alleged that pedophilia is even a worse problem in Hollywood. In the case of Weinstein over 30 women have complained of sexual assault by him and over 50 are now admitting knowledge of Weinstein's sexual molestation.

As the story of Weinstein unfolds, we learn about his 2015 contract with The Weinstein Company (TWC), which stated among other things that he could get sued over and over for sexual harassment and as long as he paid money that was good enough for the company. According to the contract, if Weinstein "treated someone improperly in violation of the company's code of conduct, he must reimburse TWC for settlements or judgments. Additionally, "you (Weinstein) will pay the company liquidated damages of $250,000 for the first such instance; $500,000 for the second such instance; $750,000 for the third such instance and $1 million for each additional instance". The contract goes on to say as long as Weinstein pays it constitutes a "cure" for his misconduct and no further action can be taken. Hollywood is almost a virtual copy of "Sodom and Gomorrah". And yet the Hollywood community in their vitriol and outrage against President Trump, would have you believe that it is a morally superior group. How hypocritical.

Harvey Weinstein was a close friend of the Clintons and has made sizeable contributions to their campaigns and their foundation. He also has contributed to top Democrats including former President Barack Obama, Presidential Nominee, Hillary Clinton, Senators Elizabeth Warren, Al Franken, Cory Booker, Charles Schumer, Martin Heinrich, Patrick Leahy and Richard Blumenthal. All but Hillary Clinton returned or donated to charity the contributions from Weinstein. The Clinton's have chosen to keep the $250,000 Weinstein donated to the Clinton foundation.

The vast majority of the Hollywood entertainers are liberal Democrats. From some sense of superiority and power they vilify and abuse President Trump unceasingly. They will discredit, ridicule and condemn the President for almost everything he does or says, yet readily remain silent and even accept the sexual misconduct of their colleagues, even with full knowledge of the sexual atrocities. The "casting couch" in Hollywood is alive and thriving in Hollywood along with the molestation of young children.

Oscar Night is the highlight of the Hollywood culture. While people are living on the streets, have little food and shelter, or working hard to live from paycheck to paycheck, the Hollywood crowd gather in the thousands, the women in their $10,000 and up gowns that leave them almost naked and wearing priceless jewels. They have spent $1000's to get properly beautified for the occasion. They are driven to the festival in stretch limousines, coming from their multi-million-dollar homes and will party on champagne and caviar before the night is over. They have distanced themselves in every way from the common man, enjoying their million-dollar yachts, $100,00 cars and exotic vacations in far-away expensive places. And yet they would have you believe that they are the champions of the poor and down-trodden. In fact, the City in which they parade their luxurious existence, Los Angeles, boasts one of the greatest populations of homeless, drug users, and people living in abject poverty, who find themselves living on the streets in filth and slums. These are the hypocrites who support the Green

New Deal that will put millions out of work. Yet their use of fossil fuels in the stretch limousines, their private aircraft, their luxurious yachts and the massive usage of fossil fuel energy in their mansions is exponentially greater than the CO_2 emissions from the average American.

The hypocrisy of the moral compass that Hollywood would have you believe emanates from their special world never ceases. In February 2019, it was Jussie Smollet who would be charged with felony disorderly conduct and filing a false criminal report that he was a victim of a racist and homophobic attack in Chicago and the media supported him and tried to lay blame on Donald Trump and the Conservative Right. Then there was the college and university scandal where actress Felicity Huffman was sentenced to 14 days in Jail for spending $15,000 to bribe and falsify SAT scores to get her daughter into college. This was topped by Actress Lori Laughlin who along with her husband spent $500,000 to get her child into a college, thereby depriving some one of his or her rightful place in the college. There are apparently over 50 of the Hollywood crowd who have taken steps to fraudulently manipulate their children into the colleges of their choices. And look at the Liberal left colleges that participated in the fraud and deceit: Yale University, University of Southern California, Stanford University, University of San Diego, University of Texas, Wake Forest University and Georgetown University. These are all prestigious schools, who along with the Huffmans and Loughlins of Hollywood, would have you believe that they are defenders of Democracy and care for the poor, the common man and the disadvantaged; and are for eliminating fossil fuels. Yet their actions consistently belie this. And it is the same Hollywood crowd that wishes to assassinate the President of the United States and I have previously covered this in detail.

When we look closely at the hypocrisy and immorality and life-style exhibited by so many of the Hollywood entertainers, we wonder why so many revere them, trust them, and listen to them?

Yet it is the sexist, anti-feminist deviant Hollywood culture that calls President Trump the sexist anti-feminist. The hypocrisy of the liberal left is so prevalent here, yet there are so many people who align themselves with the hypocritical Democrat Party, because their hatred of President Trump and the Republicans overwhelms any possibility of logical, objective thinking. Wake up America. it is the Liberal Left that sponsors and supports anti-feminism of the worst kind, not the Conservative Republicans.

Sanctuary Cities and States.

Along with the Socialist Democrat's ardent devotion to tearing down Walls and ridding the U.S. of ICE, so that immigrants can freely cross our borders and take part in a life which requires nothing of them; the Democrats openly flaunt the laws of the land to help assure that all can partake of the American dream, without doing anything to attain it. This was not the way past immigration worked. People from Ireland, Italy and Germany and other countries came to the United States with nothing, were given nothing but the freedom to succeed by hard work and acceptance of the rules of our country. They did not come looking for a handout. They were welcomed but they had to earn their way. This is not so any more. All an immigrant has to do is get one foot on U.S. soil and he no longer has to work. He will get food, shelter, medical care and even free education. And if the Democrats have their way, a steady income even if the immigrant is unwilling to work.

The Illegal Immigration and Immigration Responsibility Act of 1996 was signed into law by President William Clinton after passing both houses of Congress. The act states that immigrants unlawfully present in the United States for over 180 days but less than 365 days must remain outside the U.S. for three years unless they obtain a pardon. If more than 365 days, they must stay outside the U.S. for 10 years unless they obtain a waiver. The bill is rather lengthy and has many provisions but it does call for mandated detainment of Illegal Immigrants that have been arrested for a crime followed by their deportation. The Federal Government has looked to the states and counties to assist them in carrying out the provisions of the Immigration Law, by detaining a criminal illegal alien for up to an additional 48 hours. The law has been amended in the past and has been subject to numerous Federal cases. The law requires the mandatory detention and ultimate deportation of criminal aliens, national security risks and persons under final orders of removal, who have committed aggravated felonies, are terrorist aliens, or have been illegally present in the country.

No doubt the law needs to be revisited and amended, and that some of the objections raised are valid. But it is the law and has been the law for over 20 years. Anarchy and tyranny arise when people choose to disregard any laws that they don't like. And this is what we are facing with the conduct of some cities, counties and states in the United States, which have come to be known as "Sanctuary cities"

A sanctuary city is one which permits residence by illegal immigrants (whether criminal or not) to help them avoid deportation. There are approximately 300 U.S. jurisdictions that have chosen to disregard Federal law.

Regrettably, Los Angeles Mayor Eric Garcetti, stated that his city will defy orders from the office of the Attorney General and continue offering a safe place for illegal aliens to stay. Likewise, Chicago Mayor Rohm Emanuel said his position of providing sanctuary to illegal immigrants will never change. And New York City Council spokesperson Melissa Mark-Vivirito said in continuing the City's opposition to Federal Law, "We are going to become the Administration's worst nightmare". The rape of a 14-year-old girl in Montgomery County, Maryland by an illegal immigrant apparently does not stop the State of Maryland seeking to become a sanctuary state.

New York City has roughly 500,000 undocumented residents. In 2017 New York City passed a bill that prohibits city agencies from working with the Federal Government to enforce existing Immigration laws and also prevents the use of city resources and funds for Federal Immigration enforcement. Chicago's Mayor Rahm Immanuel introduced in 2012 the "Welcoming City Ordinance" to protect illegal immigrants from being detained or deported.

In November 2017, the Washington Post stated that in the 168 counties in the United States where 11 million illegal immigrants live, 99 counties accepted Federal requests to detain arrestees. 69 sanctuary cities declined including major cities like Los Angeles, San Francisco, Chicago, Washington, DC, Seattle, Denver, Miami and New York. These cities are all in violation of information sharing laws.

No state in the union is more left leaning or more willing to violate the laws of our country than the state of California. Yet California has the highest poverty rate in the country, the highest state taxes, the highest cost of living and the highest disparity between the rich and the poor. The rich represented by the Hollywood rich and famous, does little to help the less advantaged. They enjoy their $10 million mansions, their limousines, their beautiful life styles, while those around them are in abject poverty. This has caused a rapid exodus of the middle class, which seems to be the case where-ever the Democrat socialist rule. One only has to look at the Oscar Night extravaganza to see how out of touch the entertainment community is with the poverty around them. These entertainers are quick to express their hatred, even calling for the assassination of the president, yet separate themselves from the working masses with their walled in mansions and their extravagant life styles. And as their voices of hatred are raised from the comfort of their million-dollar life styles, droves of the middle class are leaving the state because they cannot afford to live there anymore.

The Federal Administration is most concerned about the estimated 820,000 criminals that have been reported among the 11 million illegal immigrants in the U.S. These too are protected by the sanctuary cities.

To unilaterally flaunt Federal law is wrong. To help Illegal Immigrants who are also criminals to evade deportation is unlawful. The mayors of the sanctuary cities suggest no remedies, no compromises, no substitutes for the Illegal Immigration Act. This is where rational thought and logic break down and once again, we see the avoidance of Discourse and Dialogue, leading us to lawlessness and anarchy. And the problem at our borders continues to expand with over 1 million illegal immigrants expected to find their way into the United States over our Mexican border this year along with a massive import of illegal drugs from our Mexico neighbor, that will lead to more deaths of our American citizens. Our border patrol and ICE are overwhelmed. They have exhausted their detention facilities, there are 1000's of cases of illegal immigrants bringing diseases with them that need medical treatment. The human trafficking is controlled by the Mexican cartels, who are finding this almost as lucrative as the drug trade itself. Yet the Socialist Democrats continue to say there is no crisis even though every government agency connected with the border cry out that it is the worst crisis they have ever seen. This is just another example of how the Socialist Democrats seek to tear our nation apart. Why don't they listen to those who are on the scene and see with their own eyes the mounting crisis on the borders instead of deceiving their constituents into believing there is no problem on our border with Mexico? The only aim of the Democrat leaders is to gain power for themselves and so many of us are duped by them.

The Mueller Investigation

The Mueller Investigation, that went on for 2 years has more significance to our history than it deserves. It was a catalyst to a level of hatred never seen before in our history; a hatred by one group of our leaders and those that support them, the Democrats. Ever since Donald Trump defeated Hillary Clinton, the Democrats have spent literally no time on the affairs of state and wellbeing of its citizens, with their total focus being to delegitimatize and overthrow the government under President Trump, ignoring all else. We immediately learned of the direction that the Democrats would take in dividing our country on President Trump's Inauguration Day in January 2017 when fully one-third of the Democrat members of the House of Representatives, refused to attend the inauguration. This led the entertainment industry, our educational institutions and our media to take on the mantle of hatred and direct it towards President Trump and his administration. The Democrats had chosen to do battle with half of the country that supported Trump and see how it could destroy the Republican government under Trump regardless of what damage they would mete out to the citizens of the United States. Hatred is a terrible thing and to build on a foundation of hate always leads to the destruction of a society. And to sustain the hatred, the Democrats made the Mueller investigation its cornerstone to bring down President Trump. And even after the failed attempt, the Democrats continue to insist they will find a way to impeach President Trump. The Mueller investigation wasn't enough. 67 Democrats by boycotting the Inauguration, established that they would be harbingers of hate. This is their legacy and the legacy they wish to bestow on our country.

The Special Counsel Investigation of 2017-2019, also referred to as the Robert Mueller Investigation and the Russian Investigation started as an investigation of the Russian government's efforts to interfere in the 2016 U.S. Presidential election. It began on May 17, 2017 and would last 675 days. The purpose of the investigation was to determine if President Trump and his campaign had illegally worked with Russia to sway the 2016 Presidential election. The Mueller report released on Friday March 22, 2019, concluded that there was no collusion on the part of President Trump or his campaign. The hypocrisy of the Mueller Investigation and the Democrat unending attack on President Trump for supposed collusion with the Russians is that the Russians donated $0.00 to the Trump campaign but donated $145.6 million to the Clinton Foundation and yet only Trump was investigated.

It took 19 attorneys and $25.2 million spent between May 2017 and September 2018 and that docs not include expenditures form October 2, 2018 until March, 2019, which are estimated to bring the total costs to over $40 million. 2,800 subpoenas were issued, 500 search warrants executed; 230 orders for communication records; 50 orders authorizing use of pen registers, 13 requests to foreign governments for evidence and approximately 50 witnesses. 34 people were indicted or pleaded guilty, of which 26 were Russians and 8 were Americans. Of the 8, six were former advisors or associates of Trump and 2 were neither advisors or associates. None of those charged was on the issue of collaboration.

During the two years in a rush to judgment and with no evidence, President Trump was accused of everything including Treason by the media, the entertainment industry and the Democrats. Day after day we heard of cries for impeachment and statements that there was solid evidence that President Trump colluded with the Russians ad obstructed justice. You would think that after the Mueller investigation had unequivocally found that neither Trump nor his advisors or associates had colluded, the Democrats would if not willing to apologize at least stop the aptly named "witch hunt". For two years the Democrats have done nothing other than go after The President and the Republicans. Yet, the Democrats still seek to find a way to oust President Trump and they continue to vilify him with their hatred and still seek his impeachment. Other than daily attacks on Donald Trump by the likes of Adam Schiff, Chuck Schumer, Maxine Waters, Cory Booker, Elizabeth Warren, Chris Coons, Bernie Sanders, Al Green, Jerry Nadler, Mark Warner, Ron Wyden, Diane Feinstein, Dick Durban, Benjamin Cardin, Jeff Merkley, Brad Sherman, Steve Cohen and Richard Blumenthal just to name a few, the Democrats have done nothing to further the interests of American citizens. The one thing they have in common is their enormous hatred for President Trump and willingness to do virtually anything to gain power and control over our government. Other than vilifying the President for the past two years and seeking a way to get him out of office, the only things the Democrats have accomplished is to prevent a wall at our border and come up with the crazy and dangerous Green New Deal, a plan which would effectively destroy our country, putting many millions out of work, destroying the lives of all on fixed income and increasing those on welfare by 10's of millions. The Democrats would reduce our economy to the rubble we are witnessing in Venezuela today.

Recently, as a take-off on College Basketball's NCAA championships, a tournament sheet was put together called "Mueller Madness" and based on peoples' votes, the outcome would determine what liberal pundit ranks the worst at peddling the Trump-Russia Conspiracy Theory. As in the March Madness Basketball tournament, there were rankings of each pundit. Here are some of the excerpts from the rankings:

1. **Bill Kristol** – in the print category, Bill Kristol, in August 2018 predicted: Mueller will find there was collusion between Trump associates and Putin Operatives; that Trump knew about it and that Trump sought to cover it up and obstruct its investigation. Kristol made his comments on the basis of no evidence no facts; yet he was willing to promulgate his unfounded claims to further his own hatred of Trump. And of course, contrary to Kristol's claims, Trump never attempted to obstruct Mueller's investigation.

2. **Max Boot** – Columnist for the Washington Post in July 2017 wrote: "President Trump's mantra is no collusion, something he says as if sheer mind-numbing repetition can make it true. There is copious evidence of collusion".

3. **Rachel Maddow**, MSNBC commentator with her own nightly show provided her audience with interminable rants about the Kremlin not only electing Trump, but of colluding with Trump and practically running the U.S. Government. From February 20 to March 31 of 2017 her dossier focused broadcasts accounted for 53% of her time. Far from being an objective reporter, she was seen crying after the Mueller report concluded that there was no collusion. And for almost two years, Maddow treated her audience with her lies about President Trump and consistently displayed her hatred for Trump. In many ways she should have been ranked first, not only because she was the most virulent, but she ranted nightly. Truth and facts are totally foreign to Rachel Maddow and that can be said for many of the commentators on MSNBC.

4. **Joe Scarborough** another MSNBC commentator, who along with his sidekick Mika Brezinski

host the "Morning Joe" show. Over the past two years these two have pursued President Trump with hatred and vitriol – never with facts and reason. Scarborough constantly predicted President Trump's downfall at Mueller's hand saying: "The noose is tightening" He called the President a "White Racist", never explaining what President Trump had done to earn that epithet. Yet even today, Scarborough is unwilling to accept the findings of the Mueller investigation, even suggesting that the Attorney General William Barr has tampered with the report as much as he could. A once distinguished commentator for MSNBC, Scarborough has reduced himself to a peddler of pathetic, anti-Trump ramblings and lies.

5. **Laurence Tribe**, Harvard Law Professor tweeted in July 2017: "When Senior Democrats say: "There is evidence of both collusion and obstruction, you can take that to the bank. Trump beware". His words about Senior Democrats, once words of praise for them have turned out to be indictments of Senior Democrats, since there was no evidence of collusion or obstruction of justice.

6. **Alec Baldwin** – a has been movie actor has revived his career by his impersonation of a clueless jailbird, President Trump. Not exactly the model of a good citizen, it is amazing that Baldwin's only way back into the limelight involved a demonstration of vitriol and hatred toward our President.

7. **Joy Behar** – Host of ABC's show "The View" confidently predicted that Trump was going to prison, before a cheering live audience repeating: "He goes to jail; He goes to Jail; He goes to jail".

8. **John Brennan** – Former Director of the Central Intelligence Agency under Barrack Obama's administration and now a paid contributor to MSNBC as a National Security Analyst, once tweeted regarding Trump's press conference performance in Helsinki, that Trump's performance; "rose to and exceeded the threshold of "high crimes and misdemeanors" He went on to say that it was "nothing short of treasonous and he (Trump) is wholly in the pocket of Putin". In 2018 Brennan stated that Trump should prepare for the "forthcoming exposure of your malfeasance and corruption". On August 16, 2018 Brennan stated that President Trump's claim of no collusion with Russia was "hogwash". In 2019 after the release of the Mueller report, Brennan attempting to do his best to explain why he perpetuated a hoax about collusion between President Trump's Campaign and Russia for two years, became somewhat contrite stating that he had received bad information and he suspected there was more than there actually was. After becoming a contributor to MSNBC, Brennan's security clearance was revoked because: "Brennan's lying and recent conduct characterized by increasingly frenzied commentary is wholly inconsistent with access to the nation's most closely held secrets". Yet this action was widely condemned by the Democrats. I ask, should our former directors of the CIA ever be allowed to maintain the highest level of security clearance and know detailed and current highly classified intelligence and at the same time be paid as a national security analyst by a public network? MSNBC was counting on a direct "leakage" into the innermost activities of the CIA and would have had it if Brennan's clearance weren't revoked. The terrifying aspect of Brennan working for MSNBC is that he has much already existing top-secret information,

which he can share with MSNBC for top pay, and yet this doesn't bother the Democrats.

9. **Adam Schiff** - Democrat Congressman from California and Chair of the House Intelligence Committee refuses to accept the Mueller report saying that: "there may be for example evidence of collusion or conspiracy that is clear and convincing, but not proof beyond a reasonable doubt as is needed for criminal conviction." Despite Mueller's findings, Schiff continues to proclaim that there is significant evidence of collusion. As a result, the Republicans on the House Intelligence Committee have sought Schiff's removal as head of the committee saying that: "your willingness to continue to promote demonstrably false narrative is alarming. The findings of the Special Counsel conclusively refute your past and present assertions and have exposed you as having abused your position by knowingly promoting false information and having damaged the integrity of the committee and undermined the faith in U.S. government institutions". Later in this book we will discuss, how Schiff created his own report of the famous July phone-call between President Trump and the President of the Ukraine, rather than read from the official transcript of the phone call.

10. **Chris Hayes** – MSNBC host of the "Up with Chris Hayes" show, repeatedly vilified the President with the following statement just an example – ""A cornered president storms out as the Mueller Probe closes in". Hayes recently quipped on his television show that we only have 12 years to reduce our CO_2 emissions by 50%. The shear insanity of this statement is so symptomatic of the Democrat party that has promulgated and supports the Green New Deal.

11. **Jimmy Kimmel** – Host of the "Jimmy Kimmel Live "on ABC; quipped among others: "The president appears to be on a collision course with the law".

12. **Steve Colbert** – Host of the Late Show on CBS not only had the indecency to quip on National TV, that President Trump performed a vulgar act on Putin and that Trump was Putin's puppet, he also stated on National TV: "No collusion is Trump's Aloha. It means hello and I'm guilty". The audience found this funny.

13. **Kathy Griffin** – "Not contrite about holding up a severed, bloody effigy of Trump's head, the sick humor of this comedian, would say: "Just shut the f.. k up and prepare for prison"

14. **Paul Krugman** – New York Times – "There's really no question about Trump/Putin collusion"

15. **Jonathan Chalti** – New York Magazine suggested that President Trump has been a Russian asset since 1987.

16. **Donald Deutsch** – MSNBC contributor – "Donald Trump has been owned by Russians because of money".

17. **Adam Davidson** – Writer for the New Yorker: "We are at the end stages of the Trump presidency"

18. **Jenifer Rubin** – Washington Post. Evidence of collusion was her constant watchword

19. **Ana Navarro** – CNN contributor: "It's beginning to look a lot like Christmas and its beginning to look a lot like collusion".

20. **John Oliver** – Host of HBO's" Last Week, Tonight" – "A scandal with all the ramifications of Watergate."
21. **Richard Painter** – Law professor University of Minnesota claimed that: "Trump was colluding with the Russians". What is particularly disheartening here is that a law professor should know better that there is a presumption of innocence that can only be overturned by a preponderance of evidence in a civil case and proof beyond reasonable doubt in a criminal case.
22. **Senator Chris Coons** – liberal Democrat from Delaware as late as February 2019 claimed during a televised interview that yet undisclosed transcripts of recorded phone conversations conclusively prove that elements of the Trump campaign explicitly colluded with the Russians during the 2016 Presidential election.
23. **Richard Blumenthal** – Democrat Senator from Connecticut in 2017 raised the issue of impeaching President Trump.
24. **Angus King** – Senator from Maine a Democrat/Independent said that impeachment of President Trump should be considered without giving any reasons for impeachment.
25. **The U.S. Senate Intelligence Committee** - split along party lines with all Democrats stating that there was enough circumstantial evidence to support collusion by President Trump and his campaign team. The Democrats so willing to condemn without any proof included; Mark Warner -Virginia; Diane Feinstein – California; and Ro Wyden -California. There were at least 6 Democrat led Congressional committees probing whether President Trump colluded with Moscow or tried to obstruct justice.
26. **The Impeach Trump Leadership Political Action Committee (PAC)** this was started by Democratic Party congressmen Boyd Roberts from California.
27. **Maxine Waters** – Congresswomen from California, noted for living in a large mansion outside her district as well as an upscale home in Washington, DC, has based her total visibility to the public and to the district she is supposed to be serving on perpetually crying out for the impeachment of President Trump. She is a constant reminder of the hypocrisy of the Democrats, who constantly speak loudly against the disparity in income in the United States, while taking for themselves every benefit of the disparity, living a life of luxury that the average American cannot even comprehend. In addition to Watters, notorious for living the good life, while professing to be for the common man are: Democrats, Pelosi, Sanders, Feinstein, Schumer, Gellibrand, Booker, Schiff, Nadler, Warren, Blumenthal, Coons Durban just to name a few.
28. **Brad Sherman** – Democrat Congressman from California, in June 2017 joins Al Green in drafting Articles of Impeachment against President Trump for obstruction of justice.
29. **Steve Cohen**- Democrat representative from Virginia in August to November 2017 announced he would introduce Articles of Impeachment for "failing to provide moral leadership"
30. **Al Green** – Representative from Texas early on called for Donald Trump's impeachment for obstruction of justice. In December 2018, Green brought Articles of Impeachment to a vote in the House based on: "Associating the Presidency with White Nationalism, Neo-Nazism and

Hatred and Inciting Hatred and Hostility". The Resolution was defeated 364 to 58 with all 58 being Democrats on the grounds presented by Al Green. In January 2018, Green brought up the Resolution for a second time and this time it was defeated by a vote of 355-66, again all voting for the motion were Democrats.

31. **Anthony Bourdain** - celebrated chef, Anthony Bourdain, host of the CNN show "No Reservation", in September 2017 stated that if he were the cook for President Trump, he would serve him poison, specifically "Hemlock".

32. **Senator Cory Booker (New Jersey) and Representative Maxine Waters (California)** - These leaders of the Democratic party call upon their constituents to riot against the Conservative Right and to "get in the face" of Conservatives in restaurants, elevators and on the streets. Booker would also mandate that we give up eating beef and that cattle be removed from our country because of the methane gas they produce. Cory Booker is a candidate for President in 2020.

33. **Eric Holder**. Former Attorney General under Barack Obama calls for kicking Republicans, when they go low.

34. **Hillary Clinton** – remember her saying that half of Republicans are deplorable? And she applauded Madeline Albright when Albright said "there was a special place in hell for all women" who didn't vote for Hilary Clinton. Well now she tells her liberal Democrats to throw civility toward Republicans out the window until the Democrats retake Congress. Does this sound like a party that would represent and treat fairly the 50% of the people in the United States who are Conservative Republicans?

35. **Tom Perez**, elected by the Democrats as Chairman of the Democratic National Party, who stated on July 3, 2018 that Socialist political candidates like Alexandria Ocasio-Cortez is the future of the party. He went on to say that along with Ocasio-Cortez, Ben Jealous a socialist running for governor of Maryland is another "spectacular candidate and represent the party's future. "We are no longer a country where the differences in parties were simply along liberal and conservative lines". Now capitalism and our basic freedoms of life, liberty and pursuit of happiness are under attack. Socialist implies dictating to the constituents what they can have and what they can do. Freedom of choice will be abolished. Never has our way of life been so threatened and the irony is it is at a time when the United States is doing so well by almost every measure of economic well-being.

36. **Kamala Harris – Senator** from California and candidate for President. known for her unrelenting attack on Supreme Court Justice candidate Brett Kavanaugh, is also pro-choice, quipping: "can you think of any laws that gives the government the power to make decisions about the male body?" She ignores entirely that it is not the women's body that is being interfered with, but the body of the unborn child that the government seeks to protect. Harris, along with most of her Democrat colleagues sanction abortion right up to the time of delivery and even after the child is born. She is also for legalizing marijuana because it will "bring joy to people".

37. **Elizabeth Warren** - Senator from Massachusetts and candidate for President, known for using her fraudulent claim of being a significant part Native to get her a cushy and extraordinary high paying job as a Harvard Law professor. Along with Bernie Sanders, Warren is the most vocal liberal left, and has consistently vilified the President and called for his impeachment

38. **Michael Avanatti** – One-time presidential candidate for 2020, and a Trump antagonist, representing porn-star Stormy Daniels in a fraudulent claim against Trump, has now been arrested and charged by the Federal government in two separate fraud cases. The attorney for porn star Stormy Daniels was put forth by the Democrats as a candidate for president. Really? Not anymore. Avanatti has been arrested on Federal charges in two separate cases. The U.S. attorney for the Southern District of NY has charged Avanatti for allegedly trying to extort $20 million from Nike. In California, Avanatti has been charged with wire fraud where he used $1.6 million settlement for a client for personal use and to pay expenses for his coffee business. CBS news in November, 2018 placed Avanatti on its list as one of the Democrats that could be our next president

What do the liberal left media, our liberal Senators and Congressmen, our liberal left entertainers and our liberal left educators have in common? They join together in their hatred and vilification of the President and will seduce the public, with false information and a steady bombardment of hatred toward the Trump administration and Republicans. Remember it was their leader, Hillary Clinton that was quoted as calling Republicans the "deplorables" and vigorously supported Madeline Albrights statement that "there is a special place in hell for women who didn't vote for Hilary Clinton". When interviewed by Anderson Cooper on National TV, he asked her who was her greatest enemy and Hillary without hesitation quipped "The Republicans". This remains the mind-set of the Democrats, especially those who are going to run for President in 2020. The Democrats are on record that they have no interest in representing anyone other than Democrats.

Further, the Democrats have introduced time and again a new concept into the American way of thinking. They not only raise the presumption of guilt, but they indict and convict on the unsupported, uncorroborated evidence and in some cases have falsified documents and information to raise the presumption of guilt. The Democrats even seek to pack the Supreme Court by raising the number of Justices to 12. If nothing else, the Liberal Democrats are prepared to destroy American Jurisprudence in order to gain power and control of our government and our lives.

And yet it still is not over. Even though the Mueller Report has found Donald Trump not guilty of collusion or conspiracy, the Democrats now spend all their time trying to find "obstruction of justice" on which to build a case for impeachment. Are the Democrats ever going to get down to the business of government? 2.5 years have been wasted by the Democrats and between $40 and $50 million dollars. If there is no collusion how did President Trump obstruct justice? And we have yet to hear the grounds for impeachment, although the cries for impeachment continue almost daily from the likes of Maxine Waters, Adam Schiff, Jerry Nadler and many others on the liberal left.

Rounds Two and Three of the Mueller Investigation

Just when most of us felt that the investigation by Robert Mueller and his team of radical left supporters had been finally ended by their report, which found no collusion or conspiracy by the Trump campaign, the Democrats remain dissatisfied. Regardless of the cost to America not only in money but in getting the issues facing the United States attended to, the Democrats decided that they needed to interrogate Robert Mueller further and have him explain the findings in his report. Over Robert Mueller's strong resistance to such an interrogation, the Democrats House Judiciary Committee Chaired by Democrat, Jerry Nadler and the House Intelligence committee, chaired by Adam Schiff, compelled Mueller to be subject to two separate interrogations on the same day covering a total of 7 hours. On July 24th in the morning, Chairman Nadler opened the interrogation of Mueller and in the afternoon, Adam Schiff, presided over a second interrogation.

Strangely, Mueller brought his chief counsel to both meetings, presumably to protect him. Robert Mueller insisted that his longtime aide, Aaron Zebley be sworn in as a witness at both hearings to advise him on his answers. Zebley was Mueller's Deputy Special Counsel and had day to day oversight of the Mueller investigation. The two hearings would lead to the conclusion that Robert Mueller was clearly not the author of the report, nor was he familiar with it. Although he dedicated his name to the report, it was written by his deputy and the many Trump-hating, Hillary Clinton supporting attorneys hired by Mueller to undertake the investigation.

It was interesting to note that Mueller couldn't even remember which President appointed him U.S. Attorney. When asked he named President Bush and had to be corrected that it was President Ronald Regan

Early in Mueller's testimony before the House Judiciary Committee he was asked by Ted Lieu, Democrat representative from California if the reason Mueller hadn't pushed for an indictment of Trump for obstruction of justice or any other crimes was because of an opinion by the Justice Department's Office of Legal Council (OLC) that a sitting President cannot be indicted so long as he is in office. "Is that correct?" Lieu asked and Mueller said "correct".

Later in the afternoon at the House Intelligence Committee hearing, he corrected himself that as was stated in his "Mueller Report": "We did not reach a determination as to whether the President committed a crime" and the OLC opinion had other things to do with his findings. The President wasn't indicted simply because there was no reason to indict him and fundamental to our Democracy, which the Democrats seem to endlessly disregard is that one is innocent until proven guilty.

Mueller further contradicted himself (and his report) when he told Republican representative from Georgia, Doug Collins that collusion and conspiracy were not the same thing.

Mueller's apparent personal conflict of interest was pointed out by Republican representative from Texas, Louis Gohmert, when before Mueller's appointment as Special Counsel he had a meeting with Trump just one day before as a job interview for the position of Director of the FBI. Mueller claimed he was not a candidate; he was just an advisor to the President regarding potential candidates for the job. Let the reader decide, but can anyone believe that an obvious candidate for Director of FBI such as Mueller, meets privately with the President at the exact time the President is seeking to nominate a Director of the FBI, that he was not there as a potential candidate?

Even after Jerry Nadler's all morning interrogation of Mueller that revealed nothing new, even after 2.5 years and $40 million of expenditures in an attempt to find an indictable offense of collusion or conspiracy, New York Congressman Jerry Nadler and Adam Schiff are still seeking ways to impeach the President. They have done nothing for their constituents during that time. They have been derelict in providing representation to the people they were elected to represent. They, like almost all the other Democrat members of the House of Representatives and Senate have spent almost no time on anything other than seeking to indict or impeach the President. And further, the Democrats have sought in every way to obstruct any legislation that would be beneficial to the country, that could be credited to the President. I have gone into detail throughout this book, how the Democrats have sought to disrupt our country and establish a totalitarian state. Jerry Nadler and Adam Schiff and their respective committees are examples of how the Democrats seek to obstruct the business of our government and try to make it appear that it is the fault of the Republicans and the Trump Administration.

We cannot overlook the work of Adam Schiff, representative from California and Chairman of the House Intelligence Committee. In his closing remarks at the wind-up of his committee's interrogation of Robert Mueller he made a very telling statement that is very probative of the mindset of the Democrat Party. He said: "It doesn't matter whether the Trump Campaign's contacts with Russia or President Trump's attempt to obstruct special counsel Robert Mueller's investigation amount to a crime. It is Trump's disloyalty, although not criminal, but it violates the obligation of citizenship, our devotion to a core principles". Think of what this saying to all of us American citizens. We can be prosecuted and put in jail even if we have not committed a crime if the state finds for any reason you are deemed disloyal. This is exactly what a Totalitarian state preaches. This is what justified Hitler's assassination of 6 million Jews. This is what justified Stalin's purges of millions in Russia. History tells us of Stalin's "Great Purge" from 1934 and 1939 when over 1 million dissidents were imprisoned and 700,000 executed. They had been found disloyal for one reason or another. But the full count during Stalin's regime totaled 6 million deliberate killings and 18 million incarcerations in their Gulag system. This is what justified Castro's murdering all that did not support him. Disagreement with him became a crime and the supposed disloyal Cuban was executed. This is what justified Kim Jong Un's purges in North Korea. Supposed disloyalty or disagreement with his regime and you were executed. And this was the justification for the purges and annihilation of millions under China's dictator Mao Zedong from 1943 to 1976. Mao Zedong, Chairman of the Communist Party caused the deaths of as many as 70 million from starvation, prison labor or mass execution. Fidel Castro followed a policy of mass executions of his political adversaries and the internment of thousands of gays and lesbians. In addition to purges of those in his own party that he believed to be disloyal, Castro punished dissident artists, writers and journalists. Yet at the height of his power, he was strongly supported by the liberal left in America.

Long time Democrat and Counsel to the ACLU, Alan Dershowitz, remarked about the interrogations of Mueller by the Nadler and Schiff Committees on July 24, 2019. He said: "It's a sad day for Robert Mueller. It showed he wasn't in charge. Don't call it the Mueller Report. It should be called the Staff Report. I am concerned who was really in charge of the report. The staff, who wrote the report were haters of Trump. Why did Mueller select so many who were so active in destroying Trump?" The reader should take note that highly respected liberal Democrat, Alan Dershowitz has found the Mueller report biased and unjust. Would that more Democrats examine the facts on both sides carefully and objectively and with humility recognize that maybe they have been dead wrong in their quest to impeach President Donald Trump.

When we are willing to seek impeachment of the President, when there is no crime and where the impeachment carries the potential of being put to death for treason, we are seeking to carry out the same purges and genocide that the totalitarian governments of Hitler, Stalin, Mao Zedong, Kim Jong Un and Castro had previously imposed on their citizens. It is not just Nadler and Schiff that would lead us to a totalitarian state and impeach the President even though no crime has been committed. We can accuse the whole Democrat party as being willing to indict, convict, impeach and purge President Trump, without any evidence of a crime. And included in these totalitarian members of the Democratic Party besides Schiff and Nadler are such highly ranked members of the party as: Maxine Waters, Bernie Sanders, Cory Booker, Elizabeth Warren, Kamala Harris, Tom Perez (Chairman of DNC), Keith Ellison (Deputy Chief of the DNC), Al Green and of course The Squad. The totalitarian radical left members of our House and Senate are too numerous to identify here, but I have mentioned most of them somewhere in this book.

Fusion GPS and Christopher Steele- Before Robert Mueller was appointed special prosecutor on May 17, 2017 to launch a probe into Russian Interference in the U.S. Presidential election of 2016 and whether Trump's campaign associates were involved in these efforts. In July, 2016 the FBI began investigating the Russian Government's attempts to influence the presidential election. Fusion GPS, a firm that was founded by former national journalists was right in the middle of the investigation, before Mueller became appointed.

It was the firm that funded Christopher Steele, with monies received from Hillary Clinton's campaign and the Democratic National Committee and gave rise to the infamous Steel Dossier which led to the obtaining of FISA warrants to be used in efforts to indict Trump. This led to the most unbelievable statements by Robert Mueller, who claimed he did not know who Fusion GPS was and that the FISA warrants were not within the purview of his investigation, because they were before his time. How can a special counsel claim that material facts occurring before his appointment are not within his purview? How can an investigation team costing $40 million and involving 15 lawyers investigating for almost two years, claim that they had no knowledge of Fusion GPS, or that the Christopher Steele Dossier and FISA warrants were not within their purview? There is either a severe dereliction of duty on the part of Mueller and his staff or there is outright perjury. It is one or the other.

Christopher Steele is a former British intelligence officer with the Secret Service Intelligence Service – M16 from 1987 until his retirement in 2009. He ran the Russian desk at M16 headquarters in London between 2006 and 2009. In 2009 he co-founded Orbis Business Intelligence, a private intelligence firm. He would author the infamous Steel Dossier, which although based on unverified and uncorroborated information was used to obtain a FISA warrant

Steele's Dossier contained a listing of unverified almost unspeakable allegations about President Trump and it emerged in the news on January 10, 2017, just 10 days before President Trump's inauguration. Fusion GPS was paid by the Clinton campaign and the DNC to retain Christopher Steele to conduct the research that led to the Steele Dossier. The Dossier prepared by Steele contained lurid allegations about Trump's supposed activities in Russia. Steel himself acknowledged that the information in his memos "needed to be analyzed and further investigated and verified". Nevertheless, he shared his Dossier with the FBI and the Justice Department relied on it to obtain a FISA warrant to conduct surveillance on a Trump associate, Carter Page. Although Steele's Dossier circulated the media during the fall of 2016, news organizations were unable to verify any of its claims. The dossier made 6 claims about Trump's ties to Russia, none of which were ever subsequently confirmed. The unverified, if not fraudulent dossier was used as the basis of a FISA warrant.

A FISA warrant is issued by the Foreign Intelligence Surveillance Court or FISA court, allowing wiretapping and electronic surveillance of someone suspected of spying for a foreign government. The court's actions are carried out in secret. The court has 11 members and the warrants are issued for up to 12 months. Since 2013 the FISA court has denied only 12 warrants and granted more than 34,000 requests. Robert Mueller, while Director of the FBI, once was hauled before the FISA court to address a large number of instances in which the FBI cheated in obtaining a FISA warrant. The sin that plagued the FBI almost two decades ago involved omissions of material fact by agents applying for FISA warrants. These instances occurred before Mueller became director of the FBI, but was a problem the FISA court expected him to address. Omissions are a very serious matter at the FISA court, because it is the only court in America where the accused gets no representation or chance to defend himself. And this means that the obligation is paramount for the FBI to disclose all evidence of both guilt and innocence about the target of a FISA warrant. Robert Mueller based on his experience with the FISA court clearly knew the importance of objectivity and truthfulness required in a FISA Application, yet during his whole investigation, he made no effort to examine the veracity of a key investigation and report, namely the Steele Dossier, which gave rise to the initiating of the Mueller special investigation.

The Steele Dossier was composed of hearsay based on hearsay. It was based on anonymous sources hearing things from other Russian anonymous sources. Steele did nothing to verify any of the anonymous claims made in the Dossier.

James Comey - The then FBI director, James Comey said in his testimony, that the FBI relied upon Christopher Steele's dossier. This was a clear self- indictment of James Comey, because he signed off on the FISA application under oath, by which he certified that the FBI had corroborated the facts and claims that were specified in the application. Comey was blatantly misleading the FISA court and the FISA judge would never have issued the surveillance warrant, if he had known that the information in the warrant had never been verified. Further, the FISA court was unaware that the Steel dossier had been funded by the DNC and that fact alone would have killed the FISA warrant. The FBI agents who signed the FISA application have actually perpetrated a fraud on the FISA court, which is an actionable crime that so far has remained unpunished.

That Comey had politicized the FBI in his unsuccessful attempt to keep Donald Trump from becoming president became clear with the August 29, 2019 release of the Justice Department's Inspector General Michael Horowitz's report. This 83-page report dealt harshly with the FBI director Comey's conduct. And we can all remember how brutal the criticism came from the left after President Trump's firing of the FBI Director, which in fact is an unlimited right that President Trump had. It would turn out to be the right thing considering Comey's severe dereliction of duty. Horowitz's report berated Comey for leaking memos about conversations with the President for his personal and political gain. Specifically, the report concluded that Comey had improperly released FBI material in order to launch the Special Investigation into the Presidential Election by Robert Mueller. Here are some of the specific points raised in the Inspector General's report:

1. Comey set a dangerous example for over 35,000 current FBI employees.
2. Comey kept FBI memos after he was discharged without authorization.
3. Comey failed in his responsibility to safeguard sensitive information.
4. Comey broke the law by the unauthorized disclosure of sensitive information for personal gain
5. Comey, after removal from office violated his employment agreement by failing to surrender copies of memos, some of which were classified confidential.

The report went on to say that: "Comey's characterization of the memos he disclosed as personal records has no support in the law and is wholly incompatible with the plain language of the statutes, regulations and policies defining Federal Records and the terms of Comey's FBI employment agreement. And yet, all we heard from the Democrat leaders and the biased press, that Comey was a trusted and wonderful FBI director and President Trump's discharge of him was possibly a reason for Trump's impeachment. How many of us were convinced by the left that Comey was mis-treated and President Trump was at fault?

Peter Strzok – He was a former FBI agent and Chief of the Counter-espionage section. He was born and raised in Iran, went to school there and speaks Farsi fluently. Strzok led the FBI's investigation of Hillary Clinton's unauthorized use of her private e-mail server to communicate and distribute classified documents. He also led the FBI investigation into Russia's interference in United States 2016 Presidential election. In June and July 2017, Strzok became the most senior FBI agent on the Mueller team charged with the investigation of links between Donald Trump's presidential campaign and the

Russian Government until August 2017 when he was removed from the investigation and assigned to the FBI Human Resources Branch. Mueller removed Strzok from the investigation when he became aware of Strzok's personal hatred of Donald Trump, described particularly in Strzok's text messages he exchanged with his adulterous lover, Lisa Page. Lisa Page also worked on the Mueller Team and was an FBI counsel until May 2018. Lisa Page and Peter Strzok kept their clandestine affairs hidden from their respective spouses and text messaging was one of their secret means of communication. It wouldn't be until August 2018 the Strzok would finally be fired by the then FBI Deputy Director David Bowditch and thereby lose his security clearance.

On July 12, 2018 Strzok was questioned by members of Congress and denied that his and Page's text messages of unfettered hatred for Donald Trump influenced his investigation into Hillary Clinton, which led to no criminal charges. In one instance according to a Washington Post report on June 14, 2018, the U.S. Inspector General's report revealed that Strzok told page that Trump's election would be stopped. "Trump's not going to become president, right? (Page). "No, no he won't, we will stop it" (Strzok). This text correspondence between Strzok and Page was sent in August, 2016 just a few months before the election. There were apparently thousands of text messages between Strzok and Page, but unfortunately, they were destroyed. In December, 2018, the Dept. of Justice's (DOJ), Office of Inspector General (OIG) released a report stating that Mueller's team had deleted thousands of text messages between Strzok and Page before turning the iphones over to OIG. Both Strzok's and Page's phones had been scrubbed clean by the Mueller team.

The extent of Strzok's and Page's hatred and loathing of President Trump, would suggest that they would do anything even within the FBI to prevent Trump from becoming President. There were others beside Comey, Strzok and Page within the FBI that through their hatred sought to block the presidency of Trump. Bias, hatred and vendettas should never be part of our FBI. They should and must be above that.

Mueller would claim under oath that he knew nothing about Peter Strzok's bias against Trump or of Strzok's texts of limitless hatred toward Trump and that Strzok was on a personal mission to stop Trump from becoming president. Mueller further stated under oath that he was not involved in approving the fourth FISA warrant against Carter Page which occurred in June 2017 the month after he was appointed special investigator. Mueller stated under oath that he was not in the approval chain for the FISA application. How can that be? Who was running the investigation if the head is not involved in obtaining the FISA Warrant? A FISA warrant is one of the most special and important documents, which is granted by a FISA Court based on an application of the highest integrity and credibility and under oath. How can Mueller, the signer of the report named after him, not be involved in obtaining or approving the FISA application?

The Democrats latest Attempt to Impeach Trump –
The Ukraine Controversy and the "Whistleblower".

For over three years, the Democrats have tried to impeach Trump and drive him and the Republicans from office. After spending $40 million, the Mueller report came back finding that there was no collusion with Russia by Donald Trump. The Democrats tried vigorously with hatred and vitriol to prevent Bret Kavanaugh from becoming a Supreme Court Justice. They did everything they could to disrupt President Trump's negotiations with China and North Korea. The public heard almost every day that President Trump was guilty of something and should be impeached, although they could never tell you exactly what. There were many of the radical left Democrats that were calling his acts treasonous without ever saying what was the basis for their claim. Meanwhile, under President Trump, the economy and the welfare of the people improved spectacularly. The lowest unemployment in 50 years at 3.7% for all ethnic and racial groups; real wage increases especially for minorities; lower taxes and more income in workers' paychecks, a solid increase in the stock market, low borrowing rates for loans and mortgages and a huge expansion of jobs, especially in the manufacturing sector. The Democrats and the media never even mention these very significant accomplishments during the past three years. All the Democrats have done for three years is try to find a way to impeach President Trump. Outside of that, what have the Democrat Legislators done for their country or for their district?

So, a new charge had to be made by the Democrats to unseat President Trump. In their only goal of gaining power, the Democrats are prepared to increase your taxes; render many unemployed, sink our country into levels of unsustainable debt and allow illegal immigrants, including many criminals and members of MS-13 and more drugs into our country through open borders and by doing away with border patrols and ICE. We are already losing 70,000 lives a year from drug overdoses and the Democrats are prepared to have this expand many times over this number in order to gain power and control over our country. Homelessness in America is uncontrolled and getting worse, in the cities around the country run by Democrats. Think just how much worse it will be with increased unemployment and millions of new illegal aliens taking part in the Democrat created welfare state. I have covered in detail how the National Health plan and the Green New Deal will destroy our country by increasing our unemployment exponentially; placing an unbearable tax burden on our citizens; creating such a debt burden on our country that our interest rates and inflation will soar and our stock market will lose 80% to 90% of its value. I have covered this in detail elsewhere in this book.

This Whistle Blower episode is more about the Democrats destroying "due process", and the right to confront your accuser and the abrogation of our rights guaranteed by the U.S. Constitution.

The Whistleblower Act of 1989 – The whistleblower Act of 1989 is a Federal Law that protects "whistleblowers" who work for the government and report the existence of an activity constituting a violation of laws, rules and regulations or mis-management, gross waste of funds, or abuse of authority, or a substantial and specific danger to public health and safety. All the "Whistleblower" needs to do is to give his opinion that someone in the government has breached any of these widespread reasons for misconduct. Normally, he must have first-hand knowledge of the wrong-doing, but the Democrats have expanded it to hearsay. The Whistle-blower is protected from incrimination or loss of job arising out of his "whistleblowing" even if he has performed some dereliction of duty, such as breach of trust, or publicizing, private, privileged or top-secret information. He or she is also entitled to "anonymity" that flies in the face of Amendment 6 to the Constitution.

Amendment VI to the Constitution requires that: "in all criminal prosecution, the accused must be informed of the nature and cause of the accusation, be confronted with the witnesses against him; to have compulsory process for obtaining witnesses in his favor and the assistance of counsel for his defense" The Democrats, under Adam Schiff, have breached Amendment VI, in its entirety. The Democrats would have you believe that an inquiry initiated by a whistleblower for the specific purpose of impeaching someone, in this case the President, does not fall under Amendment VI. What is the goal of impeachment in this case? To find the President guilty of high crimes and misdemeanors and remove him from office. Does anyone believe that the actions taken by Adam Schiff's committee related to the Ukraine controversy is not a form of prosecution for a crime?

Adam Schiff and his committee are applying the same "Gestapo" tactics that existed under Hitler during the Rise of the Socialist Reich. A "whistle blower" would go to the Gestapo and claim that his neighbor was reading banned books; or was making statements against the third Reich and Hitler or worst of all was protecting a Jewish family from certain death at the hands of the Nazi enforcers. It would even get so bad that the "Whistle Blowers" were often children indoctrinated by the Socialist State to turn in their parents for violations of the Third Reich's edicts. The German "whistleblower" was roundly applauded by the Gestapo and the Nazi Government leaders for spying on their neighbors and turning them in. The Gestapo would break and enter into the home of the Whistleblower's neighbor early in the morning, forcibly take him away and incarcerate him without any "due process". There would be no trial; the Gestapo would merely order the execution of the accused and he would disappear without any record of his existence remaining. In a similar fashion the Democrats and their socialist left press have presumed the president's guilt and convinced many with the help of the radical left media that there is no need for due process or the assumption of innocence in the case of President Trump. They have used force and early morning raids to take witnesses from their families and homes. History tends to repeat itself and the tactics of the Democrats are really not any different from the Socialist state under Hitler. Fortunately, there is still some small amount of Democracy left and the Democrats did not get away with their first attempt of impeachment through the Mueller Investigation Now they are looking at the Ukraine Controversy as a way to get rid of President Trump. Remember the Democrat presidential candidates" s principal platform is impeaching Trump. They have done nothing in three years. Beyond impeaching Trump, the only plans the Democrats have are ones that will destroy America.

The Ukraine Controversy – The charge made by the Democrats is that President Trump attempted to solicit foreign interference in America for Trump's personal and political benefit during a private, confidential telephone call in July, 2019 with Ukrainian President Volodymyr Zelensky. The controversy was launched by an un-named "Whistleblower" who reported that he knew from second hand sources that the President Trump had asked Zelensky to investigate Joe Biden and his son Hunter Biden, in reference to their private dealings with a large Ukrainian Natural gas company. It appears that huge economic benefits were granted to Hunter Biden at the very time his father then Vice-President Joe Biden was officially representing the United States in its dealings with the Ukraine. Although the "Whistleblower" had not heard the Trump conversation with Zelensky, he was reporting what someone who had overheard the conversation had reported to the "Whistleblower". Based on what the Whistleblower had been told, he concluded that President Trump may have cancelled a trip to the Ukraine by Vice President Michael Pence and briefly with-held the delivery of $400 million to the Ukraine. President Zelensky voluntarily and strongly confirmed that he had experienced no pressure or no "quid pro quo" from President Trump and confirmed President Trump's assertion that there was no coercion, nor any impropriety related to the telephone call. President Trump's concern was with the improper if not criminal misconduct by Presidential candidate Joe Biden and his son's dealings with the Ukraine, while Biden was Vice-President. The "Whistleblower", without first-hand knowledge, which had been the standard for all prior whistleblowing cases, had breached his duty of non-disclosure of confidential and potentially classified information, thereby damaging all future communications between the United States and the heads of states around the world, on his questionable opinion that President Trump's phone call was potentially an impeachable offense that his fellow-Democrats could use to unseat the President and thereby allow the Democrats to regain the Presidency. The Democrats, headed by Adam Schiff, immediately concluded that the Ukraine controversy could replace the failed Mueller investigation and now the Democrats could once again be off and running on their "purge through impeachment. Schiff's lack of personal integrity was made abundantly clear when he opened his impeachment hearing by supposedly quoting the transcript of the telephone conversation between President Trump and Ukrainian President Volodymyr Zelensky. The words Schiff read to the world and were written into the Congressional Record as Trump's official conversation with Zelensky were a fictional, fraudulent rendition created by Schiff, himself. It was an audacious fraud.

In 2014, then Vice President Joe Biden was appointed by President Obama to be the diplomatic lead in trying to support the new post 2014 revolutionary Ukrainian Government under Arseniy Katsenyuk. Subsequently, on April 18, 2014, Joe Biden's son, Hunter Biden became a member of the board of Burisma Holdings, a Ukrainian energy exploration and production company, and one of the largest producers of natural gas. Hunter Biden, although he had no energy background, did not speak Ukrainian and had no relationship with the company until his father had become special U.S. representative to the Ukraine, was suddenly being paid $50,000 per month as a director and Hunter Biden's company was hired at the same time receiving over another $100,000 a month as a consulting fee. Hunter and his company were taking down $166,000 per month. Vice President Biden had been given the task in April 2014 to help the Ukrainian government expand domestic production of natural gas and the U.S. was prepared to provide the Ukraine with $1 billion in loan guarantees.

In 2015, Viktor Sorkin became Prosecutor General of the Ukraine and inherited the investigation of

Burisma's owner Mykola Ziochovsky over allegations of money laundering, tax evasion and corruption. The investigation of Burisma would unquestionably raise serious concerns as to why and for what purpose Joe Biden's son, Hunter had been placed on the Board of Burisma receiving $50,000 per month and what if anything Hunter Biden was contributing to Burisma. The apparent indication was absolutely nothing. It became a bit clearer in December 2015, when Vice President Joe Biden visited Kiev and informed the Ukrainian government that he, Joe Biden, would withhold U.S. loan guarantees to Ukraine unless Vicktor Shokin was removed as Prosecutor General. Joe Biden would even brag publicly in a televised interview how he unilaterally orchestrated the removal of Viktor Shokin by withholding $1 billion of U.S. loan guarantees and this effectively shut down the investigation of Joe Biden's son, Hunter. In a separate deal, this time with China, Joe Biden flies to Shanghai aboard Air Force Two along with his son. He talks to leaders there and the next thing you know, Hunter Biden's investment company receives $1.5 billion in funding from the Chinese.

What is the difference between Trump's private call to the President of Ukraine requesting an investigation of Hunter Biden's dealings with Burisma and Joe Biden's actual threat to withhold $1 billion of loan guarantees unless Ukraine performs a specific act, namely, the removal of the Ukraine Prosecutor General? In Trump's case, it involved a private communication between Presidents being revealed by a "whistleblower" who had no direct knowledge of the communication. The transcript of the call and the affirmation by Ukrainian President Zelensky, substantiated that there was no "quid pro quo", yet the Democrats under the leadership of Adam Schiff opened yet another investigation in the Democrats' on-going attempts to impeach President Trump. In the opening of his inquisition, instead of reading the transcript of President Trump's call, Schiff fraudulently gives his own rendition of the transcript and implies it is word for word, yet his rendition bears no resemblance to the actual transcript. This is another example of just how far the Democrats will go to overthrow our government. Fraud, deceit and perjury play important roles in everything they have done to remove President Trump. And even assassination has been mentioned numerous times by the liberal left as a means to remove our President.

By way of comparison, Joe Biden demands a "quid pro quo"; he orders the Ukrainian government to fire the Prosecutor General Viktor Sorkin, or he would personally withhold $1 billion of U.S. loan guarantees. As a result, Joe Biden and his family gained an immediate personal benefit. The investigation of Burisma and Hunter Biden was dropped.

Do the actions of either rise to an impeachable offense or high crime, misdemeanor or treason? Maybe not. But the Democrats ignore Joe Biden's obvious "quid pro quo", using government funds for his personal benefit, while seeking to prosecute President Trump for a questionable quid pro quo at best. The hypocrisy is self-evident. It is just another example of the Democrats trying to bring down our government at all cost. And if they succeed, they will inflict on all of us a level of pain we cannot even imagine even in the wildest of our dreams. I have been pointing this out to the reader in detail throughout this book.

The Cost of public disclosure of communications between heads of state

What is the cost of the public release of a private communication between a president of the United States and a leader of a foreign country and the attending cost of impeachment?

We will no longer be able to have frank and open discussions with the heads of state of other countries, especially at times of serious peril to our security. The foreign leaders will never speak openly with our President ever again, especially where multiple third parties can hear or record the communication. "Quid pro Quos" are not a bad thing. They are most often the means of compromise. Our President needs to be able to explore different alternatives with his counterparts in foreign countries. Give and take may be required that may not be totally acceptable to either party. But our President should not be second-guessed and criticized where those criticizing have the ulterior and sole motive to obtain power for themselves, Thanks to the Democrats, our foreign relations have taken a massive step backward and at this time, with the world's ability to initiate the delivery of nuclear weapons in a matter of minutes, an important trusted call between our president and the potential adversary can no longer be assured.

CHAPTER 18

The Democrats and the Law

IN NOVEMBER 2010, the citizens of Oklahoma by a 70% majority passed a "Save our State Amendment" which: "forbids courts from considering or using Islamic (Sharia) law. The U.S. District Court Judge Vicki Miles-La Grange a long time Democrat and appointee of Bill Clinton, overturned the law claiming it was unconstitutional on the grounds of religious freedom to ban the laws of foreign entities or religions and her decision was confirmed by the 10th Circuit Court of Appeals. How can a law that protects its citizenry from having their rights violated by the application of law other than U.S. be deemed unconstitutional? Although a law banning the use of Sharia law in Federal or State courts is still unconstitutional in Oklahoma according to the 10th District Court of Appeals, this is not applicable throughout the United States. There are 7 states that have passed similar bans against Sharia law that have not been challenged and are still the law in seven states, namely: North Carolina, Alabama, Arizona, Kansas, Louisiana, South Dakota and Tennessee, all of which voted overwhelmingly for the ban of Sharia law.

Abortion

This is an appropriate time to mention the "pro-life", "pro-choice "controversy that pervades our country. Particularly disconcerting is that "pro-choicers" seek to extend their right to murder fully formed babies as late as the ninth month and even after the baby is born. This is not any different from making life and death decisions about the elderly. It would seem that not only any disability or incapacity of the fully formed baby would give rise to the right to murder it, but also if the baby is just not wanted or cannot be afforded would be sufficient for the Government to sanction and even perform the murder at any stage of the pregnancy right up to childbirth and even beyond. The Governors of the States of Virginia and New York have specifically endorsed the extension of the right to murder and in the case of the Virginia Governor, the taking of the life even after birth would be acceptable. Once the state has opened the door to making life and death decisions whether for the elderly or fully formed babies, we have set the stage for far reaching reasons for putting to death certain humans. In the late 1930's and early 1940's, the right to murder 6 million Jews was justified by Hitler and his Nazi-Socialist party to the predominately Christian community as necessary to achieve "ethnic cleansing" and the majority of Christians bought into it. How we deal with the right to life and the Government's rights to determine life and death decisions for its constituents starts with how we sanctify life in the later days of a pregnancy after the baby becomes "viable". The Democrats open the door to the expediency of euthanizing when the government finds it necessary.

Remember the outcry against Justices Neil Gorsuch and Bret Kavanaugh and the attending vilification was over the Democrats concern that they would over-rule Roe v. Wade. Well now the liberal left wants to go far beyond Roe v. Wade and the later case Planned Parenthood v. Casey. To see where we are now in the "pro-life", "pro-choice" controversy we need to briefly review the law of the land as embodied in these two cases.

Roe V. Wade

There are moral and legal considerations that go beyond the pronouncements of the Church or the various advocating groups. We turn to the 1973 U.S. Supreme Court case of Roe v. Wade. This case concerned the constitutionality of state laws that criminalized or restricted access to abortions. The court ruled 7-2 that a right to privacy under the Due Process Clause of the 14th Amendment extended to a woman's decision to have an abortion, but that right must be balanced against the state's interest in regulating abortion to protect a woman's health and protecting the potentiality of human life. Arguing that the State's interest becomes stronger over the course of the pregnancy, the Court resolved this balancing test by tying state regulation of abortion to the third trimester of the pregnancy. Note, most pro-choice advocates believe that Roe V. Wade gives the woman the unfettered right to choose an abortion at any time during the pregnancy. What is often overlooked regarding the Roe v. Wade decision is that the state does have the right to prohibit a woman's free choice of abortion within parameters, the parameter being the third trimester.

Planned Parenthood v. Casey

However, Roe v. Wade was significantly modified by a later court decision. In the 1993 case of Planned Parenthood v. Casey, while the case affirmed Roe v. Wade it rejected the Roe v. Wade trimester framework and, in its place, established that a woman has a right of abortion only until fetal viability. The court defined "viable" as "potentially able to live outside the mother's womb, albeit with artificial aid" and justices in Planned Parenthood v. Casey acknowledged that viability may occur at 23 or 24 weeks **OR** sometimes earlier in light of medical advance.

Why pro-choicer's make such an ado about the overturn of Roe V. Wade is amazing when Planned Parenthood v. Casey could eventually remove a woman's choice completely if and when medical advance makes it possible for a fertilized egg to live and grow outside the womb. Planned Parenthood v. Casey, would actually change the Supreme Court's thinking in favor of "pro-life" over "pro-choice".

What has been the impact of Roe v. Wade? In the United States there are approximately 1 million abortions each year representing about 20% of U.S. pregnancies. With an infant mortality rate of only 0.6%, the overwhelming percent of infant death is the result of the abortion of an otherwise healthy baby. The reason for an abortion is because the baby is unwanted, for economic reasons or simply the woman doesn't want to take care of a child. Contributing to the large number of abortions is the high percentage of out-of-wedlock births. According to the National Center for Health, statistics show that 42% of children born in 2015 were out-of-wedlock. There would seem to be logic that the state has the responsibility to preserve life once the baby becomes viable, that is can survive outside the mother's womb. It would seem at that point the rights of the human fetus would take precedence over the woman's right to kill.

Although the pro-choice advocates have raised vigorous concern over Supreme Court Conservative Justices Gorsuch and Kavanaugh, that they might seek to overturn Roe V. Wade, the liberal pro-choice outlook on abortion seems to want to go beyond Roe V. Wade into new territories. Virginia Governor, Ralph Northam is not content to promote the killing of children all the way to child birth; he even advocates the killing of children that have survived abortion and have been delivered alive if the mother so wants for her well-being. This is infanticide. Governor Northam supported a Virginia bill called the "Repeal Act", which would allow the mother and her doctor to decide whether or not to kill the newborn baby. The bill would have even allowed abortions after labor had started. The bill was defeated by Republicans.

And in New York, Governor Cuomo has promoted and passed liberal abortion legislation, guaranteeing the right of a woman to abort her unborn child at any time until birth for vaguely defined reasons of health, including social well- being. Cuomo stated that those who oppose abortion have no place in his state. Cuomo signed a bill in February 2019 clearing the way for late term abortions, which removed the death of the unborn from the criminal code. Other bills are pending to expand access to abortion in New Mexico, Rhode Island and Vermont. In Vermont, the Democratic House voted to pass a bill that would allow abortion at any stage of pregnancy and for any reason whatsoever. It passed by a margin of 106 to 36. The bill would strip unborn children of any rights or recognition of their personhood. Even Nancy Pelosi stated that: "it is really quite sad that Trump is calling for the end of late term abortion".

If we are willing to kill babies with heart beats and brain waves, even if they have been delivered, how far a jump is it to imagine legislation permitting the putting to death those with handicaps or infirmities?

U.S. Constitutional Arguments concerning abortion

We must first understand that whether "pro-life" or "pro-choice", the issue goes beyond the concerns of the mother. The issue is whether or not the unborn child has any rights that should be protected, even if those rights may conflict with the desires of the mother?

The Fourteenth Amendment of the U.S. Constitution passed in 1868 declares that no state shall "deprive any person of life, liberty or property without due process of the law nor deny any person within its jurisdiction the equal protection of the law". We have now brought the controversy between "pro-life' and "pro-choice" down to its common denominator. What is a "person"? If we can agree on that, then the pro-life/pro-choice controversy ceases.

In an Article in the Harvard Law Journal in May, 2017, law student Joshua Craddock attacked this question and claimed that states that allow abortion violate the Constitution. Craddock looks back before the 14th Amendment as to what was the definition of a "person" and the anti-abortion laws of the time. 23 of the 27 states explicitly called the unborn child a "child" in their laws and six of the eleven territories did so as well. In 1859 the American Medical Association demanded the government protect the independent and actual existence of the child before birth.

Thus, pre-14th Amendment the general consensus treated unborn beings as "persons" and the pre-born were included within the public meaning of the term persons at the time the 14th Amendment was adopted. Thus, claims Craddock, if the state allows the unborn child to be killed, but prosecutes the murderers of other groups of people, it denies the unborn "person" the equal protection of the law.

Where are we today on abortion rights?

In the light of Governor Northam's and Governor Cuomo's actions seeking to expand abortion all the way to birth and even the right to murder a baby after birth, The Senate Republicans in February 2019, sought to enhance protection for newborns who survive abortion. Senator Ben Sasse, Nebraska Republican asked for the "Born-alive Abortion Survivors Protection Act" be approve by unanimous consent. Forty Republicans and no Democrats co-sponsored the bill.

Are we heading toward a similar abortion policy that has existed in China for years? For years, China has imposed limits on the number of children a family can have. Its policies have spawned countless human rights abuses. The policies of China have forced generations of Chinese parents to pay fines; submit involuntarily to abortions, submit involuntarily to sterilization or raise their children in secret. In China, abortion is legal at any time during pregnancy.

Starting in January, 2018, families in China were allowed to have two children, up from the one previously allowed. After the second child, women were required to be sterilized and as early as 1983 China ordered the sterilization of 20 million women. A usual mode of punishment for failing to follow government policy were fines which were at the level of between 5 and 10 times the parent's annual disposable income. If the couple were too poor to pay, the government would take property from the house. Part time enforcers would come as a team of three and take washing machines, bicycles and tables and sell the confiscated property and give the proceeds to the township. And of course, the enforcers would keep some of the property for themselves. This is a clear example of how a socialist government, controls their subjects and deprives them of the rights to life, liberty and property. Do those who support the liberal left, really want the state to dictate your right to have children; the right not to be sterilized; or the right not to have an abortion?

When you combine triage, with late term abortion in the delivery room and beyond and couple these with National Health Care, we are closing in on how life is treated in China. What will keep our government from euthanizing any little baby or infant that has some physical challenge or handicap? Think of all those wonderful children with physical challenges that have received care from facilities such as St. Jude Hospital and go on to become constructive, contributing human beings; that serve as role models for others? And how soon will the government be ordering parents to abort their child even though the parents are willing and able to care for them and desire to nurture them? The argument between the "pro-choicers" and "pro-lifers" becomes moot, when the Government makes the decision for them. And this is assuredly what will happen if the programs presented by the liberal left ever get implemented. I'm sure many of the readers are credulous, but read on and hear about the devastation of America that will be wrought upon us by the liberal left. And as a final note, it is so hard to understand how one can claim that a wall is immoral, but the killing of an unborn child (even after it is born) is not?

The focal point of the abortion issue should not be whether women have the right to do what she wants with her body. The question is whether or not the unborn child is human, from the beginning of conception or at any time that it is in the womb? Pro-choice, only is a successful argument, if we agree that the unborn baby is not a human until it is born. Once we humanize the unborn baby, then we must recognize its rights. Somewhat analogous is how Hitler convinced so many people that Jews were not human and therefore it was all right to kill them. In a strangely similar wave, slavery was justified by convincing people that blacks were not human. To claim that unborn babies, Jews, or Africans were not human is more than insane. It is an attempt to justify what is inherently morally wrong.

Further, when we start dehumanizing certain classes of humans, we need to ask ourselves where does it stop? When the sick or elderly is on life-support, should he or she no longer be considered human so that we can justify putting them to death? Also, there is no need to kill an unborn human as there is always the alternative of putting the unborn human up for adoption, after he or she is born. What puzzles me is how vehemently the pro-choice advocates hate and vilify the pro-life advocates, merely because the pro-life advocates believe that the unborn child is a human being and should be protected. It is also interesting to note that it is Tom Perez, the Chairman of the Democratic Party that insists that you must be willing to kill the unborn baby to be a Democrat. What an indictment of the Democratic Party. How can any Christian, particularly Roman Catholics who believe that life begins at conception, support a party that is so ready to kill a human, just because it is unborn?

Where does the American Public stand on the "pro-life" v "pro-choice" controversy? Once again, we found the liberal left mis-leading the American people on where the sentiment lies regarding this controversy. The liberal left and the supporting media, would have you believe that the majority of people believe that the woman has the right to an abortion any time she chooses. Those who are pro-life are continually castigated by the liberal left and the biased media and the entertainment industry. The women's rights are sacrosanct and damn the life of the unborn child is the outcry of the liberal left. The unborn child has no rights. His life can be snuffed out at the will of the woman bearing the child.

A Gallup poll taken in May, 2019 regarding the pro-life versus "pro-choice" sentiments in the United States, contradicts the harsh and unanimous "pro-choice" doctrine of the liberal Democrats. The Gallup poll found that only the age group from 18 to 29 chose "pro-choice" over "pro-life" with 62% in favor of choice, 33% in favor of life and 5% having no opinion. Over-all, the most significant finding was that the majority of women in the United States are "pro-life". Yet the Democrats would have you believe that pro-choice is by far the dominant position of women and that it was even immoral to be pro-life. Another interesting fact from the survey was that the lower the household income the more likely the person would be pro-life rather than pro-choice. Those in the pole with household income under $40,000 were 59% pro-life and only 34% pro-choice. This flies into the face of the Democrat pro-choice argument that women want the right to an abortion at any time for any reason, because of financial considerations and the inability to afford having a child. The Gallup Poll found that as we go up the income scale, people swung toward pro-choice over pro-life:

Yearly Household Income	Pro-choice	Pro-life	No opinion
Less than $40,000	34%	59%	7%
$40,000 to $100,000	48	48	4
Over $100,000	59	38	3

So, it would appear that the Democrats at least on the issue of abortion are catering to the wealthy.

Another interesting observation is that pro-choice is the dominant position of the 18 to 29 age group, while all other age groups favor pro-life.

Age Group	Pro-choice	Pro-life	No opinion
18 to 29	62%	33%	5%
30 to 49	44	51	5
50 to 64	41	54	5
65 and older	37	56	7

And yet, a major concern of the Democrats has been the potential threat that conservative Supreme Court Justices may overturn Roe v. Wade. Their position runs counter to over 50% of the adult citizens of the United States.

Another observation of the Gallup poll is that the Democrats find support for their pro-choice doctrine, which is one of their major platforms, among college graduates and not among non-graduates. This is a further example of the Democrats supporting the elite and wealthy as opposed to the wishes and beliefs of the less wealthy and less advantaged. Here are the findings of the Gallup poll based on the level of education one has:

Education Level	Pro-choice	Pro-life	No opinion
No College	35%	58%	7%
Some College	40	55	5
College Graduate	57	37	6

Finally, how does pro-choice verses pro-life stack up by party affiliation?

Party	Pro-choice	Pro-life	No opinion
Republican	21%	75%	5%
Democrat	68	29	4

It is so important for each of us to analyze what are the real positions taken by each party and be sure that what they say is true. And further, it is important to evaluate what political leaders actually do as opposed to just what they say.

CHAPTER 19

Patriotism

Taking a Knee

BEFORE A GAME against the Green Bay Packers in September, 2016, Colin Kaepernick, a fading NFL quarterback for the San Francisco 49ers, gained nationwide recognition when he protested by not standing for the United States National Anthem before the game. He was motivated by what he viewed as the oppression of people of color. His statement given in an interview after he had taken the knee was: "I am not going to stand up and show pride in a flag of a country that oppresses black people and people of color. Kaepernick cited a few examples of events that led to the "Black Lives Matter movement", specifically relating to some wrongful deaths at the hands of white policemen. Colin Kaepernick in affect is saying that most whites are racists and white supremacists. He was saying this to all the white fans in the stadium, who had come to enjoy a game of football and root for their team. Surely there were a few racists fans in the seats, but they would be a minority and in supporting the Black Lives Matter movement instead of suggesting all lives matter, he too was being racist. And why doesn't he take note at the black on black carnage in many cities in the United States, but more specifically, Chicago. Nor does he acknowledge that here in the 21st century, black on black slavery is rampant in many parts of Africa. **Compounding his refusal to stand for the National Anthem, Kaepernick chose to wear socks that depict little piggies wearing police hats as a symbolic reference to what he asserted was police brutality and police repression in America.** He in fact was showing his hatred for all police, condemning them to the public for the wrong actions of the few. This is the fundamental accusation of the Black Lives Matter movement and on college and university campuses and at riots staged by the "Black Lives Matter'" movement. The terms pigs and police are considered synonymous all because of the belief that on the whole, the 1,000,000 police across America are brutal and repressive. If those supporting the Black Lives Matter movement would just take a moment to examine the facts, they would realize that their outrage directed toward police in America is just wrong.

It is important to look at the actual statistics to realize how Black Lives Matter movement is not based on facts, but is based on racism, against whites. In 2016, 963 people were killed by police, throughout the United states. 466 were white; 233 Black and 160 Hispanic. In 2015, nationwide 995 people were killed by police; 497 were white, 259 black and 172 Hispanic.

In 2016, 16 unarmed black men were killed by police out of a population of more than 20 million. In 2015 the number was 36. If we were to assume that all 56 killings were unjustified because the individual was unarmed, we would all agree that this is intolerable. However, it should be put in the proper factual perspective. In 2016 there were a total of 1.2 million violent crimes in the U.S. including robbery, rape, murder and aggravated assault. Of the 1.2 million violent crimes only .08% (that's less than 1/10 of 1 %) resulted in the death at the hands of police and approximately 50% of them were white and another 17% were Hispanic. When we factor in that approximately 20% of police are non-white, we arrive at .03% (That's less than 1/20 of 1%) of all violent crimes resulted in the death of a black by a white cop. And this makes no distinction between a justifiable and unjustifiable killing by a policeman.

By contrast, let's just look at only one city, Chicago. In 2016 there were 762 murders and 3,550 shooting incidents and 4,331 victims. One child is killed every week in Chicago. Most of the murders are the result of warfare among the 59 gangs in the city. 762 murders in Chicago alone is equal to 79% of all those killed by Police nationwide and 3.27 times the number of blacks killed by policemen nationwide. And we are only looking at Chicago and not some of the other high murder rate cities around the country. Why does the left ignore black on black crime and focus on white killing of blacks which pales by comparison?

With these facts in mind, we turn to September, 2017 and the beginning of NFL football season. It was then at stadiums around the country, their seats filled with fans who have come to be entertained by their favorite players as they do battle on the gridiron, that many NFL players decided to take a knee rather than stand at attention for our flag and our National anthem. Their protest was purportedly against police brutality and white supremacism and white racism and that led to their disrespect of the flag and national anthem. As the protesting NFL players looked out on the fans that had come only to watch them perform, they were in affect saying all among you who are white, are racists. At least they had to believe that the vast majority of whites in the stadium were racists, otherwise what reason to protest at that time and place? The protesting NFL players argued their actions were within their rights as guaranteed by the Constitution's 1st Amendment protection of free speech. However, when Pittsburgh Steeler's Alexandra Villanueva an army vet stood alone holding his hand over his heart, he was criticized by the head coach and he later apologized to his teammates for not showing solidarity with them.

What most people fail to understand is that the Constitutional Amendment I only applies to actions by the Federal Government. Employers are allowed to place restrictions on free speech in the work place, including personal appearance and standing for the National Anthem. Further, even freedom of speech may be limited in some instances by the government without being in violation of the 1st Amendment Rights. The official NFL game operations manual pertaining to the National Anthem is found on pages A62-63 which states: "The National Anthem must be played prior to every NFL game and all players must be on the sideline for the National Anthem. During the National Anthem, players on the field and bench area should stand at attention, face the flag, hold helmets in their left hand and refrain from talking. It should be pointed out to players and coaches that we continue to be judged by the public in the area of respect for our flag and our country. While it is a bit fuzzy in the NFL as to the requirements to stand for the National Anthem because there are the Official Rules Manual and the Game Operations Manual and only the latter is the source of the above wording.

There is no lack of clarity in the NBA where the rule specifically states: "Players, coaches and trainers are to stand up in a dignified position along the sidelines or on the foul line during the playing of the National Anthem. So, we have two concerns about the taking a knee in protest. First and foremost is concern with the validity of the objections the NFL players have raised regarding police brutality and white supremacy. They just are not supported by the facts. And second, the right of the NFL players to use the Stadium on game day as their forum for protesting.

But nothing angered or saddened me more than the protest at Wembley Field in London, England by the NFL teams, the Jacksonville Jaguars and the Baltimore Ravens on Sunday, September 24, 2017. The players chose to kneel in defiance of our National Anthem and then stand for the playing of the British National Anthem. This was the most divisive and unpatriotic attack on the United States, of all the NFL kneeling episodes.

And then I think of our men and women in harm's way in different corners of the world, our true patriots, who are ready, willing and able to give up their lives to protect our country. I think of all the veterans who have returned disabled and living lives with missing limbs; all the soldiers who have died on the battlefields, giving up their lives in places like the beaches of Normandy, the islands in the South Pacific, in Korea, Vietnam and the Middle East. I think of the heroes still on the battlefields in foreign lands, living in extremely uncomfortable living quarters, serving their tour of duty away from their family and loved ones; lonely; many scared; some to face death. They are all patriots. They love their country and have volunteered to protect it regardless of the personal cost. For many of military men and women, our veterans, our wounded warriors, the NFL football games are one of the few opportunities to put aside their hardships, their pains, their worries and just forget for a few moments the tragedies and travails they face each day. That moment comes on Sundays when they can watch the NFL games with their comrades in arms or fellow patients, or family. Yet the NFL athletes, with all their money, luxury, medical benefits that are poured upon them by their doting fans have chosen to throw it back in their faces by defaming the flag and the National Anthem of our great nation.

Who are the true heroes and contributors to our lives and well-being? Our military men and women, our police, our medical staffs of Doctors and Nurses and our first responders. Yet in the case of our Police and Military personnel, they are constantly vilified by those associated with the liberal left.

There is another group of unsung heroes of America, that are ignored. They are our builders, our farmers, our electricians, plumbers, factory workers, mine workers, shippers, all who make it possible for us to live.

Never has it become clearer how important all these contributors are until the aftermath of the devastating blows from the three hurricanes Harvey, Irma and Maria that struck South Eastern United States, Puerto Rico and the Virgin Islands in August and September, 2017. Puerto Rico in particular was decimated; where all things essential to life were brought to a standstill. Food, water, medicine, electricity, means of transportation; all shut off in an instant. And yet during this time of tragedy, the NFL players choose to kneel and defame our flag and country. How sad.

Our Flag and Our National Anthem as Symbols – Our flag and the National Anthem are symbols of the strife and sacrifice endured in our past history so that we could all enjoy liberty and freedom, albeit for blacks it did not come immediately. On the contrary it took many years to achieve. But, regardless, of what our country leaders, the politicians did, regardless of the slavery imposed on blacks before the 13th Amendment and the segregationist policies imposed on blacks after the passing of the 13th Amendment, this does not change what the flag and National Anthem stood for. It was our leaders, almost solely Democrats, that imposed segregation, racism and white supremacism on blacks after the civil war and this did not change the symbolic meaning of our flag and National Anthem. It was the Democrats that decided the Dred Scott case confirming that: "Once a slave always a slave". The court consisted of 7 Democrat Judges and 2 Republicans. All 7 Democrats voted to sustain slavery and the 2 Republican Judges dissented. It was also the Democrats that promulgated and enforced the repulsive "Jim Crow" laws In the South and further showed their hate and disdain for blacks by forming the Ku Klux Clan that hung innocent Blacks and burned down their homes and churches.

The demonstrations in the last weekends of September 2017 by the NFL players, mostly African American sought to denigrate and change the symbolic meaning of our flag and National Anthem. It doesn't take a large number of people to change the meaning of symbols. Just a small minority as was the case with the NFL player protest against our flag and National anthem as they sought to change the meaning of these symbols by desecrating them.

Let us turn briefly to the history of the Swastika. The Swastika in ancient times was a sacred symbol of the Buddhist and Hindu Religions. In Hinduism the Swastika Icon reminds the viewer of something conducive to well-being, something like a good-luck charm. Similarly, to the Buddhist, the Swastika is an auspicious symbol, promising success, prosperity and good fortune. To Chinese, Japanese and Korean the Swastika represents the number 10,000 and is commonly used to represent the whole of creation. In the Western World it was historically a symbol of good luck and seen as such in America as late as the early 20th Century, until the 1930's when it was adopted by the Third Reich in Germany. It became the main Nazi symbol as an emblem of the Aryan race and during WW II it became identified in the West with racism, hate and mass murder. So, from being a symbol of good fortune or well-being in many parts of the world, it became a symbol of hate, persecution and death. Is this the aim of those NFL football players in vilifying our anthem and flag? Are they trying to condemn our flag and our anthem as symbols of hate and white supremacism? Or is it just that they know not what they do?

The denigrating of our flag raised its ugly hatred once again on July 4, 2019. Once again Colin

Kaepernick, turns on America using hatred to promote his own notoriety. Kaepernick convinced Nike to withdraw its introduction of an "Independence Day" sneaker which displayed the "Betsy Ross" Colonial American flag on the back of the sneaker. Nike succumbed to Kaepernick's demand to withdraw the sneaker from the market, because Kaepernick told them that the flag connoted white Supremacism and therefore offensive to blacks. From the days of the American Revolution, until today the American flag has been the symbol of unity and American freedom although it has changed as new states were added to the Union. No-one has ever questioned this meaning of our flag until now. But based on the complaint of one person saying that our flag is offensive to blacks, Nike has chosen to accept this complaint. Now we even have members of the liberal left comparing our flag with the Swastika.

Nike made the decision to halt its distribution of the Air Max 1 Quick Strike Fourth of July Sneaker because one man, Colin Kaepernick said that it was offensive to Black America, because slavery existed at the time of the Revolution. It would appear that Nike purposely intended to make a statement by first offering the sneakers with the flag and then withdrawing them. Why did it not discard the sneakers along the way before even introducing them? Why even put the sneakers out for distribution unless you wanted to use its withdrawal as a statement against white supremacism, with the hope that it would promote its sale of other sneakers to the African/American community? The flag has never before in over 240 years been deemed offensive or a symbol of white supremacism, or stood for anything other than liberty, democracy and unity.

Yet one man, the new poster boy for Nike, Colin Kaepernick, who could not make it as an NFL football player, has parlayed his hatred of America into tens of millions of dollars, more than he could have ever earned as an athlete, by promoting hatred and by denigrating our National Anthem and American Flag. And Nike pays him millions of dollars every year to do this. How sad.

Kaepernick claims that the American Flag is offensive because of its connection to an era of slavery. And Nike apparently accepts this to be true. Nike and those that believe that the Betsy Ross flag (as well as all other U.S. flags) to be offensive to all black Americans must also seek to tear down the Washington Monument, the Jefferson Memorial, Washington's home at Mount Vernon; Jefferson's home Monticello and all other monuments and symbols which were created during the time of slavery in the United States. And maybe the George Washington Bridge should be re-named and Grant's tomb removed from New York City and the City of Washington renamed and all monuments that depict someone that had been a slave owner at some time should be removed. In short, the history of America according to Kaepernick and endorsed by Nike, needs to be rewritten to excise any marker, symbol or monument that in any way is implicated with the time when slavery existed.

The actions of Kaepernick and Nike imply that all White Americans are white supremacists and racists. Yet less than ½ of 1% of our population has ancestors that took part in slavery in any way. Think of all the immigrants into the United States since the civil war, whose ancestors had nothing to do with slavery. Think of all the Northern, mostly Republican soldiers who gave their lives or came back severely wounded. They are to be deprived of their cherished symbols of the American flag and the National Anthem, because one man and one company says they are offensive?

Kaepernick and Nike should examine closely their own ignorance; ignorance which is one of the principal by-products of hate. Look back at where slavery began many years ago and where it is most prevalent today. Slave trade existed in Africa as early as the 7th century, when Africans captured their fellow Africans, kidnapped their women and children put them in yolks and chains and sold them to the Arabs who castrated the males and raped the women. Millions of blacks died on the way to the sea to be sold to the Arabian slave traders and more died from the process of castration. But their fellow Africans did not seem to care. And without the initial slavery by Africans of their brothers, there would be no slave market available to the colonists. The duplicity of Africans in the evils of slavery seem to be totally over-looked. Then let's look at today. Slavery is more rampant in Africa than any other part of the world, where 38 of the 54 African countries still enslave their fellow Africans.

Kaepernick's hatred of America goes beyond the American flag. His hatred of police and law and order is also conveyed by the socks he wears, that depict pigs in policeman's uniform.

Megan Rapinoe

Following in the footsteps of Kaepernick, is women's soccer player, Megan Rapinoe. And for Megan, Kaepernick is her idol, because he showed her the way to disrespect our flag, our National anthem and our country. She is on the same quest to leverage hatred and disrespect into a lot of money. She may well become Nike's poster girl, not for her soccer play, but because of her loud protests, her abusive language and her disrespect of America. Can't you envision that next July 4th, Nike plans to start a line of sneakers with the White House on the back, only to have the pre-agreed protest from Megan Rapinoe that they must be removed because the White House (for some unexplained reason) is an offense to the LGBT community. And Megan Rapinoe seeks not to capitalize so much on her skills as a soccer player, which she cannot use to stand her apart from her teammates, all of whom contributed to the success of the U.S. women's soccer team. No, she seeks to stand apart from her team-mates with her pink hair her vulgar language and the disrespect of the major symbols of our American heritage. Who do we see on TV being interviewed; at the ESPY awards, in photographs, and the newspapers? Not any of the other stars of the Team, just Megan. She is making herself more valuable at the expense of her teammates as if she has earned it totally on her own.

Who are the true heroes?

The U.S. Women's Soccer team, have a great accomplishment in winning the Gold Cup. Congratulations, but you are not heroes. You got the welcome of heroes in New York City, but you are not heroes. You are very skilled athletes and deserve congratulations, but the true heroes are the 400,000 lying in graves in Arlington Cemetery, who gave their lives protecting our freedom and way of life. It is men lying in graves throughout Europe who gave their lives in World War! and World War 11 who are the heroes. It is the thousands of first responders on 9/11/2001, who saved many lives and witnessed the death of 2,997 as a result of the direct attack by radical Islamic Terrorists. There were more than 16,000 responders to the 9/11/2001 attack performing rescue, recovery, demolition and debris cleanup. There were 23 New York Police and 348 firefighters that gave their lives that day and many more have died of related illnesses since. They are the heroes, and we so easily forget them. And visit the Veterans hospitals across the United States, where there are so many survivors of combat that have lost their limbs, their eyesight, their hearing or are suffering from PTSD. They are our or heroes. And think of all the mothers and fathers, husbands and wives and children that must cope with their loss of loved ones and must struggle to survive, without the help of their father or husband. They are the heroes. They all love our country; they respect our National Anthem and our Flag and our Whitehouse. And if that isn't enough, what about the half of the citizens of the United States, that respect our President, the White House, the Flag and the National anthem? Megan Rapino like Colin Kaepernick before, tell us that none of these counts.

There is another group of heroes that we so easily disregard. The ones that have been physically challenged at birth or by some tragedy that has occurred during their lives. We read about the special children that St. Jude Hospital has dedicated itself to help. The child Bella and her brain tumor; or two-year-old Joseph and his battle with large tumors in is eye; or little Charlotte, and her battle with aplastic anemia or David valiantly trying to survive leukemia or Isabella, Olivia and Jordyn fighting to survive every day of their lives. They too are the unsung heroes, coping with their maladies every day. And what do each of these children display to all of us. These heroic children persevere with love in their hearts, not hate; with joy at being alive, not anger for what pain and suffering has been given to them.

I also pay tribute to one of them most inspiring yet unsung heroes, that I had no knowledge of until the ESPY Awards Show on TV in July 2019. ESPN put together a magnificent story about Rob Mendez a 36-year-old football coach from California. Rob Mendez was born without arms and legs. Active participation in sports was never open to him, but he loved sports. He did not despair; he did more than cope. Who would think it possible to be a football coach without arms and legs? But Rob Mendez persisted; his resolve was unlimited and as a result he has made an impact on the lives of all the boys he has coached. As one of his players said: "He's willing to do that, then what are we willing to do?"

And then there is Jeff Tweedle a ventilator dependent quadriplegic, injured in a rugby accident in 1994, giving back to the sport community as an assistant coach for Winthrop/Monmouth Middle School football team in Maine. He doesn't have a very strong voice because of the ventilator, but as soon as the boys here Coach Tweedle, they come over to him and stand next to him to hear what he has to say. And the list of Quadriplegics who have risen above their misfortunes, do not merely cope, but really contribute to society. There should be a book about these un-sung heroes and there are so any of them. And you will not find one of them hating or vilifying our flag, our National Anthem or our White House.

What gives Magen Rapinoe the right to be spokesperson for anyone but herself? What has she accomplished? She is extraordinarily good at kicking a little ball into a net. But she couldn't have done this on her own, without all her teammates. She was not even the best player on the team, according to the Espy awards. Without her teammates, Megan Rapinoe would be nothing special. Her hate, arrogance and abusive language are products of being on a team that catapulted her to notoriety and allowed her to leave her teammates behind, the teammates that has made the notoriety possible for her.

She wants President Trump to do more and talk less. Wouldn't that be something she too should adhere to? At least under President Trump, we have already seen the increase in wages above the inflation rate and across the board for all ethnic groups and minorities. We have seen interest rates, the lowest in decades. We have seen economic growth consistently higher than 3%, a level never achieved in any year under Obama. We have seen the incomes of families rise through the tax cuts authorized by the Trump administration and we have seen manufacturing jobs return to our country and our unemployment rate drop below 4%, a rate of unemployment never achieved by any Administration in this century. The Trump Administration has strengthened our military that had become dangerously inadequate obsolete and in terrible disrepair. We have become energy independent. We have opened channels of dialogue with China, North Korea and Russia, although Megan Rapinoe might not believe that dialogue is important, since she is unwilling even to speak to our President. Everyone's pensions, annuities, IRA's and 401K's are now stronger and richer, significantly improving the quality of life for the 60 million retirees in our country. And the Trump Administration has obtained better medical care for our Veterans and also more timely, allowing them to go to the doctors and medical centers of their choice, that are nearby and will provide immediate medical attention as opposed to the Veterans Hospitals where many veterans died waiting for medical treatment. Rapinoe completely ignores these successes of the Trump Administration saying he must do more for all people. There is always more someone can do, but that does not mean giving a President no credit for what he has done.

So, what does Megan Rapinoe say? She protests the National Anthem and vows to continue her protest while representing the U.S. calling it "a good f...you" to the Trump Administration. She says "I'll probably never put my hand over my heart or sing the National Anthem again. A month ago, she was quoted as saying "If the U.S. wins the World Cup, I'm not going to the "F...ing Whitehouse". Further, she tells us that she speaks for all of her teammates, although I have not heard one teammate confirm this. And in this regard, she has been quoted as saying: "I don't think anyone on the team has any interest in lending the platform we worked so hard to build" to the Trump Administration. Somehow the hubris of Rapinoe leads her to believe that she and her team has a special platform to lend to our country, because she can kick a little ball down the field and put it into a net. And that somehow, she can hurt our country by not lending it her platform. Megan Rapinoe, the self-proclaimed spokesperson for the radical left even went as far as to say; "So many more people that I would like to talk to that could really affect change in Washington, rather than go to the White House". What planet is she living on? Who in the United States can affect more change than the President of the United States not just our Nation but the world? Regardless as to how one believes or accept his policies, what is possibly achieved by being unwilling to even dialogue with him? This is the philosophy of the adolescent, who disagrees with a fellow classmate and shuns or stops talking to him or her. I might add, that I have run into numerous adults who will refuse to talk to you if you disagree with them. How childish some of our adults are. Nothing is ever accomplished by hate and the refusal to dialogue.

The hypocrisy of Rapinoe is overwhelming. At one point she says we "have to come together", "we have to collaborate". But her words are divisive, hateful, unpatriotic and she refuses to dialogue with anyone with whom she disagrees. She tells us that she cannot hold a substantive meeting with our President, but welcomes more meaningful meetings with Nancy Pelosi, Chuck Schumer and Alexandria Ocasio-Cortez, people with whom she agrees with. What could be more useful than for someone with opposing beliefs with another welcomes a meeting to dialogue with him, especially when one of them is the President of the United States? But that is something Megan Rapinoe not only refuses to do, but disparages with abuse and profanity.

And to make it very clear how vulgar this self-proclaimed spokesperson of our Women's World Cup Champion soccer team, in almost her last public words during the ticker tape parade in New York City in front of adults and little children, is her loud cheer referring to us all as "mother-f…ers".

Megan Rapinoe claims to represent all the U.S. Women's Soccer team members. They remain silent and therefore it must be true. Are we to believe that every woman on the U.S. World's champion soccer team that is supposedly representing the United States, believes that our Flag, our National Anthem and our White House should be treated with hatred and vitriol? If that is so, then we have just welcomed as heroes back to our country that hate our country and treat it with disgust. These soccer players are not heroes for winning a soccer game in the first place and they are not patriots as clearly demonstrated by their hatred and vilification of our country. Rapinoe will certainly make her millions of dollars, probably from Nike, while the rest of the team will just fade from history, forgotten, but if remembered it will be for their vilification of our country.

The Bladensburg Case

A similar attack on Patriotism in the United States deals with Bladensburg, Maryland and the memorial cross put there in 1925 in dedication to the memory of the 49 soldiers from that town who gave their lives serving their country during World War I. In 2014, a liberal left organization, the Humanist Associates, argued that the memorial cross violated the Establishment Clause of the First Amendment of our Constitution. Three U.S. Court of Appeals for the Fourth Circuit agreed and declared the cross Unconstitutional and must be torn down. The cross had long been a memorial to those who had died, not only to honor them, but to honor their beliefs and their family's beliefs that something after death existed for them. Even those who are of other religions or are atheists, should not seek to deprive those of their right to memorialize those that have died, but also to do so in a way that is in keeping with their traditional beliefs. Why should that be so repugnant to those of different faiths or beliefs?

First Liberty Institute, representing the American Legion asked the Supreme Court to overturn the decision and the Supreme court did so on June 20, 2019 by a 7-2 decision with the two liberal judges Ruth Bader Ginsburg and Sonia Sotomayor dissenting.

The reasoning of the majority opinion was a bid shaky. While the court ruled that the 40-foot cross, was a memorial to fallen soldiers in World War 1 that had been consecrated for almost 100 years of public devotion and that tearing it down would show "unconstitutional hostility". It also ruled that the cross had earned "special significance" over the years as a war memorial and an expression of a community's grief for its lost sons. But the Justices were unable to come to any consensus about how to approve hundreds of other religious themed memorials across the country, leaving them to be fought over one by one.

So, all the Federal memorial cemeteries where brave soldiers lie buried, even those on foreign soil are still threatened to be rendered extinct, especially if Ruth Bader Ginsburg and Sonya Sotomayor ever got their way. The United States operates and maintains 26 military cemeteries in 17 foreign countries and in the United States, all commemorating the service and sacrifice of our American soldiers who have served in WWI and WWII. Each cemetery has rows and rows of crosses and in many instances the Star of David, marking the grave of a soldier. If the controversial ruling of the 4th Circuit Court had been upheld these crosses would have to be removed. The Arlington Cemetery here in the United States would be decimated and the soldiers lying buried there would no longer have a cross marking his grave. Why can't people understand that the crosses are symbols of the faith, hope and memories of the husbands and fathers who have lost their lives in protecting our country? This has nothing to do with demeaning the beliefs of others and I would expect those that complain know this and it is only their hatred of those who are not like them to seek to destroy all that is dear to those who only want to remember their lost loved ones.

CHAPTER 20

Black Lives Matter versus All Live Matter

WE CANNOT DENY that African American history is marked with slavery and mistreatment of blacks that continued well beyond their emancipation in January 1863. But the Democrats have made it an issue to gain the support of Black Americans, that the Republicans are the racists and have caused all forms of repression against the Black community. There were 56 signers of the Declaration of Independence in 1776 and although the second paragraph of the Declaration states: "We hold these truths to be self-evident, that all men are created equal, that they are endowed by their Creator with certain unalienable Rights, that among these are Life, Liberty and the Pursuit of Happiness, yet 41 of the 56 signers owned slaves. Certainly, this is a strong argument in support of "Black Lives Matter" v. "All Lives Matter". In 1789, thirteen years after signing of the Declaration of Independence, the U.S. Constitution would be ratified, which confirmed the Declaration of Independence, when in its pre-amble, it includes as reasons for the creation of the Constitution "to establish justice, insure domestic tranquility, promote the general welfare and Secure the Blessings of Liberty to ourselves and our Posterity." Further, the Constitution in Article I section 2 makes a distinction between slaves and freemen as to how they are to be counted in elections, a slave to count only as 2/5 of a freeman. Again, our founding fathers provided a strong argument for the position that "Black lives" (and American-Indian lives) did not matter as much as White lives. And finally, 12 of our first 18 presidents owned slaves. Historically, it is certainly a strong argument that racism was prevalent in the United States in the 18th and 19th centuries and still existed in the 20th century in the U.S., not in the form of slavery but in the denial of equal rights and privileges for blacks.

Let's fast forward to the Presidency of Abraham Lincoln, the Emancipation Proclamation and Amendment XIII of the Constitution, abolishing Slavery which was ratified December 6, 1865. Maybe more important than the Article XIII itself was the 596,670 Union soldiers out of a total of 1,532,278 who fought to free slaves and who were killed, captured or remained missing. This was more than WWI and WWII combined. My grandfather and his brother, my Great Uncle and my Great grandfather all fought for the freedom of slaves serving in the Union Army from September 3, 1861 to September 16, 1864 when they were mustered out. They were part of company G 46th Regiment of the New York Infantry of Volunteers. They fought at Bull Run, Petersburg, Virginia and

James Island, South Carolina and were all fortunate to have survived. Didn't this amount to some atonement for the sins of the forefathers? This does not mean that we should ever forget how wrong slavery was (and is) or forget that at its peak there were 385,000 slave owners in the United States owning 4 million slaves.

And what about the duplicity of African blacks in slave trade? Are Africans themselves blameless? Africans were vastly complicit in the African Slave Trade. Of course, this does not absolve whites of guilt, but the question is why do we focus on one wrong and ignore the black contributions to slavery in Africa? By the time the slave trade was abolished in the West, there were many more slaves in Africa (black slaves of black owners) than in America. The tribal chiefs of the Western Coast of Africa were for ages accustomed to selling their captives into bondage and as early as 700 AD Arabs conducted a thriving slave trade, in Africa, castrating the male captives before selling them into bondage to other Arabs, and then enslaving black women to serve as concubines to their Arab masters.

Historians estimated that ten million of abducted Africans never made it to the slave ships. Most died on the march to the sea, chained, yoked and shackled by their African captors long before they laid eyes on a white slave trader.

In October 2013, the Los Angeles Times noted that African countries dominate a new global index of slavery with as many as 38 of 54 African nations still supporting slavery, but most notably: Mauritania, West Africa, Benin, Ivory Coast, Gambia, Gabon and Senegal.

In June, 2014 Ta-Nehisi Coates wrote an essay entitled: "The case for reparations". Born in 1975 in Baltimore, he is an award-winning writer, including the National Book Award for non-fiction and the George Polk Awards in Journalism in 2015 for his "Case for reparations". Coates contends that reparations should be paid to African-Americans for crimes against them during slavery. Coates argues that the idea of reparations should result in our nation considering what the nation might owe the black population for the slavery and abuse at the hand of white supremacists.

It is not questioned that African-Americans have in the past been abused by slavery and segregation. But Coates does not even discuss the slavery and abuse imposed by Africans on fellow Africans long before slave trade began by whites, when they so actively participated in the Arab slave trade in the 7th and 8th centuries. During that period Africans captured and sold their fellow Africans to the Arab slave traders. Nor does he acknowledge that there would have been no slave trade with white slave traders if it hadn't been for the willing participation of Africans in attacking and capturing blacks, placing them in chains and yolks to be sold to the white slave traders and resold into slavery. Nor does Coats acknowledge that slavery today exists almost exclusively in Africa. Nor does he mention that the killing and abuse of blacks by blacks is rampant in cities such as Chicago, Baltimore and St. Louis. Nor does he mention the hundreds of thousands of white soldiers in the Union Army, who during the Civil War, gave their lives to free the slaves, the slaves of the Democrat plantation owners of the South.

We turn to what African leaders today have to say about the Atlantic slave trade. Ugandan President

Yoweri Museveni said: "African chiefs were the ones waging war on each other, capturing their own people and selling them. If anyone should apologize it should be the African chiefs". King Kpoyo-Zoynme Hakpon IV of Benin to a black audience in Alabama in 2013: "I want to apologize for the role my ancestors played in the slave trade". At the Civil Rights Conference in Nigeria in 2009 the Congress concluded: "We cannot continue to blame the white men; as Africans, particularly the traditional rulers are not blameless…. It would be logical, reasonable and humbling, if African traditional rulers accept blame and formally apologize for their collaborative and exploitive slave trade". Former Ghana diplomat to the U.N., Kofi Awoonor, as early as 1994 said: "There is a shadow over Africa…dealing with our guilt and denial of our role in the slave trade. We too are blameworthy in what was essentially one of the most heinous crimes in human history". Finally, Senegal's President, Abdoulaye Wade urged Africans to acknowledge publicly and teach openly about their (the blacks) share responsibility for the Atlantic Slave Trade".

The Civil War – Dread Scott Case and Fort Sumpter

Probably no two causes contributed so much to the start of the Civil War than the Supreme Court, Dread Scott Case and the firing on Ft. Sumpter in South Carolina. Both were Democrat led and provoked. It was Democratic racists, Democratic White supremacists and Democratic slave owners who would bring our country into a Civil war, which would result in the death of 620,000 to 750,000; more than all other wars engaged in by the U.S. combined. It amounted to 2.4% of our population at that time which would be equivalent to 7.5 million today.

Approximately 60% of those killed were Union soldiers who supported Republican President Abraham Lincoln and voluntarily gave their lives to free the slaves owned by Democrats in the Confederate South. Once again, we hear from the Democrats, threats to assassinate the President, overthrow the government, bomb the White House. The history of hatred and violence imbued in the Democrats in the past is once again with us.

The Dread Scott Case. Dred Scott v. Sandford, commonly referred to as the Dread Scott Case, was an 1857 Supreme Court Case that would be a landmark decision and would ultimately lead to the Civil War. It held that "a negro, whose ancestors were imported into the U.S. and sold as slaves, whether enslaved or free could not be an American Citizen and therefore had no standing to sue in a Federal Court. Dred Scott an enslaved man of "the Negro-American race" had been taken by his owners to free states and attempted to sue for his freedom. The decision was written by Chief Justice Roger B. Taney and by a 7-2 decision, the court denied Scott's request. The seven justices in support of the decision were Democrats. The two dissenting justices were Republicans. The decision would prove to be the catalyst for the American Civil War. The decision spurred intense dissent from Northern anti-slavery proponents. Today most historians and legal scholars consider this decision to be the worst decision in the history of the U.S. Supreme Court. The holdings of the Supreme Court in this case included the following: "Persons of African descent cannot be nor were ever intended to be citizens under the U.S. Constitution. The two Republican Justices John McLean and Benjamin R. Curtis voiced their dissent.

Mclean wrote that: "there was no basis for the claim that blacks could not be citizens". Justice Peter V. Daniel, Democrat from Virginia summed up the opinion of the seven Democrat justices as follows: "the African negro race never has been acknowledged as belonging to the human race". Of the seven Democrat justices who voted to support slavery, five were slave owners, namely, Chief Justice Roger Taney and Associate Justices James M. Wayne, John Catron, Peter V. Daniel and John A. Campbell.

Fort Sumter – The major event after the decision of the 7 Democrat Justices of the Supreme Court had decided that slaves did not deserve the rights of freemen as they were less than human, was when the Southern Democratic leaders and their followers actually started the Civil War by firing on the U.S. and the Union Fort Sumter in Charleston, South Carolina. On April 12, 1861 for thirty hours. 4,000 shells were fired on Ft. Sumpter and finally the battered fort raised the white flag. The Union soldiers left the fort and no one on either side had been killed. It would be a bloodless beginning to America's bloodiest war.

Jefferson Davis, a Democrat served as President of the Secessionist Confederate states from 1861 to 1865. He was a member of the Democratic party representing Mississippi in the U.S. Senate and House of Representatives prior to becoming the President of the Confederacy.

And so, the bloodiest war began and the responsibility rested with the pro-slavery, white supremacist Democrats, that led to the tragedy and horror of the Civil War and caused so many of the young northerners who supported freedom for the blacks to give their lives voluntarily in this just cause.

The Democratic party today wants us to believe that it is the Republicans that are the racists and white supremacists. What a hypocrisy; what a falsehood. It is the Democrats that for over 125 years have defended slavery, started a Civil war to sustain slavery, even provided legal justification for slavery and fought in Congress against every civil rights act. And we certainly must not forget the racism of the Democrat party in relation to the Japanese Americans during WW II where Democrat Franklin D. Roosevelt issued Executive order 9066 which interred 127,000 Japanese because they were of Japanese descent. His order was confirmed by a Democratic court consisting of 7 Democrat justices and 2 Republican justices.

Emancipation Proclamation

Abraham Lincoln, by Executive Order on January 1, 1863, issued Proclamation 95, better known as the Emancipation Proclamation, which changed the Federal legal status of more than 3 million enslaved people. Approximately two years later the !3th Amendment to the Constitution was finally passed, which abolished slavery and involuntary servitude. The Senate voted overwhelmingly for the Amendment and by a vote of 38 to 6, passed it on April 8, 1864. But the House on June 15, 1864 voted 93 in favor and 65 against, 13 votes short of the two-thirds needed for pass. The split was along party lines with the Republicans supporting and the Democrats opposing. This opposition was strictly from Northern Democrats, since no Southern States were represented. So even in the North, where slavery was virtually non-existent, there were many Democrats that supported slavery. It wasn't until the following year that enough Northern Democrats changed their vote and finally supported the Constitutional Amendment 13 that freed the slaves.

Carol Swaim's Essay

Carol Swain an African American and professor of political science and law at Vanderbilt University, faced a petition in November 2015 signed by over 1,000 students asking administrators to terminate her from teaching and requiring her to attend diversity training sessions. The students accused Swain of becoming: "Synonymous with bigotry, intolerance and unprofessionalism". The University administration sided with Swain stating that the University was committed to free speech and academic freedom. A pro-petition was started by supporters, suggesting that the student petition against Swain was reminiscent of China's Cultural Revolution where student Red Guards made false and ridiculous accusations against their professors. In January 2017, Swain announced she would retire from Vanderbilt in August, 2017 stating: "I will not miss what American Universities have allowed themselves to become". Maybe the best example of Carol Swain's position against the Democratic Party that ultimately gave rise to the quest for her termination by the Vanderbilt students on the liberal left is found in her essay entitled "The Inconvenient Truth About the Democratic Party". Here is the essay for which Swain was vilified and condemned by the liberal left:

"When you think about racial equality and civil rights, which political party comes to mind? The Republicans? Or, the Democrats? Most people would probably say the Democrats. But the answer is incorrect.

Since its founding in 1829, the Democratic Party has fought against every major civil rights initiative and has a long history of discrimination.

The Democratic party defended slavery, started the Civil War, opposed Reconstruction, founded the Ku Klux Klan, imposed segregation, perpetrated lynchings and fought against the civil rights acts of the 1950s and 1960s.

In contrast, the Republican Party was founded in 1854 as an anti-slavery party. Its mission was to stop the spread of slavery to the western territories with the aim of abolishing it entirely. This effort, however, was dealt a major blow by the Supreme Court in the case of Dred Scott v. Sanford. The court ruled that slaves aren't citizens; they're property. The seven justices who voted in favor of slavery? All Democrats. The two justices who dissented? Both Republicans.

The slavery question was, of course, ultimately resolved by a bloody civil war. The commander-in-chief during the war was the first Republican President, Abraham Lincoln – the man who freed the slaves.

Six days after the Confederate Army surrendered, John Wilkes Booth, a Democrat, assassinated President Lincoln. Lincoln's vice President, a Democrat named Andrew Johnson assumed the presidency. But Johnson was adamantly opposed to Lincoln's plan to integrate the newly freed slaves into the South's economic and social order.

Johnson and the Democratic Party were unified in their opposition to the 13th amendment which abolished slavery; the 14th Amendment, which gave blacks citizenship and the 15th Amendment which gave the blacks the vote. All three passed only because of universal Republican support.

During the era of Reconstruction, Federal troops stationed in the south helped secure rights for the newly free slaves. Hundreds of black men were elected to southern state legislatures as Republicans, and 22 Black Republicans served in the US Congress by 1900. The Democrats did not elect a black man to Congress until 1935. But after Reconstruction ended, when Federal troops went home, Democrats roared back into power in the South. They quickly re-established white supremacy across the region with measures like black codes -laws that restricted the ability of blacks to own property and run a business. And they imposed poll taxes and literacy tests, used to subvert the black citizen's right to vote.

And how was all of this enforced? By terror – much of it instigated by the Ku Klux Klan, founded by a Democrat, Nathan Bedford Forest. An historian, Eric Fonner – himself a Democrat – notes: "In effect, the Klan was a military force serving the interests of the Democratic Party".

President Woodrow Wilson, a Democrat, shared many views with the Klan. He re-segregated many federal agencies and even screened the first movie ever played at the White House – the racist film Birth of a Nation" – originally entitled "The Clansman"

*A few decades later, the only serious congressional opposition to the landmark Civil Rights Act of 1964 came from Democrats. Eighty Percent of Republicans in Congress supported the bill. Less than 70 percent of Democrats did. Democratic senators filibustered the bill for 75 days, until Republicans mustered the few extra votes to break the logjam. And when all of their efforts to enslave blacks, keep them enslaved and then keep them from voting failed, the Democrats came up with a new strategy. If black people are going to vote, they might as well vote for Democrats. As Democrat President Lyndon Johnson was purported to have said about the Civil Rights Act, I'll have them n****s voting Democrat for 200 years.*

So now the Democratic Party prospers on the votes of the very people it has spent much of its history oppressing. Democrats falsely claim that the Republican Party is the villain, when in reality it is the failed policies of the Democratic Party that have kept the blacks down

So, when you think about racial equality and civil rights, which political party should come to mind?"

For sure, Black lives matter, but more importantly, All lives matter. It is time for Blacks to realize that their African ancestors made slavery possible, for without Africans enslaving their own brothers and aiding and abetting the slave traders, there would have been no slavery as we know it. It is also time for African-Americans to realize that the Democrats not the Republicans have been your oppressors and sought mightily to keep African-Americans in bondage. And it is time for African-Americans to look at how they have fared under Democrat rule in the major cities and urban areas in our country.

Robert Byrd

The historical hatred and suppression of blacks by the Democrats before the Civil war and for over 100 years after the civil war cannot be better demonstrated than by Robert Byrd, U.S. Democrat Senator from West Virginia for over 51 years. He died in office in June 2000 and he was a revered colleague of Joe Biden, who eulogized him at his funeral. During the 1940's Robert Byrd was a high-ranking member of the Ku Klux Klan in West Virginia. In 1944 he wrote: "I shall never fight in the armed forces with a negro by my side. Rather I should die a thousand times and see Old Glory trampled in the dirt never to rise again rather than see this beloved land of ours become degraded by race mongrels a throwback to the blackest specimen from the wild" Then, in 1946, Byrd wrote to the Grand Wizard: "The Klan is needed today as never before and I am anxious to see its rebirth here in West Virginia and in every nation". In later years Byrd appeared to have a change of mind and would concede that his hatred of blacks was wrong and that intolerance has no place in America. Even so, Byrd was the lone Senator to vote against the confirmation of the only two African-Americans nominated to the United States Supreme Court, opposing Thurgood Marshall in 1967 and Clarence Thomas in 1991.

Byrd joined the Senate Dixiecrats in filibustering the Civil Rights Act of 1964, a filibuster that lasted over 80 days. Byrd's personal filibuster of 14 hours, 13 minutes remains the 11th longest filibuster in history. Byrd would also vote against the Voting Rights Act.

It is interesting to note, that two Democrat candidates for President Joe Biden and Cory Booker in trying to put a racist, white supremacist label on President Trump, compare him to another African-American hating, white supremacist George Wallace, Democrat Governor of Alabama for 20 years. Wallace chose to run for President as a segregationist candidate, who gained nominal support from black hating white-supremacist, Democrats.

The Ku Klux Klan

We have discussed the role of the Democrats in suppressing blacks for over a century after they had gained their freedom by the proclamation of Republican President Abraham Lincoln and the willingness of Northern Republican men to sacrifice their lives and limbs to achieve freedom for the blacks. But it was not long after blacks obtained their freedom, that the Southern White Democrats founded the terrible, hateful, murderous organization called the Ku Klux Klan. President Abraham Lincoln had been assassinated by a radical Democrat, John Wilkes Booth on April 15, 1865. On December 24, 1865 the hateful American White Supremacist organization, the Ku Klux Klan, was founded in Pulaski, Tennessee by six former officers of the Confederate Army. Klan groups rose across the South as an insurgent group, promoting resistance to freedom for blacks. Another Confederate veteran, John W. Morton, founded a chapter in Nashville, Tennessee as a secret vigilante group. The Klan targeted freedmen and any that supported them. The Klan sought to restore White Supremacy by violence including the murder of blacks, by hanging, shooting or even burning them in their homes and churches. The Klan also targeted white northerners, and supporters of the rights of freedmen. In 1868 Confederate General Nathan Bedford Forrest was elected the first Grand Wizard and became the Klan's first national leader. He stated that the Klan's primary target were Republican State governments.

In effect the Klan became a military force, serving the interests of the Democrat party, specifically against black freedmen. The aim of the Ku Klux Klan in the 1860's was no different form the aim of today's Democratic Party, to destroy the Republican Party and launch a reign of hatred and violence against those that disagree with them (i.e. Republicans)

The Ku Klux Klan continued to ravage the South and Republican efforts led by President Ulysses Grant issued Enforcement Acts in 1870 and 1871 to suppress and prosecute the KKK. In 1871 Grant asked for and Congress passed the Enforcement Act of 1871, also known as the Civil Rights Act of 1871 and also known as the Ku Klux Klan Act. The Enforcement Acts of 1870 and 1871 were criminal codes which protected African-Americans' right to vote, right to hold office, right to serve on juries and have equal protection under the laws.

This was not enough to stave off the atrocities of the Southern White Democrats. And no travesty better exemplified the Democrat white hatred for blacks than the Massacre of 150 black men in Colfax, Louisiana on Easter Sunday, April 13, 1873. A group of White Southern Democrat KKK members armed with rifles and small canon overpowered black Republican Freedmen and black state militia. Most of the freedmen were killed after surrendering and nearly 50 were killed after being held prisoners for several hours

In contrast to the atrocities of the Southern White Democrats, Ulysses Grant and the Republican party lobbied hard for the 15th Amendment, which guaranteed that blacks would have full citizenship and suffrage. It was passed. Despite Democratic opposition, the Republicans steadily won ratification and the necessary ¾'s of the states finally passed the 15th Amendment on February 3, 1870, which reads as follows:

15th Amendment to the Constitution

Section 1 – The right of citizens of the United States to vote shall not be denied or abridged by the United States or by any State on account of race, color or previous condition of servitude.

Section 2 - The Congress shall have the power to enforce this article by appropriate legislation.

The Jim Crow Laws

The white supremacist attitude of the Democrats toward Blacks in America was not going to be thwarted by the law of the land. And so, in response, the Democrats in control of the South found a way to keep blacks in their place; the so-called **JIM CROW LAWS.** The African American community in the south would be segregated and punished by these laws created by the Democrats for almost 100 years after gaining their freedom.

The Jim Crow laws were state and local laws that enforced racial segregation in Southern states in the late 19th and most of the 20th century, by white Democrat dominated legislatures. These laws were enforced until 1965, when they were finally declared unconstitutional and "separate but equal" would supposedly no longer be tolerated. So, the Democrats were the white supremacists, the racists, who singularly persecuted the Indians, the blacks and the Japanese for over 250 years.

In practice, the Jim Crow Laws mandated racial segregation in the states that were the former Confederate States at the time of secession. The pro-slavery, white supremacist Democrats ran and controlled states included: South Carolina, Mississippi, Florida, Alabama, Georgia, Texas, Virginia, Arkansas, Tennessee and North Carolina. Although President Lincoln's Executive Order, the Emancipation Proclamation, issued on January 1, 1863, changed the legal status of 3 million backs from slaves to free, the Jim Crow laws in the Democrat South would create a new level of oppression for the Blacks and lead to a high level of lynchings coupled with limited employment opportunities for black Americans. This would lead to a Great Black American migration to the North, Midwest and the West. That occurred even into the early 1970's. Prior to 1910, more than 90% of African Americans lived in the South. Six million would migrate North, Midwest and West during the next 60 years. Only 10% of African Americans living in the South in 1900 lived in urban areas and by 1970 more than 80% of African-Americans lived in cities nation-wide. And the cities would almost be entirely controlled and run by Democrats, who have done virtually nothing for them other than to count their votes. We have seen how the cities with the highest crime rates, highest black unemployment rates, the highest murder rates are all run by Democrats.

Martin Luther King –

The Jim Crow laws continued to repress the Blacks and subjected them to violence imposed by the Southern Democrat political leaders, until Martin Luther King came on these scene and King's peaceful confrontation with the policies of segregation under the Democrat South began in 1955. Note that Martin Luther King championed the black quest for equality, not in opposition to whites, rather in opposition to white Democrats

Montgomery Alabama movement 1955 - The Montgomery, Alabama boycott by African-Americans against the policy of racial segregation on the public transit system of that facility achieved little. However, it was a start. Martin Luther King was now President of the Southern Christian Leadership Conference (SCLC),

The Albany Movement, 1961 - King mobilized thousands of citizens for a non-violent confrontation on every aspect of segregation within the city. The movement was doomed because the confrontation was too general. Although the rallies themselves failed and the Southern Supremacist Democrats continued their illegal suppression of the Blacks, the movement learned to distrust the media and journalists. The media and journalists were banned from mass meetings and conferences of SCLC. Does this sound familiar. Today's Democrats flaunt the laws of our country as they see fit and they control a biased media that promulgates information to incite the voters to hate and to vilify the Republican right.

The Birmingham Movement, 1963 -In April, 1963 Martin Luther King began a non-violent campaign against racial segregation and economic injustice in Birmingham, Alabama. The protesters occupied public spaces with marches and sit-ins, openly violating the City of Birmingham and State of Alabama laws. The response of the Birmingham police department under Police Chief "Bull" O'Connor was swift and deadly. He turned high pressure water jets on the Blacks and turned police dogs against the protesters including children. King himself would be arrested (one of the 29 times he was arrested).

The March on Washington, 1963 – On August 28, 1963 Martin Luther King marched on Washington. The march made specific demands: an end to racial segregation in public schools; meaningful civil rights legislation; laws prohibiting racial discrimination in employment and protection from police brutality; all evils imposed on blacks by the white supremacist Democrats. More than 250,000 people of diverse ethnicities attended the event sprawling around the Lincoln Memorial and the National Mall. This was the largest gathering of protestors in Washington's history up to that time. It was here that Martin Luther King delivered his 17 minutes: "I have a dream" speech, one of the finest speeches in the history of America. It is worth recounting some parts of it here. Martin Luther said:

"I have a dream that one day in Georgia the sons of former slaves and the sons of former slave-owners will be able to sit down together at the table of brotherhood".

How can we ever have brotherhood when all the Democrats do is consistently hate and vilify not only our President, but also all that support him. How can we all sit down at a table of brotherhood, when the Democrats claim that all Republicans are deplorables; or that there is a special place in hell for any woman that doesn't vote for a Democrat woman, or that one cannot be a Democrat if he or she is pro-life? Or how can we sit down as brothers, when we are told that the President we voted for (and that's roughly 50% of us) should be shot for treason, hung from the highest tree, have his head cut off, be assassinated by gun or knife, or be blown up with his wife in the White House? And these words of hate and vitriol from the left have been incessant; every day for almost three years.

"I have a dream that one day even the state of Mississippi, a state sweltering with the heat of oppression, will be transformed into an oasis of freedom and justice".

How can we find freedom and justice, where Democrats cry out for the impeaching or jailing of the president, without any proof of wrong-doing, which they have been searching for almost 3 years and spending millions of taxpayer money for investigations and have found nothing? And during those almost three years, they have done nothing to improve the lives of their constituents particularly the black community. And they have violated time and again the very foundation of our justice system that one is presumed innocent until proven guilty. And they have flaunted the very laws that they had previously not only supported but approved, specifically in the case of the creation of sanctuary cities.

"I have a dream that one day in Alabama with its vicious racists, with its governor having his lips dripping with words of interposition and nullification, one day right there in Alabama little black boys ad black girls will be able to join hands with little white boys and white girls as sister and brother."

How can that ever be when the Democrats encourage blacks to believe that all white Republicans are white supremacists and racists and when they seek to indoctrinate the black community to hate those on the Conservative right and to hate the white police across our country.

In his "I have a dream" speech, Martin Luther King was specifically drawing attention to Southern Democrats as the white supremacists and racists by mentioning three of the most racists states in the south, namely, Alabama, Missouri and Georgia.

Selma, Alabama 1965 (Bloody Sunday) – Even the passage of the Civil Rights Act of 1964 did little in some parts of the South, to restrain Southern White Democrats from denying Blacks their basic rights. In January 1965, Martin Luther King came to Selma, Alabama in a peaceful protest of the City for denying Blacks the right to vote. Alabama's Governor, George Wallace in response to King's plan to march 54 miles from Selma to the state capitol in Montgomery, ordered his troops "to use whatever measures are necessary to prevent the march". John Lewis, 25 years old at the time and recently deceased Congressman from Georgia was one of the leaders of the march along with Martin Luther King and his wife Coretta King. King, Lewis and Coretta King set out from the Brown Chapel AME Church in Selma and began crossing the Alabama River over the Edmund Pettus Bridge (named after Confederate General Pettus who was reputed to have been the Grand Dragon of the Alabama Ku Klux Klan).

Waiting at the bridge for the Kings, Lewis and the other marchers totaling approximately 600 was a wall of state troopers. When the marchers had arrived within 50 feet of the troopers, John Lewis requested to have a word with Major John Clod, the leader of the state troopers. "I have nothing to say to you", responded Cloud and his troopers wearing gas masks and carrying clubs advanced. The troopers knocked the marchers to the ground, beat them with clubs, unleashed tear gas and ran them down on horseback. The troopers even used whips and rubber tubing wrapped in barbed wire. The protesters did not fight back. John Lewis himself was severely injured. His skull was fractured and the scars remained. All the marchers wanted to do was to dialogue peacefully in the hope of getting justice and freedom from the Jim Crow laws. The brutality of Bloody Sunday in Selma, Alabama galvanized public opinion and as a result Congress passed the voting rights act which was signed into law on August 6, 1965. John Williams is to be admired and respected for his contributions to the movement that would begin removing the repression that was imposed upon them by the white Democrat supremacists.

Death of Martin Luther King – On April 4, 1968, Martin Luther King was assassinated by James Earl Ray, as King stood on the second-floor balcony of the Lorraine Motel in Memphis, Tennessee. James Earl Ray hated black people, was a segregationist and supported for president the radical Democrat Governor of Alabama George Wallace.

What about Native Americans? – The Indian Removal Act -The Trail of Tears-

The racism and hatred of non-whites by the Democrats, even preceded the conflict between Republicans and Democrats over slavery that eventually gave rise to the Emancipation, the civil war and the on-going persecution of blacks by the Democrats. We need to turn back to the Presidency of Andrew Jackson, a Democrat whose pro-slavery, anti-black beliefs carried over to the Native American.

Democrat President Andrew Jackson –

A Democrat white supremacist President, Andrew Jackson proposed the "Indian Removal Act of 1830", which would disrupt 5 Indian tribes in the South East and force them to travel over 1,000 miles without their belongings, many to die along the way. In his inaugural address to Congress in 1830, Jackson talked about the Indian Removal Act saying: it will enable them to pursue happiness in their own way under their own rude institutions…. It will retard their decay, which is lessening their numbers and perhaps cause them gradually under protection of the government and the influence of good counsels, to cast off their savage habits and become an interesting civilized Christian community". He then went on to say: "And is it supposed that the wandering savage has a stronger attachment to his home than the settled civilized Christian? The policy of the General government toward the red men is not only liberal but generous". And so, it was with the Democrats even 30 years before Republican President Abraham Lincoln freed the black slaves. President Jackson's successor, Martin Van Buren, another white supremacist Democrat, who was President from 1837 to 1841 strongly enforced the actions against Native Americans started by President Jackson. And from 1829 when Andrew Jackson took office through 1841 when Martin Van Buren was succeeded by William Harrison, the Senate and the House were both controlled by Democrats. Leaders of the Whig party often referred to as the Anti- Jacksonian Party and the fore-runner of the Republican Party, were strongly opposed to this treatment of the Native Americans. In particular, Henry Clay and Daniel Webster, both of the anti-Jacksonian (Republican to be party) vehemently raised their objections to the Indian Removal Act and the unconstitutional use of it to remove Native Americans from their homes. There is no worse example of white supremacism against Native Americans than the "Trail of Tears".

The Indian Removal Act was overwhelmingly voted for by the Democrats providing a 28 for and 19 opposed decision in the Senate. The decision in the House was much closer, although again the Democrats prevailed with a vote of 101 to 97.

Trail of Tears - From 1838 to 1839 as part of Andrew Jackson's Indian Removal policy, the Cherokee nation was forced to give up its lands East of the Mississippi River and migrated to an area in present day Oklahoma. The 1,000-mile journey became known as the Trail of Tears. 60,000 Native Americans were forced to make this journey and 13,000 to 15,000 died along the way.

U.S. Supreme Court Decision – Worcester v. Georgia (1832) - In this case, the Supreme Court ruled that the states did not have the right to impose regulations on Native American land, because they have sovereignty within the nation and therefore, the Georgia Act that forced the Cherokee Nation to leave their lands in Georgia (The Indian Removal Act) was unconstitutional. This decision did not deter Andrew Jackson. He decided to ignore this Supreme Court decision. Instead, he sent Federal troops to take over the Cherokee Nation's land and to force the removal of the Native Americans. The Cherokee families were not even allowed to gather up their belongings as they left and whites looted their homes. But the Cherokees were not the only tribe that was illegally disrupted and driven from their homes. So were the Creek, Choctaw, Chickasaws and Seminole. The breakdown is as follows along with some interesting numbers of black slaves of these tribes who trekked with them on their journey on the Trail of Tears.

Tribe	Number Removed	Deaths From Journey	Black Slaves Included
Cherokee	20,000	4,000	2,000
Creek	19,600	3,500	900
Choctaw	12,500	4,000	500
Chickasaws	4,000	800	1,200
Seminole	2,800	700	-
Totals	58,900	13,000	4,600

Democrat President, Woodrow Wilson – 1913 to 1921

Another Democrat president that was racist and white supremacist was Woodrow Wilson, even by the standards of 1910. He oversaw the resegregation of multiple agencies within the Federal Government. Upon taking office, President Wilson, himself fired 15 of 17 black supervisors and replaced them with whites. The head of the Internal Revenue Service in Georgia, fired all of his black employees saying: "there are no government positions in the South for Negroes. A Negro's place is in the cornfield. To enable hiring discrimination going forward, the Federal Government in 1914 began requiring photographs on applications.

Wilson was a vocal defender of the Ku Klux Klan. Wilson attacked reconstruction on the ground that: "the dominance of an ignorant and inferior race was justly dreaded". His radical racism went even so far as being against black suffrage. He said: "It was a menace to society itself" Woodrow Wilson praised those slaves who: "stayed very quietly by their masters and gave them no trouble".

Wilson's racism wasn't a matter of a few unfortunate remarks here and there. It was a core part of his identity.

What About Japanese Americans During World War II?

On March 18, 1942, Democrat President Franklin D. Roosevelt by Executive order created the War Relocation Authority (WRA) to handle the relocation and internment of Japanese-Americans during World War II. These were American citizens, men, women and children many who had been born in the United States. The concentration camps would eventually house 120,000 people of Japanese ancestry. On April 22, 1943 the whole Japanese race is condemned by the President stating: "As a race, the Japanese have made themselves a record of conscienceless treachery unsurpassed in history". By these words, every Japanese in America had been condemned by their Democrat President and in turn by the whole country.

Milton Eisenhower, brother of future President Dwight Eisenhower, was appointed the first Director of the War Relocation Authority. Although a proponent of FDR's New Deal, he disapproved the idea of mass internment. Early on he had tried to limit the internment to adult males, allowing women and children to remain free. Milton Eisenhower wrote: When the war is over and we consider calmly this unprecedented migration of 120,000 people, we as Americans are going to regret the unavoidable injustices that we have done". Milton Eisenhower is most likely better known for his contributions to education as a University Administrator serving in the capacity of President of three universities, namely: Kansas State (1943-1950); Pennsylvania State (1950-1956) and Johns Hopkins (1971-1972).

The Little Rock Nine

On September 25, 1957 under escort from the U.S. Army's 101st Airborne Division, 9 black students enter the all-white Central High School in Little Rock, Arkansas. Three weeks earlier, Arkansas Governor, Orval Faubus had surrounded the school with National Guard troops to prevent its Federal Court ordered integration. After a tense standoff, Republican President Dwight Eisenhower federalized the Arkansas National Guard and sent 1,000 Army paratroopers to Little Rock to enforce the Federal order. Under heavily armed guard, the "Little Rock Nine" entered Central High. The 101st Airborne Division ,known as the "Screaming Eagles" was founded in 1942 and would be considered the elite of the airborne divisions during WWII. They parachuted into Normandy and cleared the was for the infantry divisions at Omaha and Utah beaches and were called into action at the Battle of the Bulge to defend a critical transportation hub. The "Little Rock Nine" incident was just another episode, where Republicans reached out to defend the rights and freedoms of blacks that were consistently being repressed by the Democrats and their political leaders.

Jackie Robinson

One of my greatest memories was accidentally meeting Jackie Robinson in New York City, sometime in the late 50's. I was walking down John Street from Broadway, toward my place of business at Chubb and Son at 90 John Street. I was just passing the Chuck Full o' Nuts store on John Street, when I almost bumped into Jackie Robinson, about to enter the store. I got up my nerve and said "Mr. Robinson". He stopped and I went up to him and offered him my hand. As we were shaking hands I said to him: "Mr. Robinson, I know of of no other man that has done more for blacks and the human race." With that he smiled and we departed.

Jackie Robinson was a life-long Republican as was Branch Rickey and together they broke the barrier that precluded black athletes from playing major league baseball. In 1960, Jackie Robinson campaigned rigourously for Richard Nixon against John F. Kennedy, citing Nixon's support of the 1957 Civil Rights Act, which Kennedy and many other Democrats opposed.

Time and time again over a period of 200 years that Democrats have either outwardly opposed the rights of blacks to liberty and freedom or time again have made false promises to them to get their votes. They have been responsible for running every major crime ridden city in the United States and allowed the murdering of blacks in these cities to run rampant. Yet for some reason, the blacks keep voting for Democrat leaders even though they have consistently thwarted their attempt to obtain their God given rights to life, liberty, property and the pursuit of happiness. Does this make sense? Is it time for blacks to re-examine their loyalties to the Democrat party?

CHAPTER 21

President Trump's Accomplishments in his first Two Years.

DESPITE THE ONGOING, vilification and hatred that has led the Socialist Democrats, the Media, the Entertainment Industry and most of our educators to ignore or make little of the accomplishments of the Trump Administration, there have been many and it would seem that most should be acknowledged by everyone to be good for the country. This chapter will highlight just a few of the accomplishments and benefits achieved by the Trump Administration in just two years. For the most part this list has been compiled from a release in October 2018 by the Washington Examiner. The underlying premises of President Trump's actions are based on his fundamental beliefs that:

1. Capitalism as an economic system is far better than socialism.
2. The fundamental rights of human beings are the right to freedom and liberty
3. That the fundamental moral values as taught by Jesus Christ, should be guidance for everyone regardless of their religious beliefs
4. That the power of the National government should be restricted and where possible returned to the states.
5. A strong military is essential to protecting our rights to liberty and freedom
6. A strong Domestic police force is necessary to protect the rights of everyone and should be respected.
7. The U.S. Constitution must not be tampered with or misconstrued, or its interpretation and meaning changed without an agreement from the people in the form of an amendment
8. Socialism must not be allowed to take over our country either politically or economically.
9. Unlimited abortion is morally wrong and the unborn child is a person with the rights of any other human being.
10. Unless and until the Second Amendment is changed, the right to own guns should not be limited, but may be regulated.

The Economy - Employment: Pre Covid-19

1. 7.0 million jobs have been created since President Trump took office. More Americans are now employed than ever before in our history. Jobless claims are at the lowest level in nearly 5 decades. Job openings are at an all-time high and outnumber job seekers for the first time on record. Unemployment claims are at an all-time low. African-American, Hispanic and Asian-Americans unemployment have reached a record low and women's unemployment is at the lowest rate in 65 years at 3.6%. Youth unemployment rate at 9.2% is the lowest since July 1966 and Veteran's unemployment rate at 3.0% reached the lowest rate since May 2001. The unemployment rate for Americans without a high school diploma reached a record low. Blue Collar jobs grew at the fastest rate in more than a three decades.

2. In a poll 85% of blue-collar workers believe their lives are headed in the right direction. Job satisfaction of American workers hit the highest level since 2005

3. More than 500,000 manufacturing jobs have been added since President Trump took office, thanks to the corporate tax cuts. The pace of manufacturing job growth over the first 21 months of President Trump's leadership is more than 10 times that of President Obamas last 21 months in office.

4. 3.9 million Americans have come off food stamps since Trump took office.

5. Poverty rates of African-Americans and Hispanic-Americans have reached the lowest levels ever recorded.

6. 9 of 10 American workers saw their paychecks increase due to the tax cuts and more than 6 million workers have received wage increases and bonuses directly attributed to the tax cuts.

7. In 4th quarter of 2018, wages across the board rose more than 3% for the first time in more than 10 years. Minorities achieved equal or even better wage increases and labor participation rates reached its highest level in six years

8. In April 2019, average hourly earnings increased at a 3.2% pace for the ninth straight month in which wage growth topped 3%

9. Increased the exemption of the estate(death) tax to help save family farms and small businesses from being sold to meet the confiscatory estate tax burden.

10. On April 25, 2017, President Trump issued an Executive order Promoting Agriculture and Rural Prosperity in America. This created a task force, headed by the Secretary of Agriculture that will identify policy options to promote U.S. Agriculture and business growth in rural America. It will specifically look into regulations that impede U.S. Agricultural growth and look at ways to encourage the use of agricultural products in America.

11. An Ernst & Young survey found that 89% of companies surveyed planned to increase workers' compensation in response to the Trump tax cuts.

12. Established a National Council for the American worker to develop a strategy for training America's workers for high demand industries

13. Signed the first authorization since 2006 providing more than $1 billion to states each year to fund vocational and career educational programs

These results will be suspended immediately if the Socialist Democrats take over. Gone will be all the jobs associated with fossil fuels, airlines, cattle, private medical care, gas stations, convenience stores, small businesses and all the indirect support businesses for these activities. We have covered this in detail. All these accomplishments will be reversed as our unemployment levels reach staggering heights of 15% or even higher.

1. $500 Billion of foreign investment has flooded back into the United States as a result of the corporate tax cuts introduced by President Trump
2. Steel and Aluminum producers, imperative for our national security have re-opened plants and these industries have been revived.
3. Corporate tax rates were reduced significantly. Prior to the reduction the United States had the highest corporate tax rates in the developed world. As a result, an Ernst and Young survey found that 89% of companies polled planned to increase investment in plant and equipment.
4. The Dow Jones Industrial Average, S&P 500 and NASDQ have all reached record highs and at the fastest rate of any president in the first two years of office. The private retirement plans and investment portfolios of millions of Americans have been vastly improved as a result of the increase in corporate earnings due to the tax cuts; the low interest rates associated with alternative investments, and the expanding consumer and investor confidence in our economy.
5. For the first time our country is confronting China not only for its cyber-espionage, but for its unfair trade practices that is causing over $450 billion in trade imbalance. President Trump has been roundly criticized by the socialist left for imposing severe tariffs on Chinese goods, but they offer no suggestions for what is the alternative. The Democrats would have us suffer from severe trade imbalances forever, rather than create some short-term burden on our farmers, small businesses and manufacturers. The trade imbalance must be addressed. The lower corporate tax rates, subsidies to farmers and tax cuts for individuals have more than offset any cost to our individuals and corporations, yet the Socialist left still vehemently criticize the Trump administration. This can only be explained by either their ignorance or their treachery. The damage done by the trade imbalances with China and Mexico has been discussed elsewhere but it is a severe threat to our jobs, our economy and our country's security.
6. February 24, 2017 President Trump issued an executive order to enforce his regulatory reform agenda. Each agency must designate an official as a Regulatory Reform Officer (RRO) who will be responsible for reviewing current regulations and make recommendations to their agency, how to modify or eliminate them. The objective is to make business more efficient and less hindered by the time and cost associated with over regulation.
7. Small Business creation hits an all-time high.

The Economy - Trade: Pre Covid-19

I have discussed in length the damage to our economy caused by large trade deficits, which expanded every year under the Obama Administration. This will only get much worse if the Democrats were to succeed in obtaining unlimited power in our government. Our country would lose our growing exports of fossil fuels and with the replacement of air travel with rail transportation we would lose our important exports of commercial aircraft. Our total trade deficit in 2018 was $621 Billion, $500 billion of which was with China ($419 billion) and Mexico ($81 Billion). We exported $109 billion of fossil fuel products in 2018 and $130 billion of Commercial Aircraft. Overnight, the Democrats would increase our balance of trade deficit by $239 billion. This tragic occurrence would increase our trade deficit by almost 50%, above a level which is already unsustainable. We do not even discuss here the damage to our national security, resulting from the doing away with fossil fuels and air flight. Our country will be exposed for the first time to being overtaken by our enemies. Unfortunately, our enemies are all socialists and our Socialist Democrats will probably thrive under the dictatorship by either Russia or China.

1. March 31, 2017 – Omnibus Report on significant Trade Deficits. President Trump directed the Commerce Department to compile a report on trade practices contributing to the trade deficit. The report will examine all trade partners to assess if their practices unfairly discriminate against the U.S.

2. April 18, 2017 -Executive order – "Buy American, Hire American". The order has two parts: 1) Hire American tightens the rules that allow businesses to hire workers outside the United States and 2) gives U.S. companies priority when hiring contractors or purchasing goods, specifically reducing waivers and exemptions to current laws.

3. September 16, 2018 – President Trump signed the new U.S./Mexico/Canada trade agreement which among other things expanded access to the U.S. Dairy and Poultry markets, fulfilling President Trump's promise to bolster American Farmers. The USMCA Trade Agreement assures freer and fairer trade among the three countries.

4. Enacted steel and aluminum tariffs to protect our vital steel and aluminum producers, so essential to national security. The result was the reopening of steel and aluminum factories, the re-employment of steel workers and a move to self-sufficiency in these industries so that the United States would not be subject to foreign coercion.

5. Approved $12 billion in aid for farmers affected by unfair trade retaliation for U.S. mandated tariffs.

6. Confronted China's unfair trade practices after years of Obama's administration looking the other way.

7. Imposed heavy tariffs on China's goods and services, with the objective of reaching a fair-trade agreement with China. China had consistently had higher tariffs on Amirian goods than those imposed by the U.S. on goods and services from China. The onerous balance of trade deficit with China continued under the Obama administration and only got worse. When was this

imbalance going to stop? When would a Democrat leader take strong and necessary action? The Trump Administration has been consistently criticized by the Democrat leaders and its controlled media for placing tariffs on Chinese goods as it results in higher cost of Chines goods for Americans and also hurts the farmer in the sale of their products to China when retaliatory tariffs are put in place. The Democrats would have our country remain at status quo, continue to lose jobs to Chinese workers and see more and more money flow out of our economy. To do nothing is not an option. To do something may cause a little pain, but Trump's $12 billion in aid to farmers and the tax cuts for the American tax payer, should offset most if not all the pain caused by the tariff war between China and the U.S.

8. Issued Executive order establishing better enforcement of anti-dumping and other trade laws
9. Conducts 82 major actions protecting U.S. Trade an increase of 58% over the Obama Administration.

Domestic Infrastructure

Even though the total government debt of the United States doubled under President Obama and more debt was created under the Obama administration than all the debt previously created under all the other presidents from the beginning of our country, we have nothing to show for it. The Obama administration left our military with obsolete and malfunctioning equipment to a level that was cited as very dangerous for the security of our government. In his 8 years he presided over a country whose infrastructure deteriorated every year to the point where over 60,000 of our bridges and tunnels had become unsafe and need immediate rehabilitation. What did we get for the $10 trillion of new debt imposed on the taxpayers of the United States? **NOTHING!** This was one of the biggest travesties of the Liberal Left government, which is now heading to go even further left and become socialist. Look at what local Democrat leaders have wrought on the major cities of the United States to see what we can expect from them about or infrastructure. We have discussed in detail the filth, crime and high murder rates that exist in all the major cities that are run by Democrats. Those who are considering voting for the Socialist left, based on the performance of the Democrats in your states and your cities, can you really trust that they will make your lives better if you entrust them to undertake the rule of our country as a socialist state? What has the Trump Administration done to improve our infrastructure?

1. The Trump Administration has proposed an infrastructure plan that would utilize $200 billion in Federal funds to spur at least $1.5 trillion in investment in infrastructure across the country. Note that the massive infrastructure program undertaken by the joint effort of the Liberal left government of California and the Obama Administration to build a high-speed rail from Los Angeles to San Francisco had a time over run of 15 years over the original planned 10 years and after the spending of $3 billion had to be totally abandoned. And Obama's government's brief sally into solar energy ended abruptly with the failure of Solyndra at a cost to the tax-payer of $500 million. Can we really permit our Democrat leaders the power to invest $10's of trillions of dollars in infrastructure and alternative energy, when their initial investments in this area

have been a total failure?

2. The Trump administration issued an executive order to reduce the time for environmental reviews and approvals for critical infrastructure projects from 10 years to 2 years.

3. The Trump administration issued an executive order requiring government agencies to reduce the number of regulations by two for each new one issued. The cuts of Obama Administration regulations and red tape has already resulted in saving $378 million annually.

4. President Trump directed the Chairman of the Council of Environmental Quality (CEQ) to within 30 days of a submission of a project to determine the project's environmental impact.

5. President Trump created the Presidential Advisory Council on Infrastructure - an advisory council within the Department of Commerce in order to advance infrastructure projects. The Council will be composed of up to 15 members with expertise in: finance, real estate, construction and environmental policy. The Council will submit a report on potential infrastructure projects that could be carried out over the next 10 years.

6. President Trump issued an Executive Order to establish discipline and accountability in the environmental review and permitting process for infrastructure projects. The order aims to increase the efficiency of Federal Infrastructure permitting process and revokes an Obama Executive Order that created environmental review standards that resulted in environmental reviews taking as long as 10 years. The order set as a goal a 2-year target to complete environmental reviews. A prime example of the 10-year environmental review process concerned the infrastructure proposal in California to build a high-speed railway. 10 years after initiating the project, the environmental studies were still on-going and the high-speed railway was abandoned. Can you just imagine what the Democrats will have in store for us in environmental reviews for a $100 trillion worth of projects to meet their fossil fuel free environment? The Democrats could not even start, let alone complete a $3 billion railway, initially to be completed in 10 years that eventually expanded to a $10 billion railway to be completed in 24 years and finally abandoned.

Health Care

At a cost of $33 trillion ($52 trillion estimated by Presidential candidate Elizabeth Warren) the Democrats are proposing a national health care plan for everyone including illegal aliens. This works out to $3.3 trillion per year, which is equivalent to 83% of our current total Federal budget, and over 100% of our total government revenues from taxes. It is cost that cannot be met, even though rationing medical care and limiting to the young and healthy. The 180 million people currently insured by private plans provided through private insurance or corporate plans, will lose their right to choose plans; will lose their right to choose their doctor or medical facility they wish to go to and in many instances, particularly in the case of the aged and infirmed, will be refused medical treatment. The performance of the Government in running medical services has been demonstrated by the disaster in medical care for Veterans in Veterans Hospitals, which represent only 20 million not 320 million people. Every Democrat candidate would have our country forsake all private medical care and force every person to look to the Federal Government to make their health decisions for them. And more grievous is that many will be denied medical services because a Federal panel will determine whether or not a person should be treated, or how much medical service should be allocated to him. And the $3.3 trillion/year cost cannot be sustained, so medical services and choices will have to be cut back somehow. Those who will suffer most will be the retired, the elderly, the bed-ridden and severely sick and disabled. The healthy and young will get the benefits of the Nationalist medical program, while the aged and infirmed will have to bear the burden of less medical services in order to better manage costs. We have also previously covered the monumental loss of jobs in the health care industry, which is just another serious burden placed on our economy. By her own count, Elizabeth Warren has suggested that 2 million jobs would be lost

The Trump administration will sustain private health insurance. He would expand the right of insurance companies to offer insurance nationally and not be restricted to individual states. This would greatly enhance competition. He also has made it clear that he supports coverage for pre-existing conditions. Here are some of the accomplishments of the Trump Administration, regarding Health Care.

1. Signed right to try legislation expanding health care options for terminally ill.
2. Enacted changes in the Medicare program resulting in saving seniors an estimated $320 million annually in drug costs.
3. Repealed Obamacare's burdensome individual mandate. Individuals and families under Obamacare were forced to pay a fine, if they chose to self-insure. Anecdotally, a middle-income family of 4, had chosen to self-insure because they couldn't afford to pay $2,000/month premium, coupled with an $8,000 deductible. Under Obamacare the family would have to spend $32,000/year before any medical benefits kicked in. Thankfully, the Trump administration eliminated the mandate and the family could self-insure.
4. President Trump also repealed Obamacare's Independent Payment Advisory Board also known as "death panels". This panel would have made life and death decisions, determining who should or should not get medical treatment. The "death panels" would be restored under any national health plan as a major cost controlling tool of the plan.
5. Approved $6 billion of new funding to fight the opioid epidemic, which had greatly expanded during Obama's administration and will even get worse if the Democrat plan for open borders and doing away with ICE is ever implemented. The Democrats are even suggesting legalizing all drugs and opening drug clinics so that addicts can get their "fix" with clean needles.
6. The Department of Justice (DOJ) secured the first ever indictment against Chinese Fentanyl manufactures.
7. The Trump Administration created a commission to combat the drug addiction and opioid crisis and declared the opioid crisis as a national public health emergency in October 2017. This crisis was ignored for 8 years under the Obama Administration.

8. April 27, 2017 – Executive order for Improving Accountability and Whistle Blower Protection. This order was specifically aimed at improving accountability within the Department of Veterans' Affairs. During the Obama Administration dozens of veterans died needlessly while on a wait-list for medical care. The incompetence, fraud and abuse of thousands of veterans at the hands of VA hospitals across the country clearly demonstrates the incompetence and incapability of the Federal government to run a National Health Care system. If the Federal Government could not provide adequate medical care for the treatment of 20 million veterans, how can we expect that the Democrat Run National Health Care system will be able to provide adequate health services for 330 million?

9. October 12, 2017 – Executive order promoting Health Care choice and competition across the United States.

Veterans Affairs

The Obama Administration failed miserably in the treatment of our Veterans particularly in the area of medical services. Fraud and incompetence were rampant in the VA under Obama and it festered for the full 8 years of his administration. The elimination of fraud and the increasing of accountability of the VA executives were major goals for Trump at the time he took office.

1. President Trump signed the VA Accountability Act and expanded walk-in clinics to provide same day urgent primary and mental health care.

2. Signed legislation that provided $86.5 billion in funding for the Department of Veterans Affairs, the largest dollar amount in the history of the VA

3. Signed legislation to modernize the claims and appeals process of the VA

4. Signed the Veterans Choice and Quality Employment Act of 2017 which authorized $2.1 billion in additional funds for the Veterans Choice program

5. Created a White House VA Hotline to help veterans. The Hotline would be principally staffed with veterans

6. VA Employees are now being held accountable for poor performance and under Trump Administration, 4,000 VA employees have been removed, demoted or suspended.

Law and Order

The major concerns of the Trump Administration deal with the direction of the Supreme Court in terms of strict construction or revisionism. We have covered previously the dangers of allowing the Supreme Court to change the meaning of the U.S. Constitution and its amendments thereto, to fit their political beliefs as to what is best for the country. The Supreme Court is supposed to be only an arbiter, not a legislator. The separation of powers is greatly watered down, when the judicial branch is free to interpret and change the meanings of different clauses and amendments to our constitution.

- **Supreme Court** - The Trump Administration has appointed 2 Associate Judges of the Supreme Court, 43 judges to the United States Courts of Appeal and 99 Justices to the United States District Courts.

- **Enhancing Public Safety in the Interior of the United States**

    1. Strips grant money to so-called sanctuary cities
    2. Hires 10,000 new immigration officers
    3. Calls on local and state police to detain and apprehend people in the United States Illegally
    4. Directs Federal funding to construct a wall along the Mexico/U.S. border (Note a wall previously endorsed by Obama, Biden, Pelosi, Schumer, Bill Clinton, Hilary Clinton and many others Democrats)
    5. Calls for the ending of the "catch and release" protocol
    6. Directed the hiring of 5,000 more Border Patrol Agents

- **Enforcing Federal Law with Respect to Transnational criminal Organizations nd Preventing International Trafficking**

    1. Outlines Administrative approach to cutting down crime, including gangs, cartels and racketeering organizations
    2. Enhanced cooperation with foreign governments and improved sharing of information and data between countries
    3. Identifies human trafficking, drug smuggling and cyber-crimes as threats to public safety and national security. The DOJ secured its first-ever indictment against Chinese Fentanyl manufacturers
    4. ICE's Investigative Division arrested 796 MS-13 members and associates in 2017 an 83% increase over Obama's Administration.
    5. Created a commission on combating Drug Addiction and the Opioid Crisis. Declared the Opioid crisis a nationwide public health emergency in October 2017. This crisis was ignored for 8 years under the Obama Administration.
    6. Justice Department establishes working relationship with partners in Central America Security forces. Criminal charges are brought against 4,000 MS-13 members and Border Patrol arrests 228 illegal aliens affiliated with MS-13.
    7. ICE made 11,691 narcotics related arrests of illegal aliens in 2017. Their job is continually made more difficult as Democrat leaders: refuse to support the securing of our borders with a wall. They actually seek open borders; seek to do away with ICE entirely and provide sanctuary for illegal aliens including criminals in major Democrat run cities in the United States. Further compounding the problems with immigration is the constant disparaging of

the Trump Administration for attempting to close our borders and even lying to constituents that there is no crisis at our borders. This lie is overwhelmingly disputed by video proof and affidavits from every ICE worker at the border, that a crisis exists.

8. In 2017 ICE enforcement and Removal operations arrested more than 127,000 illegal aliens with criminal convictions or charges including: 48,000 with assault offenses; 11,000 with weapons offenses; 5,000 with sexual assault offenses; 2,000 with kidnapping offenses and over 1,800 with homicide offenses. And the Democrat leaders keeps telling us there is no crisis on our borders.

Education

Our education system has been indoctrinated by the liberal left. We have previously discussed how the overwhelmingly socialist liberal left educators are indoctrinating our children from elementary school right through college. The teaching and celebration of Judaism and Christianity has been removed from our schools and Islam has been substituted. Capitalism is criticized and Socialism is embraced. Unrest and riots on college and university campuses throughout the United States have been encouraged as a First amendment right even if it quashes the rights of the conservative right. Our educators even teach our children to admire Russian and Chinese Communism and our leaders reflect on Venezuela as the model for our economic system. The Democrats seek to control our education system and move us even closer to the society depicted in George Orwell's book, "1984". The Trump Administration is the only adversary standing in the way of the Democrats from reaching their goal of a socialist, totalitarian state.

- On April 26, 2017, President Trump issued an executive order **Enforcing Statutory Prohibitions on Federal Control of Education.** The Secretary of Education is directed to study Federal overreach into local and state education systems, particularly in areas such as curriculum, school administration and textbook or library content. It should be noted that during the Obama Administration a vast National program was sponsored by the Department of Education to provide texts, curriculum and studies to teach the wonders of Islam to students from 3rd grade and up. This included learning Islamic prayers, dressing up in Muslim attire and placing posters of the "Five Pillars of Islam" in school hallway. In some schools, children were told to pretend to be Muslims for a week. This occurred even as any mention or display of Judeo/Christian theology in schools was strictly prohibited.
- On February 28,2017. President Trump issued the White House Initiative to Promote Excellence and Innovation at Historically Black colleges and Universities.

Foreign Policy

We do not hear the Democrat presidential candidates talking much about foreign policy. This probably is a reflection of the fact that none of them have any knowledge or experience with foreign policy, except possibly Presidential contender Joe Biden. On the contrary, almost everything the Democrats did during the Obama Administration and are now proposing for a Democrat administration will lead to the demise of our country. Let's just summarize some of the disastrous moves the Obama Administration made and a New Democrat admiration proposes.

- The Obama administration with the help of Secretaries Kerry and Clinton negotiated a one-sided treaty with Iran that gave them everything they wanted, most importantly $150 billion that would guaranty their ability to become a nuclear power in a very few years. Inspections in Iran were so limited that they were virtually useless. Iran was not prohibited from developing delivery systems and actual missile development and technology was readily available from their belligerent partner, North Korea. We are now learning just how absurd a treaty with Iran was as we see them attacking Saudi Arabia's Oil fields, destroying foreign ships and carrying on other acts of war throughout the Middle East either directly or through their support of ISIS. The naivete or downright stupidity of Obama, Kerry and Hilary Clinton should be obvious even to the most supportive of the Treaty.

- We saw the Obama Administration back down in Syria, after firmly stating that the use of Chemical weapons by Bashar al-Assad against his own people would be "crossing a red line". Assad killed thousands with Saran gas and Obama did nothing. Then the Russians attacked Crimea and again Obama did nothing. Then the Chinese began to usurp sovereignty over the China Sea and Obama did nothing. And then Kim Jung Un tested nuclear missile after nuclear missile and Obama did nothing. Then a resolution came up before the U.N. to condemn Israel for its inhuman acts against Palestinians and for the first time in its history, the United States turn away from Israel and by abstaining to vote allowed the resolution to pass. And then the Obama Administration did nothing as our trade deficit grew especially with China and Mexico. And the Obama Administration did nothing to protect our borders as the waives of illegal immigrants kept crossing our borders with Mexico. His bowing to Arabs on his visit to the Middle East did not go unnoticed. Under the Obama Administration our military equipment not only became obsolete, a substantial portion of it was out of service for maintenance and there were no parts to fix them.

Now we look at the 20 candidates for President. No foreign experience; little or no contact with the leaders of the world and no discussion of what they would do to promote and protect the safety of the United States and its people. Here's what will impact our safety if the Democrats get into power.

1. We will have no oil of our own to rely on if there is a military confrontation with super powers such as China and Russia.

2. We will have no aerospace industry, no jet fueled airplanes, no fossil fuel powered military vessels. We will see the demise of Boeing, McDonald Douglas, Lockheed Martin and Northrop Grumman as well as many other companies in the aerospace industry. Our research into air flight will dry up. Air weaponry is where our country leads and it is paramount to our defense. The Democrat goal of eliminating all our fossil fuel energy within 10 years is an invitation to

China, and Russia to just sit back and wait and then they can walk in and take over our country

3. With Democrat proposals calling for $13 trillion a year to be spent to provide National health care and to reduce fossil fuel usage to 0, the funding must come from somewhere. Doubling taxes for everyone, individuals and corporations alike will only raise $2.0 trillion at most. Where is the rest of the money going to come from? The Democrats will have to cut military spending and our military capacity and military quality will deteriorate to levels even below those we experienced during the Obama years. The Chinese and Russians know this. They can just sit back and wait as we become a defenseless third world country.

4. If the devastation of our military is not enough, the proposed policies of the Democrats will destroy our country internally as unemployment levels rise beyond the levels experienced during the great depression of the 1930's. Inflation will set in, interest rates will rise, the cost of food and shelter will increase even 1000%. Just look at Venezuela, Bernie Sanders role model for a political and economic system. You see the homelessness in the many Democrat run cities in the United State. Imagine it only getting 100 times if not 1000 times worse under the Democrat administration. We have previously covered this in detail elsewhere.

5. It isn't enough that the Democrats are proposing programs that will destroy our country economically and militarily. They actively and on a daily basis, condemn and ridicule every attempt made by the Trump administration to foster relationships with the leaders of foreign governments, particularly the ones that are our adversaries. According to the Democrat leaders, we shouldn't be talking to Vladimir Putin, Xi Jinping, or Kim Jong-Un. On the contrary, the Democrats actively seek to undermine President Trump's meetings with these heads of state. Dialogue with your enemies is so much more important than dialogue with your friends. Dialogue is also the best way to avoid confrontation that could lead to military action. In today's nuclear age this could result in terrible consequences. The Democrat leaders in shunning meetings with the heads of state because they don't like them or don't trust them are not valid reasons for avoiding dialogue. It is only through dialogue that common ground can be reached and compromise is the only way to avoid military confrontation. Unfortunately, the Democrats and none of their presidential candidates understand this. The risk of confrontation and war will increase immeasurably under a Democrat presidency as a result of our weakness, our ignorance and the policies that the Democrats would put in place.

With this preamble regarding the expected failure of leadership under a Democrat government, let's briefly look at the accomplishmnts of the Trump Administration in a very short period, regarding foreign policy.

1. **Meeting with the leaders of 50 Islamic Nations in Riyadh in May, 2017 at the Islamic-American Summit.** At that meeting, President Trump publicly urged the Muslim leaders to "stand together" with the United States against the murder of innocent Muslims, the oppression of women, the persecution of Jews and the slaughter of Christians. He called on the Muslims to confront: "the Islamic Extremism and Islamist Muslim terror of all kinds". (Do

we not remember when Obama and his fellow Democrats refused to call the terrorism of Al Qaeda, ISIS, Hezbollah and Hamas "Islamic Terrorism"?). Trump continued in his address to the Arab nations: "Religious leaders must make it absolutely clear: Barbarism will deliver you no glory; piety to evil will bring you no dignity. If you choose the path of terror, your life will be enmity, your life will be brief and your soul will be condemned. A better future is only possible if your nations drive out the terrorists and extremists. Drive them out. Drive them out of your places of worship. Drive them out of your communities. Drive them out of your Holy lands and drive them out of the Earth. The Democrats welcome the Muslim extremists to their party and even placed one as a leader of their party. They welcome the support of Louis Farrakhan and promote the teaching of Islam in our public schools. We should recall when President Obama met with Arab leaders his only response was to bow to them, symbolic to the Arab leaders as subservience, nor did he even mention Islamic extremism. President Trump added: "This is not a battle between different faiths, different sects or different civilizations. This is a battle between barbaric criminals, who seek to obliterate human life and decent people in the name of religion".

The response from the Arab world was notable and refreshing. President Abdel Fattah el Sisi of Egypt told Trump: "You are a unique personality that is capable of doing the impossible". The Saudi government applauded President Trump for taking a "very bold and historic step". Saudi Foreign minister Abel al Jubeir told reporters: "If we can change the conversation in the Islamic world from enmity towards the U.S. to partnership with the U.S. and if we can change the conversation in the U.S. and the West away from enmity toward the Islamic world toward a partnership we will have changed our world. We will have truly drowned the voices of extremism and terrorism and we will have drained the swamp from which extremism and terrorism emanates". Abel al Jubeir's analogy to draining the swamp from which extremism emanates is so fitting here in the U.S., where Democrat extremism will surely sustain the swamp in the United States, forever.

President Trump has taken the first steps toward finding a peaceful and positive resolution to the enmity of extreme Islamists toward the West. Does it make sense to throw away all that President Trump has accomplished in seeking world peace and friendship and start from scratch with new leadership with no international experience and no personal contacts with the leaders of the world and who have consistently ridiculed any attempts made by President Trump to negotiate with our adversaries to find common ground? Can we afford to turn over our negotiations with the rest of the world to Joe Biden, Elizabeth Warren, Bernie Sanders, Mayor Pete Buttigieg or Kamala Harris?

2. **Developed Personal Relationships with leaders of the World** - President Trump has personally met and developed friendships or at least had friendly dialogues with 100's of leaders in the world. Here are some of the most notable. This is so important, because dialogue is the first step to obtaining understanding, compromise and ultimately peace in the world

Benjamin Netanyahu – Israel Prime Minister	Angela Merkel - Chancellor, Germany
Emmanuel Macro -President France	Vladimir Putin -President, Russia
Boris Johnson – Prime Minister. Great Britain	Queen Elizabeth II – Queen of England
Li Keqina – Premier o China	Narendria Modi – Prime Minister, India
Xi Jiniping – President of China	Li Keqina, Premier, China
Shinzo Abe – Prime Minister, Japan	Justin Trudeau – Prime Minister, Canada
Joko Widodo - President Indonesia	Andres Obrador – President, Mexico
Mahmoud Abbes – President, Palestine	Recep Erdogan – President, Turkey
Pope Francis – The Vatican	Ashraf Ghani – President, Afghanistan
Lee Loong – Prime Minister, Singapore	Reuven Rivln – President, Israel
Abdel Fattah el-Sisi – President, Egypt	Mohammad bin Salman – Crown Prince Saudi Arabia
Mohammad bin Zayed al Nahyan – Crown Prince United Arab Emirates	
Scott Morrison – Prime Minister, Australia	Nguyen Xuan Phuc – Prime Minister, Vietnam
Kim Jong-un – President, North Korea	Saad Hariri – Prime Minister, Lebanon
Abdullah II – King of Jordon	Adil Abdul-Mahdi – Prime Minister, Iraq (current)
Mauricio Macri – President, Argentina	Sergio Mattarella – President, Italy
Imran Khan – Prime Minister, Pakistan	Haider al-Abadi – Prime Minister, Iraq (former)
Volodymyr Zelensky – President, Ukraine	Andrzej Duda – President, Poland
Maurico Macai – President Argentina	Jair Bolsonaro, President, Brazil
Jans Stoltenberg – NATO Sec. General	Sauli Niinisto - President, Finland
Rodrigo Duterte – President, Philippines	Kalinda Graber-Kitarovic, President, Croatia

This is by no means a complete list, and many other heads of state have been left out. But these are important heads of state that President Trump has developed a personal relationship with and is able to discuss with them at a moment's notice urgent issues affecting the World and our country. It is important to have personal meetings and dialogues with all the leaders of the world, but in particular with those who are unfriendly or adversaries. The rationale is that even if you don't like them you have to dialogue with them and nothing is accomplished by just abusing them with hatred and vitriol. Nor is anything accomplished by ignoring them. Can we afford to give up these relationships and leave it to any of the Democrat candidates to initiate new relationships with all of these leaders? At the time of world unrest, this may be the most vital role that the next president of the United States will undertake. Are we prepared to throw away all the dialogue and open communications established by President Trump? We may recall that Hillary Clinton and many other Democrat leaders, sought to raise fear and trepidation in the minds of the voters, that President would be trigger happy and lead us into a third world war. The Democrat leaders also constantly told the public, that President Trump was an isolationist. The press relentlessly pursued this argument. Do these actions by President eve hint of isolationism, or war-like? The opening of dialogue and communications with world leaders has never been so great under any prior president. President Trump seeks peace throughout the world, but calls for strength at home. These are the right ingredients for successful foreign relations. Instead of the constant criticism from the left, the efforts of President Trump should have received by-partisan support. Yet the Democrats have time again demonstrated their willingness if not their desire for the United States to fail economically at home and fail in our pursuit of peace through improved foreign relations, just to obtain power in our country. Radicalism of any kind is about achieving power. And the Democrat Party has swung so far left that it is now clearly a Socialist Party with Totalitarian overtones. Is this what the people of the United States want?

3. **Moved U.S. Embassy to Jerusalem** -Over the objections of the Democrats and with the praises from Israel, President Trump moved the U.S. Embassy to Jerusalem. He has time again made it clear that the U.S. is a friend and ally of Israel and would stand beside them in any military confrontation and Israel has many enemies. Israel is threatened in the North by Hezbollah in Lebanon; Al Qaeda and ISIS in Syria and Iran to the West and South and Palestinian Hamas in the Gaza and the West Bank. The Democrats on the other hand not only criticized the embassy move to Jerusalem, but they also supported the condemnation of Israel for acts against humanity in relation to Palestine and it is the Democrats who spawned the Boycott, Disinvest, Sanction (BDS) movement against Israel. With an anti-Jew, Muslim in a leadership position in the Democrat National Party (DNC), Deputy Chief Keith Ellison (He resigned in November 2018) and a number of outspoken Jew-hating congress women, whose public comments about their hatred of Israel remain unchallenged by their Democrat colleagues, what can we anticipate for Israel's future? Note it is the Palestinians and its leading Party HAMAS that will not accept a two-state solution in Israel and will not be satisfied until the Jews are either killed or thrown out of Israel. Yet it is Palestine and HAMAS that the Democrats support and the future of Israel is at best uncertain if the Democrats come into power.

4. **Withdrew from the disastrous Iranian Nuclear Ban Treaty** – President Trump withdrew from the disastrous Iranian Nuclear ban deal, that the Obama Administration and in particular Secretary of State John Kerry imposed on our country. All the Democrat leaders, long after the Treaty had been shown to be fatally flawed, would continue to claim it was a success and continued to criticize President Trump for terminating the treaty. President Trump reimposed sanctions on Iran that had been lifted under the Obama Administration. The United States, thanks to Obama gave Iran $150 billion, which in fact provided them funds to continue to develop their nuclear capabilities. We received nothing in return. The Obama Administration and particularly Secretary Kerry continued to dupe many Americans to believe that they had averted a nuclear build-up in Iran. This assertion was either fraudulent or negligent on the part of the Obama Administration. Obama was so determined to make the Iranian Treaty along with Obamacare his legacy, he did not even mention the fatal flaws of these so-called achievements. Development of nuclear missile capability by Iran continued without slow-down thanks to its cooperation and partnership with North Korea. Since the institution of sanctions by President

Trump, Iran's crude exports have fallen dramatically; the value of its currency has plummeted and international companies have pulled out of the country. The only thing that has allow Iran to continue its acts of terrorism and acts of war has been the $150 billion released to them by the Obama Administration.

We need to be reminded of the weak-willed, spineless actions taken by the Obama Administration that have so exacerbated the international problems we face today. Besides the Iranian deal, how can we forget the "red line" drawn by Obama in response to Syrian President Assad's use of chemical weapons against his own people. Obama made it clear that there would be consequences to any further use of chemical weapons by Assad. When Assad once again used Syrian gas (similar to the Zyclon B that Hitler used against the Jews in Germany) against his own people, Obama did nothing. When Russia attacked the Crimea and claimed sovereignty over it, Obama once again did nothing. And then the Obama Administration ignored the build-up of a nuclear capability by North Korea; the expansion of China's control over international waters; the ongoing cyber-attacks and unfair trade practices by China; the bowing to the heads of state in the Middle East; and his withdrawal of support of Israel in favor of Palestine when he had his U.N. Ambassador abstain from vetoing a resolution condemning Israel for its actions against Palestine.

Beside funding a substantial portion of the development of Iran's nuclear capability, a substantial portion of the funds went to support terrorism in other countries. Very little went to help the people of Iran. Here are some of the ways Iran has dispensed the money received from Obama's ill-conceived if not treacherous deal:

- Helped fund Assad's regime in Syria, a regime which has murdered over 120,000 of its own people and created millions of refugees.
- Funneled money to the Houths, fanatics of Yemen (May well have been involved in the missile attack on Saudi oil fields)
- A big chunk of the money went to Hezbollah in Lebanon in order to add thousands of rockets to their arsenal; rockets aimed directly at Israel.
- Some money is used to infiltrate Iranian agents across the Mexican/U.S. border along with other illegal immigrants, who make their way to the Democrat sponsored sanctuary cities throughout the United States.
- Helped fund the unprovoked missile attack on the Saudi oil fields in mid-September 2019, which shut down more than half of the Saudi oil production. President Trump's measured response was to order new sanctions on Iran and increase deployment of our military into the Middle East region.
- In late June 2019, Iran shot down a U.S. Navy Drone, which nearly prompted a military response from the United States. President Trump called off a retaliatory response stating that it would not be proportional to the downing of an unmanned aircraft. Again, the

President, contrary to what the Democrats would have one believe, had shown a measured response. President Trump has shown time and again that he is not the belligerent, trigger happy leader that the Democrats, the Media, the entertainment industry and our liberal educators would have one believe.

- In July, 2019, Iran seized a British flagged oil tanker in the Gulf
- On June 13, 2019 two oil tankers were attacked by Iran near the Strait of Hormuz, while they transited the Gulf of Oman. The Japanese "Kokuka Courageous" and the Norwegian "Front Affair", both sustained fire damage
- On August 4, 2019 Iran's Revolutionary Guard seized another tanker.

The belligerence and the support of terrorism by Iran is monumental and all Obama and Kerry accomplished was to aid and abet it. But nothing is more telling about the naivete, ignorance and downright stupidity of the Obama Administration than the strategic partnership forged between Iran and North Korea dating back to 1979. Each country had something to provide. From Iran came oil and from North Korea came military expertise and hardware. Iran's nuclear and ballistic programs have always depended on external assistance and North Korea was and is a particularly valuable partner. The Iranian nuclear program was not delayed one minute in its development of a nuclear capability and now they had $150 billion additional funds. Our adversaries are just waiting and hoping that the Democrats will return to power, so that once again they can obtain such incredibly great deals, that are almost laughable if they weren't so sad and dangerous. The Obama Administration must have known about the close ties between Iran and North Korea. After all, they had been in place for over 30 years. But the Obama Administration did not make mention of them to the public. Obama and Kerry sold it as a wonderful deal. It was another so-called "legacy" deal for Obama and he must have it regardless of the cost to his own country. Obama and Kerry were ready to sacrifice their own country to achieve their personal legacy. So, what did Obama's administration leave us? A failed Obama Care; A failed Iranian Treaty; A weakened military, a seriously deteriorating infrastructure, serious breaches of security from Russia and China and $10 trillion more debt. And now the new radical left/socialist Democrats plan on increasing our debt not by $10 trillion to $20 trillion, but from $20 trillion to over $100 trillion. Their legacy will be the total destruction of our country.

5. **Imposition of Additional Sanctions on North Korea** – In September, 2017, President Trump ordered additional sanctions on North Korea. These wide-ranging sanctions not only penalize North Korea, but also anyone doing business with North Korea. The sanctions seek to cut off sources of revenue to North Korea and impose penalties on anyone trading goods, services or technology with the country. Further, any ship or plane that enters North Korea will be barred for 180 days from entering the United States. Finally, the Secretary of the Treasury is to sanction any foreign financial institutions that conducts business with North Korea.

6. **Withdrew U.S. from Paris Climate Accord** – The Paris Climate Accord was just another

example of the folly of the Obama Administration. Here the United States committed in good faith to reduce CO_2 emissions at a substantial cost to our country, anticipating that the other countries would fulfill their commitments also. Well they didn't and while the U.S. cut its CO_2 emissions by 15% over the past 10 years, the rest of the world, including the other signers of the Accord have actually increased their emissions by 35%. Why should the United States commit itself to an accord, that is breached by most of the other members?

7. **First-ever National cyber-security summit** - bringing together industry leaders and Federal officials to examine and improve critical controls against cyber-intrusions

8. **Actions for Peace and De-nuclearization on the Korean Peninsula** – As a result, North Korea halted its nuclear and long-range missile test. Even President Trump's efforts in this regard have been actively frustrated by the Democrats. The Democrats, with the help of the liberal left media, with their hate and vitriol have interfered with President Trump's ability to negotiate with North Korea, Iran. China or Russia, since the leaders of these countries know that by waiting, they will possibly have new Democrat Socialist leaders, who are more supportive of and in tune with the socialistic practices of their countries. Why would any of them not wish to postpone dealing with a capitalist, when in just a bit over a year they may have fellow socialists to deal with. The vilification of the liberal left and their media supporters and entertainers has immensely hurt our country's ability to negotiate and it is just another example how the Democrats are willing to bring down our country to gain power. Further, based on Obama's performance in the past and looking at the candidates the Democrats have running; our adversarial nations know that the waiting game is to their advantage and they will have ignorant socialist American leaders to deal with. Russia, North Korea, China, Iran could not have orchestrated the future better and the American citizens may actually vote in a group of politicians that will give them the United States on a silver platter. Can we really afford to have Joe Biden, Elizabeth Warren, Bernie Sanders, Pete Buttigieg or Kamala Harris, negotiating for our country's right to remain free and at peace?

9. **Directed a strike Against Syrian air bases used to deliver deadly chemical gas to innocent civilians** - In response to Syrian President Assad's use of chemical weapons against his own people, President Trump authorized a strike on the airfields in Syria used to deliver the Saran gas against its own innocent Syrian civilians. (This is in contrast to Obama reneging on his promise to take action if chemical warfare was used by Assad against his own people).

10. **Change of Rules of Engagement** - Changed the rules of engagement against ISIS and empowered U.S. commanders to take the fight to ISIS. As a result, ISIS lost almost all its territory and the Capital City of Raqqah was liberated in October, 2017. Further, all Iraqi territory had been liberated from ISIS

11. **Expelled dozens of Russian intelligence officers from the U.S. and ordered the closing of the Russian Consulate in Seattle.**

12. **Banned the use of Russian developed Kaspersky labs software on government computers** – This was in response to learning of Kaspersky labs ties to Russian intelligence.

13. **Support for the Ukraine** -Provided enhanced support for Ukraine's armed forces to help Ukraine better defend themselves from Russian interference. (President Trump has provided Ukraine with missiles and armaments for their security, which President Obama had refused to do. Yet the Democrats under Adam Schiff; Jerry Nadler and the liberal left Democrats, seek to impeach President Trump, for allegedly holding back the delivery of weapons for five weeks, which according to the Ukrainians themselves caused no damage to their security and more importantly were not even aware that there had been a holdback on the delivery of any weapons or funds from the United States.

14. **Sanction of Russian Companies** – Sanctioned twelve Russian Companies which profited from Russia's destabilizing activities. Sanctioned 100 targets in response to Russia's occupation of Crimea and aggression in East Ukraine.

15. **Began removal of troops from Afghanistan and Syria** – Although this has faced much criticism, particularly from the left, the rationale behind it is overlooked by most. Since 2001 the United States has spent between $6 and $8 trillion dollars (depending on how you treat interest and future medical costs for wounded soldiers) to fight terrorism and conflicts in the Middle East, with little or no aid from their allies. Our American men and women have been engaged in fighting the battles between different tribes and sects in the area, battles that have gone on for centuries if not millenniums. The factions are still at war with each other and as the proficiency of weapons becomes greater, more lives are being lost, including men, women and children who are civilians. Our loss of life and casualties during this period breaks down as follows:

	Deaths	Casualties	Total
Iraqi War	4,424	31,952	36,376
Afghanistan	2,216	20,030	22,246
Intervention Against Syria	76	81	147
Totals	6,716	52,063	58,779

These are our men and women who have come home in body backs or are missing limbs. When do we stop placing our men and women in harm's way to fight wars that are not ours and are never ending? In return, Afghanistan has been the major source of the heroin and cocaine that has reached our shores ad is causing the death of so many of our young people. We have severe homeless and drug addiction problems here at home and inner city crime rates are at all-time high. Why don't the lives of our own people receive the same concern as those in faraway places where the foreign countries are at a constant state of war? What about the families who have lost their loved ones in the Middle East, or have their sons and daughters returning with missing arms and legs?

Yet the Democrats will criticize President Trump for being dishonorable in abandoning the Kurds who fought side by side with us. You must be the judge, but for those of you with young children or grandchildren, do you want them to be fighting all over the world in battles that are not ours?

Military

By every account, our Military preparedness had deteriorated under the Obama Administration. Equipment particularly our airplanes were in such poor condition that they were permanently grounded and mechanics had to search plane graveyards to find replacement parts to make our aircraft serviceable and able to fly. The heads of every branch of our Military were at an unacceptable level of operation. Further, the United States was funding a disproportionate amount of the total NATO defense funding. Military personnel were getting little or no pay raises for over a decade. As the military implications of space became more and more apparent, the Obama administration was ignoring it. Here are just some of the steps taken by President Trump and his administration to address "the legacy" of an ill-equipped, poorly maintained military left by Obama.

1. **Military pay increases** – Implemented the largest military pay raises in a decade.
2. **$716 Billion Defense Budget Approval** – approved the largest military budget to renovate, repair and replace obsolete equipment with new equipment to reverse the deterioration and decay of our military during the Obama Administration
3. **Increase NATO Members Share of Cost of NATO's Defense** – Under threat of leaving NATO, President Trump told NATO allies to increase their defense spending to their agree to levels. Every member state subsequently increased spending and NATO allies spent over $42 billion more on defense, then the last year under the Obama Administration.
4. **Launched the Space Force as a new branch of military** – recognizing the need to focus on space as critical to our country's security, President Trump created a new military branch and re-launched the National Space Council.

Energy

1. **Withdrawal from the Paris Climate Agreement** – We have already mentioned this previously but it should also be noted that our country's continued commitment to the Paris climate agreement would have cost the U.S. nearly $3 trillion nd led to 6.5 million fewer industrial sector jobs by 2040.
2. **Keystone Pipeline** – Cleared roadblocks so that the construction of the Keystone Pipeline and the Dakota Access pipeline could be completed
3. **Energy Independence** - The U.S. has become a net Natural gas exporter for the first time and has become totally energy independent. Along with the revival of our steel and aluminum mills, our national security is no longer dependent on securing fuel, steel and aluminum from foreign sources.

There is much more for the Trump Administration to do. There are the very important additional issues of Abortion, gun control and climate change and there is more to do on the issues already being address as outlined above.

CHAPTER 22

Summary of My Observations

I START WITH the premise that in my lifetime (but before COVID 19), our economy has never been so strong. Employment is at the strongest levels that it has ever been, including all minorities. Wages are rising, the economy is booming, the stock market is surging, taxes are down and disposable income is up and there is virtually no inflation. It is historically unheard of that in a time of prosperity, that so many crave socialism. We only have to look at Venezuela, Russia, North Korea and China to see the level of failures achieved by these Socialist economies. Those of you that are old enough can remember the Berlin Wall that separated West Berlin from East Berlin and the contrast between the Capitalist West and the Socialist East was so dramatic that those in the East would expose themselves to being shot by their fellow countrymen just to escape over the wall and enter West Berlin. (The wall was very effective in keeping East Berliners prisoners in their own country).

Let us summarize what we have already covered as a ready reference to the reader. What does Socialist Democrats beliefs and plans do for the country? Maybe as important, what will the Socialist Democrats do for you?

1. **Hatred** – The single most significant attribute of the Liberal Left is hate-mongering. We have shown that our Democrat government leaders, their supporting media; the entertainment industry and our educators are not only full of hate, but actively and on a daily basis, seek to convince all their constituents, students and audience to hate as they do. I have seen this level of hatred only once before in my lifetime and I was too young to fully understand it. I am referring to Hitler and his Nazi party who stirred the German people to hate Jews so much that they were willing to put all their moral convictions aside and participate in the extermination of 6 million Jews. Once the Democrats achieve a frenzied level of hate among its constituents, they will no longer listen to reason and logic, nor will they be willing to dialogue. Hate is a terrible thing. It is irrational it is emotional, subjective, frenzied, and ignorant. Hitler understood this and selected Joseph Goebbels to be Reich Minister of Propaganda a position Goebbels would hold from 1933 to 1945. He was raised a Roman Catholic and almost went into the Catholic priesthood. He became responsible for presenting a favorable image of the Nazi regime to the German people and they went for it. Goebbels' tactics included using provocation to bring

attention to the Nazi party along with violence at party meetings and demonstrations. Violent incidents included young Nazis randomly attacking Jews in the streets. Goebbels was particularly interested in controlling radio which was the new mass media. He also sought to gain control over all cultural and intellectual life and his major focus was to glorify Hitler and the Nazi party and at the same time vilify the Jews. We all know the truth. The Hate promulgated by Goebbels and the Nazi party, was spread so successfully, that the German people were willing to participate in the most heinous crimes of the century; the annihilation of 6 million Jews. The hatred fostered by the Democrats is being aided and abetted by their constant attacks on Christianity particularly in the public schools, where any expression of Christian faith or belief has been prohibited. The Democrats have even gone further by glorifying Islam in our public schools. And how can we ever forget Barack Obama's own mentor Protestant Minister Jeremiah Wright who would say: "God D.. n America" three times from his pulpit to his congregation at Sunday worship service. Do the Democrats ever refer to our Lord, Jesus Christ in public? Whether one is Christian, Jew, Muslim or any other religion, we should all be able to agree that Jesus teachings of love not hate, humility not hubris is truly something to strive for. I began this work with some teachings from Jesus Christ: Do unto others, what you would have them do unto you; love one another; love your neighbor as yourself. And in his story of the Good Samaritan, Jesus taught us that even if we are sworn enemies, we help others in time of need. And he taught us not to judge others without first examining one's own motives and beliefs, your own prejudices and hatreds. And maybe the most important teaching of Jesus, was the need for HUMILITY, for without humility we cannot dialogue; we cannot perceive that we may be wrong; we cannot rise above our hatred or lack of caring for our fellow man. We should all be able to agree to at least care for one another; to "do unto others as you would have them do unto you"; to "remove the log in one's own eye so that you may better see the spec in your brother's eye". What is wrong with these teachings of Jesus? Why can't we at least listen to them?

I was never fully aware of the level of hatred that the Democrats show towards 50% of the population of the United States until Tuesday night, October 13, 2015. That night of a Democratic debate Anderson Cooper asked Hillary Clinton: "which enemy that you made during your political career are you most proud of?" Hillary Clinton promptly responded "probably the Republicans". To declare approximately half of the country your enemy, certainly should be concern to us all, whether Democrat or Republican. Then on Saturday, February 6, 2016, Hillary Clinton had former Secretary of State Madeline Albright introduce her at a campaign rally in New Hampshire. To the cheers from Hilary Clinton and the audience Madeline Albright said: "and just remember, there is a special place in Hell for all women who don't vote for each other". Then on September 10, 2016 Hillary Clinton declared Republicans were a "Basket of deplorables" characterized by: "racist, sexist, homophobic, xenophobic, Islamophobic views". So, let's be clear on this, Hilary Clinton, representing the prevalent thought of liberal Democrats declares half the people of our country to be her enemy because they are Republicans and condemns all women to hell if they vote for someone other than she.

And she considers Republicans to be deplorable. This was her belief even before the election that she would lose to Donald Trump. Let's do the math. Roughly 50% of the voting citizens are Republicans and 50% are Democrats. The Democrat leaders consider Republicans to be: deplorables, racists, white supremacists or doomed to hell. To this hated 50%, we need to add the 29% of unwanted Democrats who are "pro-life". Thus 29% of the 50% Democrats equals 14.5% and therefore 64.5% of all Americans are hated or unwanted by the Democrat leaders. Hatred and the accompanying vitriol are the focal points of all the Democratic Congressional leaders and where hatred is the focal point, as history has proved time and time again, the nation is doomed.

And the hatred and vitriol expressed by Democrats towards Republicans, especially the President has become much worse. We only need to listen to the constant tirades from the leftist Democrats.

2. **The crisis at the Wall** -The crisis at our border with Mexico keeps growing. In April 2019 alone, it was estimated that 150,000 illegal immigrants would storm our borders and that there will be well over 1 million during the year. Everyone who is on site and trying to protect our borders is telling us that there is the worst crisis at our borders that our country has ever had. Yet the Democrats, who have never even visited the border, along with the liberal media, tell us every day that there is no crisis and that everyone in the Trump administration that claims there is a crisis is lying. The Democrats have spent most of their time, when not vilifying President Trump and trying to oust him from office, in frustrating the completion of a Wall, which all authorities tell us is necessary to protect our borders. The Democrat claim that it will cost too much is absurd, when they are planning projects and programs that will cost the country upwards of $100 trillion. A support of Democrats, is a support for open borders; elimination of ICE and an influx of illegal immigrants that will displace millions of jobs in the United States. Is this even rational?

3. **International Issues** – We first look back on what occurred during the Obama Administration with the support of the Democrats. During his 8 years our military fell into such a state of disrepair that it was barely functional. One of the first actions taken by the Trump administration was to fund drastically needed upgrades in military equipment. We look at Obama's Administration and how he reacted to the Syrian Crisis where thousands of Syrians were being gassed by their president, Bashar al-Assad. In response to Assad's chemical attack on his own people in April 2018, President Trump ordered a military strike in conjunction with France and Great Britain against Assad's military aircraft and ship-based missiles. Trump, unlike Obama, showed compassion and concern for the innocent men, women and children of Syria and even in the face of strong criticism from the liberal left, he authorized a military strike on Syria to let the Syrian President know that genocidal attacks by Assad would not be tolerated. A far different response when Obama was President. He just backed down.

In May, 2017 President Trump delivered a speech in Riyadh, Saudi Arabia on global terrorism.

Before the representatives of 55 Arab-Islam nations, President Trump urged the Muslim nations to take a stand on global terrorism and share the burden of eradicating extremism in their religion. The Democrats roundly criticized Trump for seeking to dialogue with the Arabs as being much ado about nothing. That may be so, but for diplomacy to work anywhere in this nuclear age, it starts with dialogue, even with your potential adversaries. And we all remember that Democrats have consistently refused to call terrorism by the term "radical Islamic terrorism".

President Trump was also roundly criticized by the Democrats for initiating dialogue with Kim Jong Un North Korea's President; with Xi Jinping, General Secretary of the Chinese Communist Party and Russia's leader Vladimir Putin. China, Korea and Russia are clearly our adversaries. They all have nuclear arms capable of destroying millions of people. Instead of supporting President Trump's opening of lines of communications and actually entering into dialogue with these dangerous adversaries, President Trump and his administration have received constant ridicule and criticism from the Democrats and their supporting media. Many have suggested even in vile terms, that President Trump is merely a pawn of Vladimir Putin. When adversaries are talking, they are not shooting. Dialogue is a necessary starting point. The Democrats even sought to assure failure of President Trump's discussions with Kim Jong Un in Singapore by scheduling its public interrogation of Trump's former lawyer Michael Cohen on the very day Trump was meeting with Kim Jong Un.

By way of comparison, look at what diplomacy under the Obama Administration accomplished aided and abetted by John Kerry and Hilary Clinton. Obama had stated he would take action against Syrian President Bashar al-Assad, if Assad used chemical weapons on his people. Assad did so, killing and seriously injuring thousands of his people using a gas similar to what Hitler used to murder millions of Jews. Obama responded by doing nothing. During Obama's administration there was no attempt to meet with Kim Jong Un and his administration just stood by as Kim Jong Un ran nuclear missile tests again and again, even sending missiles over Japan. The Obama administration did nothing to: 1) react to Russia's invasion of Crimea in 2014; 2) intervene in Syria in 2015 or 3) react to the Russian interference in the U.S. Presidential election in 2016, although being fully aware of this.

The Obama Administration by entering into a treaty with Iran assured that Iran will become a nuclear power and a threat to the security of U.S. citizens in just a few years, even funding the nuclear research of Iran with $150 billion with full knowledge that North Korea was an ally of Iran and was already assisting Iran in the development of missile technology. The treaty did not prohibit Iran from developing delivery systems, so with the aid of North Korea, Iran will be fully capable of delivering missiles almost anywhere in just a few years, thanks to the Obama administration.

The United States had a long-standing rule that it would not pay ransom for hostages; yet on

January 16, 2016 on the same day four Americans detained by Iran were released, under cover of night a jumbo jet carrying $400 million in Euros, Swiss Francs and other foreign currencies landed in Tehran and soon after $1.3 billion followed. Why wasn't the normal transfer of funds accomplished by wire transfers between banks? This was a blatant attempt by the Obama government to hide his illegal action, which cost our country another $400 million.

Then there was the sale of 20% of the total uranium supplies of the United States, which were secretly sold to Russia under the authorization of the Obama Administration and the then Secretary of State Hilary Clinton. Coincidentally, at the same time $millions wound up in the coffers of the Clinton Foundation, paid by Russian agents.

The terrible record on International affairs included the following:

- Benghazi where our Ambassador and three soldiers are killed when our Embassy is overrun. There had been 569 requests to Hilary Clinton by her Ambassador that there was a critical need for more security in Benghazi, and Secretary of State Hilary Clinton and the Obama administration ignored them all.
- Failure to support Israel, even under threat of annihilation by Palestine and Iran
- Leaving Iraq too soon and thereby allowing ISIS to take over
- Continued failure to call ISIS a radical Islamic movement
- Paying $5 billion and releasing 5 Taliban terrorists in trade for American deserter Bowe Bergdahl
- Failure to secure the border with Mexico although a border wall had been previously approved.

The record on the Domestic front under the Obama Administration was equally bad, although this does not compare to what is in store for us if the Democrats were to achieve the presidency in 2020 and take over both houses of Congress.

- Our Debt was doubled from $10 Trillion to $20 Trillion and our country lost its Triple A bond rating
- Failure to stop illegals from bringing guns and drugs across the border.
- Failure to provide adequate health care to our Veterans through the scandal ridden Veterans Hospitals
- Stalled the passing of the Keystone Pipeline which under Trump would create many jobs
- Imposing a failed health care system on Americans, which has not only lead to sky-rocketing costs in premiums and higher deductibles, but included an unconstitutional provision, namely a mandate under which a person could not freely choose to be self-insured without paying a penalty to the Federal Government.

- Under the Obama Administration the highest number of Americans over 16 were not working. The number was 93 million
- The Obama Administration achieved the lowest labor force participation rate since the 1929 depression at 63%
- The highest percentage of Americans were on food stamps and Medicaid during the Obama Administration

4. **The New Green Deal** - I have spent much time in this book, describing the shear insanity of the Green New Deal. The fact that we do not have economists attacking the Green New Deal with vigor, tells us that almost all economists are socialists or at least liberal Democrats. How can anyone accept a plan that could put 13.6 million people out of work (and more likely much more) and after adding in their families, add over 50 million to the welfare rolls of our country? Can the future unemployed and their families really vote for the party that will take away their jobs and render them and their families destitute? Remember when the Democrats, under the leadership of Hilary Clinton during the 2016 election campaign said "we are going to put a lot of coal miners out of business". This was just the tip of the iceberg. While the Democrats claimed to be the friends of the working class; under the Obama Administration thousands of jobs left our country and wound up in foreign lands. Now, the Democrats are not just going after Coal miners to render them jobless, homeless and surviving on welfare. Think of all the workers in the energy fields, the oilmen, who drill, refine, ship by pipeline and truck and distribute through gas stations, that will be rendered jobless. Think of all the convenience store workers who will be rendered unemployed. Think of the airline industry, the pilots, stewardesses, baggage handlers, aircraft maintenance crews. Think of all the ranchers and cowboys who will no longer have jobs. And think of all the indirect jobs that count on the existence of the fossil fuel industry. airline industry and ranching industry, that no longer are their customers. And the Green New Deal would accomplish nothing, unless the rest of the world joined in as we only represent under 5% of the world's land mass and world population. Even if we were able to reduce our fossil fuel emissions by 100% in 12 years, it would have no impact unless the rest of the world participated. And to think this could be accomplished in 12 years is just folly.

5. **Debt Crisis** – We are already there, yet the plans of the Democrats which include the Green New Deal, National Health Care, free college tuition for everyone, guaranteed income for even those unwilling to work and free child care will cost upwards of $130 trillion over the next 10 years or $13 trillion per year, which is 4 times the current annual expenditures of our Federal Government. What would be the sources of funds to meet the costs of the Democrat plans:

- Reduce current spending on existing programs such as Social Security, virtually depriving those over 65 of their basic sources of income;
- Reduce military spending so drastically that the security of our country would be so severely impaired that we would become easy pray for China or Russia.
- Increase taxes on everyone by 50% or more.

- But doing all the above will barely dent the severe deficit that would be imposed on the United States, even if only part of their plans were actually implemented. The Democrat plans can only be financed by an explosive increase in Government Debt. Interest rates will soar, the stock market will tumble and inflation similar to what is experienced in Venezuela will undoubtedly happen. This is a realistic course of events, certainly a lot more realistic than the global warming scenario the Democrats would have you believe. What does this mean for the 40 million of our citizens that are over 65? These are the people on fixed income. As prices on the necessities such as food, clothing and shelter skyrocket, those over 65, counting on social security, pensions, 401k's, IRA's, Annuities and Investments in the stock market will see all the income from all these sources, rapidly disappear. At the same time, they will see their income tax rates rise substantially. All taxes rates will have gone up; not only on the wealthy. For the 40 million of us over 65, if the Democrats succeed in taking control of the White House and the legislative branches, you will see rising subsistence costs accompanied by a drastic reduction in income. This will not occur sometime in the future. It will start happening immediately if the Democrats take over the government and start to install: The Green New Deal; National Health Care; Guaranteed income; Free College tuition; and Free child care. The stock market will crash, more than just reversing all the gains that have been enjoyed under the Trump Administration. Our 401k's, IRA's Annuities, and pension plans are all tied to the stock market and the underlying companies that pay the dividends that provide the source of our retirement incomes. Can you the 65-year-old retiree afford the economic disaster that will be brought upon us by these insane programs of the Democrats. And make no mistake, they are insane.

6. **National Health Plan** – It has been estimated that the Democrat proposed National Health Care plan will cost $33 trillion over the next 10 years or $3.3 trillion a year. Even forgetting the Democrat proposed Green New Deal plan, this alone will be more than enough to bankrupt the United States and put millions of workers out of work and on welfare And yet the Democrats continue to tell us that they are for the common man and for more jobs, while planning programs that will destroy jobs like no other programs in the history of man. The National Health plan will control what doctors we can go to; what medical services will be provided us and when we can get access to medical services. Looming over all, especially those over 65 is the practice of triage. Triage is the assigning of priority order in allocating medical treatment on the basis of where limited funds and other resources can best be used. Medical care will have to be limited and the first to suffer will be those over 65, who in some cases will be denied any medical services because they are too old and the services are better used on younger more productive members of society. Then to, we know how well our government serves our citizens, especially in the area of medical care when we see the atrocious performance of the Veterans Hospital over the years. There are only 20 million veterans and the Federal government's operation of VHA hospitals has been worse than inadequate. Performance had been falsified time and time again, so the staffs could earn huge bonuses. Do you really think that based on VA hospital performance; the Federal government can manage health care for

320 million people?

7. **Elimination of air flight, gas fueled vehicles and buildings heated and air-conditioned with fossil fuels** – How many of you, regardless of age will be able to purchase electric powered cars or refit your homes to be all electric? How many of you will be able to even trade in your car for an electric car, since your gas fueled car will be worthless? How many of you will accept being denied the ability to fly anywhere in the United States, whenever you want either for business or pleasure? And how are people from Hawaii, Puerto Rico or the Virgin Islands supposed to get to mainland U.S? And how many are ready to give up eating meat, particularly beef as the Democrats propose eliminating cattle? And the cost of this insanity is approximately $10 trillion a year; 3 times our current total annual budget. If the National Health Care plan didn't bury our country, this certainly would, resulting in the elimination of many more millions of jobs. And for what? As we previously pointed out, our country represents only 4.5% of the world's population and only 4% of its land mass and the rest of the world has been increasing their CO_2 emissions each year faster than we have been reducing ours. For even if we could reduce our emissions to 0 while the rest of the world continued to increase theirs, nothing in our environment will change as world CO_2 emissions will continue to rise faster than we reduce ours. And there are also strong arguments by 1000's of scientists and meteorologists that global warming is not caused by CO_2. Are you willing to sacrifice your way of life; your freedoms; your jobs; your homes, your ability to travel? And even with these sacrifices are you ready to accept an economy, ravaged by inflation, high unemployment and burgeoning debt that will bankrupt our country and leave us defenseless against countries such as China and Russia?

8. **The Building of the Wall and the related raging drug problem** – The Democrats insist on no walls, open borders and doing away with border patrols and the Immigration and Customs Enforcement agency (ICE). We have the worst drug epidemic in our history and its coming from Mexican cartels, that enjoy the ease of entry into our country. We have Democrat run cities and states refusing to assist the Federal Government in enforcing existing immigration laws even to the extent of releasing known criminals back into society. Then to, there are the Democrat controlled sanctuary cities and states, where the liberal Democrats would rather release, violent criminals into our society, rather than hold an illegal immigrant for the Federal Immigration authorities. The Democrats insist that there is no crisis at our borders between Mexico and the United States; even though every professional assigned to border security at every level is telling us there is the worst border crisis that the United States has ever experienced. Not one Democrat government official; not one Democrat candidate for president has chosen to visit the border, where the immigration crisis exists, yet they will tell their constituents that they know better than those who have been working the area and serving our country to provide border security for 10 or more years. How is it that so many are willing to listen to the sheer ignorance and nonsense of the Democrats and their supporting liberal media, over those who have factual and recorded evidence of the crisis existing at our border? Then too, how many of you, who provide basic services to our community such as farming, landscaping,

ranching, maintenance and so many other skilled and un-skilled services are willing to support the Democrats free borders proposals that will allow millions of illegal immigrants to come into the U.S. and take your jobs for less pay? And not only will the illegal immigrants come in and replace many of our American citizens in their jobs. In many instances the immigrants will be unable to find jobs and will receive free medical; free education, food, childcare, housing and a guaranteed income even if they are unwilling to work. The total rejection of the wall and the ongoing adversity to border security by the Democrats is beyond comprehension, since there is nothing positive that Democrats can claim benefits their constituents by the rejection of a border wall.

9. **Free income for everyone** – There is the old saying that nothing is truly free. Who will pay for those extra costs of welfare and income for the illegal immigrants? And should the hard-working citizen of the United States be expected to pay for those who are unwilling to work?

10. **Reparations for the Black Community** - Yet another proposal of the Democrats is paying reparations to the black community for being enslaved by white Americans. We have discussed how the ancestors of today's African-Americans, were far from blameless in initiating black slavery. We have discussed how Africans enslaved their fellow blacks in Africa and sold them in the market place first to Arabs and then eventually to White slave traders. Without, the black's enslavement of their brothers by the millions in Africa, there would have been little if any slavery in the Americas. The blacks made it happen. We have also noted that the greatest amount of slavery today is black on black slavery in many African nations. We also noted that there were many free blacks that owned slaves in America prior to the civil war. We also noted that most white Americans did not own slaves; that the Democrats were the party that insisted on subjecting Blacks to some form of slavery, through their establishment of the Ku Klux Klan and the institution of the Jim Crow laws in the South. And finally, I have noted that the overwhelming majority of Americans did not own slaves and that the Northern, basically Republican White Americans, fought for and gave their lives for the freedom of the slaves. And what about all the immigrants from Europe over the centuries, whose ancestors in Europe as well as in the United States, never owned slaves. And what about those who are the descendants of survivors of the Holocaust, should they be required to pay reparations to Blacks for the historical slavery of blacks?

11. **Why do African Americans gravitate toward the Democrat party?** There are approximately 40 million African-Americans, most of whom are committed to the Democrat Party. The Democrat Party leaders keep informing the black community that the Democrats are the party that endorses: "black lives matter" as opposed to "all lives matter". Yet through the years as I have already discussed, it has been the Democrats who have sought to keep the black community in slavery. We have already discussed how the 7 Democrat Supreme Court Justices with two Republican justices opposed decided in the "Dred Scott" case that: "once a slave, always a slave". It was the Southern Democrats who started the Civil War by firing on Fort Sumpter and the Southern Democrats that sought to secede from the Union in order to sustain slavery. It was the mostly Republican North who volunteered to sacrifice their lives in order to free the slaves. And it was a

radical Democrat that assassinated Lincoln (and we note today that there are radical Democrats calling for the assassination of President Trump). It was the Democrats that started the Ku Klux Klan and it was the solidly Democrat members of the KKK who hanged and burned blacks, men, women and children, burned their homes down and beat them incessantly. And it was the Democrats who enacted and enforced the Jim Crow laws that would exist into the 1960's, in order to keep the black community in a continuous state of bondage. And it would be Democrat President Woodrow Wilson who was not only the only President to be a member of the Ku Klux Klan, but also enforced segregation among all Federal employees.

And today, what have the Democrats done for the Black community, other than try to convince them that they, not the Republicans have their interests at heart? The Democrats run the 25 cities with the highest crime rates and murder rates in the country. The most to suffer from the ineptness and apparent insensitivity of Democrat leadership is the black community. Take Chicago for example. Each year more than 700 blacks are murdered; many are innocent lives of men women and children and in over 8 years the Democrats who run the city have done nothing about this. In 2016 there were 785 murders of blacks in Chicago and 4,368 shootings. Yet in 8 years, Democrat Mayor Rohm Emmanuel has done nothing to make things any better for the black community. We can look at many other cities under Democrat control that have failed the black community as much or even more than Chicago. These cities have not been able to deal with the steady stream of violence and loss of innocent lives. These cities include: St. Louis, Baltimore, Detroit, Newark, Memphis, Cleveland, Birmingham, Oakland and Miami to name a few. Why does the African-American community hold such an allegiance to a party that has failed them consistently prior to, during, after the civil war and even today?

What about the Jewish Community? – The Jewish population in the United States is just under 7 million. They are among the strongest liberal Democrat groups in U.S. politics according to a Pew Research Center Report: "A portrait of Jewish Americans" with approximately 70% identifying themselves with the Democrat Party. But why this allegiance to the Democrat Party, especially now? The Democrat party, in action after action is hostile toward Jews. Look at their anti-Jew congressmen that are taking on leadership positions in the Democrat Party. Remember how the Democrat party had turned its back on the Jews in the U.N. and supported Palestine and denigrated Israel and the Jews claiming they had performed acts against humanity, even though their Palestinian adversaries have undertaken terrorist attacks in Israel and vowed to annihilate all Israelis?

During the Obama Administration the Democrats showed their adversity toward Jews when the U.N. Security council voted against Israel on December 23, 2016. The United States rebuked Israel when it abstained on a Resolution demanding an end of Israel settlements in the Gaza and the West Bank. The U.S. was one of the five members of the U.N. Security Council that had a veto and for the first time in 40 years refused to exercise the veto and the Resolution passed 14-0.

The Democrats had placed Keith Ellison, an avid anti-Jew Muslim and rabid supporter of Louis Farrakhan, as Deputy head of the Democrat Party. Farrakhan has demonstrated time and again his hatred for the Jews, even suggesting they should be treated like termites and exterminated. The Democrat party opposed President Trump's move of the U.S. Embassy to Jerusalem. The Democratic party unanimously refused to criticize the anti-Jew comments of one of its four Muslim representatives, namely, Congresswomen from Minnesota Ilhan Omar, one of the two Muslim women elected to Congress in 2018 that are openly anti-Israel and anti-Jew. Ilhan Omar an avid supporter of Palestine recently accused pro-Israel Americans of allegiance to a foreign country. Then there is the Muslim representative from Indiana, Andre Carson, who would have the United States adopt the Muslim educational system. The Democrats have also elected Rashida Tlaib a Muslim from Michigan who is also anti-Jew and like so many of the Democrats in Congress seeks to put pressure on the U.S. to cut military ties to Israel, boycott certain products produced in Israel and disinvest from companies that are believed to be pro-Israel and anti-Palestinian. This refers to the infamous BDS (boycott, disinvest, sanction) movement in the United States against Israel, supported by Democrats, although not necessarily the majority.

It is not the Republicans that have anti-Jew sentiments as the Democrats would have you believe. On the contrary, the Trump Administration authorized the move of the U.S. Embassy to Jerusalem, affirming his close affinity with Israel and the right of Israel to exist. It is the leadership of Israel, most notably Benjamin Netanyahu. Prime Minister of Israel, who has repeatedly stated that President Trump and his administration is the greatest friend Israel has ever had. Yet the Democrats support the Palestinian Nation, a nation whose only objective as specifically outlined in the Charter of Hamas the ruling party of Palestine, is to kill every Jew, or at least drive every Jew out of Israel. In addition, the Charter of Hamas states that there can never be a two-state solution for Israel to continue. And as a final straw, it was the Democrats that negotiated a treaty with Iran that not only guaranteed that Iran will have a nuclear capability to destroy Israel, but provided $150 billion to fund a nuclear arsenal and the means of delivery. Why does the Jewish Community so strongly support an adversary such as the Democrats, who if given a chance would remove the U.S. Embassy from Israel, deny military aid to Israel, and effectively give Iran the nuclear capability to destroy Israel in just a few years?

12. **The Hispanic Community** – While it is true the Hispanic Community is understandably concerned with the threat of deportation, seven out of ten of all Hispanics said it was important for Congress to pass new Immigration laws. But also ranked as extremely important were the economy, jobs and education. These were not well addressed during the Obama Administration and the Democrats today certainly do not intend to assist this community as it seeks to flood the United States with illegal, undocumented immigrants, which is at the current rate of over 1 million a year. The Democrats oppose a wall; are in favor of free borders and seek to do away with Immigration and Customs Enforcement Agency (ICE) altogether.

Under the Trump Administration the Hispanic Community has seen a significant reduction in unemployment levels for the first time in decades along with the black community and a significant increase in wage rates as a result of the increase in job demand, which has been aided by the return of over 500,000 manufacturing jobs as a result of the corporate tax rate reductions put in place by the Trump administration over the strong and unanimous objections of the Democrats. How can the Hispanic Community believe that supporting Democrat leaders, that is helpful to their community?

Furthermore, the Green New Deal and the National Heath Care Plans proposed by the Democrats, as I have previously discussed will cause an incredible increase in unemployment. It is safe to say that the Hispanic Community will not only suffer from the proposed mass influx of illegal immigrants, but also from the massive loss of jobs that will occur because of the Democrat proposals. How does the Hispanic Community so strongly support the Democrats, whose policies will clearly lead to their suffering?

13. **Abortion rights** – We have discussed abortion at length. It is more than a moral issue. It is primarily an issue as to whether the unborn child that is perfectly healthy, with all the attributes of a human being, should have any rights before birth and beyond. The Democrats and the "pro-choice" women, believe that the unborn baby is just a part of their body and has no rights of its own and therefore the pregnant, woman can terminate the child at will, even up to the time of delivery and sometimes beyond. The Democrats would have you believe that it is solely the mother's right to take the life of an unborn baby at any time. Even those who are "pro-choice" should be concerned that once the state says the killing of an unborn baby is all right, it is not much of a reach for the state to demand abortions and sterilization of women as we see in China, in order to control population growth as a method of cost control. The State of Georgia, has recently passed legislation that is "pro-life" referred to as the "Fetal Heartbeat law", which protects the unborn baby when a heartbeat is encountered. The position of the Democrats is that this is an "immoral" law and: "bad for business". Now we see the Democrats even supporting infanticide, killing a child even after it is born. What are the possible implications of this for a Democrat government that would seek to control your medical health, your education, your income, your travel and what you can eat? With their support of infanticide, the Democrat moves toward controlling your right to live. If the Democrats would sanction the killing of a baby because he or she is on life support and therefore not a human being, then what about any person through an accident or illness Is on life support? Does he or she also qualify as other than a human being and therefore can be deprived of life by the government? This is not much different from the rationale of the Nazi's, who convinced the German people that Jews were not human and therefore could be exterminated. Are "pro-choicers" willing to accept the risk that the state will be allowed to determine when one can be deprived of his or her life, even when no crime has been committed? Or are they willing to accept that abortions in the first trimester is enough protection for the pro-choicers?

14. **Other plans that the Democrats would impose on us if they become the majority** –

- The Democrats including many of those expecting to run for president in 2020 believe that convicted felons should be allowed to vote even while serving their sentences in jail. There are rural communities where the population of the penitentiary is greater than the law-abiding citizenry. The wholly illogical scenario of the felons running the town is actually possible.

- The Democrats advocate that 16-year-olds should be allowed to vote. The typical 16-year-old has little or no responsibilities; lives at home; is still in high school; his or her major concern is the party or prom that he or she will be attending. The typical 16-year-old is dependent on his parents for support and has little or no responsibilities. Yes, there are exceptions, but a right to vote is not based on the exception but rather the rule. There is only one reason why the Democrats are pushing so hard for the 16-year-old vote. They know that statistically, the 16-year-old has been indoctrinated through school by socialism and the left and therefore will be generally a candidate to vote Democrat. It is for the same reason that the Democrats want open borders; to expand their voting base by adding illegal immigrants who will also gravitate to the Democrats because of all the free things they Democrats promise: free health, free education, guaranteed income; free child care, free housing and free food.

- The Electoral college- The Democrats sorely want to do away with the Electoral College so that the liberal left that controls our cities will gain control over the country. The United States is now a country of primarily urban dwellers. The farmers and ranchers who provide the food for our subsistence and the miners and producers of energy have lost their voting significance to the urban dwellers, who provide little if anything for our subsistence. The hard-working ranchers, farmers, miners, and other mid-America workers no longer have much say in our government; Further, the taxpayers would see their voting rights erode also as the country became more controlled by illegal aliens, those on welfare, those who don't want to work and convicts in prison. There would be nothing in the way of enacting the New Green Deal; National Health and guaranteed income for those unwilling to work. And this will result in the demise of the U.S. as the majority of the votes would be in the hands of those who enjoy receiving everything for free. The electoral college is a buffer that helps us stave off the harsh reality of the promises and programs of the liberal left. It doesn't eliminate the threat of having a voting public, whose majority would have as its objective voting in more and more socialist programs to benefit themselves.

What's happens to American Citizens if the Democrats take control?

The plans and proposals of the socialist Democrats will hurt if not destroy the lives of any group of voters that we can conceive. I have pointed this out throughout this book. Who are our voters? There are 253.8 million people in the United States of voting age, broken down by race and ethnicity as follows:

	Millions
White	160.6
Hispanic/Latino	41.2
African-American	30.8
Asian	15.0
Mixed	3.9
Native American	1.8
Other	<u>0.5</u>
Total	**253.8**

There is another breakdown which is along the line of shared interests. This number totals 357.8 million. The large discrepancy (almost 100 million) is that some adults fall in more than one category and therefore are double or even triple counted. But the breakdown by groups of shared interest follows:

	Millions
Over 65	52.0
60 to 65	20.3
18 to 60	164.0
Hispanic/Latino	41.2
African American	30.8
Veterans	20.4
Asians	15.0
NRA Members	5.5
Jewish	4.4
Native American	1.8
Military service	1.3
Police (includes, ICE)	<u>1.1</u>
Total	**357.8**

Over 65 – This is probably the most vulnerable group to the Socialist Democrats' plans for the future of America. They are the Traditionalists and a segment of the Baby Boomers, discussed further on in more detail. But these will suffer the most from, the Medicare for all plan; the Green New Deal and the free and open borders that will bring in millions of undocumented immigrants. Inflation, high cost of living, high taxes and loss of the value of homes and loss of income from investments will result

in vast numbers being driven from their homes and finding it almost impossible to meet their daily cost of living.

60 to 65 – These are the oldest of the Baby Boomers and they will soon be on fixed income like the Traditionalists and they depend on their Social Security, Pensions, Annuities, IRA's, 401k's, and Investments they have built up through putting aside part of their earnings each year for retirement. Higher taxes, inflation, and loss of value of their assets and the accompanying loss of dividend income will destroy their way of life. There will be no part-time jobs available as unemployment will have sky-rocketed by tens of millions. Even the new Medicare for All plan cannot be counted on, for the prohibitive cost of the plan will mean health services will be rationed and the first place that will occur is with the elderly. The Green New Deal Plan, the Medicare for All Plan; the free college tuition for everyone, the open borders and unlimited immigration proposed by the Democrats will cost the nation $13 to $15 trillion a year. Our total Federal budget today is only $4 trillion which has a built-in deficit of $1 trillion. High debt and attending high interest rates, inflation and the loss of asset values is a given. Are you prepared to accept these catastrophic events that will virtually destroy your life in retirement?

18 to 60 - This is the single largest group of adults and the main source of workers and employees. You may not worry about Medicare for all, but you should be concerned about massive unemployment, because that means many of you will not be able to find jobs and many of you will lose your jobs as most if not all fossil fuel related industries go out of business. We have covered this previously in detail. And even as our unemployment rates soar, the Democrats will have opened our borders to millions of new undocumented immigrants, who will flood our country and compete for your jobs. Free college tuition will be meaningless since there will be no jobs waiting for the youngest in this group. And for those in their late 40's through 60, there will be no retraining available, for who is going to train someone that only has 5 or 15 years left in the labor market. You too will experience the rampant inflation, the high cost of goods and services, the high rates of interest and the accompanying lowering of your standard of living. Even your ability to take a vacation will be limited as there will no longer be airplanes to fly you to destinations of your choice. And will you be able to afford a new electric car, when your existing car can only be turned in for scrap?

Hispanic and Latino - 69% of Hispanics voted Democrat in the 2018 mid-term election. Look at how well you have fared in the cities run by Democrats. How does open borders allowing millions of new undocumented immigrants into our company benefit you? Are you prepared to have your taxes doubled, and your cost of living explode? And worst of all, how many of you are employed in the very industries that will be quashed by the Democrats? Finally, 57% of Hispanic and Latinos identify themselves as being Catholic. The Roman Catholic Church strongly advocates the right to life, and that abortion is wrong at any time. Yet the Democrat party advocates abortion at any time, even in the third trimester. Tom Perez, the leader of the DNC publicly and proudly tells our American citizens that the Democrats don't want those who believe in the right to life as members of the Democrat party. If you don't accept abortion at any time, according to Tom Perez, you cannot be a

Democrat. The Democrat Governor of Virginia, Ralph Northam goes as far as supporting the killing of a baby in some instances even after it has been born. New York State, Governor Andrew Cuomo, a Roman Catholic, would extend killing of unborn babies into the third trimester, not just because the mother's life is threatened, but for any reason that her health may be threatened. The positions of the Democrats as reflected by these two governors is in direct conflict with the U.S. Constitution, specifically Article 14: which states among other things that: "no State shall deprive a person of life, liberty or property without due process of the law, nor deny any person within its jurisdiction the equal protections of the law". At the time the 14th Amendment was passed (on July 9, 1868), the American Medical Profession, the scientists and the law agreed that an unborn child was included in the category of protected persons and a state legislature does not have the right to negate a preborn person's fundamental and Constitutional right to life.

African Americans – 90% of African Americans, voted Democrat in the mid-term elections of 2018. Yet many of the travesty's that the Liberal Left will impose on other shared interest groups will befall the shared interests of African Americans. Some we have discussed elsewhere.

The gains in employment, the reduction in income taxes will be reversed under a Democrat administration. Millions of jobs will be lost in the African American community. But what has the Democrats previously done for you? Look at the massive murder of African-Americans that is rampant in all the many cities controlled by the Democrat Mayors and their Democrat City Councils. And look at the past history of the Democrats. For over 100 years the Democrats did everything to suppress you as a group; treat you as inferiors and sustain what amounted to bondage and slavery, far after the Republican President obtained your freedom through the passage of the 13th Amendment, which abolished slavery. I have reviewed all the policies of the Democrats through the years, starting with the Dred Scott case; seeking secession form the United States so that they could sustain slavery in the South, assassinated President Lincoln, passed the Jim Crow laws and vigorously enforced them in the South. They also established the Ku Klux Klan, which not only enforced the Jim Crow laws, but went on killing sprees, hanging thousands of innocent African Americans, burning them out of their homes, beating them and shooting them at will. There was the Democrat President Woodrow Wilson, who demanded segregation throughout the Federal government and the military and then there was Democrat Governor of Alabama, George Wallace who ran on a platform, "segregation now and segregation forever". It was mostly northern Republicans that gave their lives to free African Americans and it was the Democrats that insisted that African Americans remain as slaves. And even today, the Democrats do nothing for the African-Americans living in their cities across the nation. The Democrats would have you believe that White Republicans are racist, yet the Democrats are the ones throughout most of American History that have tried desperately to keep you in bondage. And today, the failure to help the African Americans in their districts, where crime and murder runs rampant, is just a new form of bondage perpetrated by the Democrats. Nothing was done for you during the Obama Administration and now the only issue that gets any attention from the Democrats is how to impeach President Trump, the President who, among other things, has reduced unemployment, lowered taxes and raised income for the African American community.

Veterans - This is the group, who have been mistreated at the hands of the Veterans Administration. During the Obama Administration, wait times and performance reviews were fraudulently documented and administrators were paid substantial bonuses on the basis of their fraudulent reports. Many veterans died, because of delays. President Trump changed that and made private health care available to Veterans at no cost, when the VA hospitals could not meet their responsibility for efficient timely medical services. The Veterans know that government administered health means, inefficiency, long wait times, stifling regulations and paperwork, and arbitrary medical treatment. Do you really believe that the Federal Government that could not effectively administer health care for 20 million people, that you will now get better treatment when the Federal Government is administering health for 320 million, including you?

Asians – This group has in the past experienced persecution at the hands of the Democrats. Remember how, during World War II, Democrat President Roosevelt issued an Executive Order which incarcerated Japanese-American men, women and children? This group has experienced in the past how the Democrats can deny their freedom. 77% of Asians vote Democrat. The group must think that deprivation of their rights is a thing of the past and it could not happen again. What do you think the Democrats have in store for you and every other American? The Democrats are going to double your taxes, take away your right to choose your own doctors and your own hospitals; they are going to obsolete your vehicles and prohibit you from flying anywhere. You will see huge increases in interest rates, substantial loss of asset values on your homes and investments, pensions, annuities, 401k's and IRA's. Without airplanes, how will you even be able to visit your families in faraway lands? And what about an unlimited number of immigrants crossing our borders with Mexico? Either they will replace some of you in your jobs, or you will pay higher taxes to cover their welfare costs. Some Democrat leaders are even suggesting the banning of eating meat.

NRA Members – There are 5.5 million members of the National Rifle Association. And there are many in addition that believe we have the right to protect ourselves and that includes owning guns. True, there have been devastating murders of men, women and children by assault weapons and the loss of loved ones is a tragedy that stays with the families for the rest of our lives. I know the feeling. My wife and I watched our two sons run down by a drunk driver while they were changing a tire. Our oldest son was killed and our youngest son, was close to death, but after months of pain and suffering, he miraculously survived. One life lost to assault weapons is one to many. But how can we forget the tens of thousands that are killed each year by hand guns? The answer is not confiscation of guns. We need to do better background checks, register guns better and maybe even require written tests and tests dealing with the proper use and maintenance of guns.

In 2017, 39,773 people died from gun related injuries. Of that number, 23,854 (60%) were gun-related suicides, while 14,542 (37%) were murders. Of that number, 373 were killed by mass shootings. We must never forget those who lost their lives in mass shootings, nor can we forget the anguish borne every day by the families left behind. I know what you are feeling. But we shouldn't disregard, or ignore the 14,000 other murder victims and their families, almost all of whom were killed by handguns. The right to own guns is guaranteed by the Constitution. The Democrats would confiscate your guns. This will surely happen under a Democrat administration.

The Jewish Community - There are approximately 4.4 million Jewish voters in the United States. 64% of the Jewish community identify themselves as Democrat. This is the party of Louis Farrakhan who is radically anti-Jew, even referring to Jewish people as "termites" to be exterminated. Then there is Keith Ellison, former Congressman from Minnesota and Deputy Chairman of the Democrat National Committee from February 2017 to November 2018 and avid supporter of Farrakhan. Then there is Andre Carson, Congressman from Indiana who advocated in a public speech that American schools should be modeled after Islamic Madrassas. A typical Islamic Madrassa school offers two courses of study: 1) A course teaching memorization of the Qur'an and 2) a course leading the candidate to become an accepted Islamic scholar in his community. A regular curriculum includes courses in Arabic (Qur'anic Interpretation); Islamic Law (Shariah); the study of recorded deeds and sayings of Muhammad (Hadiths) and Muslim History.

Then there are Ilhan Omar, a Minnesota Congresswoman and Rashida Tlaib, a Michigan Congresswoman, whose anti-Jewish diatribes are never criticized or sanctioned by the liberal left Democrats.

Nor can we forget how President Obama instructed his representative to the U.N. to abstain from voting against the Resolution condemning Israel rather than using his vetoing vote of "no". As a result, for the first time in our country's history we failed to support Israel and allowed a resolution to be passed in the U.N. condemning Israel for acts against humanity in its dealings with Palestine.

Finally, there is the Boycott, Divestment and Sanctions Movement (BDS), supported solely by the left. This is a Palestinian campaign promoting various forms of boycott against Israel until it meets what the campaign describes as Israeli obligations under international law; most importantly withdrawal from Israeli occupied territories and removal of the separation barrier (the wall) in the West Bank.

The leading force behind the BDS movement is a Palestinian activist named Omar Barghouti. Barghouti supports the destruction of Israel and opposes any two-state resolution to the Israeli/Palestinian conflict. He demands "the right of return" for all Palestinians to Israel, which would quickly overturn its Jewish majority and turn the Jewish state into the 22nd Arab state. The BDS movement blames the entire conflict on Israel and fails to acknowledge that HAMAS, the leading party of Palestine calls for the murder of all Israelis. Bottomline, the BDS movement, is motivated by obsessive hatred of Jews and opposition to the Jewish state. The Palestinians are unwilling to accept a two-state solution and are even unwilling to sit down with Israel for direct peace talks without any preconditions. They will not be satisfied until Israel is extinguished as a Jewish State. The Republicans strongly support Israel and President Trump is recognized by Israel as a great friend of Israel and applauded Trump's moving the U.S. Embassy to Jerusalem, in recognition that Jerusalem is the Holy city of Israel. The Democrats to the contrary are adversaries of Israel. They have shown that in leadership positions they give to those who hate Jews; by criticizing the move of the U.S. embassy to Jerusalem and by lending support to the BDS movement and by allowing Israel to be sanctioned for acts of inhumanity against Palestine.

The Muslims have their two holy cities, Mecca and Medina and they want nothing more than to annihilate the Israelis and deprive them of their holy city even though the city has been the holy city of the Jews for several thousand years before Mohammad was even born. And the Democrats, based on their actions to date will aid and abet the Palestinians to accomplish their goal to deprive Jews of their rightful claim of Jerusalem as the Holy city of the Jews (and secondarily of the Christians).

Native Americans - Historically, the Democrats have not treated racial minorities well. In fact, for over a hundred years they have singularly mistreated minorities First, under Democrat President Andrew Jackson, we had the Trail of Tears, where Indians were uprooted from their homes, not allowed to take any of their belongings and forced to march over 1,000 miles to Oklahoma, with many dying along the way. We have covered, how the Democrats led our country into a civil war, costing the lives of so many, in order to preserve slavery. And after slavery was abolished by Republican President Abraham Lincoln, the Democrats Assassinated him. And when that wasn't enough to satisfy their desire to keep African Americans in a constant state of slavery, the Democrats came up with the Ku Klux Klan and the Jim Crow Laws. And then the Democrat President, Woodrow Wilson made sure that segregation was maintained in the Federal government. Then during World War II, it was a Democrat president who herded Japanese-Americans into concentration camps; men women and children. And today, we look around the country, at the 25 major cities with the highest crime and murder rates, the majority of murders being black men, women and children. Every one of the cities has been run by Democrats for Decades.

In 1988, Republican President Ronald Reagan signed into law the Indian Gaming Regulation Act. After Reagan signed the Act, Native American gaming revenue sky-rocketed from $100 million in 1988 to $33.7 billion in 2018. Native Americans received $4 of every $10 of Casino revenue. The Native American Casinos employ 628,000 Native Americans, nationwide, which equates to 17% of the total Native American population of voting age. What happens to the Casinos, if the Democrats come into power and start to implement its $13 trillion a year programs relating to the New Green Deal, Medicare, and free tuition. Even the Democrat plan to double taxes for everyone won't come close to covering the $13 trillion of new expenditures. I have discussed in detail the 10's of millions of jobs lost, the millions of new illegal immigrants that will join our unemployment roll, the attending high interest rates, high inflation rates and loss of investment values that will hit our economy. Discretionary funds of almost all Americans will drop precipitously. Who will be able to afford to come to the Native American Casinos? Not only will there be a substantial loss of income to the Native American Community, but the 628,000 jobs supported by Native American casinos will disappear.

There is no better an example of how Democrats use Native Americans for their own selfish personal gains, than presidential candidate Elizabeth Warren. For years, Warren successfully used her claim to be of Native American ancestry for her own personal gain. What an insult to the Native American and the Cherokee Nation spoke out in criticism of Elizabeth Warren saying that Senator Elizabeth Warren was: "undermining tribal interests with her continued claim of tribal heritage."

Military Personal - We saw how during the Obama Administration, our military capabilities deteriorated so significantly that our security was deemed inadequate. President Trump has mandated an immediate improvement in military equipment, higher compensation for military personnel and restored our nation to a level of security not achieved during the Obama Administration. The Trump Administration has taken important steps to achieve necessary and proper care for wounded soldiers; care that was fraudulently overstated under the Obama Administration. We see those on the left leading protests against patriotism with burning the flag, kneeling for the national anthem and generally demeaning our military. But most importantly, the huge expenditures that the Democrats propose for our country, will require cutbacks from somewhere. And the cutbacks will have to come from the largest areas of expenditures such as defense. The Democrats under President Obama allowed our military to deteriorate to a level of inadequacy. What can we expect for cutbacks in our military, if the Democrats come into power? The Democrats were satisfied with an inadequate military before. Now cutbacks will be mandatory to fulfill their programs. Is this something that our military will accept by voting for Democrat leadership? Are you prepared to go into harm's way without adequate military supplies and weapons?

Police (including ICE and Border patrol) - The constant disrespect and vitriol against our police throughout the United States comes solely from the left. From referring to police as pigs; to calling white police racists; to establishing the "Black lives matter" as a political movement aimed at police, to condemning ICE and Border Patrol for acts of inhumanity; to establishing sanctuary cities across the United States to flaunt the law and frustrate our police in performing their duties, the Liberal Left has shown us constant hatred and vitriol for all who serve gallantly to protect our lives, freedom and security. Yes, there are some incidents, where police have made mistakes; may have used unreasonable force but to condemn police throughout the country for the acts of a few is irrational and unjust. Police are necessary and should be revered for their service in providing safety and security of our country. The Democrats would expand their catch and release program; even legalize heroin and cocaine and other drugs that will just make the job of law enforcement that much harder. We have discussed all the cities throughout the United States with the highest crime rates. They are all managed by Democrats. I have discussed the major cities that are overrun with homelessness and drug addiction. They are all run by Democrats. Requests for more police are often denied by the incumbent Democrat leaders of these crime ridden cities. With the anticipated exploding increase in illegal immigrants and the attending influx of more drugs, and the rapidly expanding unemployment rate and homelessness resulting from the policies of the liberal left, does it make sense to vote for Democrat leadership, which will virtually make your jobs impossible?

For All who believe in our Constitution

The flag and our National Anthem are the symbols of our Democracy and Freedom and also of the Document that protects are individual rights and freedom, namely the U.S. Constitution. The liberal left has denigrating our flag and our National Anthem time and time again. Burning of our flag and kneeling in protest at the playing of our National Anthem are symbolic of the radical left that pervades our country. That it can be argued that the right to desecrate our flag and insult our anthem is protected by the First Amendment, it would seem that it should be an equal right to criticize these actions. Not so, because anyone who stands for the National Anthem or looks upon the flag as a symbol of freedom are swiftly labeled by the liberal left as supremacists.

The Democrats would create dissent and division among us by denigrating the very symbols that unite us.

Further, the Democrats wish to violate the provisions of our Constitution, by claiming that an unborn child is not a person (violation of the 14th Amendment and 5th Amendment); by eliminating the Electoral College (violation of Article II); confiscating our guns (violation of Amendment 2); and depriving churches and religious organizations of tax exemption if they don't accept doctrines demanded by them (violation of Amendment 1). Since the inauguration of President Trump, the Democrats have spent all their time seeking to impeach the President, and over three years have spent $40 million and not found any "High crime or misdemeanor" that is demanded by the Constitution to impeach a President. Again and again, the Democrat vindictive tribunals and their endless impeachment proceedings have breached Amendment 6 of the constitution which states that the accused " shall enjoy the right to a speedy and public trial by an impartial jury; shall be informed of the nature and cause of the accusation; be confronted with the witnesses against them, and to have a compulsory process for obtaining witnesses in his favor". For the past three year the rights of the President of the United States have been violated by the Democrats, incessantly and un-interrupted. This is what typifies a totalitarian state, where the freedom and rights of individuals can be totally ignored. The Democrats will argue that Amendment 6 does not apply to Impeachment proceedings. Are the Democrats really saying that they are above the law and they do not have to abide by our Constitution? This is the very first step toward a totalitarian state.

There is a third breakdown by shared interests and that is generational. Each generation shared characteristics that defined them and differentiate them from other generations. These generations and their numbers are:

Generation	Period	Numbers (Millions)
Traditionalists -	Before 1945	32.1
Baby Boomers	1946 and 1964	75.5
Generation X	1965 and 1980	65.7
Generation Y (millennials)	1981 and 1999	79.4
Generation Z	1996 and 2016	73.6
Total		**326.3**

What are some of the common values of these different generations? We will briefly discuss each with the exception of Generation Z, where a large percentage are not of adult age.

Traditionalists, also referred to as the "**Silent Generation**, experienced tough times and sacrifice relating to the Great depression, high unemployment and World War II, all of which occurred during their lifetimes. They believe in hard work, sacrifice, respect for authority, old time moral and safety and security. How does the socialist Democrat values match any of the common values and shared interests of the Traditionalists? They will increase your taxes, erode your investment portfolios, use your money to provide more and more entitlements, including to illegal immigrants. As to safety and security, the Democrats are in control of the 25 cities with the highest crime rates in the country; they vilify the police at every opportunity, even going as far as displaying pigs in police uniforms. The military capability became severely decimated, during the Obama Administration. The Socialist Democrats are proposing on allowing free immigration across our borders, no border patrol, no wall and millions will flood into our country, including many bringing drugs and more crime into our country. And finally, the Democrats support murdering unborn babies at any stage of a pregnancy. Is this consistent with your traditional moral values? And what about your medical care? The cost of $3 to $5 trillion a year is so prohibitive, that if it were to be implemented, some health costs will have to be cut. All of us traditionalists are over 75. Our medical care will be triaged out of existence. Immediate medical attention will not be available and just like Veterans, who died while they waited weeks and months for treatment at the VA hospitals, you will be facing the same kind of treatment, only worse. The Federal government could not take care of 20 million veterans. Moreover, corruption prevailed throughout the system; records were falsified to make it appear that the VA was doing a good job and the administrators by their fraud, received huge bonuses for their falsified performance.

Your Health care will be minimized and will be administered by "death panels" that will determine, which of us are entitled to kidney, liver or heart transplants. Anything that isn't death threatening will be denied us. No hip replacements; no knee replacements, no removal of cataracts. And even treatment of serious life-threatening conditions will be denied such as open-heart surgery, tumor removals, cancer treatment and costly drugs. You think this just won't happen? Where do you think $3 trillion is going to come from, without severely cutting services and medical treatment? And we are on the top of the list.

How in the world can the Socialist Democrat government take care of 320 million Americans? What else will the Democrats deprive you of? You won't be able to go anywhere by air travel and you probably will not even own a car, because your gas fueled car will become worthless and will have no trade-in value. You probably will not be able to do any travel anyway, without cars and airplanes. And your cost of living will soar so high, as interest rates go through the roof and inflation rushes past 100% per year. At the same time, you will watch your savings, your IRA's, 401k's, your pensions, your annuities and your home values drop 50%, maybe 75% and even more. You may have already realized this, if you read this far, that your future is dire if not abysmal under Democrat Socialism. Will you vote for your own demise?

Baby Boomers - This generation is characterized as having a strong work ethic; they are self-assured, competitive, goal oriented and resourceful. They are motivated by a desire to quickly rise to the top of the corporate ladder. They are capitalists at heart and instinctively want the freedom to attain success through hard work. They want to compete hard with others and be rewarded for their personal achievements. This is an anathema to the socialist Democrats. Their proposed policies will take away not only the ability to achieve success, but also any rewards for achieving success. Your earnings will be controlled by an income ceiling and where that is not enough, onerous taxes will be imposed so that you will receive no benefit for working hard. Regardless of how educated you are, how entrepreneurial you are, how hard working you are, you will achieve little more than those less industrious, less willing to work hard. And more importantly, you will be called to pay for those who are not just unable to work but who are also unwilling to work.

Many of you are already, in the over-65 category or very soon to be there. You will first see a reduction of your benefits under a Nationalized Health System, because costs must be contained somehow and the elderly will be the next group to have their health care limited maybe not as much as the Traditionalists, but it will be substantial.

But the worst tragedy that will befall many of the Baby Boomers, is the loss of jobs in the twilight of their careers. Who will retrain you if you have less than 10 years until retirement? And how will you be able to compete with the millions of young illegal immigrants that the Socialist Democrats will allow to freely cross our borders and who will take jobs that you might have otherwise been able to get? Who will hire you for any jobs that require physical labor, or require you to be on your feet for long periods during the day? I have pointed out the 10's of millions of jobs that will be lost due to the Green New Deal and the Medicare for All programs. Look at the massive industries that will disappear with the implementation of the Green New Deal: Commercial Airlines; Aerospace, Health Insurance, Oil and Gas, Coal, Resort, Hospitality and Travel, Automotive (including suppliers, dealers, car rental); Gas stations, convenience stores, fast food (particularly beef based); and all business directly or indirectly dependent on any of the named industries.

Generation X - This is the independent, resourceful, self-sufficient generation. They value freedom and responsibility in the workplace. They want to become entrepreneurs. They believe that hard work is the key to getting ahead. Most have retirement savings plan, which they expect to need after retiring. They believe that most of their retirement income will come from pensions, 401k's, IRA's annuities and other investments that they have made as opposed to social security. Many are employed in the very industries that the Democrats would eliminate by the New Green Deal. Many will lose their jobs in the twilight of their careers. They will face higher personal income taxes leaving them with substantially less to spend. Their investments will deteriorate by 50% to 75% or even more as the higher corporate taxes imposed by the Democrats, their elimination of whole industries, and higher interest rates, due to the costs of the Green New Deal, Medicare for everyone and free college tuition. And on top of all this will be devastating inflation, driving cost of living to levels that will be unbearable for most.

Millennials (Generation Y) - The millennials seemingly have many of the same traits as Baby Boomers. They have an entrepreneurial spirit, they want recognition, they are goal oriented, they are confidant, they like to travel and they are highly motivated to provide a better future for themselves and their children. Yet 70% of them think socialism is the panacea for their way of life. How sad it is that most Millennials believe that the Socialist Democrats provide the path to achieve their goals and provide the freedom to achieve them. This just is not true. The Socialist Democrats will create a political and economic structure, which eliminates competition, controls how far you can go and how much money you can earn. The socialist Democrats will create conformity in the workplace, control levels of compensation, burden you with intolerable tax rates. The Socialist Democrats will even ban air travel, and obsolete your autos, so that travel for pleasure will virtually be banned. Even a night out at a good steak house would be eliminated. And what high taxes and income ceilings doesn't impose on you, rampant inflation will. Further, the millennials need to think beyond themselves and think of what is best for your grandparents, parents and children. Your Grandparents are most likely born before 1945 and are living on fixed income, from Socials Security, pensions, annuities, 401k's and IRA's. The rapid inflation in the cost of goods and services attributable to the Socialist Democrat plans, coupled with the attending stock market crash, will see all of them struggling to survive. Their medical plans, which allows for choice of doctors and quick access to medical services, will be supplanted by a Medicare for all system, where they no longer have a choice of doctors, will be subject to long wait times for treatment and will see medical services triaged, placing them at the bottom of the list for medical treatment. Medical life and death decisions will be made by a government tribunal (often referred to as "death squads") who will distribute medical services to those deemed more deserving, such as the young, healthy and employed. The tribunals will literally do a cost/benefit analysis to determine your right to medical care. Your parents and grandparents' cars will be rendered obsolete and will be scrapped as there will be no market for them and they will not have the money to replace them. Yes, your children may have free college tuition, but there will be no jobs as all businesses relating to fossil fuel will have been abandoned, all health insurance companies, restaurants, airline industries will shut down and many other businesses will be disrupted and just go out of business. Do you really see your future under a Socialist Democrat Rule? Is this what you want for your families?

Abortion, the Right to Life, the teaching of Islam in our Public Schools

There is even a fourth breakdown that needs consideration and that is those who are predominately pro-life because of religious beliefs and they are the Evangelicals and the Catholics. Both groups believe strongly in the sanctity of life and that life begins sometime during a pregnancy. For Catholics, the tradition is life begins at conception. For evangelicals, life begins when the unborn child is viable that is can live outside the mother's womb. Any time after that, abortion is considered murder. Yet the Democrats would sanction abortion at any time before birth and the head of the DNC, Tom Perez has even gone as far as said that those who are pro-life are not wanted in the Democrat Party. Presidential Candidates like Kamala Harris has said that the unborn child is not to be protected by the Federal Government, and that the unborn child has no rights at all and the mother can do what she wants with the child right up until its birth. Some Democrat leaders are even saying that the murder of a baby may occur under some circumstances even after its birth. Yet 22% of Evangelicals and 50% of Catholics will still vote Democrat.

The number of Evangelicals and Catholics in percent and voting number (based on 253.8 million potential voters) break down as follows:

	Percent of total Voters	Number of Potential Voters (000's)	Number currently Voting Democrat (000's)
Evangelicals	25.8%	65,480 (22%)	14,406
Catholic	20.8	52,790 (50%)	26,395
Totals	**46.6%**	**118,270**	**40,800**

Thus, there are 40.8 million Catholics and Evangelicals, that are currently voting for Democrats. Abortion has not previously been so clearly a Socialist Democrat goal, where the mother is to be allowed to kill her unborn child at any time for any reason. Now it has become a prominent and vociferous issue of the Democrats, where pro-choice at any stage will be the mandate of our country if they are elected. Can someone who holds the right to life as one of their fundamental principles of morality, still willingly vote for socialist Democrats, knowing that the life of every unborn child becomes in jeopardy?

Teaching of Islam in our public schools – If the killing of our unborn children at any time is not enough to convince Catholics and Evangelicals, that the Democrats will turn us away from Christian morality, then we also need to examine how the Democrat run schools throughout our country are promoting Islam and denigrating Christianity. In October, 2019, the United States Supreme Court declined to take up the appeal from the Fourth Circuit Court, which had decided that it was acceptable under the U.S. Constitution to exclusively teach Islam in our public schools and not in violation of the "Establishment" clause in the first Amendment of the Constitution.

Caleigh Ward was an 11th grade Christian student at the La Plata High School in Charles County, Maryland. Caleigh, along with the other students was forced to write on a worksheet: "There is no god but Allah and Muhammad is the messenger of Allah. She refused to complete the assignment and was given a failing grade. Caleigh and her classmates were forced to view a PowerPoint slide presentation which stated: Most Muslims' faith is stronger than the average Christian. The students were also told to fill out a worksheet about the Five Pillars of Islam. The school refused to give Caleigh a different assignment.

The Thomas More Law Center represented Wood and claimed the assignment violated the "Establishment" clause in the first amendment of the Constitution. Richard Thompson, president and chief counsel of Thomas More Law Center stated that: "many public schools have become "hotbeds" of Islamic propaganda. The teaching in schools goes far beyond a basic history lesson. (I had previously discussed this in detail in Chapter 4). Public schools are bending over backwards to promote Islam while at the same time denigrating Christianity. It is not wrong for our children to be exposed to other religions but not just limited to Islam and certainly not without giving equal time to Christianity. As Christians, are you prepared to have unborn children murdered on demand and the expansion of the teaching of Islam to the exclusion of all other religions in our public schools? This is just another example how the Liberal left seeks to destroy our country.

All Who Will become Unemployed - I have previously discussed the specific industries where there will be a total of 13.5 million Jobs lost and 45.8 million placed on welfare. I believe these to be conservative numbers. Are you a candidate for being unemployed, if the fossil Fuel, airline, and health Insurance industries among others are eliminated? Do you work in the new and used car dealerships, gas stations, convenience stores, coal, steel, aluminum, utility, restaurant, theme parks just to name a few? If you want to view a country that Democrats wish us to emulate, look no further than Venezuela.

CHAPTER 23

The Trump Impeachment

The Beginning

HILLARY CLINTON LOST the election in November 2016, even though she won the popular vote by approximately 2.9 million votes (65.9 million, Clinton; 63 million Trump). Neither won a majority with Clinton winning 48.2% of the votes and Trump winning 46.1%.

The Electoral College vote showed a significant difference with Trump winning 304 of 531 electoral votes or 57.3%. This is what started the rage and hate in the Democrat party toward President elect, Donald Trump and the call for impeachment would emanate from the liberal left immediately after the election.

On November 8, 2016 high school students at Hope High School in Providence, Rhode Island held a walkout at exactly 11:08 A.M. in protest of Donald Trump being elected President. They carried banners saying: "F..k Trump"; "Not My President"; "Black Lives Matter"; "A Racist"; "A Sexist and a Homophobe". Madison Middle School in Seattle planned a walkout for Inauguration Day, January 20, 2017. There were similar walkouts across the country by high school and middle school students in Chicago, Oakland, Omaha, Minneapolis, Portland, Phoenix, Berkeley, Washington, DC and New York to name a few. President Trump was even burned in effigy and he had not been in office one day. Across the nation there were the following protests: "shut down Trump's Inauguration"; "Stand Against Trump"; "Resist Trump", "Rally Against Trump". Our duly elected President was vilified with anger and hate, even before he had been in office. And this anger and hatred was spurred on by the liberal left Democrat leaders, the media and the entertainment industry.

Approximately 60 Democrat Congressmen refused to attend the Inauguration. There were many claims by the Left that Trump was not the legitimate President and the media and the entertainment industry loudly proclaimed his illegitimacy.

What is interesting to note is that New York City alone consisting of five counties, cast 2 million more votes for Hillary Clinton than Donald Trump. These five counties account for only 319 square miles out of a total of 3,797,000 square miles of the U.S. Yet, 70% of Clinton's higher popular vote came from New York City alone.

There are 3,113 counties in the U.S. Trump won in 2,626 counties to Clinton's 487. Trump won 84.4% of all the counties in the United States. In New York State alone, a Democrat stronghold with 62 counties, Trump won 46 of them or 74.2%.

Finally, in 52 counties of the 487 won by Hillary Clinton, all major metropolitan areas, Clinton had 8 million more votes than Trump. This is exactly the problem that our Constitution seeks to address. In Article II Section 1 starting with paragraph 2, the Constitution describes how the President and Vice President are to be elected by electors, that will be appointed by each state. The number of electors shall be equal to the number of Senators and Representatives to which each state is entitled. That means no state can have less than three electors, as every state will have two Senators and least one House Representative.

The framers of the Constitution recognized that but for the election of electors instead of solely by popular vote, the agriculture and dairy farmers, the ranchers, the lumbermen, the fisherman, the miners and industrial workers would have little or no representation as the popular vote would come overwhelmingly from city dwellers. Those who provide our basic needs to live would be overwhelmed by the sedentary city dwellers who contribute little to sustaining our basic needs to live. The authors of the Constitution were prescient in realizing that our country would move to a largely urban society, dominated by large cities virtually removing any voice in the governing of our country from those responsible for the production of our basic needs.

The United States has become a service oriented, city dwelling economy and with it comes a strong demand for social programs by many of its constituents and a growing demand for socialism. The best way to commandeer votes, is to appeal to urban dwellers by offering them all kinds of free services and benefits and never mention by whom and how these benefits will be paid. Along with the massive growth of city population has come the increase in homelessness, crime and drug addiction. These are problems that need to be addressed and for decades the liberal left has captured the votes of those in need by promising them everything they need for a good life, for free. And like socialist programs throughout the world, decade after decade goes by and the urban problems, especially in the major cities of the United States keep getting worse and all these major urban population centers have been run for years by Democrats.

There are 538 electoral votes representing the combined number of senators (2 from each state) and the total number of members of the House of Representatives allocated to each state on the basis of the 2010 census. Each party selects 538 electors and on voting day, the voters cast their votes for the President and Vice President candidates of their choice. The voter is actually casting his or her vote to select their state's electors. There is no requirement that the electors must cast their vote in accordance with the popular vote in their state, although over 99% of the electors vote as directed by the voters.

The total population of the U.S. is approximately 327 million and the total registered voters is approximately 153 million. California and New York account for 28.5 million registered voters or 18.6% of the total voters registered in the U.S.

Yet the electoral breakdown in California, far exceeds the political breakdown of the state. Of the 19.9 million registered voters in California, 8.6 million or 43% were Democrats and 4.7 million or 23.6% were Republicans. (The difference would be voters who registered as independents and non-party affiliations). Yet of the 53 electoral votes, the Democrats had 45 (representing 86.5% of the electoral votes and the Republicans 7 (13.2%). (There was one vacancy). New York State registration showed similar results. Of the 8.5 million registered voters, 5.8 million or 68% were Democrat and 2.7 million or 32% were Republican. Yet of the total 27 electoral votes in New York, the Democrats held 21 (81%) and the Republicans 5 (18.5%). Thus, the combined 86 electoral votes of California and New York, 74 (86%) were cast for Democrats and 12 (14%) for Republicans. This under-representation of Republican voters would be even worse under a straight popular vote.

Whether or not we like the methodology for electing the President and Vice-President through the "Electoral" vote, it is the law as established by our Constitution and it has remained so for over 232 years. President Trump won the election by a landslide according to the results pursuant to our Constitution. Yet the Democrats would have you believe that the Trump presidency was illegal and President Trump was illegitimate.

The Mueller Investigation Revisited

We turn next to another look at the Mueller Investigation, also known as the Russian Investigation and the Mueller Probe that began in May, 2017 and concluded in March, 2019. The Mueller Report concluded that while the Russians attempted to interfere with the 2016 Presidential election, neither Donald Trump or his associates were found to have conspired with the Russians. Furthermore, it was concluded that the results of the election would not have been different without Russian intervention. The report left the question of obstruction of justice unanswered, but if there were no conspiracy, where is the obstruction of justice?

Yet the Democrat leaders, including Nancy Pelosi, Jerry Nadler, Adam Schiff, Maxine Waters, Eric Swalwell, Joaquin Castro, Al Green and Brad Sherman among many others persisted in proclaiming that the facts clearly showed that Trump had colluded with the Russians and needed to be impeached. And the media and entertainment industry overwhelmingly supported these false and deceitful allegations. The lines were clearly drawn between the Democrats and the Republicans. The proposed impeachment of President Trump, became the most divisive issue to hit our nation in my lifetime. Another fake and malicious claim of the Democrats was that President Trump obstructed justice by firing the FBI director James Comey, a right that every President before Trump, had and often exercised during their tenures. We would soon learn how corrupt James Comey had been from the FISA (Foreign Intelligence Surveillance Act) Court. It was James Comey who approved the FISA warrant applications to be used against President Trump and his associates a multiple of times. Comey approved the fraudulent FISA applications and was corrupt in his actions, particularly in leaks of classified materials to the press.

Less than a week after the Department of Justice, Inspector General (IG) Michael Horowitz released his investigation, detailing FBI misconduct during Comey's tenure as Director, in obtaining and approving a FISA application on a Trump presidential campaign aid, Carter Page, the presiding judge of the FISA court, Rosemary Collyer issued a scathing four page Response order on December 17, 2019. This unprecedented order by the FISA Court condemned and verified on-going wrong-doing by the FBI in its entire approach to the FISA process. Collyer, who approved the original FISA application on Carter Page said that the FBI "provided false information and withheld material information" from the Justice Department's National Security Division (NSD) and in so doing "equally misled" the FISA court The Horowitz report condemned 17 separate wrongful activities of the FBI, in the original FISA application, and in three subsequent extensions.

The IG report found in addition to serious errors in the initial FISA application, that the renewed applications from the FBI failed to advise the FISA court of the inconsistencies that the FBI knew about but refused to reveal to the FISA court.

Collyer found the frequency with which representations made by the FBI personnel turned out to be unsupported or contradicted by information in the possession of the FBI and the frequency with which the FBI withheld information in their possession detrimental to their case, calls into question whether information contained in other FBI applications is reliable. The Democrats and the media virtually ignored this and their constituents and their readers were led to believe this to be trivial, when in fact it was the worst condemnation of the FBI in its history.

The FISA establishes procedures for the physical and electronic surveillance and collection of foreign intelligence information between foreign powers suspected of espionage and terrorism. The FISA court has been established to oversee the appropriateness of the application by the FBI or CIA to surveil. The significance and of paramount importance in evaluating FISA applications and authorizing the application deals with the fundamental rights of citizens of the United States guaranteed by our Constitution, specifically Amendment 4, which prohibits unreasonable search and seizure and requires a judge to issue a warrant, justified by probable cause and supported by an oath of affirmation and it must particularly and accurately describe the place to be searched and the property to be seized. Amendment 4 was violated on all points by the FBI in its biased attempt to establish a reason to impeach Trump.

Jerry Nadler, himself, Democrat Chairman of the House Judiciary Committee was opposed to the passage of the FISA Amendments Act of 2008 as it: "abandons the Constitution's protections and insulates lawless behavior from legal scrutiny" The Act greatly expanded the ability to wiretap and surveil. For example, the Act increased warrantless surveillance from 48 hours to 7 days.

The Democrats had counted on Mueller finding President Trump guilty of some impeachable offense, but the Mueller investigation could not find any collusion. The liberal left would hang on briefly claiming that the Mueller investigation did not clear Trump of obstruction of justice. But it soon became clear to them they needed to find something else. And coming to the Democrats rescue was a 30-minute call by President Trump to the President of Ukraine and a "Whistleblower" who determined that he had been told by others about the call and he concluded that it amounted to some impeachable offense. The next round of "let's get Trump out of office", virtually the sole effort of the Democrat Representatives in the House for three years, begins.

The Impeachment

On March 6, 2019 in an interview, Nancy Pelosi, the Democrat Speaker of the House said: "Impeachment is so divisive to the country that unless there's something so compelling and overwhelming and bi-partisan, I don't think we should go down that path because it divides the country." Six months later she would renege entirely on this statement and call for the impeachment of President Trump based on a 30-minute call that went nowhere, accomplished nothing and did not impact the security or well-being of either the United States or the Ukraine. How can we forget Nancy Pelosi's comment during the Obama Administration, when she was then also the House Speaker telling her fellow Democrats (and also Republican House Members), that they must pass the Obamacare bill without reading it? And that's what the majority Democrat house members did over the objection of the House Republican members. This is the leadership she is providing our country as well as her constituents. And just how are they faring in San Francisco, while she focuses on the impeachment of the President?

Pelosi was not the only one to be concerned with the divisiveness of impeachment proceedings against a sitting President. Republicans and Democrats alike had previously insisted that Impeachment must be bi-partisan and that if it were not it would be very harmful and divisive to our country.

Democrat Representatives Al Green (Texas) and Brad Sherman (California) drafted Articles of Impeachment against President Trump in December, 2017 to force the House to consider impeachment articles. The effort was killed by a strong bi-partisan vote of 364 to 58.

Democrat Presidential candidate, Tom Steyer, an ardent advocate of impeachment would declare nationally and without any merit or factual foundation, that Trump brought our country to the brink of nuclear war and even falsely claimed that Trump took money from foreign governments (without naming which governments, how much and when). Debate after debate among the 20 to 25 Democrat Presidential Candidates have focused almost entirely on ousting President Trump from office, virtually ignoring what they would do to benefit our country. And when forced to discuss what they would do, besides removing President Trump, they all proposed outlandish, unaffordable programs; programs that would destroy our country. I have discussed this in detail elsewhere in this book.

In December, 2019 the impeachment articles were presented for a vote on the floor of the House of Representatives. The impeachment resolution passed by a vote of 232 to 196 without a single vote from the Republican House members. Two Democrats voted with the Republicans against the impeachment and one Democrat, Jeff Van Drew from New Jersey actually changed parties and became a Republican, stating that he could no longer embrace the politics of the Democrats.

The impeachment proceedings were rushed by the Democrats, who claimed that time was of the essence and Trump had to be removed immediately. It was now time for Pelosi to turn the approved Articles of Impeachment over to the Senate for trial as required by the Constitution. Almost five weeks would go by before Pelosi and the House Democrats would turn the Articles of Impeachment over to the Senate for trial, even though the Democrat House members had consistently insisted that the House Impeachment proceedings must be expedited as quickly as possible and turned over to the Senate for trial.

The July 25, 2019 Telephone Call

On July 25, 2019, President Trump had a telephone conversation with Ukraine President Zelensky. It lasted exactly 30 minutes from 9:03 to 9:33 and would become the sole basis for the impeachment proceedings against President Trump. The call had to be considered treasonous, a bribe or some other high crime or misdemeanor to rise to the level of an impeachable offense; none of these was ever established. The call itself was reported by a "whistleblower", who had no direct knowledge of the call himself; only what several people told him as to what they had heard. The unnamed "whistleblower" did not go to his superiors, but rather directly to the House Intelligence Committee chaired by Adam Schiff. Only the Democrat members of that Committee knew the identity of the "whistleblower". In fact, evidence seems to indicate that Adam Schiff's staff drafted the "whistleblower" affidavit which would serve as the basis of the prosecution of President Trump. Adam Schiff would claim that he did not know who the" whistleblower "was, although it was his staff that interrogated the "whistleblower" and assisted in the drafting of the "whistleblower" affidavit.

The transcript of the "whistleblower" affidavit provides no basis for claiming abuse of power except by far reaching surmise and inuendo. A reading of the transcript as a standalone document does not substantiate or support any of the claims made by the Democrats.

The 30-minute phone call by President Trump to the President of Ukraine on July 25, 2019, overheard by unnamed people and relayed to the un-named "Whistleblower" formed the basis of the serious claims against the President of bribery, extortion, quid-pro-quo, obstruction of justice and abuse of power. The Democrats on the Judiciary Committee would even convene a focus group to ascertain what would be the strongest charge to use to assure conviction of President Trump. Apparently, none of the focus group found any of these charges appealing or convincing. So, all of the original charges pursued by the Democrats running the impeaching committee were dropped and two new ones were created in the final moments, namely: 1) abuse of power and 2) obstruction of Congress. These charges were solely based on the July 25th 2019 phone call from Donald Trump to Ukraine President

Zelensky. President Trump was never given the opportunity to respond to these last-minute charges and neither had been raised by either impeaching committee during their proceedings

The Constitution and the Ongoing Breach by the Democrats

The authority and importance of our Constitution has never before been under such attack as we have witnessed from the Democrat leadership in the House, nor has the Constitutional conflict between strict "constructionism" and "revisionism" been so strong and significant. It started under the Obama administration and the Affordable Care Act. Within that act was the mandate that everyone must have health insurance or they would be fined. They would have to pay the Federal Government a penalty, for the privilege of not having to buy health insurance. The "penalty" or "fine" would eventually be called a tax by Chief Justice John Roberts and on that basis, he cast his vote that determined the Affordable Care Act was constitutional, in a 5 to 4 Supreme Court decision. Amendment 16 to the Constitution passed on July 2, 1909 made clear what was the taxing authority of Congress and the limitations thereon. According to this amendment, "Congress has power to lay and collect taxes on **INCOME** from whatever source derived". To consider a mandate that triggers a fine or penalty some form of income that can be taxed is a very clear example of how "revisionism" works in Supreme Court decisions. It virtually gives the Supreme Court legislative powers and undermines the very basis of our Constitution which is the separation of powers among the three branches of government.

I have previously discussed the infamous Dred Scott case, which became one of the triggers of the Civil War. This was the decision of 7 Democrat Supreme Court Justices in opposition to the 2 Republican Supreme Court justices. In violation of the basic guarantees to all citizens of the United States as provided in the First amendment of the Constitution, the court held: "Once a slave, always a slave". This was arguably the worst decision by the Supreme Court in its history and it was decided by the Democrat controlled Court.

We proceed to the current day and the Trump administration. From the day of Trump's election, the Democrats were claiming that he was an illegitimate President; that Hillary Clinton won the popular vote and therefore should be President. None of the Democrat leaders, talked about the procedures carefully laid out in the Constitution for electing a President and Vice President. No Democrat, no representative of the liberal left media ever mentioned to their constituents how the Constitution provides for the election of the President and the Vice President. Based on the election pursuant to our Constitution, President Trump won by a landslide. He won 306 electoral votes to Hillary Clinton's 232. That's 57% of the electoral votes. Trump won 30 states (60%) and Hillary Clinton 20 (40%). This was never mentioned in the press or by the Democrat leadership. All we would hear for weeks; months and years was that President Trump was illegitimate and many people took the Democrats and the media at their word.

Next, the Democrats decided to attempt to make President Trump a participant in Russian interference in the 2016 Presidential election. The Democrats cried out "collusion" and their leaders claimed time and time again that they had solid proof that President Trump had colluded with Russia to win the election and that his firing of FBI director James Comey was "obstruction of justice" and "abuse of power". We would later learn how fraudulent or at least incompetent, Comey was in a series of FISA applications for which he was responsible.

The Mueller investigation would be initiated and after 2.5 years and 500 witnesses, thousands of documents and the expenditure of $40 million, even the severely anti-Trump bias of the Mueller team could not find any collusion by President Trump or his campaign staff. Although the report did not come to a conclusion about obstruction of justice, one could argue if there were no collusion, what justice was being obstructed?

The Whistle Blower

The Whistle Blower Memo

The "whistleblower" wrote a memo on July 26th, based on a conversation the "whistleblower" had with "White House Officials", who allegedly overhead the July 25th conversation between President Trump and Ukraine President Zelensky. This memo preceded the official complaint regarding the hearsay conversations the "whistleblower" had with unnamed officials who claimed to have overheard the telephone call. The memo was reduced to an official "whistleblower" complaint, well-crafted by Adam Schiff's Staff. Adam Schiff was the Democrat Chair of the House Intelligence Committee. The complaint was no longer the words of the "Whistleblower". Rather, it was carefully constructed by a bunch of lawyers on Schiff's staff, who virtually dictated the "Whistleblower's" affidavit, even incorporating footnotes and language associated only with lawyers. The complaint alleged that President Trump had used his July 25th call to persuade Ukrainian authorities to investigate Trump's potential political rival Joe Biden and his son Hunter Biden. At no time did the "Whistleblower" or his "hearsay" sources ever consider that the so-called "favor" asked for by Trump could have been because of a valid and justifiable concern that there had been a valid obstruction of justice and bribery actually and successfully undertaken by Joe Biden in demanding the then Ukrainian General Prosecutor, Viktor Shokin be removed from office before Biden would authorize $1 billion be provided the Ukrainian government. At the time the General Prosecutor was investigating the Ukrainian natural gas company, Burisma, a company known to be corrupt and a company where Biden's son, Hunter served on Burisma's board and was paid close to $1 million a year for doing nothing and having no background in the oil and gas industry. Hunter Biden became a director, soon after his father, then Vice President Joe Biden had taken on the lead position in our country's relationship with the Ukraine. Joe Biden gave the Ukraine 6 hours to fire the General Prosecutor, or the Ukraine would not get the $1 Billon from the U.S. Joe Biden had successfully bribed (or extorted) the Ukraine Government and the Prosecutor General was immediately fired.

The Democrats would claim that the withholding of funds for a theoretical maximum of 55 days (a shorter time is more likely) damaged the Ukraine's national security and therefore so was the National security of the U.S., even though the President of the Ukraine, Voldymr Zelensky insisted there was no damage to his country's security and in fact he was unaware of any delay.

The Democrat leaders and the far-left media, failed to mention to their readers and constituents, that in April 2018, President Trump had arranged the delivery of 210 Javelin anti-tank missiles to strengthen Ukraine's defense in order to repel Russian aggression. The Ukrainian government was extremely grateful for the decision of President Trump to support the Ukraine in defense of freedom and democracy. By way of comparison, during the Obama administration only non-lethal aid was ever provided to the Ukraine. The very fact that Trump provided the Ukraine with deadly missiles for defense against Russia would seem to run contrary to the Democrats constant and unfounded complaint that President Trump was in collusion with Russia. After Russia seized the Crimea and later sent troops to Eastern Ukraine in 2014, U.S. General Breedlove strongly urged the U.S. to sell Javelin missiles to Ukraine. Obama refused to do so, only opting to provide non-lethal assistance. The claim of collusion with Russia would be far more applicable to President Obama, who stood by as Russia over-ran the Crimea and attacked the Ukraine and refused to come to the aid of Ukraine with weapons of defense.

The Formal Whistle Blower Complaint

The Whistleblower's complaint, dated August 12, 2019 was formally addressed to "The Honorable Adam Schiff, Chairman Permanent Select Committee on Intelligence, United States House of Representatives. It was 9 pages crafted in a very legalized format as one would only expect from a professional legal staff. The "Whistleblower" describes the specific "whistleblowing procedures" outlined on 50 USC 3033(5)(A) (a detail one would not expect from your "everyday Whistleblower"). The Whistleblower then says: "This letter is unclassified when separated from the attachment". My immediate observations were: 1) The "whistleblower's" formal complaint was crafted by a group of lawyers, probably Schiff's staff; 2) how could Adam Schiff consistently claim that he did not know who the "Whistleblower" was, although the "Whistleblower's" letter was addressed to him; 3) Adam Schiff's staff admitted to having met with the "Whistleblower" and if this is the case, how could Adam Schiff not know the accuser who was providing the very foundation for the impeachment of the President?; 4) The whistleblower states "I found my colleagues' accounts of these events to be credible. Since when does a complainant verify that his own witnesses are credible? and 5) The complaint is abundantly annotated, typical of a document crafted by lawyers. Why isn't the complaint in the "whistleblowers" own words?

The letter than states: In the course of my official duties I have received information from multiple (unnamed) officials that the President of the United States is using the power of his office to solicit interference from a foreign country in the 2020 U.S. election." This is classic hearsay and would be inadmissible in any judicial venue in the United States.

The "whistleblower" then goes on to say that the President's "interference includes among other things the pressuring of a foreign country to investigate one of the President's main domestic political rivals".

The "whistleblower" then claims that "over the past four months, more than a half-dozen (unnamed) U.S. officials informed me of various facts (again unidentified) related to this effort." (What specific facts and what specific effort?) This is the basis for the impeachment of our President. "Whistleblowers" are often trouble-makers; often have ulterior motives and try to convince people of the righteousness of their actions. Sometimes this may be true. However, in many of the worst instances in history of whistleblowing, it has been the source of some of the most hateful and tragic episodes to have ever been undertaken by man against his fellow man.

A Short History of Past Whistleblowers

1. **The Trial of Jesus**. One of the most infamous "Whistleblowers" in history was Judas Iscariot who turned Jesus over to the high priest Caliphas for 30 pieces of silver. Even though Pontius Pilate would find Jesus innocent and no legal basis for condemnation, the Pharisee leader of the people stirred them to cry out for Jesus' crucifixion. This historical event was not much different from the Democrat leaders, supported by the media, convincing so many of our citizens that President Trump is guilty of something, although it was never clearly established as to what. And further, the Democrats kept changing their arguments and reasons for impeachment, when they turned out to be fallacious or without merit.

2. **Spanish and Roman Inquisitions** – In 1478, the Catholic monarchs began the Inquisition as a tribunal to identify heretics and bring them to justice. It was designed to purify Catholicism. The Roman Inquisition developed by the Roman Catholic Church in the latter part of the 16th century was responsible for prosecuting individuals accused of a wide array of so-called "crimes" relating to religious doctrine or alternate religious belief. The Roman Inquisition also began the early witchcraft accusations, where numbers from 100,000 to over 1 million witches, mostly women were tortured and put to death. Common to both the Spanish and Roman Inquisitions was the role played by "whistleblowers", where mere accusation was sufficient to incarcerate, torture and eventually kill. The accuser did not have to factually prove his accusation. So long as he was a respected member of the community, his or her accusations of heresy or witchcraft were enough to send the accused to his or her death after first being tortured.

3. **The Salem Witch Trials** – Between February 1692 and May 1693, the colonial settlement at Salem, Massachusetts held a series of hearings and prosecutions of people accused of witchcraft. More than 200 were accused in the small community by "whistleblowers". Thirty were found guilty, nineteen of whom were executed by hanging. The episode is one of Colonial Americas most notorious cases of mass hysteria. It provides a vivid tale about the dangers of false accusations and lapses of due process. The trials were started after people had been accused by "whistleblowers" who were primarily teenage girls. Even Dorothy Good, a four or five-year-old girl was accused of witchcraft. No due process was required; no confrontation of the accusers ("Whistleblowers") was allowed; no facts were put into evidence. The accused were just found guilty.

4. The prosecution of someone charged with witchcraft started with a "whistleblower" concluding that a loss, illness or death had been caused by witchcraft and the "whistleblower" would enter a complaint against the alleged witch with the local magistrate. If the complaint were deemed credible (which it almost always was) the accused would be arrested; often on the accusation of one sole person. It was then up to the accused to prove his or her innocence. It was not up to the tribunal to prove the guilt of the accused. My observation is that the prosecution of the witches of Salem was no different than the impeachment proceedings against President Trump today. President Trump is considered guilty unless and until he proves his innocence.

5. **Nazi Germany and the contribution of "Whistleblowers "to the reign of Terror.** In his book: "Backing Hitler, Consent and Concern in Nazi Germany, Robert Gellately discusses his major study which investigated the role of the secret police in Nazi, Germany in the 1930's and 1940's. His book demonstrated conclusively that the much-feared Gestapo relied on widespread public support to function effectively. Denunciations of fellow citizens and relatives by members of the public initiated many Gestapo investigations even though the "whistleblower" understood that those denounced could suffer torture, be assigned to concentration camps or be executed without due process. In this way, the Nazi German Socialist State succeeded remarkably in policing all aspects of human behavior and assured that the Nazi party could eliminate any opposition, through fear or threat of execution. While one may rightfully claim that the outcome of today's "whistleblower" accusations is not so drastic, it yields the same objective that the Nazi Party had, namely, to get rid of any opposition in order to obtain and maintain political power for a Democrat Socialist Party. The danger is clear and overwhelming. Like the Nazi Third Reich, the Democrats are willing to abuse and ignore our laws, control our media, suppress diversity of opinion, disrupt our government, eliminate opposition and impose socialism with all its control over our freedoms guaranteed to us by our Constitution.

First, we had our children carrying signs as vicious and appalling as "f..k President Trump". Then we had many Democrat members of the House refusing to attend the inauguration of our President; then we had those calling for his assassination, by cutting off his head, hanging, shooting or knifing to death. Then we had suggestions of a military coup. Then we had many Democrat House Members claiming he was illegitimate and that he stole the election with the help of the Russians. Then we had the Democrats claiming the President had committed Treason, without giving any reason and needed to be impeached. Then we had the media falsely claiming that the President committed crimes and the House spent $40 million on the Mueller Investigation, which found that the President innocent And finally when all the charges they could think of didn't work, at the last moment the Democrats come forward with two new specious charges of: "abuse of power" and "obstruction of Congress", neither of which are impeachable offenses.

Whistleblowing can be used for good or evil, but like this one, the most significant whistleblowing cases in history have all been evil. Ponder this along with all my observations in this book. Can we really support a far-left Socialist Party, who will do anything to gain power and take away our liberty, justice and freedom?

The Response of the Evangelical Community

Mark Galli, editor of the Evangelical "Christian Today" wrote an op-ed stating that Trump: "should be removed not as a matter of partisan loyalties but loyalty to the creator of the 10 commandments." ".... the impeachment hearings have made it absolutely clear in a way the Mueller investigation did not; that President Trump has abused his authority for personal gain and abused his Constitutional oath. None of the President's positives can balance the moral and political danger we face under a leader of such grossly immoral character. It was claimed that Galli represented the beliefs of as many as 20% of all Evangelicals. The Democrats were overjoyed. Here was a bastion of support for President Trump and it was crumbling. But this was short-lived.

Nearly 200 Evangelical leaders stepped forward to soundly criticized Galli and made it clear to all that he was not a spokesperson for at least 80% of the Evangelical community. Their public statement would make it abundantly clear that Galli had strayed from his claim of being an Evangelical. The 200 leaders said in a formal release of their criticism: "It would appear that he (Galli) has forsaken his fundamental Evangelical beliefs to make a political statement. Nearly 200 Evangelicals slammed Galli for questioning their Christian witness. They said that Galli, offensively dismissed the majority of Evangelicals on the far right as if Christ is only for the far left". The faith leaders, the signatories of their rebuttal, decried Galli for "offensively" dismissing their far-right point of view stating that: "we are not far right Evangelicals. Rather we are Bible believing Christians and patriotic Americans who are grateful to a President who has sought our advice as his administration has advanced policies that: protect the unborn, promote religious freedom, reform our criminal justice system, contribute to strong working families through paid family leave, protect the freedom of conscience,. prioritizes parental rights and assure that our foreign policy aligns with our values, while making our world safer, including through the support of Israel".

The Evangelical respondents also denounced assertions made by Galli in an essay published last year entitled "Still Evangelical" deriding 80% of Evangelicals who support President Trump. Galli described those Evangelicals as: "who often haven't finished college, and if they have jobs, which most of them don't are blue collar jobs or entry level work. In the same piece, Galli referred to himself as belonging to a different group of Evangelicals, the "elite" Evangelicals.

The foundation of Evangelicalism is the belief in the teachings and authority of Jesus Christ and that belief is the path to salvation. You cannot cherry pick which of the teachings of Jesus are acceptable to you and ignore those that are not. Also fundamental to all Christians whether Evangelical or other Protestant Sect or Catholic is supposedly the strong sense of love and humility. If we do not love our neighbors. If we let hate rule our lives, if we are never humble enough to admit we may be wrong, then how can we claim to be a Christian?

There are some important teachings of Jesus, which seem to be overwhelmingly ignored today. These teachings should be considered by all Christians, whether their political leanings are Democrat or Republican; whether one is Protestant or Catholic. And beyond Christianity, these teachings of Jesus should make sense to any human being, whether Christian, Jew, Muslim, Hindu, Buddhist, atheist or any other religious belief for that matter. There are two in particular that I believe should be considered by all man-kind, regardless of religious background or persuasion:

1. **Matthew 7 verses 1-5** - Jesus said: "Judge not that ye be not judged. For what judgment ye judge, ye shall be judged and with what measure ye mete, it shall be measured to you again. And why behold the spec in your brother's eye, but do not consider the log in your own eye? You hypocrite, first remove the log from your own eye and you will see more clearly to remove the spec from your brother's eye.

2. **John 8 verses 3-11** – And the scribes and Pharisees brought unto him a woman taken in adultery and when they had set her in the midst, they say unto him, Master, this woman was taken in adultery in the very act. Now Moses in the law commanded us that such should be stoned: but what says thou?......So when they continued asking him he lifted himself up and said "He that is without sin among you, let him first cast a stone at her.........And they which heard him being convicted by their own conscience went out one by one and Jesus was left alone....... Jesus said unto the woman "Woman, where are those, thine accusers? Hath no man condemned you? She said "No man and Jesus said unto her: Neither do I condemn thee, go and sin no more".

What powerful teachings. We need to avoid biased hypocritical judgments; we must avoid false accusations. We must be sure that we are guiltless before accusing others of immorality and most of all we must forgive. Apparently, a minority of Evangelicals and most Democrat leaders fail to accept any teachings of Jesus that would suggest that their condemnation of President Trump is mostly based on hatred, lack of humility and their own hypocritical conduct.

The Articles of Impeachment

Congressman Jerry Nadler, Chairman of the House Judiciary Committee, delivered the Articles of Impeachment (the Resolution) against President Donald Trump on December 10, 2019. The Resolution impeaching the President for High Crimes and Misdemeanors raised two articles: Article 1 – Abuse of Power and Article 2 – Obstruction of Congress. Bribery, Extortion, Quid Pro Quo, Obstruction of Justice, the original charges that the House Intelligence and House Judiciary Committees had sought to prove were dropped and in its place were these vague, non-criminal claims challenged by all the Republicans in both Houses and questioned by approximately 50% of the citizens of the United States. These Articles of Impeachment, promulgated solely by the left would be the most divisive action taken by either party in my lifetime and at a time under the Trump administration when our economy unquestionably has been the best in our history. It has been virtually a miracle, that with all the hatred, vitriol and attempts to bring down our government by the Democrats, that so much positive could be accomplished and but for the Democrats, so much more could have been accomplished that would have been a benefit to all our citizens. Let us briefly look at each Article of Impeachment so biased and unsupported by all the Republicans Senators and Republican House Members and approximately 50% of the people.

Article 1 – Abuse of Power

This article stated that President Trump solicited interference of a foreign government (Ukraine) in the 2020 Presidential election, requesting the government to investigate Joe Biden and his son Hunter Biden (who had obtained the position of Director of a corrupt Ukraine Company, Burisma; was paid close to $1 million a year by Burisma for doing nothing and had no knowledge or experience in the natural gas business of Burisma). Hunter Biden became a director of Burisma coincidentally at the same time his father, Joe Biden, then Vice President of the U.S., became the lead U.S. government official in dealing with the Ukraine. At the time, the Ukraine General Prosecutor, Viktor Shokin, was investigating the corrupt activities of Burisma, which would have involved looking into the background and motivation for hiring Hunter Biden as a director and paying him such incredible sums of money for doing nothing. To make the dealings between Joe Biden and the Ukrainian government more incredulous, Joe Biden ordered the Ukrainian government to fire The General Prosecutor and thereby desist from investigating Burisma. If they failed to do so in 6 hours, Biden told them, he would not release the approximate $1 billion that the U.S. had agreed to. Joe Biden would publicly brag on National TV about how he extorted the Ukraine government into firing Victor Shokin. The Ukraine Government immediately complied and fired Shokin within the 6 hours demanded by Joe Biden. (Viktor Shokin, himself would claim that he had been told to back off investigating Burisma and Hunter Biden). Is this not abuse of power by the then Vice President, Joe Biden? And is it unreasonable to expect that our President would want to look into this? And certainly being one of 25 candidates for President should not exclude Biden from being investigated. Are candidates for President above the law? After all, that is what the Democrats consistently said about President Trump regarding his 30-minute call on July 25, 2019.

Article 1 of the impeachment suggests that President Trump was enlisting a foreign power in corrupting Democratic elections. Isn't it equally appropriate to say that Trump's actions sought to expose improprieties and abuse of power by an American citizen? This also could be a logical and appropriate intent, and if so, we do not reach the threshold of even "preponderance of evidence" for a civil case, let alone "beyond reasonable doubt", the threshold for a criminal case.

Article 1 goes on to say that the July 25th call compromised National security. After all the achievements by President Trump in enhancing our National Security, how does this 30 minute call, which resulted in no quid pro quo, no investigation into Burisma, no public statement by Ukraine officials that Ukraine would investigate Burisma; no non-delivery of missiles to Ukraine and even a lack of awareness on the part of the Ukraine President that there had been any delay in the delivery of the missiles, amount to abuse of power or damage to our National security?

Let's digress for a moment and look at the achievements of President Trump's administration regarding the security of our country:

1. Rebuilt our military that had deteriorated to levels under President Obama, severely impairing our National Security

2. Provided anti-tank missiles to the Ukraine to assist them in holding off Russian interdiction. You may recall that the Obama Administration looked the other way as Russia invaded the Crimea and refused to provide any armaments for the defense of Ukraine during his administration.

3. Reacted forcefully to Syria using chemical weapons against its own people. You may recall, Obama drawing a "red line" regarding Syria's use of gas against his people and then reneging.

4. Placed strong sanctions against Iran. You may recall that during the Obama Administration, $150 billion was made available to Iran as the quid pro quo for the weak Obama Nuclear Ban Treaty, which allowed international inspections of nuclear sites only with the permission of the Iranian Government. In addition, under the cover of darkness, the Obama Administration secreted $1.5 billion of cash in different currencies into Iran. These monies have been used to provide arms, missiles and fund terrorist armies, under the direction of Iranian Terrorist leader Qasem Soleimani, recently eliminated by U.S. military action. Our U.S. government under, President Obama through the Nuclear treaty with Iran has effectively funded the growing ranks of terrorists throughout the world and has allowed Iran to expand proxy armies throughout the Middle East, particularly in such terrorist groups as HAMAs Hezbollah and ISIS. The weapons that the U.S. have funded under the Iranian Nuclear Arms Agreement have unquestionably been used to kill our American Soldiers and bomb our bases in the Middle East. You may also recall the insane "Fast and Furious" project under the Obama Administration, where we delivered thousands of weapons to the Mexican Drug lords, who in turn used them against our border patrol agents, leading to some deaths and injuries on our border.

5. Provided strong sanctions against North Korea in contrast to the Obama Administration which permitting North Korea to expand its nuclear capabilities unhindered.

6. Obtained a step-up in contributions to our defense from our NATO partners, substantially improving the security of our NATO allies.

7. Shored up our support and joint security relationship with Israel. You may recall that the Obama Administration, turned against Israel for the first time, in allowing Israel to be condemned by the U.N. for its actions against Palestine. This resulted in a strengthening of support for Palestine at the expense of Israel.

8. Continued to build the wall on our borders, although continually frustrated by Democrats who want open borders, sanctuary cities and unlimited rights for any who cross our borders, whether legally or illegally.

9. Developed the U.S./Mexico/Canada Trade agreement, which the House of Representatives finally passed. This agreement not only improves trade relationships among the three countries but also bolsters our North American Security.

10. Started a campaign to promote cyber security particularly with China. The U.S. took virtually

no steps to harness the cyber-security threat during the Obama Administration.

And yet, the Democrats would have you believe that the one thirty-minute call on July 25, 2019, which resulted in nothing happening, was a threat to our national security, while ignoring all the obvious threats to our security during the Obama Administration.

Article 2 – Obstruction of Congress

This Article of Impeachment deals with the defiance of subpoenas issued by the Democrat members of the House of Representatives. The fundamental question here is when does the House of Representatives" subpoena power over-ride the President's right to executive privilege? The power of the Legislative branch in this case is co-equal and the rights or abuses should be left to the Judiciary to determine. The Obstruction of Congress is a specious and invalid article, because there can be no obstruction of justice until the Supreme Court determines whether the President's right to Executive Privilege, prevails over the House's power of subpoena. It is interesting to note that every time a President vetoes a bill approved by Congress, he has obstructed it.

Finally, the decision of the Democrat members of the House of Representatives in approving Articles of Impeachment was based solely on evidence from an unnamed "Whistleblower" who could provide only hearsay evidence, which is inadmissible in any court of law. The House Intelligence Committee and the House Judiciary Committee, both controlled by the Democrats, would argue that they are not subject to the rules of law like everyone else in the United States. Isn't it ironical and hypocritical of the Democrat members of the House to claim that "nobody is above the law"; yet their actions in promulgating the Articles of Impeachment disregarded our Constitution repeatedly and clearly demonstrated that they, the Democrats to a man were "above the law"? The Democrats had already violated our Constitution with the fraudulent and corrupt FISA warrants obtained against Carter Page, specifically Amendment IV, which states that "no one shall be subject to unreasonable search and seizure". The repeated fabrication of the FISA warrants gave rise to unreasonable search and seizure, particularly illegal surveillance.

As to the hearings of the Foreign Intelligence and House Judiciary Committees, they repeatedly violate Amendments V and VI to the Constitution. Amendment V tells us that no-one can be deprived of life, liberty or property without due process and Amendment VI tells us what we need for due process. In any criminal prosecution (which the impeachment hearings clearly were) the accused has:

1. A right to a speedy trial;
2. An impartial jury – The Democrats were biased against President from the beginning. They were far from impartial. They presented their case on the basis of inference, presumption, inuendo and hearsay and in their bias said this was enough, although all their evidence would have been thrown out of any court in a real trial.

3. The accused must be informed of the nature and cause of the accusation. In the Mueller investigation it was "collusion" and President Trump was found innocent The Democrats still claimed Obstruction of Justice, until it was pointed out to them if there were no collusion, what justice was being obstructed? For that reason, they replaced obstruction of justice with obstruction of Congress.

4. Probably the most important right guaranteed the accused by the Constitution is Amendment VI, the right to be confronted by his accuser and witnesses against him. In this case not only was the "Whistleblower's" identity kept from the accused, the President was not allowed to confront him on cross-examination. Amendment VI also provides for a compulsory process for the accused to obtain witnesses on his behalf. President Trump was also denied this. Democrat Chairman Schiff would not allow minority members to call any witnesses.

The law is quite consistent on the disallowance of hearsay evidence. Yet the case against President Trump is totally based on hearsay. Adam Schiff would even comment that hearsay evidence can be better than direct corroborative evidence. This is the mindset of the Democrat prosecutors that President Trump faced. Even the direct statement of Ukraine President Zelensky that he did not feel any pressure from President Trump during the 30-minute telephone call and that there was no bribery, no demand, no quid pro quo, was ignored by the Democrats. President Zelensky even commented that he was unaware that any aid from the U.S. had been withheld. Yet the Democrats would not even consider this. Also irrelevant was the fact that aid was delivered within the time constraint and President Zelensky never mentioned publicly nor did he undertake any investigation of Burisma, Hunter Biden or Vice President Joe Biden. This struck at the very heart of the Democrat claims against President Trump and it too was ignored. The actions of the Democrats here are no different from their past. Remember, they were the party that founded the Ku Klux Klan and established illegal tribunals that killed and tortured blacks after the Civil War and it was the Democrats who also established the Jim Crow laws, which they enforced in opposition to the Constitution and specifically Amendment 13 which freed all from slavery and involuntary servitude.

U.S. Ambassador to the European Union, Gordon Sondland

Finally, the Democrats bring forward as their star witness, Gordon Sondland, Ambassador to the European Union, who was supposed to provide the direct testimony regarding a call he had with President Trump that would prove beyond reasonable doubt, that Donald Trump was guilty of something on his telephone call to Zelensky on July 25, 2019. Sondland, changed his testimony that his private conversation was not incriminating, to appearing to admit there was a "quid pro quo" linking U.S. aid to Ukraine with an investigation into President Trump's political rival, Joe Biden. Yet Sondland would testify that his direct telephone call with the President on September 9, 2019, was as follows. The President said to him: "I want nothing, I want no quid pro quo. I want Zelensky to do the right thing". Sunderland then asked the President: "What does that mean" and the President responded: "I Want him (Zelensky) to do what he ran on". Gordon Sondland had changed his testimony and the "bombshell" he supposedly offered against the President was that Trump had offered a "quid pro quo". Then during the Republican cross-interrogation, Sondland was asked; "No one told you that Trump was tying aid to investigating Burisma and the Bidens? To which Sondland answered "yes". The follow up question: "So you really have no testimony today that ties President Trump to a scheme to withhold aid from the Ukraine in exchange for these investigations?" Sondland's answer: "**No. Other than my own presumptions**".

Let us summarize the results so far. Our Democrat leaders, persecuted and prosecuted our President based on a 30 minute private telephone conversation on July 25th, with Ukraine President Zelensky, released by an unknown third party, the so-called "Whistleblower", who had no direct knowledge of the phone call, having had it revealed to him by other unknown parties; the "Whistleblower's affidavit were not his own words, but carefully drafted by the staff of Adam Schiff, whose only intention was to impeach President Trump regardless of the truth or factual basis of the charges which were based solely on hearsay; in violation of the Constitution, particularly the right to due process; the right to confront his accuser and witnesses against him; and the right to present witnesses in his defense and most importantly failed to establish an impeachable offense. It should be noted that the impeachment was totally bi-partisan, with not one Republican supporting the impeachment. It should also be noted that close to 50% of the voting population of the United States were opposed to the impeachment.

The Four Law School Professors – Witnesses before the House Judiciary Committee.

The House Judiciary Committee called four law professors as witnesses during the first day of its impeachment inquiry into President Trump. These four witnesses were:

1. Noah Feldman, professor of law at Harvard Law School. His opinion was that the Democrats had legitimate grounds to impeach President Trump for abuse of power in office.

2. Pamela Karlan, professor of public interest law at Stanford Law school. She had not previously commented on Trump's impeachment proceedings, but also concluded that Trump had performed impeachable offenses in his July 25, 2019 telephone call to the Ukraine President.

3. Michael Gerhardt, professor of jurisprudence at University of North Carolina School of law and former media director for Democrat Al Gore's Senate campaign, who also concluded that Trump had performed impeachable offenses and

4. Jonathan Turley, professor of public interest law at George Washington University School of Law. He was the only one selected by the Republican members of the committee.

All four were Democrats and had voted for President Obama and then for Hillary Clinton in the 2016 election. All admitted having no personal knowledge of the telephone call. Feldman, Karlan and Gerhardt were clearly strongly biased against the President. Karlan in particular revealed her bias and hatred for President Trump by attacking Trump's son, Baron for having the name Baron. "The Constitution doesn't allow titles of nobility", Karlan Said: "so while the President can name his son Barron, he can't make him a Barron". Law professors are not supposed to be biased, and not supposed to exude hatred toward those appearing before them. The law is to be above politics and yet this particular professor Karlan demonstrated unrelenting bias that reflects terribly on the whole legal profession. In a serious and monumental inquiry concerning the possible impeachment of a sitting President of the United States, one of the Democrat's star witnesses, Pamela Karlan, brings the President's 13-year-old son Baron into the prosecuting forum. This was despicable and hardly what should be expected from a supposedly respected law professor.

But, more importantly the three biased professors never should have provided opinions convicting the President. They were supposed to be Constitutional authorities, but concluded that President Trump was guilty, even though Amendments IV and VI to the Constitution were clearly violated in the prosecution of the President. The evidence was virtually all hearsay, open to several interpretations and never reached the level necessary to find "beyond a reasonable doubt" or even "preponderance of evidence". The one call between Sondland, the U.S. Ambassador to the European Union and the President, the only testimony not based on hearsay, by Sondland's own recount, raised only his "surmise" that there was a "quid pro quo". Nothing more than a surmise.

Further, the three law professors should have mentioned that President Trump by law has the right to confront the witnesses against him, particularly the "whistleblower". They should have either recused themselves or at least pointed out that vital rights under the Constitution had been violated and therefore a valid conclusion could not be reached on their part.

Jonathan Turley

Finally, Jonathan Turley was the last to address the Committee. Although a Democrat and supporter of Hillary Clinton, he was selected by the Republican members of the committee to put forth a rebuttal to the three other witnesses. Turley opened his testimony by declaring that he had voted for Hillary Clinton and that he was a Democrat. But he could not bring himself like the others to just forget his responsibility to be faithful to the law and to justice. He said: "21 years ago, I sat here before you, Chairman Nadler and other members of the Judiciary Committee to testify on the history and meaning of the Constitutional Impeachment standard as part of the impeachment of William Clinton. I haves spent decades writing about impeachment as an academic and a legal commentator. I tend to favor Congress in disputes with the Executive branch and I have been critical of the sweeping claims of presidential power and privileges made by modern administrations." He then went on to say:

"If the House proceeds solely on the Ukrainian allegations, the impeachment would stand out among modern impeachments as the shortest proceeding, with the thinnest evidentiary record and the narrowest grounds ever used to impeach a president. The law does not bode well for future presidents, who are working in a country often sharply and at times bitterly divided. As with the Clinton Impeachment, the Trump Impeachment has again proven Alexander Hamilton's words to be prophetic: "The stifling intolerance for opposing views are the same."

Turley goes on to say: "I am not a supporter of President Trump. I voted against him in 2016 and I have previously voted for Presidents Clinton and Obama. I have been highly critical of President Trump, his policies and his rhetoric in dozens of columns. These points are meant to drive home a simple point; one can oppose Trump's policies or actions, but still conclude that the current legal case for impeachment is not just woefully inadequate, but in some regards, dangerous, as the basis for the impeachment of an American President. My personal and political views of President Trump are irrelevant to my impeachment testimony as they should be to your impeachment vote.... I am concerned about lowering impeachment standards to fit a paucity of evidence and an abundance of anger. If we are to impeach a President for only the third time in our history, we will need to rise above this age of rage and genuinely engage in a civil substantive discussion"

Turley's 53-page testimony decries every illegal action proposed by the Democrats against President Trump including Bribery, Extortion, and Obstruction of Justice. For obstruction of justice, Turley pointed out that many came forward despite the request of Trump to not testify and they still have their jobs. And those who refused to testify should have a judicial determination as to whether Executive Privilege should prevail over Congressional subpoena power.

As to extortion, Turley sited the Hobbs Act, which defines extortion as" "the obtaining of property from another with his consent induced by wrongful use of actual or threatened force, violence or fear or under color of official threat. None of this stated Turley was attained here.

Turley then challenged among other things the charge against Trump that he failed to yield to Congressional demands in an oversight or impeachment investigation. He questioned how the Democrats distinguished the Trump case from a long line of cases where prior presidents withheld witnesses and documents. As an example, he pointed out the Obama Administration's position on the investigation of "Fast and Furious "which he stated: "was a moronic gun-walking operation in which the government arranged for the illegal sale of powerful weapons to (Mexican) drug cartels in order to track their movement. One such weapon was used to murder border patrol agent Brian Terry and Congress, justifiably so, began an oversight investigation. Some members called for impeachment proceedings. But President Obama invoked Executive Privilege and barred essential testimony and documents. The Obama Administration even went so far as to assert that the President's Executive privilege to withhold witnesses and documents was not reviewable. Turley would say; "The position of the Obama Administration was "extreme and absurd."" Nevertheless, President Obama had every right to seek judicial review of his opinion." (No more than what the Trump administration was seeking). I will go no further in the review of Turley's detailed condemnation of the specious, illegal proceedings by the Democrats.

Turley concludes as follows: "My Democrat friends are mad; my Republican friends are mad. We are all mad and where has it taken us? Will a slipshod impeachment (supported by less than 50% of the population and not one Republican member of the House) make us less mad, or will it only give invitation for the madness to follow in every future administration? For two years, members of the

Committee have declared that criminal and impeachable acts were established for everything from treason to conspiracy to obstruction. However, no action was taken to impeach. Suddenly, just a few weeks ago, the House announced it would begin impeachment inquiry and push to a final vote in a couple of weeks. It proceeded on a record composed of a relatively small number of witnesses with largely second hand (hearsay) knowledge. The only three direct conversations with President Trump did not contain a statement of "quid pro quo" and two expressly denied such a pre-condition. The House was moving forward based on conjectures. The military aid was released after a delay, which witnesses testified was not uncommon for this or prior administrations. In this age of rage, there seems to be no room for nuance, or reservation. Yet this is what the Constitution expects of us. Expects of you (House Members)."

Turley goes on to say: "In this age of rage, many are appealing for us to simply put the law aside and "just do it" You can declare the definition of crimes alleged are immaterial and that this is an exercise in politics, not law. However, the legal definition and standards that I have addressed in my testimony are the very things dividing rage from reason".

In the final analysis, Turley is appealing to reason not hate and that our Constitution is being overwhelmed by the hatred from the left and our country will not survive unless anger and hatred are set aside and freedom and justice exists for everyone.

Impeachment Final Chapter

"If we do not act now, we will be derelict in our duty" cried out Democrat Speaker of the House, Nancy Pelosi. The Democrats to a man stated they could not wait to the election. They had to get rid of President Trump now. Historically, whenever there is a rush to judgement there is an unsavory and unconscionable reason often flamed by hatred. This was true of the Ku Klux Klan lynchings, the Salem Witch Hunts, the Spanish Inquisition and all the purges and mass murders of the historic socialist regimes of the 20th and 21st century.

On December 18, 2019 by a vote of 220 Democrats and all 195 Republicans plus two Democrats crossing the isle in dissent, the House voted for impeachment of President Trump for only the third time in the history of our nation. There were two counts of impeachment, namely: Abuse of power, and obstruction of Congress, neither of which appear in the Constitution or are even remotely inferred. Then the rush seemed to stall as Nancy Pelosi refused to send the articles of impeachment over to the Senate for almost one month as she sought to dictate the procedures that the Senate was to follow in performing its sole right and duty to try the President for impeachment. Finally, on January 15, 2020, Pelosi agreed to send the Articles of Impeachment to the Senate and the House voted to transmit the Articles and formally appointed seven Democrats to serve as impeachment managers to prosecute the Democrats' case before the Senate.

We learn near the opening Democrat arguments in the Senate Trial from Jerry Nadler and Adam Schiff that "A crime need not be committed to impeach a president". How do we arrive at that conclusion? The Constitution says that a President and Vice President may be impeached for, treason, bribery and high crimes and misdemeanors. Where is the ambiguity? In every instance the Constitution is only mentioning the commission of a crime as a requisite for impeachment.

For 22 hours we will hear the droning of the Democrat managers as they vilify and exude their hatred for the President. They are very selective in the evidence they present; they would have the listener believe that hearsay evidence is more substantive than real and factual evidence. They will dazzle the listening audience with how they can read the minds of our founding fathers as to what they meant or what they intended in the framing of the section on impeachment. And somehow, they know the state of mind and intent of the president, based on the hearsay of witnesses and their suppositions of what the president meant or intended. They flat out refused to accept any alternative to the intent they supposed was that of the president.

Conjecture, surmise, hearsay, were the catchwords, the very backbones of the process by which the Democrats created the appearance of impeachable offenses but this was not enough. The Democrat systematically and intentionally violated the Constitution of the United States again and again. We have discussed this previously, but just look at Amendments 4 and 6 to our Constitution. I'll reiterate them again Amendment 4 protects every citizen against unreasonable search and seizure and: "no warrant shall issue, but on probable cause, supported by Oath and affirmation". The FISA warrants were unauthorized from the very beginning and were fraudulently doctored and submitted under Oath as to their truth. Amendment 6 guarantees every citizen certain rights in the case of criminal prosecution among which include: a trial by an impartial jury; the right to be confronted by the witnesses against him (i.e. the secret whistleblower); to be informed of the nature and cause of the accusation (you may recall, that the nature and cause kept changing, from bribery to quid pro quo, to extortion, to obstruction of justice and then in the very final moments, abuse of power and obstruction of Congress, neither of which had been the initial accusations); a compulsory process for obtaining witnesses in his favor and to have assistance of counsel in his defense. (none of these were allowed by either the House Intelligence Committee under Democrat Chair Adam Schiff or House Judiciary Committee, chaired by Democrat Jerry Nadler).

The so-called Constitutional experts that appeared before the House Judiciary Committee, even Professor Turley, claimed that a crime need not be committed to impeach a president. If not, then what is the standard for determining on what grounds a sitting President can be removed from office? We learn in law school that ambiguity is a nemesis to good law and is to be avoided in crafting any legal documents. While I do not pretend to know what the framers intended by their language other than what the language actually says, I would expect that they would not strive for ambiguity. If impeachment were to be applicable to instances that did not involve a crime, why then did not the authors of the Constitution make that clear? That a law professor is recognized as an "authority" on the Constitution does not make him or her clairvoyant, with the ability to read the minds of the deceased authors of our Constitution or for that matter read the mind of our President.

What does expanding the understanding of grounds for impeachment to include: "Obstruction of Congress", mean? Well, for one thing, every President of the United States has obstructed Congress. Every time a President vetoes a bill passed by Congress; he is obstructing it. President Roosevelt was the all-time leader in obstructing Congress with the veto of 635 bills while in office. Harry Truman, 250, Ronald Reagan 78; Bill Clinton 37; Barack Obama 12, Donald Trump, 6. All of a sudden, obstruction of Congress would immediately encumber the Presidential right to veto.

What about "Abuse of Power". Could not the presidential "power to pardon" be claimed in some instances to be an abuse of power? Franklin Roosevelt pardoned 3,687; Harry Truman 2,044; Dwight Eisenhower, 1,157; John F. Kennedy, 575; Lyndon B. Johnson 1,187; Richard Nixon, 926; Bill Clinton 459: and Barack Obama 1927.

Let's just look at three that Bill Clinton pardoned.

1. Roger Clinton – Bill Clinton's brother.
2. Susan McDougal – Bill Clinton's business partner in the scandalous "White Water" venture
3. Mark Rich - Convicted of Tax evasion and illegal trading with Iran. President Clinton pardoned Mark Rich after Rich's ex-wife made large donations to the Democratic Party and the Clinton Foundation.

Then look at two by Barack Obama

1. Oscar Lopez – Sentenced in 1981 to 55 years in prison for sedition, use of force to commit a robbery and conspiring to transport explosives with intent to destroy government property
2. Chelsea Manning – U.S. Army "Whistleblower" court-martialed and sentenced to 35 years in prison for violating the Espionage Act after disclosing nearly 750,000 classified or military sensitive documents to Wikileaks. She was charged with 22 offenses, including aiding the enemy, which could have resulted in the death penalty.

The expansion of the definition of "impeachable offense" to mean anything you want it to mean, plays right into socialism and provides just another tool for the liberal left to overthrow our government. The liberal left has used propaganda through the media and the entertainment industry; indoctrination in our schools, hatred and vilification of all that oppose them and even the suggestion to overthrow the government. Those are the sticks. The carrots are all the free things that the left promises you. Free medical, free college and university education, a guaranteed income; all things they will never be able to deliver. They preach insanity and then rely on the people's ignorance. In my lifetime, there has never been one successful socialist economy. On the contrary without exception, every socialist regime has provided death, famine, homelessness, and despair to its constituents. Yet time and time again people are convinced this is the best system for them. **Yet, they have always failed.**

I look at all the purges, mass murders, genocide, the execution or incarceration of the opposition and, the promulgation of hatred and fear that occurred in my lifetime. And what do I find they all had in common? They are all Socialist regimes and they have all failed. I will not mention all of them. There are so many. But I have included in the next chapter, the ones that destroyed so many lives and wreaked havoc on everyone they were supposed to serve. They all started by saying the law didn't matter; that they could create their own laws to be whatever they wanted them to be and ignore the laws they find unacceptable. The Democrats violated the law with their sanctuary cities, allowing illegal immigrants to not only stay in the U.S., but also to receive all the benefits of a citizen. They ignore the Constitution, or create their own interpretation to fit their needs. And they make promises of vast benefits for their constituents that they know they can't provide.

Once the President can be removed from office without committing a crime; once the President of the United States can be subject to indictment without due process; once the President is not allowed to confront his accusers or to bring forth witnesses in his behalf; once the President is not allowed to mount a defense, what does that mean for the rest of us? If our political leaders can do that to our President, they can do that to any of us. The Democrats have shown that they are ready to destroy our economy and take away the very freedoms and rights guaranteed by the Constitution in order to gain power for themselves.

CHAPTER 24

Conclusions

THE DEMOCRATS SEEM to have something bad to offer everyone. They have consistently put their objective to achieve ultimate power and control over the Citizens of the United States and ahead of their well-being. Yet despite the constant hatred and vilification of the Trump Administration by the liberal left; despite all the efforts by the Democrats to frustrate the Trump Administration both at home and abroad, much has been accomplished for the benefit of all Americans. There have been $1.6 trillion in tax cuts, giving the average American more disposable income. There have been substantial cuts in Corporate taxes which has led to 500,000 new manufacturing jobs. Under the Trump administration we have seen a total of 6 to 7 million new jobs created and in 2019 applications for unemployment benefits fell to a 50-year low. We have seen great steps in improving the health care of our veterans by establishing a policy that Veterans can go to the doctor of their choice rather than wait for availability of medical services from the scandal plagued Veterans Hospitals. We have seen our country for the first-time reach energy independence that even allows us to be a net exporter of oil. We have seen a drastic reduction in regulations that were stifling our industries. We have seen unemployment fall to the lowest it has been in over 50 years; a level consistently under 4%. We have seen the IRA's and 401K's of our retired citizens grow substantially as the stock market has made phenomenal gains during the Trump Administration. We have seen the Trump Administration open dialogue with the Arab Nations, North Korea, China and Russia; dialogues that the Democrats have criticized or even sought to obstruct whenever possible. We have seen the Trump administration renew our support of Israel after years under Obama's Administration's policy of supporting Palestine in its conflict with Israel. We have seen our military restored to a level of capability that had deteriorated dramatically under President Obama. We have seen low interest rates sustained, making investments and capital formation less expensive and more easily realized.

We have watched the Democrat party contribute nothing to the wellbeing of our country for almost four years, during which time the Democrats have constantly cried for President Trump's impeachment and even that he should be tried for treason. For three years the Democrats have sought to find President Trump guilty of collusion with Russia. After spending $40 million through the Mueller Special Counsel, the Commission concluded there was no collusion, yet the Democrats are still spending all their time targeting President Trump, as opposed to promulgating and passing meaningful legislation. The Democrats will tell you that the following will be of benefit to all: (Remember our total Federal tax revenues today is approximately $3.2 trillion)

1. $100 trillion Green New Deal; (cost $10 trillion/year)
2. $50 trillion National Health Care Plan ($5 trillion a year)
3. free college for everyone;
4. $12,000/yr. income for everyone including those unwilling to work; ($3.8 Trillion/yr.)
5. elimination of airplanes, gas powered cars and cattle;
6. eliminating all jobs associated with fossil fuels, Health insurance and gas fueled vehicles
7. supporting open borders, allowing free entry of immigrants from anywhere at any time
8. providing free healthcare and education and even the right to vote to immigrants
9. doing away with ICE;
10. supporting and expanding sanctuary cities;
11. Refusing to negotiate with our adversaries without pre-conditions;
12. eliminating sanctions on Iran and restoring the Nuclear Ban Treaty, (initially only a 10-year treaty signed in 2015; now with only 5 years left to run).
13. increasing substantially corporate and personal income taxes on everyone;
14. providing voting rights for illegal immigrants;
15. doing away with the electoral college;
16. packing the Supreme Court, so that it becomes another legislative arm under Democrat control;
17. Implementing socialist programs throughout the economy virtually doing away with free enterprise;
18. Reducing our military budget, in the face of mounting pressures of terrorism and nuclear threats around the world.

Why do so many people gravitate toward the socialist Democrats? First because of all the promises of free benefits that will descend on them with a Socialist Democrat Government. But more insidious and the catalyst behind everything the Democrat Party says and does is their constant promotion of hatred for the Trump Administration. And this emanates from our public schools, our colleges and Universities; the media and the entertainment industry. Hatred spawns ignorance and is fed by hubris. Hatred clouds reason and unifies mobs, who follow what they are told by the hate mongers. Hatred is the enemy of Wisdom and Humility. Jesus taught us how to live and react in society. His teachings were based on love, and along with love he prescribed humility.

Who are the Real Dictators?

The liberal left including our Democrat Congressmen, our college and university professors, talk show hosts, the reporters and the entertainment industry have often suggested that President Trump is a dictator, even comparing him to Hitler, Stalin, Putin and Mussolini all liberal socialist regimes. Where is the logic or rationale in this statement? When do any of these members of the liberal left provide us with a logical, factual basis for these statements? Do you think for one moment that a dictator would put up with the on-going vilification of his regime, or would be placed before a tribunal that was seeking to oust him from power? President Trump seeks to reduce the size of our Federal government and return many of its activities to the states. He seeks to repeal the Affordable Care Act, a Nationalist health program aiming at becoming a single-payer system and return it to the states. He wants to reduce taxes on the middle class so that they may better enjoy the fruits of their labor. He wants to reduce taxes on corporations and small businesses so that they may be more competitive with the rest of the world. He wants to restore Judaism and Christianity to its proper place of recognition within our society. He wants to bring back "Christmas" into our lives. He wants to reduce the burdens of regulations on our businesses, especially small business. He wants to return control of education to the states and increase individual choice for the education of their children. He wants to eliminate Government departments and agencies that usurp functions that rightfully belong to the states. He wants a "Constitutionalist" conservative interpretation of the Constitution so that the judiciary no longer has the power to legislate through wild interpretation of the Constitution. And finally, he wants to drain the Washington, DC "Swamp" of corruption fraud, deceit and self-dealing. Does this by any means sound like a dictator or fascist?

The liberal left seems to better reflect the policies and objectives of Hitler, Mussolini Stalin, Putin. We also might want to add Mao Tso-Tung and Castro as dictators that the liberal left seems to emulate. Let us examine the objectives of the liberal socialist that seem to closely emulate the fascists, communists and dictators of the past (and present).

1. Seeks to centralize under government control (or actual operation thereof) of all industry
2. Dictate what and how products are to be produced (i.e. shut down coal mining, prohibit expansion of oil production and oppose building of new pipelines)
3. Allow arbitrary changes to the Constitution by fostering arbitrary interpretations (i.e. the fine imposed on individuals who choose to opt out of Obamacare; removal of any reference or symbols of Christianity or Judaism in our schools).
4. Control the legal system by appointing political activists to the bench willing to give biased interpretations of the Constitution
5. Control education from k-12, indoctrinating the children along the way (i.e. imposing on the student's special Islamic studies including Islamic Prayers, the wearing of Islamic clothing and the learning of passages from the Qur'an).
6. Take control of education at the college and university level and indoctrinating the students;

refusing to allow the expression of opposing views with threats of reduced grades, or even removal from class; disallowing speakers with opposing views; providing students with "safe places" so they can avoid confrontation and dialogue; encouraging protests, demonstrations, vandalism and violence against any who oppose their doctrines and beliefs.

7. Attack and berate the opposition with hatred and vitriol in order to turn the masses against them.

8. Suppress any news or information which may reflect negatively on the liberal left.

9. Spread negative and unsupported propaganda against the conservative right.

10. Control the media to assure that propaganda against the opposition is sustained on a daily basis.

11. Control of the press which can continually promulgate unfounded and even false accusations against the Conservative right. Control the entertainment industry (including talk show hosts) who will continually vilify the opposition

12. Use every means possible to disparage, destroy or block any plan or program proposed by the opposition and at the same time never give the opposition credit for positive occurrences on their watch. (i.e. stellar stock market performance, substantially lower unemployment, new job creations; higher consumer and business confidence)

13. Seek to promote anarchy and thereby gain control of the government rather than seeking some bipartisan approach to achieving a better life for its constituents. (i.e. sanctuary cities)

That the liberal socialists are ready and willing to impose their credo on its constituents at any cost and by any means has been clearly demonstrated in the past by the bloody revolutions they have launched followed by violent periods of terror in Germany, Italy, China, Cuba, North Korea and most recently in Venezuela. Whether Communism, Fascism or Nazism, they are all socialist regimes that were established through purges of the opposition and terrorizing the citizens to get them to conform to the will of the state. The liberal left in America so far falls just short of this, but all the elements are there as every step the liberal left takes is targeted to overturn our government. The liberal left has made hate and vilification a centerpiece of their movement. The disruption and violence and suppressing of free speech on our college and university campuses is a strategic element of a successful coup. The constant attacks by the media and the entertainment industry calling for the assassination of the president or at least his impeachment and even suggesting at one point a military coup are typical of the beginning of a socialist revolution. (Former Department of Defense official in the Obama Administration, Rosa Brooks, publicly suggested military insurrection against the Trump administration). We did not see anything like this coming from the Conservative Right during the Obama Administration. It is not the Republican Conservatives that should be condemned. It is the liberal socialist left in our country that is putting on the mantel of Nazism, fascism and Communism that are to be condemned and they are the ones who would take our country into a bloody revolution. There is reason to fear such an outcome by the Conservative Right. They can't even agree among themselves. They do not toe the line as far as a Conservative Credo is concerned. No, not like the

Liberal Left who all walk in lockstep. The Conservative Right can disagree openly among themselves; criticize each other and even vote against their party if their conscience directs them to. But the Liberal left has strongly indicated its willingness to do anything to achieve a centralized government, even if they must overthrow the existing government and throw the country into turmoil. Our country is in a crisis, much of which has been brought upon us during the 8 years under Obama's administration. There is the crisis in North Korea, one that should not have been ignored these past 8 years. There is the serious if not equal crisis in Iran where the Obama Administration chose to make such a weak and one-side agreement favoring Iran that he virtually assured that Iran would be a nuclear power in the near future. The Obama Administration even provided Iran $150 billion to fully fund not only Iran's quest for a nuclear war capability, but to build proxy armies of terror throughout the Middle East. And part of the $150 billion given to Iran was used by Iran or its allies to kill American soldiers Obama stood by as Russia took over the Ukraine and Crimea. He backed down on his threat (his so-called "red line") in Syria; and he even sided with Palestine against Israel by not voting against the condemnation of Israel for acts of inhumanity against Palestine. Disruptions throughout the world have been allowed to fester and now the Liberal Left is dividing our country at the very time we need a united country the most. By the liberal left's constant promulgation to the world of their hatred and contempt toward President Trump and his administration, they portray to the world a weakness and divisiveness that encourages our enemies and rogue states that this is the best time for them to confront the United States.

We conclude our discussion of the real dictators in our midst by once again referring to Mark Levin's book "Liberty and Tyranny". The liberal left, Levin tells us: "misuses equality to propose uniform economic and social outcomes. The radical liberal must continually enhance his power at the expense of self-government and must violate the individual's property rights at the expense of individual liberty, for he believes that through persuasion, deception and coercion he can tame man's natural state. Further, Levin tells us: "the radical liberal must claim the power to make that which is unequal, equal" and "if only the individual surrenders himself to the all-powerful state, only then can the impossible be made possible". Levin then quotes from the writer-philosopher C.S. Lewis, who wrote: "of all the tyrannies, a tyranny sincerely exercised for the good of its victims may be the most oppressive. Those (the liberal left) who torment us for our own good, will torment us without end, for they do so with the approval of their own conscience".

What should we seek to achieve as a united country?

Here are 14 things I believe most important.

1. We need first and foremost more open and objective discussion (Socratic discussion) among liberals and conservatives to arrive at truth. We must promote more bi-partisan and friendly endeavor in our Congress and the hatred expressed by the liberal left must be curtailed. We so infrequently hear the truth from any politician and as long as the entertainment industry, the media, our educators and our government spin propaganda, we will never have a government

of the people, by the people and for the people.

2. We must be free from excessive regulation. My experience with government contracting is that the government is woefully incapable of running anything successfully, but must at least provide for the safety of the citizens. It is arguable beyond that what the Federal government is really better equipped to do than private enterprise? The Veterans Administration is the classic example of how incapable our government is in running socialistic programs.

3. Many if not most of government programs and regulations should be pushed back to the states. They are far better equipped at handling their own problems. This would eliminate a lot of "pork barrel" trades among Congressmen. We wouldn't see bridges to nowhere built and probably no ill-conceived investments like Solyndra.

4. A health care system with less Federal regulation and more state regulation; allowing insurance to be marketed across state lines, and allowing the individual to have a freedom of choice as opposed to being dictated by Federal or state governments.

5. The life of the unborn child should be protected as a human being at a point where science defines it as a human being (i.e. heart beat; brainwaves)

6. Less meddling by the government in the lives of its constituents

7. A balanced budget where the government doesn't spend more than it takes in. (This goal may not necessarily be achieved overnight)

8. Reduce the overall size of the Federal government.

9. Simplify and reduce our taxes, particularly corporate and small business to render them more competitive with the rest of the world

10. Make "Made in America" a real goal. We must reduce trade imbalances.

11. Control outrageous cost overruns on government purchases and require contracts to be completed on budget and on time. Recently the U.S.S. Gerald Ford Aircraft carrier was delivered at a cost of $13 billion. It was delivered 3 years late and $2 Billion over budget. It still will not be ready for deployment for another 4 years. This is outrageous. Does anyone remember in the past, Senator Proxmire's monthly "Golden Fleece Award", pointing out some of the wasteful spending on useless projects by the U. S. Government and the outrageous costs for a simple screw or a toilet seat?

12. Term limits for Senators and Representatives.

13. Congressmen should have the same health insurance as everyone else.

14. Make Homeland Security a vital element in determining any immigration policy.

Complacency, the fertile ground of Radicalism

Complacency coupled with apathy and topped off with ignorance eventually brings down nations. No better example is Germany under the Third Reich. Our opinions and conclusions should be reached as a result of research and objective reasoning. **WE NEED TO REVIVE SOCRATIC DIALOGUE**. How many of you have read the Qur'an? How many have read the Charter of Hamas or Hitler's, Mein Kompf?".

We need only to look at the family trees of Jewish families. Many of these trees have limbs which have abruptly ended, without any branches because a grandparent, parent, brother or sister had been put to death in one of the many death camps in Poland such as Auschwitz, Treblinka and Chelmo, or were starved or beaten to death in slave labor camps such as Buchenwald and Dachau in Germany.. And Mein Kompf, a best seller in the Arab World reveals the roots of Hitler's genocidal nature. In one passage, he states: "if at the beginning of the war and during the war, twelve to fifteen thousand Hebrew corrupters of the nation had been subjected to poison gas…. the sacrifice of millions at the front would not have been in vain".

Hitler knew how to bend the will of Christians to hate and even kill. He realized early on that if you controlled the media, you could bombard the citizens with lies and deceit and create an environment of such hatred as to make otherwise peace loving, law-abiding citizens willing to murder millions of people just because they were Jews. Like Kaepernick referring to all police as pigs; Hitler repeatedly called all Jews, pigs and not humans. Once he was able to convince the population that they were not really killing humans, murdering them was all right. Yes, there were a few Germans who did not go along with the exterminating of the Jews, but the majority were complacent, and did not want to get involved. They let this upstart radical socialist, Adolph Hitler lead them to the greatest atrocities in the history of mankind.

Our American moral values are diametrically opposed to Islam. We seek love and peace with all people, all nations and do not wish to interfere with their beliefs. Islam on the contrary wants to conquer and impose their beliefs on all people, through terror and war if necessary. It is time for Americans whether Christians, Jews or Atheists, to stand up for what is morally right and no longer be swayed by the constant hate and vitriol from the liberal left.

There are key words that describe where our nation is and to some extent where our churches are. Multiculturalism, inclusiveness, secularism and political correctness have truly pervaded all areas of our culture. Our government, our schools, our universities, and our churches seem to have allowed these key words to dictate our lives and consequently resulted in the country's divisiveness. Are Lincoln's words "United we stand, divided we fall" no longer resonant in our community? How about the words of Jesus Christ found in Mark 3:24-25: "and if a kingdom be divided against itself, that kingdom cannot stand and if a house be divided against itself, that house cannot stand". Do we not believe this? Does Jesus' admonition fall on deaf ears?

We have leaders of our country boycotting the inauguration; we have celebrities supporting the imposition of martial law and we have protestors marching in droves calling the past election illegitimate. In California seventh graders are subject to an intense three-week course in Islam in which they are required to pray to Allah and memorize Koranic verses. They must wear a Muslim robe, adopt a Muslim name and stage their own Jihad. They must memorize 25 Islamic terms, six Arabic phrases and 20 Islamic proverbs along with the Five Pillars of Faith. Nothing like that is presented concerning Christianity. In Wisconsin, Maryland and Georgia there are similar issues of the imposition of Islamic religion on the students at certain schools in those states. Yet by contrast, Christianity has been virtually eliminated from our schools.

What has happened to our media? Most of our TV and radio commentators and our newspapers no longer even attempt to hide their bias. Where are the likes of Edward R. Morrow, John Cameron Swayze, David Brinkley, Chet Huntley, Tom Brokaw and Walter Cronkite? We could count on them to report the news in a fair and balanced way. We could trust them. Now the reporting in most of our media is more like the propaganda of Joseph Goebbels, Reich Minister of Propaganda of Nazi Germany from 1933 to 1945. He succeeded in centralizing control over all aspects of German cultural, political and intellectual thought. By bombarding the German nation with his hate and lies, he was able to get a nation to back Hitler in his quest to kill all Jews. Who is calling for the murder of our president by hanging, shooting, assassinating, knifing? And short of killing the President, who is constantly bombarding us with diatribes of hatred calling for the President's impeachment, or claiming that he is a dictator, white supremacist, racist or dictator like Hitler? It is our liberal left socialist Democrats, the vast majority of the media, the entertainment industry, and the education institutions. And like propaganda minister Goebbels who was able to gain the support of the citizens of Germany to murder 6 million Jews, a vast number of our American citizens are actually listening to and believing in the far-left diatribes.

What is happening in our churches, universities and schools? In pursuit of multiculturalism, inclusivity, secularism and political correctness, we see the divinity of Christ being questioned if not actually being eliminated, the holding of Christian pageants in schools being abolished, and the promotion of Islam on our college and university campuses while at the same time diminishing or abandoning the moral values associated with Christianity.

In their 1938 book "The War Against God", Sidney Park and R.S. Essex noted that the Christian Church had lost its vitality in Germany. In February 1937, Hans Kerr, Minister of Religion for the Third Reich said: "The question of the divinity of Christ is ridiculous and unessential. A new answer has risen as to what Christ and Christianity are: Adolph Hitler." And the University Nazi in Kiel wrote in 1935: "We Germans are heathens and want no more Jewish religion in our Germany. We no longer believe in the Holy Ghost; we believe in the holy blood."

Which party had as the Chief of its party an outspoken supporter of the most avid anti-Jew in the United States, Louis Farrakhan. That was, until recently, Keith Ellison, Deputy Chief of the DNC. And we have previously discussed the outrageous anti-Jew sentiments of House of Representatives Ilhan Omar and Rashida Tlaib, whose anti-Jew rantings go unchallenged and uncensored by her liberal left compatriots.

And since when is Hollywood our moral and political compass? When in our lifetime has the entertainment industry, spoken out so viciously and seditiously? From Hollywood, we have some suggesting a military overthrow of the government; boycotting performing at the inaugural and even claiming vociferously that the new presidency is illegitimate.

And what about our Democrat political leaders, who were unwilling to even attend the inaugural on the grounds that an illegitimate president will be sworn in. Or the Democrat leaders who consider those who do not side with them as "deplorable" or if they are women, "there is a special place in hell for them".

The divisiveness in our country; the unwillingness of so many to even want to try to unite; the constant cry of illegitimacy, the constant promotion of dissent, even threats of government overthrow, surely provides our enemies with much glee that the U.S. is falling apart. There is nothing more damaging to our country and our way of life, than to show such disunity, to show that we are a "house divided".

Likewise, the abstention from voting at the U.N. Security Council on the recent resolution against Israel was the decision of one-man, former President Obama without review, without discussion, without consensus. Was this an abuse of power?

These are troubling times and they call for unity and good will not adversity and contempt.

I believe the two greatest virtues one can have are Wisdom and Humility. Wisdom is achieved through acquiring knowledge and applying it correctly to find the truth of a matter. Humility is needed so we can learn to listen to others and accept the possibility that we may be wrong.

I recall a short fairy tale written for children by Danish author Hans Christian Anderson published in 1837 and entitled the" Emperor's new Suit of Clothes". It seems there was a vain Emperor who hired two weavers to make him the most beautiful suit of clothes. The two weavers were con-men and they promised the emperor a new suit of clothes, that would be better than any other suit of clothes ever made, but could only be seen by intelligent people and the leaders of the kingdom. The weavers pretend to dress the Emperor in the invisible clothes and all his ministers and members of his court, pretended that they could see the suit of clothes for fear of appearing unfit for their positions or hopelessly stupid. After the weavers dress the Emperor in his "invisible clothes", the Emperor marches naked in procession before his subjects. All the townspeople admire the "new suit of clothes" not wanting to be considered stupid. Finally, a child cries out that the Emperor is naked and then the townspeople speak up. It took a little child to bring the townspeople to their senses, to see the truth and speak up.

And this sums up the Socialist Democrats attempt to delude and defraud the American voter, taxpayer and worker. The New Green Deal; the free education, the guaranteed income for life; the free child care and the free medical are like the emperor's new suit of clothes. These are programs and projects that will never occur because they would cost 4 or 5 times our total annual national budget. They must never occur, because they will destroy our country. They will be applauded by many, even though these programs are foolish if not insane. Yet no one will speak up. Those who cling to the belief that the Federal government can make life better by making everything free are fooling themselves. The leaders of the socialist Democrat Party, the media, the educators and the entertainment industry are collectively like the weavers. They are the con-men, who you will believe just because they say it is so.

So, take your hands away from your eyes so you can perceive; take your hands away from your ears, so you can listen; take your hands away from your mouth so you can dialogue. Seek knowledge; obtain facts, search for wisdom, speak out and find truth. Do this and you will be all right.

A Final Word About Socialism

I have spent a lot of time talking about the limitless hate, vilification and bias against our government; indoctrination of our schools, colleges and universities; hate propaganda from our media; the denial of due process; abuse of human rights; abuse of the rights of unborn children; CO_2 as a cause of climate change; the insane cost of proposed socialist government spending programs; sanctuary cities; uncontrolled immigration; and the impeachment of our president based on one 30 minute telephone call. Everything that has gone on in our political arena since the election of President Trump has been aimed at bringing down our government and imposing socialism on all Americans. Before I finish, my last observations deal with the historical deaths of many people who were adversaries of socialist leaders and the destruction of the lives and wellbeing of so many who have had failed socialist systems imposed upon them. Socialism has not only consistently failed the public it was supposed to serve, it also cost the loss of millions of lives of innocent men, women and children not from battle, but from the socialist leaders who place power above humanity as their singular goal. Let us look briefly at some of the many failed socialist systems, some of which are still on-going. This will be brief. The reader, if he or she is more interested can research the regimes described for more detail.

1. **Hitler's Germany – The Socialist Third Reich 1934-1945.**

We have discussed Hitler and his atrocities at length in this book, yet we refresh the reader's memory with the atrocities of Hitler's regime as an example of a socialist system that did not work. On the contrary Hitler's Socialist Third Reich personified a system based on hate and fear; a system that forever vilified its opponents and did not end there, leaving assassination of rivals and the murder of 6 million Jews in its wake. The "Brownshirts" and later the Gestapo acted as the enforcers of the Nazi Party, beating or killing anyone that protested. And through the control of the media and entertainment industry, the Nazis spread hate, their principal tool along with fear to accomplish their rise in power. It was short-lived and accomplished little beyond hatred, murder and genocide that became all that we remember of this Socialist system.

2. **Stalin's Soviet Socialist Republic – 1934-1953**

The Great Purges under Stalin started in the late 1930's when many prominent Bolsheviks were found guilty of treason and executed or imprisoned. Thousands of party members who protested were killed along with their wives and children. It was subsequently established that the accused were innocent, that the cases were fabricated by the secret police (NKVD) and their confessions had been made under pressure and intensive torture. Millions of alleged enemies of the people were sent to prison camps in the 1930's. All industry and private property were taken over by the Socialist regime under Stalin and none of his Socialist 5-year plans ever succeeded, leaving Russia in a constant state of poverty and famine. Finally, the USSR socialist regime could not be sustained and its failure lead to the breaking up of the Union Soviet Socialist Republic (USSR).

The dissolution of the Soviet Union began in the second half of the 1980's with the growing unrest in the member states. The USSR ended December 26, 1991, when the USSR was voted out of existence and replaced by the Commonwealth of Independent States. The last USSR President, Mikhail Gorbachev resigned, declaring his office extinct and handed over its power to the President of the newly formed Russia, under Boris Yeltsin. Of the 15 new separate states, three of them, namely the Baltic States (Latvia, Lithuania and Estonia), became members of NATO and the European Union.

The dissolution of the Soviet Union took place as a result of general economic regression under the USSR Socialist regime. Most of the former Socialist states began transition to a market economy where investment, production and distribution are guided by the forces of supply and demand as opposed to the Socialist Command (planned) economy where investment, production and allocation of capital goods takes place according to economy-wide plans imposed by a socialist government.

3. China from Mao Zedong to Xi Jinping

Another example of the evils of Socialism comes to light from a brief examination of the recent history of China and its socialist economy dictated by severe rule under a dictatorship. Almost all socialist economies are based on severe control by a governmental dictatorship, in which freedoms are severely regulated if not eliminated in their entirety. Socialism requires absolute control by governmental authority and time and time again we see it fail. This is the perfect definition of insanity, where an economic system is tried again and again and always fails.

Since becoming China's leader in 2012, Xi Jinping has undertaken a massive internal purge of opponents in which more than a million officials have been disciplined. The scale of the purge of opponents has not been seen since the days of Mao Zedong and his so-called Cultural Revolution.

The Cultural Revolution was a political movement in the People's Republic of China from 1966 to 1976, launched by Mao Zedong the Chairman of the Communist Party. The stated goal was to preserve China's Communism, by purging remnants of Capitalist elements in Chinese Society. The estimated death toll ranged as high as 20 million, while 10's of millions of Chinese people were persecuted. China's economy has been a consistent economic failure. Its performance has been abysmal and the contrasting success of Hong Kong is a thorn in the side of China's leaders. The control by the Chinese Government over its constituents is no more evident than in its demand that families limit their number of children to 1 (now 2) and failure to do so will result in such large fines. The offending couple will be driven from their homes and left with no personal property. Unemployment is very high, GDP/Capita is way below the levels of most economies, and the five-year plans have been so unsuccessful, that they have been dropped.

4. East Germany and the Berlin Wall

There was no better contrast between capitalism and socialism than the stark contrast between West and East Germany, created by the infamous Berlin Wall, imposed on Eastern Berliners by the oppressive Russian Socialist regime. In 1961, the Berlin Wall was built under the direction of the Russian Socialist occupiers of East Germany, depriving free access between the two divided areas of Germany. Until 1961, German people regularly passed between East and West Germany, to go to their place of employment or to visit their family and friends. East Germany had become the Socialist German Republic, adopting the social and economic systems demanded by the Russian occupiers. Nearly 3.5 million or 1/6th the population of East Germany fled for their freedom to West Germany. To stop the exodus, the Russian leader, Nikita Khrushchev, ordered the General Secretary of the East German Socialist Unity Party to erect a barrier between East and West Berlin; the Berlin Wall. The Berlin Wall ran 96 miles (27 within Berlin) and consisted actually of two walls. Between the walls was a 160 foot "death strip". The wall included 302 watchtowers, 55,000 land mines 259 dog runs and machine guns activated by trip wires. The Socialist East German government was prepared to kill their fellow citizens, even if they only sought to gain their freedom. At least 327 innocent civilians were shot down and killed, trying to escape and another 5,000 were arrested. President Ronald Reagan on June 12, 1987 delivered his famous speech at the Brandenburg Gate in Germany, where he said: "Mr. Gorbachev, tear down this wall". This speech would lead finally to the dismantling of the Berlin Wall on November 9, 1989. And with it came the uniting of Germany and a successful return to a capitalist economy for all of Germany. East Germany's economy would no longer lie in the shadows of the successful economy of West Germany and freedom was gained for all Eastern Berliners. The hatred, the fear, the suppression of freedom of speech and press, so much a part of socialist regimes, disappeared over night and the rights that all human beings should be able to enjoy were restored. Once again, we see that Socialism cannot exist without hatred, violence and the suppression of all rights associated with being free.

5. Castro's Cuba

Immediately after Fidel Castro's takeover of Cuba in 1959, he began the purge of his opposition and over 5,000 would be executed, mostly without trial and with fabricated charges brought against them. The number of Cuban citizens that Castro would eventually murder ranged between 35,000 and 141,000. There were also 77,000 who lost their lives trying to escape from Cuba on makeshift rafts. The murders and assassinations that Castro wreaked on his Cuban fellow citizens was for the sole purpose of sustaining a communist/socialist regime in Cuba. Castro effectively took over the control of all Cuban lives through a combination of hate, fear and the ultimate socialist weapon, death. The

Cuban economy has remained a disaster for all the years of Castro's rule. The standard of living has deteriorated so extensively that Cuba has one of the worst economies in the world. Along with that is one of the highest levels of poverty and lowest levels of health services. And to help sustain his position in power, Castro was prepared to locate Russian nuclear missiles on his island, hoping that this diversion would help unite Cubans against the United States. We see the same socialist themes here. Control of all production, elimination of private property and private enterprise. elimination of all human rights, control of the media, and creation of a society of fear sustained by the threat of brutality incarceration or assassination.

6. Kim Il Sung and Kim Jong-Un's North Korea

Kim Jong-Un and his socialist regime came into power in 2012 replacing Kim Il Sung. He solidified his power by the assassination of all his rivals. A 2014 UN inquiry into human rights in North Korea concluded: "the gravity, scale and nature of these violations, reveal a state that does not have any parallel in the "Contemporary World". The North Korean economy is heavily nationalized like any socialist economy and tried to follow the style of the former Soviet Union's 5-year plans. The plans were so unsuccessful in North Korea that after 1993, North Korea stopped announcing plans. Like all other Socialist countries, the media is heavily censored and controlled by the government, ownership of private property is very limited, any criticism is threatened with beatings, incarceration or even outright assassination. The economy of North Korea is one of the weakest in the world and the GDP/capita is very near the bottom of over 170 countries. The most poignant example of how dire is the economy of North Korea are pictures taken by satellites, showing the nation of North Korea in total darkness, in stark contrast to the bright lights emanating from South Korea with its robust capitalist economy.

7. Venezuela under Nicolas Maduro

Led by, Nicolas Maduro, the government of Venezuela is engaged in a bitter struggle with Juan Guaido, the opposition leader who has declared himself acting President in January 2019. This once proud economic jewel of South America, is now the worst economy in the world and its people the most suffering under the socialist regime imposed on them.

Nicolas Maduro was first elected in 2013 after the death of his socialist mentor and predecessor in office, Hugo Chavez. Maduro gained control of the military and the Supreme Court and has successfully banned many candidates from running, even jailing them when necessary. Millions have fled the country in fear of further loss of freedom under Maduro's Socialist regime. More than 50 countries recognize Mr. Guaido as the legitimate President of Venezuela, but Russia and China in particular back Maduro.

During Maduro's first term, the Venezuelan economy went into free-fall. President Maduro and his predecessor Hugo Chavez (President 2/1999 to 3/2013) among other things, promised to drive down Venezuela's huge levels of inequality. While they managed to reduce inequality, some of their socialist policies backfired. Price controls, for example were aimed at making basic goods more affordable to the poor by capping the price of flour, cooking oils and toiletries. Many Venezuelan businesses just stopped producing, because they could not make a profit. This eventually resulted in severe shortages.

Along with the controls placed by the socialist regime on the economy has come hyper-inflation. Business News website, Bloomberg has been tracking the price of a cup of coffee in Caracas, Venezuela. The price of a cup of coffee has increased 9,900% between January 8, 2019 and January 9, 2020.

An estimated 5 million Venezuelans have left the country since 2014 out of a population of approximately 29 million. That's over 17% of the population that has left solely because of the harsh reality of the abysmal failure of the socialist government under Maduro. This would be like 56 million Americans leaving the United States.

Today, socialism in Venezuela has left 94% of the population living in poverty according to a March, 2019 UN report and over 50% do not have enough income to meet their basic food needs. The people are killing their pets and scavenging garbage dumps just to find enough food to live. To make matters worse (if that is possible) Venezuela leads the world in murder rates with 81.4 murders per 100,000 people in 2018 and it is ranked the third most violent country in the world. This was the one-time jewel of South America.

And what does our Socialist Democrat leaders think about Venezuela, as they try to convince us that socialism is the answer to all or economic problems? Nicolas Maduro called Bernie Sanders, a leading contender for the Democrat nomination for President; "our revolutionary friend" and praised his candidacy in 2016. Back in 2011, Bernie Sanders wrote an essay, which he finished with these words:

"These days, the American dream is more apt to be realized in South America, in places such as Venezuela, Ecuador and Argentina, where incomes are actually more equal today than they are in the land of Horatio Alger. Who's the banana republic now?"

Let's review some of the comments about Socialist Venezuela coming from the far-left media:

- From the New York Times, March 29, 2017 – "Venezuela was once Latin America's powerhouse…A growing number of Venezuelans are going hungry in a food shortage; are dying from treatable ailments in squalid, ill-equipped hospitals…. Until political prisoners are released, the prospects of restoration of democratic rule are very dim…..inflation has soared to an estimated 700%, while the people in this oil-rich nation are left digging through piles of trash for scraps of food".
- CNN March 1, 2017 – "Venezuela has only $10.5 billion of foreign reserves left. For the rest of the year they owe $7.2 billion in outstanding debt payments. In 2005 they had $20 billion….it's hard to know when Venezuela will run completely out of cash. Venezuelans are suffering massive medical and food shortages as well as skyrocketing grocery prices. Massive government overspending; mismanagement of the country's infrastructure and corruption are

all factors that have sparked extremely high inflation in Venezuela. Inflation is expected to rise to 1,660% this year and 2,880% in 2018 according to IMF (International Monetary Fund)."

- Reuters January 8, 2017 – "President Nicolas Maduro announced a 50% hike in the minimum wage and pensions, the fifth increase over the last ear. The minimum wage has now been increased by 322% since February 2016. Critics say his incompetence and 17 years of failed Socialist policies are behind Venezuela's mess. (Yet Bernie Sanders considered Venezuela's socialist regime a role model for the United States.)

8. Iraq under Saddam Hussein

Iraq under Saddam Hussein was notorious for its severe violations of human rights. Secret police, state terrorism, torture, mass murder, genocide, ethnic cleansing, rapes, assassinations and chemical warfare were all the inhuman methods used by Saddam Hussein and his Ba'athist, Socialist government to maintain control over the Iraqi people. The total deaths are estimated at around 250,000 in particular the Anfal genocide in 1988 that killed between 50,000 and 180,000 Kurds. Saddam Hussein had established a one-party, Socialist government, which suppressed ownership of private property and controlled all industry, particularly oil production, which was the life blood of the economy. The people of Iraq have suffered terribly under socialism, which brought with it the destruction of human rights and the loss of freedom.

9. Syria under Bashar Assad

Syria is a highly regulated Socialist economy under the domination of its president, Bashar al Assad. In 2010 the "Human Rights Watch" and organization headquartered in New York City referred to the country's human rights record as "among the worst in the word. Arbitrary detention, torture and disappearances are widespread. The murder of thousands of civilians including the killing of children as young as two years old and the raping of boys as young as 11 years old by Assad's security forces have been reported". For the period from 2016 to 2018 the UN reported that Syria was the most violent country in the world causing more than 570,000 deaths, displacing 7.6 million internationally and causing 5 million refugees. Syria's economy has declined more than 70% from 2010 to 2017, under the socialist regime of President Assad.

10. Iran under Rafsanjani, Mahmoud Ahmadinejad, Hassan Rouhani and Supreme leader Ali Khamenei

Socialism is the political and economic ideology of Iran. It is currently a dictatorial Republic. In 1989 Iran was the most radical in terms of the application of leftist economics with state control and anti-capitalist leanings, with goals to re-distribute money to the poor. 70% of the nation's capital was under state control during Rafsanjani's era. From 1989 to 1997, the economy crept toward 100% government control, with state control being at least 80% and private control limited to no more than 20%. The current leader of Iran, Hassan Rouhani succeeded Mahmoud Ahmadinejad in August 2013. He reports, however, to Ali Khamenei the Supreme leader of the economic revolution, who is empowered to issue decrees on the economy, the environment, foreign policy, education, national planning and other aspects of governance of Iran. Even with the $150 billion returned by the U.S. during the Obama Administration to Iran in exchange for their promise not to build nuclear weapons for 10 years, the economy of Iran is still one of the worst in the world and there is now serious unrest in the country to obtain freedom from the domination of socialist control in Iran.

What do all these countries have in common? They are all failed socialist regimes, where the leaders have gained power by stirring up hatred against and vilifying their opponents and in many instances, simply assassinating them. They all sustained their power by the control of the media and the clever dissemination of lies (propaganda). All the regimes are guilty of abuse of power, denial of freedom of speech, press and assembly and ignoring due process. Hate and fear of reprisal become main weapons to sustain their position of power. These in every instance were the weapons used by socialist regimes and each regime failed, leaving death, crime, poverty and even slavery in their wake. And one more extremely important right that I have not dwelt upon is freedom of religion. In almost every case of the socialistic regimes I have discussed, the people have been deprived of freedom of religion.

The insanity of it all is that socialism has been imposed time and time again and it has always failed. Why do people believe that doing the same thing again and again will lead to different results? Never has our life choices here in America been so clear. Our voting citizens have the opportunity to choose between Republican Capitalism and Conservatism with its free economy, private ownership of property, and assurance that the basic rights of freedom of speech, press, assembly and religion are sustained, or Democrat Socialism, which will lead to the loss of our freedoms and an economy that will emulate those of the historical socialist regimes that have all failed.

Greece -one last look at the destructiveness of Socialism.

This once beautiful historical country has turned into a tragedy. Overwhelming debt nearly destroyed the country that needed three international financial bailouts to avoid default and today barely survives. Greece's disaster was created by the Panhellenic Socialist Movement founded in 1974; a radical Marxist inspired party that was a major cause of the crisis. Stephen Moore wrote in the Washington Times: It's "a place where government gives a lot of things away for free, few people work and millions receive government pensions and paychecks". These are the ingredients for a failed economy and they are the ingredients that, Nancy Pelosi, Chuck Schumer, Alan Schiff, Jerry Nadler, Joe Biden, Elizabeth Warren, Bernie Sanders, Kamala Harris, Cory Booker, Amy Klobuchar, Peter Buttigieg, Tom Steyer, Andrew Yang, Julian Castro and John Delany and so many other socialist Democrats, will mix for you and make you eat. Can any American really want this?

One more thing. Once again, we have lost our belief in the dignity of man. We lost it during slavery in America. We lost it during the Jim Crow laws and the reign of the Ku Klux Klan. We saw it lost in so many countries with socialist regimes such as USSR, Nazi Germany, Mao's China, East Germany after WWII, Castro's Cuba, and in North Korea, Syria, Iraq Iran, Afghanistan and many other countries too numerous to mention here. Along with the lost dignity of man, came the tyrannical behavior of the socialist leaders, where murders, assassinations, and genocide became rampant. And now we have seen most recently the loss of man's dignity in Venezuela, where 95% of the people are in poverty; they have to scrounge through garbage dumps for food and are even forced to kill their pets for food.

But the loss of man's dignity has returned with a vengeance here in America. It started with Hillary Clinton calling all Republicans "deplorables"; that Republicans were the people she hated the most (that's about 50% of the population, which she wanted to represent). She would then applaud, when one of her supporters would say that "there is a special place in hell for any woman that doesn't support a woman (i.e. Hillary). The dehumanizing cries from the left would become more specific, when Hillary Clinton said that she would destroy the jobs of every coal miner. She was prepared to destroy the very livelihood and existence of a group of citizens, whose human dignity was derived from working very hard in the coal mines to support their families and meet the basic needs to live; food clothing and shelter. But like a cancer the cries from the liberal left spread rapidly.

Now those on the right that support Republican Capitalism and conservatism are called racists, white supremacists, dictators and anti-feminists. They are no longer treated as human beings. The Socialist left believe those on the Conservative right deserved to be vilified and deprived of any dignity. But this was not enough for the Democrats. They called for the assassination of the president, by hanging; decapitating, destroying the White House, even knifing to death like Julius Caesar. And the Democrats even demonized and dehumanized police, even wearing clothes displaying pigs in a police uniform. The Democrats even stooped to having young boys and girls in elementary school carry signs saying "F..k Trump".

Finally, the dignity of man is dependent on his or her freedom and ability to provide for his/her family. Yet destroying the lives of all coal miners is not enough for the Democrats. The Democrat leaders, want to deprive 10's of millions of people of their jobs; render them unemployed and incapable of providing for their families. The Democrat leaders have boasted how they will destroy all jobs associated with air travel. They will destroy all jobs associated with fossil fuel. They will destroy all jobs associated with health insurance. They will destroy all jobs related to cattle ranching and dairy farming and providing beef and milk for food. They want to destroy all jobs relating to gas driven cars and trucks. And they will destroy all related industries such as the fast food industry, convenience stores, gas stations, used car dealerships, restaurants and many others. How many of you are prepared to be rendered unemployed by the very party that you may be considering voting for? And oh yes, those who survive the onslaught of unemployment and who have paid their way through college and university and worked extra hard to pay off your college debts, you will now be called upon to pay off the college debt of those currently in college and provide free tuition for all that follow you. That's $1.4 trillion of current student loans outstanding. With a total workforce of approximately 130 million in the U.S., it would cost each worker approximately $11,000 to pay off the student loans, assuming our workforce was completely employed. The annual cost of public tuition is approximately $70 Billion per year, but if free, would easily rise to $100 billion a year, costing each worker approximately $750/year, assuming every member of the workforce is employed.

We Must Not Let It Happen!!

Never in my lifetime have I seen such hatred, such vilification, such determination to destroy the opposition regardless of the cost to our nation. The liberal left, the radical socialists, have seen to it that the indoctrination of hatred and vilification pervades almost every part of our society. We see it in our public schools, our colleges and universities, in the media and in the entertainment industry. But most troubling of all is the hatred and vilification expressed by our government leaders from the liberal left toward those on the conservative right, particularly toward our president. I have tried to share with the readers some of the most outrageous examples of the tirade of abuse from the left toward those who disagree with them. I have tried to show the reader how the past 8 years of the liberal left domination under the Obama Administration has been so disastrous for our country. And I have spent time discussing dialectics as the way out. Our country so needs rational objective dialogue among all parties. We need to seek knowledge, sift through the statements made by our media and our elected officials and find unshakeable facts to arrive at truth. We must make sure our children are not indoctrinated in grade school where so many of our teachers have a left leaning political agenda. And we must encourage our young men and women at the college and university level to examine carefully the statements made by their instructors, examine carefully their own beliefs and listen to all sides of an issue. If a person is hearing only one side of an issue, he or she certainly is being indoctrinated. If we don't hear all sides of an issue, then we cannot choose and if we cannot choose, we cannot be truly free. George Orwell in his book "1984" described what would happen if indoctrination took hold and freedom of choice was denied. We must strive for knowledge, obtain truth, achieve Wisdom and arrive at justice for all. We are closing in on "1984". We must not let this happen.

Finally, I do not expect everyone to agree with all and maybe even most of what I have written here. But at least I hope that you will read my comments and observations objectively, evaluate honestly and with knowledge and wisdom and accept that if we differ, we can still like each other and be friends.

CHAPTER 25

Encore – The Corona Virus (COVID – 19)

ON FEBRUARY 10, 2020, I had completed my book… so I thought. There were some rumblings about a new virus, but no one seemed to be paying attention. Nancy Pelosi, Chuck Schumer, Jerry Nadler and Adam Schiff among others were all still hard at work trying to raise new grounds for impeaching President Trump, having failed to do so for over 3 years. They paid virtually no attention to anything else. And the Democrat focus on the impeachment of Trump has been a major distraction at the very time we needed to focus our attention on the Coronavirus plague. After President Trump was acquitted on February 5, 2020, Pelosi was still not satisfied and commented: "The President and Senate Republicans have normalized lawlessness and rejected the system of checks and balances of our Constitution". Yet how hypocritical of her when she says that she just won't accept the acquittal, which occurred from the precise following of the Constitution.

After the acquittal, as the Corona virus pandemic spirals around the world, Pelosi, Schiff, Nadler and Schumer were still looking for ways to remove Trump as president. And Sanders and Biden were exuding nothing but hate and vitriol toward President Trump. Remember, starting with Hilary Clinton and furthered by the Democratic Party, they hate 50% of the people in the United States. The Democrats consider Republicans to be "deplorables". They are hated simply if they believe in the right to life and are told that the Democrat party wants to exclude them from their party; those who are "pro-life". And women are told that there is a special place in hell for them if they don't vote for a woman. And they are told that they will have their livelihood destroyed, if they are involved with the production, supply and distribution of fossil fuels (particularly coal), as Hilary Clinton promised West Virginia and Ohio that she would put all coal workers out of work). Those employed in the Health Insurance industry, they too are also targeted for permanent unemployment by the Democrats. They will be driven from their jobs. All those involved in the airline industry or the cruise line industry, they will lose their jobs permanently. Those working in the restaurant business are told that if their restaurant's menu is one where beef is the main offering, like most fast food chains, they will be permanently terminated from their jobs. I have reviewed in detail elsewhere, how the Green New Deal will destroy so many industries, beyond those described here.

And in the first and second quarter of 2020, we have all become concerned by the rapid expanding federal debt, as the Federal government pours more than $5 trillion into our economy. Yet many of us do not seem to worry about the $13 trillion per year for the next 10 years, that the Democrats want to spend on the Democrat's programs, namely: "The Green New Deal"; National Health Care and Free College tuition for everyone.

We look back in history and what we see is that every Socialist regime that has existed anywhere in the world has been based on some or all of the following: Hate, Terror, Fear and outright murder and torture of vast numbers of the citizens. Further, they are all failed economies, with huge portions of their populations, destitute, starving and in abject poverty.

Here is a short list:

Kim Jong-Il – North Korea

Adolf Hitler – Germany

Hideki Tojo - Japan

Joseph Stalin USSR – (Also Krushev, Brezhnev and Putin)

Bashar Assad - Syria

Saddam Hussein – Iraq (Butcher of Bagdad)

Mao Zedong - China

Idi Amin – Uganda (Butcher of Uganda)

Iotollah Khomeini – Iran

Ho Chi Minh - Vietnam

Pol Pot – Cambodia

Nicolas Maduro – Venezuela

This is by no means a full list. But these leaders all could be characterized as socialists, who gained power and sovereignty over their constituents through hate, terror fear, torture and murder. Maybe our socialist Democrat leaders, whether politicians, media personalities, educators or entertainers do not spread torture or terror, but they do spread hate and fear and have often suggested the murder of our President in violent ways.

There has never been such a division between Democrat Socialism/liberalism and Republican Capitalism/conservatism as we see today. And the Coronavirus Pandemic has made these differences more clear and more poignant. Before I begin my observations about the Corona virus pandemic and how this helps make more clear the differences in our political and economic views of our country, let me first review with you the 10th Amendment of our Constitution and how that is important in discussing where the primary responsibility lies for fighting the Coronavirus pandemic. Then I will provide a short timeline concerning the Coronavirus pandemic in our country.

The 10th Amendment of the U.S. Constitution

The 10th Amendment reads: "The powers not delegated to the United States by the Constitution, nor prohibited by it to the state are reserved prospectively to the state or to its people".

No statement can be more clear as who is primarily responsible for the welfare of the citizens at the time of an emergency such as the Coronavirus. Our country has been blessed by our front line responders; our heroic warriors who are our doctors, nurses, medical technicians, hospital workers, maintenance staffs, police, firemen, sanitation workers, our military medical staff and engineers, our grocery store employees and all the many others who have been essential to keep our country running during these difficult times. These first line responders have all done well and we should all be grateful and extend our thanks and well wishes to all of them and their families for the sacrifices they have made on our behalf.

Now we turn to the managers; those responsible for the administration and direction of the 100's of thousands of front-line responders and all the citizens who may be directly or indirectly exposed to the Corona Pandemic. The managers at the very top are the governors of each state and their staff and the medical health personnel under their direct responsibility and control. It is they, not the Federal government that is responsible for the day to day management of their state. It is the state government, led by its governor who is ultimately responsible for the state having the medical supplies, equipment, facilities and personnel to meet the needs of the state. The role of the Federal government is monumental, but one of support. It can respond to the state with funds, supplies, facilities, medical personnel and even military personnel to keep peace and build facilities. But each state must initiate the request for help and actually regulate it within the state. This is what our Constitution requires.

Many states understood this, but unfortunately some didn't and chose to blame the Federal Administration for their failure to be prepared. And the Democrat Congressional leaders and their supporting media: MSNBC, CNN, ABC, CBS and NBC Newscasters and the liberal press chose to constantly criticize the Federal Administration while holding state leadership blameless. It is so convenient for the Liberal left to use the Corona Virus for political gain, just when we all need to be united in the common cause to eradicate the Coronavirus. I will provide some specific observations concerning the handling of the Coronavirus pandemic within our country and how the Coronavirus may be a wakeup call in understanding the threat posed to our country by the far left. But first I will outline a brief timeline of the Coronavirus, leading to the loss of lives and economic disruption within our economy.

The Coronavirus (COVID-19) Timeline

November 17, 2019 - a 55-year-old is reported to have contacted COVID-19 in the South China Morning Post, which is a Hong Kong English language newspaper founded in 1903. The case was not recognized in China at the time.

December 2, 2019 – the first hospitalization of a COVID-19 victim is reported.

December 10, 2019 - a 52-year-old seafood merchant, working at the Wuhan seafood market is reported as the first patient from the market. The Huanan Seafood Wholesale market was a live wild animal and seafood market in the Jiangshan district of Wuhan, China, The World Health Organization (WHO) was not notified until December 31, 2019 about the outbreak of "pneumonia" in Wuhan. By then 41 people were hospitalized in Wuhan with the unknown virus and 33 of 585 samples would be identified as coming from the market. The market would be closed on January 1, 2020 for sanitation.

December 31, 2019 – The Government in Wuhan confirms that health authorities were treating dozens of cases, which they have identified as pneumonia.

January 7, 2020 – Chinese Authorities censor the leakage of any information on the Virus.

January 9, 2020 – Chinese State broadcaster CCTV, reports for the first time that the new viral outbreak was first detected in the city of Wuhan on December 12. Almost a month had gone before the Chinese government announces through its state news channel that there is a new virus. Chinese researchers identify the new virus but state there is no evidence that the virus spreads between humans.

January 11, 2020 – China reports the first death from the unknown virus.

January 14, 2020 – WHO states: preliminary investigation conducted by Chinese authorities have found no clear evidence of human to human transmission of the now named Coronavirus.

January 20, 2020 - China finally announces that the coronavirus can be transmitted from human to human.

January 20, 2020 - WHO reports the first confirmed cases outside of China occur in Japan, South Korea and Thailand.

January 21, 2020 – The first confirmed case in the U.S. occurs in Washington state. A man in his 30's developed symptoms after returning from Wuhan.

January 23, 2020 – Wuhan, a city of 11 million is finally closed by Chinese authorities, canceling planes and trains leaving the city and suspending buses, subways and ferries within it.

January 23, 2020 – WHO director Tedros Ghebreyesus states: "It is too early to declare the coronavirus outbreak a public, international health emergency. It is interesting to note that Tedros is the first WHO director to not be a medical doctor. WHO meets with China authorities and they decide not to declare a Public Health emergency.

January 30, 2020 – WHO finally declares the Coronavirus a public health emergency of international concern amid thousands of reported new cases in China. (believed to have been severely under-reported). The U.S. State department warns U.S. travelers to avoid China.

January 31, 2020 – One day after WHO declares Coronavirus to be a public health emergency, the Trump administration suspends entry into the United States by any foreign nationals who have travelled to China in the past 14 days. By this time 213 people had died and 9,800 had been infected world-wide.

February 2, 2020 – The first Coronavirus death is reported outside China; a 44-year-old man in the Philippines. By then more than 360 had been reported dying from Coronavirus in China. It is believed by many that the number of deaths reported by China is way understated.

February 4, 2020 – WHO director Tedro urges that there be no travel bans. He states: "We reiterate our call to all countries not to impose restrictive interference with international travel and trade. It would increase fear with little public health benefit. Trump's closing our borders to China is roundly criticized by the left, calling Trump racist, Xenophobic, ignorant and unwilling to listen to the medical authorities.

February 5, 2020 – After a two-week trip to Southeast Asia, 3,600 passengers begin a quarantine aboard the "Diamond Princess" cruise ship, while anchored in Yokahama, Japan.

February 7, 2020 - A Chinese doctor, Li Wenliang dies after contracting the Coronavirus. In early January, the Chinese authorities reprimanded him for raising serious concerns about the Coronavirus. He was forced to sign a statement denouncing his warning as an unfounded and illegal rumor. The Chinese "whistleblower" had been silenced by the government and shortly thereafter he is permanently silenced by the disease he was seeking to warn the world about. How fortunate for the Chinese government.

February 12, 2020 – The death toll in China reaches 1,113 and the total number of confirmed cases rose to 44,653. There are 393 cases outside of China spread over 24 countries.

February 13, 2020 – Chinese officials announce more than 14,800 new cases added to the total infected in Hubei Province. The reported cases increase 10-fold in China and deaths more than double, following China changing its diagnostic criteria. Information out of China continues to drastically under-report extent of epidemic/pandemic

February 14, 2020 – France announces the first Coronavirus death in Europe; an 80-year-old Chinese tourist dies in a Paris Hospital. It was the fourth death outside of mainland China where about 1,500 deaths have now been reported, mostly from the Hubei province.

February 17, 2020 – China drafts legislation to curb the practice of eating wildlife, which has been identified as the probable but unsubstantiated source of the virus.

February 19, 2020 – After a two-week quarantine, 443 passengers begin leaving the Diamond Princess. A total of 621 aboard the ship were infected.

February 23, 2020 – Italy sees a major surge in cases from fewer than five to more than 150. Italy locks down 10 towns near Milan. Schools are closed and sporting and cultural events are cancelled.

February 24, 2020 – The Trump administration asks Congress for $1.25 billion for new emergency funds to bolster preparedness of Centers for Disease Control and Prevention (CDC). At this point there were 35 confirmed cases and no deaths in the U.S.

February 26, 2020 – The President names V.P. Pence to head the U.S. Coronavirus response.

February 29, 2020 – The U.S. records its first death as the number of global cases rise to 87,000. The Trump administration issues its highest-level warning to "do not travel" to Italy and South Korea. All travel is banned to Iran and all foreign citizens who had visited Iran within the past 14 days were barred entry into the U.S. Iran had become a Coronavirus "hot spot".

March 1, 2020 – U.S. reports its second death from the Coronavirus; a man in his 70's with underlying health conditions.

March 3, 2020 – U.S. administration approves widespread coronavirus testing.

March 5, 2020 – In a WHO briefing, Director Tedros praises China for its approach, even in light of the drastic under-reporting, censoring and cover-up by the Chinese government.

March 8, 2020 – The number of cases in the U.S. passes 500. Worldwide cases exceed 100,000 and deaths are over 3,400, while China is claiming only 366 deaths.

March 11, 2020 – WHO finally characterizes the Coronavirus (COVID-19) as a Pandemic.

March 13, 2020 – President Trump declares a National Emergency, making $50 billion in Federal Funds available to states to combat Coronavirus. Additionally, he would give doctors more flexibility to respond to the virus, including remote treatment of patients.

March 15-16, 2020 – CDC recommends no gatherings of 50 or more people in the U.S. On March 16, it revises the number to no more than 10. New York City finally announces the closing of public schools affecting 1.1 million students.

March 17, 2020 – France imposes a nation-wide lockdown prohibiting the gathering of any size. By this time, France has 6500 cases and 140 deaths. The European Union bans the travel outside the bloc for 30 days.

March 19, 2020 – China reports no new local infections. The veracity of this report is deemed questionable at best.

March 21. 2020 – American companies in response to the Administration's requests, including Hanes and General Motors vow to increase their effort to restock hospitals and repurpose their operations to create hospital garments and masks.

March 21, 2020 - Trump tweets about the potential of Hydroxychloroquine as a possible "game changer" in treating the coronavirus. This drug had been used for over 70 years in treating Malaria and although its efficacy in use against the Coronavirus was untested, there was significant anecdotal evidence that it was a cure even for severe cases. The point made for those severely ill and on the death bed, "what was there to lose?" The response by WHO's director Tedro was: "Using untested medicines, without the right evidence could raise false hope and even do more harm than good". This became the response that the liberal left and its supporting media rallied around to attack President Trump. Once again, the condemning and ridiculing of President Trump was put ahead of the health and welfare of the American people. Personal gain of power at the expense of lives is common to all liberal socialist regimes and it is no different here in America as the Democrats seek to impose socialism on us all.

March 22, 2020 – A vote to advance the massive Coronavirus stimulus bill failed in the Senate because the Republicans needed 60 votes to move forward on the bill and they were not able to win over any Democrats to proceed. This meant that no aid would flow to the economy including checks to individuals and help to small businesses. The bill was stalled by Nancy Pelosi and the Democrats and would not be voted on and passed until almost a week later, when it would include among other things Pelosi's demand for $25 million for the Kennedy Center for the Performing Arts and more funding for abortions through Planned Parenthood. These surely are not demands that should be attached to approving critical funds to save the lives of thousands of Americans.

March 23, 2020 - Boris Johnson locks down Great Britain. He will become very ill from the Corona Virus, but will survive.

March 27, 2020 – After almost a week's delay caused by House Speaker Pelosi and her fellow Democrats, President signs the $2.0 Trillion plus Coronavirus bill into law. There never should have been a delay, although Pelosi, fellow Democrats and the far-left media would say everything to convince the public that the delay was righteous and moral.

March 28, 2020 – CDC urges residents of New York, New Jersey and Connecticut to refrain from non-essential domestic travel for 14 days, effective immediately. They can only urge; since it is the responsibility of state governments to enact regulations restricting travel.

April 2, 2020 – Thee are now 1 million people infected with Coronavirus and 51,000 deaths worldwide across 171 countries.

April 10, 2020 - Infections world-wide reach 1.6 million with 101,000 deaths. U.S. reaches nearly

500,000 cases with more than 18,000 deaths.

April 13, 2020 – Some European countries begin loosening its lockdown and some stores open in Austria. Construction workers and some factor workers are allowed to resume work.

April 14, 2020 – President Trump with-holds funding of WHO pending a review to assess WHO's role in severely mismanaging and covering up the spread of the Coronavirus.

April 15, 2020 – U.S. Ambassador to the U.N., Kelly Craft stated that WHO had been inaccurate in its assessment of the Coronavirus. If it had been accurate, may thousands of lives would have been saved. The Coronavirus Pandemic is a war, but unlike any other. In World War II there were many American lives lost, soldiers, sailors, marines, airmen on battlefronts in Europe and the South Pacific. But except for Pearl Harbor, our homeland did not experience the ravages of war like it is experiencing now from the Coronavirus. We could associate with our friends and work our jobs during WWII. But most importantly, we were united as one nation. There was no hatred, there was no vitriol and divisiveness. There were no leaders of an opposition party, publicly ripping up the State of the Union Address of the President, or constantly criticizing and trying to humiliate the President and his administration, just when unity of purpose, and working together were of utmost importance. Many governors responded poorly to the Coronavirus, but they were quick to blame the Federal Administration for delays and poor response to the pandemic.

Almost unbelievable was the response of the New York Times, generally a far-left propaganda resource for the liberal socialist agenda, but on this occasion, would not accept blame shifting from State Governors to the Federal Government. On April 8, 2020, the New York Times published a piece entitled: "How delays and unheeded warnings hindered New York's virus Fight". It claimed that Governor Andrew Cuomo and NYC Mayor William de Blasio failed to keep up with the virus. The Times noted that despite Cuomo and de Blasio pledging to take action on March 1, 2020, they didn't follow through. On March 1, 2020, a 39-year-old women, who had returned the prior week from Qatar, tested positive for the Coronavirus. The next day, Cuomo and de Blasio at a joint news conference promised that their health investigations would track down every person on the woman's flight. They never did. The two continued repeating that their hospitals were among the best in the world and that New York had been trained for events like: 9/11, Ebola, HIV and the Zika virus. New York was not prepared and the New York Times could not blame Trump this time. In one straw poll, over 90% of the voters believed that Governor Cuomo had mishandled the Coronavirus in his state.

Andrew Cuomo was quoted as saying to a collection of reporters in March: "Excuse my arrogance as New Yorkers. I speak for the Mayor also on this. We think we have the best health care system on the planet, right here in New York. So, when you're saying what happened in other countries verses what has happened here, we don't think it's going to be as bad here as in other countries". It wasn't as bad as other countries. New York City had the worst performance against the coronavirus than any other city or country in the world. It should be noted that Cuomo also waited days to implement social distancing guidelines after President Trump put in place the Federal Distance guidelines. California acted a week before New York and although California has nearly twice the population of New York it has had only a fraction of the total deaths experienced by the State of New York.

Random Observations About the Corona Virus Pandemic

- The U.S. Intelligence Community concluded that China concealed the extent of the Coronavirus outbreak in its country, significantly under-reporting both the total cases and number of deaths it suffered from the disease. One funeral home alone in Hubei province had requested 5,000 funeral urns, which represented more than the total deaths reported by China. Deborah Birx, the State Department's immunologist said on Tuesday, March 31, 2020, that China's public reporting influenced assumptions elsewhere in the world about the nature of the virus. The medical community had concluded that the outbreak of the virus although serious, was smaller than anyone expected. She said: "We were missing significant amounts of data, now that we see what has happened in Italy and Spain". On April 7, the City of Wuhan, realizing the rising skepticism around the world about their reports on Coronavirus, revised its death toll by 50% from 2,579 to 3,869 Yet WHO wanted us to believe that China was being transparent and doing an outstanding job of reporting the nature and extent of the Coronavirus-19 in their country. China prevented international experts in January from visiting their Wuhan P4 laboratory and censored all research from the laboratory, so it could not be shared with the international public. We have even learned that the Wuhan P4 lab is undertaking bio-chemical weapons experiments. China is already the major supplier of illegal fentanyl into our country. Recently, enough fentanyl coming from China was seized by the U.S. government to kill 14 million Americans. Where are Fentanyl and other illegal drugs produced in mass quantities? In Wuhan, China. Fentanyl is 100 times more potent than Morphine and 25 to 50 times more potent than Heroin and China is flooding our country with these drugs. They are the major provider of these drugs, which are killing 30,000 to 40,000 of our citizens every year.

    Apparently, the killing of Americans by pouring vast quantities of illegal drugs into our country is not fast enough for the Chinese Communist party leaders, but the coronavirus may be just as effective by destabilizing our economy and creating vast unemployment in our country. And remember China didn't even announce the Coronavirus epidemic until January 20, 2020. We are too dependent on our major prescription and over-the-counter drugs from China, with 70% to 90% of major drugs that we depend upon are being supplied by China. We need to become drug independent as we have become energy independent.

- **Bill Maher** - I could spend pages discussing the abusive tirades coming from the liberal left media, specifically CNN, MSNBC, CBS, NBC and ABC, but I will narrow it down to only three. My choices are arbitrary. Bill Maher is the poster boy for hate and vitriol against President Trump, even willing to pray that Americans get sick and die in order for Trump to be removed from office. In August, 2019, Maher prayed for an economic recession, claiming it would tank President Trump's shot at re-election in 2020. And he went on to say that it would be worth hurting all the people of the United States to bring on the recession. Well, Maher got his wish. Think about it. At the height of our booming economy, with low unemployment and growing spectacularly, what possibly can bring down our economy other than a pandemic, that forces the shutdown of all business; massive unemployment and the deaths and sickness to 10's of thousands of people in the United States. The answer to Bill Maher's prayer was the Coronavirus. Joblessness, poverty even death is acceptable if the left can gain power and establish their socialist programs to curtail if not eliminate all our freedoms.

- **Mica Brzezinski** - Co-host if MSNBC's "Morning Joe" show with Joe Scarborough, went into a tirade about how President Trump had personal financial gain in his hawking of Hydroxychloroquine. "Follow the money" she said. Mica was parroting what the New York Times had explicitly said on April 6, that President Trump was pushing Hydroxychloroquine for personal gain because he had a personal financial interest in hydroxychloroquine. More details promulgated by reporter Brian Cohen claimed that Trump was hawking hydroxychloroquine because he had a financial interest in a French Drug maker, Sanofi, the world's fifth largest prescription drug maker, that makes a brand name version of Hydroxychloroquine. It turns out that three Trump family trusts have small investments in a Dodge and Cox mutual fund that has 3.3% of its investments in Sanofi. The three Trump Trusts have a total of under $45,000 in the Dodge and Cox fund and therefore their interest in Sanofi is between $99 and $1,485 at most.

- **Anderson Cooper** – On the "Anderson Cooper 360 degrees" show on April 7, 2020, Anderson Cooper declares that Trump uses the press briefings to cover up his own deadly dismissals of the virus for crucial weeks. He calls Donald Trump's response, "reprehensibly irresponsible". Like every other critic of President Trump, Cooper provides no specific reason for his hateful critique of Trump. Moreover, Cooper's hypocrisy becomes so evident when we look at his comments on CNN around January 29th, 2020, when he said: "if you are freaked out about the Coronavirus, you should be more concerned about the flu". What a hypocrisy. On January 31[st,] when President Trump ordered the halt of all travel to China and from China, his order was met with hollers of xenophobia from the likes of Joe Biden and Bernie Sanders and from every corner of the far-left media. Lenny Bernstein at the Washington Post wrote on January 31, 2020: "get a grip America, the flu is a much bigger threat than coronavirus". The Washington Post then published a piece on February 3rd, 2020: "Why we should be wary of an aggressive government response to coronavirus". As late as March, Sanders was insisting that he wouldn't have closed the U.S. borders to prevent the spread of the coronavirus and condemned the Presidents act as xenophobic. Now the Democrat hypocrites condemn Trump for not banning travel from China and Europe sooner.

- **The Coronavirus Team** - The criticism that the liberal left constantly levies at the Federal Administration is primarily aimed at Trump. The team he has assembled has been generally widely applauded. We start with **Mike Pence,** Vice President, who is coordinating and overseeing the activities of the Coronavirus team. He has led the team with his non-confrontational all America approach, even in the face of the constant criticism and haranguing of the president. **Debora Birx,** Chair of the Coronavirus task force. Her appointment has been widely applauded. She was the global AIDS coordinator under President Obama. **Anthoni Fauci,** Director of the National Institute of Allergy and Infectious Disease, he has been the top infectious disease expert since 1984, when he was appointed by President Reagan as NAID director. **Seema Verma,** Medicare-Medicaid administrator, responsible for overseeing both the Medicare and Medicaid program. Directed the unprecedented expansion of telehealth services throughout the country and directed hospitals across America to postpone elective services to preserve capacity. **Alex Azar,** as Health Secretary, he heads the Department of Health and Human Services with a proposed budget of $1.4 trillion. The budget encompasses Medicare, Medicate, Federal Drug Administration (FDA); National Institute of Health (NIH) and the Center of Disease Control (CDC). He controls the National Strategic Stockpile and President Trump's Defense Production Act gives Azar the authority to compel private companies to manufacture medical supplies including masks and ventilators. **Jerome Adams**, Surgeon General, the nation's doctor. **Stephan Hahn**, head of Federal Drug Administration. A longtime cancer doctor, he is responsible for fast tracking efforts for testing as well as overseeing the development and testing for coronavirus. **Steven Mnuchin**, Secretary of the Treasury, architect of financial relief for Americans laid off and businesses that were forced to close because of the coronavirus. **Chad Wolf,** Secretary of Homeland Security, oversees the reentry of thousands of Americans scrambling to return home from Europe and keeping non-citizens in Europe, China and South Korea from entering the U.S. **Robert Kadlec**, Assistant Health Secretary for planning and response, a career Air Force physician, he directly oversees the strategic national stockpile and also serves as advisor to Health Secretary, Azar. **Brett Giroir**, Assistant Secretary for Health and 4-star Admiral in the U.S. Public Health Service Corp; he is the point man for expanding the availability of test kits. **Larry Kudlow**, Director of the National Economic Council. This is the principal forum for considering economic policy matters and it is formidable. The council along with Kudlow, consists of the President, Vice President, all the members of the cabinet, plus the deputy assistant to the President for Domestic policy (Andrew Ohlman); Deputy Assistant for International policy (Clete Willems); the Administrator of the environmental Protection Agency; the Chair of the Council of Economic Advisors; the Director of the Office of Management and Budget; the United States Trade Representative; and the Advisors on Domestic policy, National Security and Trade and Manufacturing. **Robert Wilkie**, U.S. Secretary of Veterans Affairs. (VA). (The Veterans Administration employs approximately 380,000 and has a budget of approximately $250 Billio).n **Ben Carson**, Secretary of Housing and Urban Development.

This is the team that President Trump has put together overnight and these are the people that Anderson Cooper said are being bullied by Trump to cover up his own deadly dismissals of the virus for crucial weeks. And in direct response to constant criticism from the left that President Trump doesn't listen to his medical advisors; both Dorothy Birx and Anthony Fauci announced at a nationally televised briefing that their critical recommendations had always been accepted and adopted by the President. The critics from the left are not afraid to lie to the public to gain power and control over the country. We saw this during the, frivolous and false hearings on Trump's collusion with Russia; We saw this again on the false and rigged Trump impeachment hearings and we saw this during the Democrat interrogation of Bret Kavanaugh to become a Supreme Court Justice.

- **Nancy Pelosi** - House majority leader for four years, Nancy Pelosi has spent all her waking hours trying to remove President Trump from Office. Early on she accuses President Trump of being a Russian agent without presenting any evidence and her accusation was ultimately proved to be false and unfounded. Not to be deterred, Pelosi then made false and unfounded charges against, Senate Majority leader Mitch McConnell and Attorney General, William Barr. that they were part of a criminal cover-up. Pelosi was making treasonous charges, which were serious enough, if true, to call for the execution of the accused and even saying that she had proof, which was a lie.

Nancy Pelosi represents the 12th Congressional District of California, that incudes San Francisco. She has represented this district for 7 years from her $15 million gated home in the Pacific Heights area of the city; the most expensive neighborhood in the U.S.; the "Gold Coast", famous for its billionaires and record-breaking prices for homes. What has Pelosi done for the constituents of her city during the past 7 years? San Francisco has become a city with one of the highest crime rates and homelessness in the United States and the highest in California, during Pelosi's watch. In fact, the homelessness in San Francisco is so bad that whole sections of the city are overflowing with fecal matter, garbage, drug needles and litter. Yet Pelosi has done nothing to help her city. You may recall, that she criticized the Trump tax reduction for individuals, which gave a family of 4 around $2,000 more a year, calling that merely "crumbs". This is how in touch a woman living in a $15 million home with a net worth of $100 million is with her constituents. And what about her display of personal hatred for Donald Trump as she rips up his State of the Union Address on February 5, 2020? And yet the constituents choose to vote her into office again and again. Pelosi's dereliction of duty is matched by Maxine Waters, representative from the 43rd district of Los Angeles, primarily the City of Torrance and portions of Los Angeles. What has Maxine Waters (who doesn't even live in her district) done for the past four years for her constituents, other than spend every working day attacking and vilifying President Trump?

Remember it was Pelosi that called for the passing of the 1,500 page "Affordable Care" Act, stating that Congress had to pass it even though it hadn't been read by anyone. This political leader of the Democrats and the House of Representatives, would recommend to the House the passing of probably the most important bill of the Obama Administration, without having been read and over the objections of all the Republicans. The partisan Obamacare Bill was misrepresented as having conditions in it like keeping your doctor and keeping your health insurance, which were not there.

As the Coronavirus epidemic started to gain momentum, Pelosi was still focused on the impeachment of President Trump and then at the February 5th, State of the Union address by President Trump on nation-wide TV, Pelosi rips her copy of the State of Union address, that she had received beforehand as Speaker of the House. Pelosi rips it numerous times, showing her contempt not only for President Trump but for the office of the President. And as she rips the historic document, she holds it high for everyone watching on national TV to see. This was an address, where many parts were approved by both parties and even received applauds. The symbolic ripping could only be understood as a personal and emotional response by Pelosi, and her unlimited willingness to divide the country in time of a need for unity.

Pelosi, time and again claimed that Trump's delay in response to the pandemic cost the lives of many. She supposedly would have taken steps sooner. However, in late February, almost a month after President Trump had closed our borders to China, Pelosi was in San Francisco's Chinatown encouraging people to go out in public and spend their money at local businesses in Chinatown, despite national concerns regarding the spread of the Coronavirus. On February 24th, Pelosi said: "We want to be careful how we deal with it, but we want to say to people "come to Chinatown". Here we are and come and join us. And yet with her usual level of hypocrisy, Pelosi quickly accused the President for not doing more to combat the spread of the virus.

On March 25th, the Senate passed a historical $1.6 trillion stimulus package. It passed by a unanimous bipartisan vote of 96-0. It was the largest emergency package in the history of the United States. The stimulus package consisted of the following:

	$ Billions
Direct Payments to individuals and families	250
Small Business Loans	350
Unemployment Insurance benefits	250
Loans to distressed companies	500
Hospitals	130
State and Local Governments	150
Total	**$1,630**

It was primarily drafted by the Senate Republicans but the Democrats blocked its passing for two days with procedural roadblocks. It then had to be turned over to the House of Representatives for passage and of course, Nancy Pelosi.

Nancy Pelosi hogtied Congress for almost an entire week from getting the critical stimulus package passed and the critical funding distributed. How many died because of the one-week delay will never be known, but we do know that the pandemic threat that one week means 10's of thousands of more deaths in the United States What could possibly be the reasons that Pelosi would delay the vital stimulus package? Here are some that she wished attached to the stimulus package before she would allow her majority Democrats in the House, support a stimulus package:

- $25-$35 million for the Kennedy Center for the Performing Arts
- $300 million for the Corporation for Public Broadcasting
- Tax credits for solar panels and windmills
- Require every state that accepted relief, guarantee 14 days of early voting by absentee ballots mailed to all registered voters; a ban on voter ID cards and prohibition of notarization or witness of signatures to authorize absentee ballots. This one would assure that non-citizen, illegal aliens and fraudulent voters, would be able to vote and determine the outcome of an election.

Pelosi didn't get all of these add-ons, but she did get the $25 million for the Kennedy Center. At what cost of lives? Then at the end of March, just when our country is in deep distress and disaster from COVID-19; just when we require our leaders to work together for the safety of our nation's citizens, Nancy Pelosi wants to launch another investigation into the President of the United States. She has already spent almost four years, trying to remove the President from office, paying attention to nothing else and failing. Now she blames President Trump directly for the loss of lives, never providing us with the precise reasons for this claim. On CNN she will charge President Trump with "fiddling, while people die".

And Pelosi is not alone. Supporting her is Adam Schiff who led the 3.5-year unsuccessful impeachment inquisition of President Trump. Now Schiff tells the Washington Times that he will be starting another investigation of President Trump. Does the hatred and the divisiveness of the Democrats ever end? And around the same time, Hollywood actress, Debra Messing indicative of the hatred and divisiveness emanating from the entertainment industry raises her voice in a tirade saying; "He (Trump) f.. king knew 150,000 Americans died and he did nothing. Trump owns every death". And Kathy Griffin wants to kill Trump with an injection of air. The hatred emanating from the left is unmatched since the time of Hitler, when he and his advocates raised hatred of Jews to such a level that he convinced the majority of otherwise decent people to condemn, beat, imprison and ultimately put to death 6 million people only because they were Jews. The mindset the Third Reich created in Germany, is no different than the mindset the Democrat leaders seek for their followers: That all Republicans are "deplorable"; that there is a special place in hell for Republican Women; that anyone who is pro-life is excluded from the Democratic Party; that all Republicans are racists and anti-feminists; that all Republicans should be hated; and even assassination of the President should be considered, by shooting, hanging, bombing, beheading, mass knifing or lethal injection.

- **Andrew Cuomo** – Governor of the State of New York on March 1, assures New Yorkers that the general risk to the state remains low. On March 3, the day after New York reported its first case of Coronavirus (on March 2), Andrew Cuomo at his press conference said: "This isn't our first rodeo. We are fully coordinated and we are fully mobilized and we are fully prepared to deal with the situation as it develops". Cuomo went on to say: "Excuse our arrogance as New Yorkers. I speak for the Mayor also on this. We think we have the best health care system on the planet right here in New York So when you're saying what happened in other countries verses what has happened here, we don't think it's going to be as bad here as in other countries". Cuomo would turn out to be totally wrong as New York, particularly the city of New York would have the worst outbreak of the Coronavirus in the world and also the most deaths. Cuomo also waited days to implement social distancing guidelines after President Trump put in place Federal distancing guidelines. California acted a week before New York and although California has nearly twice the population of New York, it had only a fraction of the deaths experienced in New York. In a Patriot pulse poll, 93% believed that Governor Cuomo had mismanaged the state in its response to the Coronavirus pandemic. Almost a month later in another press conference, Cuomo had to admit: "we underestimated this virus". In an interview on CNN, hosted by Jack Trapper, Chuck Schumer, who had attacked Donald Trump mercilessly for delay on social distancing was asked the following question: "Dr. Thomas Frieden, former head of the Center for Disease Control told the New York Times that if New York State and New York City had adopted social distancing two weeks earlier, the death toll in New York could have been reduced anywhere between 50% and 80%. Didn't New York politicians drop the ball here to?" Schumer's response, clearly exemplified his devious character and unwillingness to admit the truth, if it would be at all damaging to his cause. Schumer said: "Well, look, I think our governor and our mayor have done a great job. I think most of America agrees. It is very hard when you don't have Federal cooperation". No cooperation from the Federal government? What about the thousands of ventilators that the Federal government delivered to New Yok City and state, a state which had not stockpiled any? What about the Army Corp of Engineers turning the Javits Center overnight into a 1,900 bed hospital facility to treat Coronavirus? What about the rapid deployment of the Federal Hospital ship to NYC? What about the thousands of Federal medical staff including doctors, nurses, maintenance staff and attendants the Federal government made available to NYC and the masks along with other medical supplies that were also provided by the Federal government? And what had the state and city done for themselves to prepare for the pandemic? Tapper then said: "San Francisco ordered schools closed on March 12. Ohio did the same with only five confirmed cases. Finally, on March 15th de Blasio ordered schools closed with 329 cases and a New York stay at home would not be announced until March 20th. Schumer's response: "Look again; we were the epicenter. There was so much to do". Wouldn't this be the very reason why NYC of all places should have been leading the shut-down of schools and social distancing? And then Schumer re-iterated: "I think both Cuomo and de Blasio get very high marks for how they handled this".

But the worst evidence of Cuomo's mis-management of the Coronavirus was his transferring of coronavirus patients to nursing homes within the state to make more room for more victims of the virus. This was more than mis-management. This was gross negligence. Instead of transferring them to Javits Center, where there was plenty of room and the facilities and staff were suited for treating Coronavirus patients, Cuomo decided to remove them from the hospitals and send them to nursing homes that were not only ill-equipped and un-trained to handle Coronavirus victims, but housed the very people who were at the most risk of death from Coronavirus. On March 25, Governor Cuomo issued an advisory to discharge elderly patients with COVID-19 back to nursing homes. This would include individuals who were not originally residents of nursing homes. The residents of the nursing homes were well over the age of 65 and many were over 80 and most had pre-existing conditions that made their vulnerability even greater. Cuomo in effect signed the death warrants for many of them. He did this, even knowing that 25% of all deaths in New York from the Coronavirus occurred to patients in nursing homes. Over 4,500 patients with the Coronavirus were transferred from hospitals to nursing homes according to the Associated Press. The AP did the survey, because the New York State Department of Health would not release the results of their survey, on how many deaths were actually attributable to Governor Cuomo's order to transfer very contagious persons from hospitals to nursing homes. Why is there no outrage from the liberal left Democrats or its supporting media? Because they will cover-up any adverse or ill-conceived actions of a Democrat, particularly of those who are their "heroes" and stand in the wing to be Democrat Presidential candidate, if candidate Joe Biden keeps demonstrating his unfitness for office.

If this wasn't enough, Governor Cuomo, proceeds to fraudulently cover-up the actual death experience of nursing home residents. He authorizes the fraudulent reporting of deaths associated with nursing homes. New York State decides in April, 2020 to report only the deaths of those actually dying in a nursing home facility and not those infected by Coronavirus in a nursing home, but subsequently dying in a hospital. This was contrary to every other state reporting of nursing home deaths from Coronavirus. As a result, New York was reporting the lowest rate of nursing home deaths among the eight states with the highest nursing home mortality rates. Whereas, the other 7 states were reporting mortality rates from 36% to 66%, New York's fraudulent figures reported only 20%, the lowest by far of any of the states.

- **Mayor Bill de Blasio** – Not to be outdone by Governor Cuomo in his mis-management and negligence, on February 2, de Blasio is telling New Yorkers that the only way to get the virus is with substantial contact from someone who has it. "You can't get it from surface or temporary contact': de Blasio said. At the same time the Center for Disease Control (CDC) was saying it was possible to get the virus from touching a surface and then touching your mouth, nose or ears. On March 2nd de Blasio urges New Yorkers to go out on the town. On March 10, de Blasio says to MSNBC: "If you are under 50 and your healthy, there is very little threat here. This disease, even if you get it, basically acts like the common cold or flu and transmission is not easy". De Blasio was fatally wrong on all counts.

On March 2nd Governor Andrew Cuomo joins de Blasio in his obliviousness to the seriousness of COVID-19 saying: "We should relax because this is what is dictated by the situation. We don't think it's going to be as bad as other countries".

In early March the NYC Health Department advised collecting information from swabs in a procedure called "Sentinel Surveillance". The Mayor's office refused to authorize testing the swabs. The effort was blocked over fear that it might create a panic. The Mayor's office would not relent until March 23, and then testing of samples began, almost a month after samples were first collected.

On March 4, de Blasio advised New Yorkers, who thought they might have the virus to go to their doctor. This was exactly opposite of what the medical experts were saying. It wasn't until March 15th that de Blasio's administration allowed the City's health department to post an advisory, advising sick people to stay home. It was mind boggling how Mayor de Blasio refused to listen to the health experts.

On March 6, de Blasio informs his constituents that the virus can only last on a surface two or three minutes. However, CDC and WHO, the country and world authorities on viruses and pandemics are claiming that the virus could last hours even days on a surface.

On March 8th, when Dr. Ivan Lipkin a leading virologist, who had been researching the Corona (COVID-19) virus pointed to a recent study that showed that that the virus could last on surfaces for days, de Blasio claimed that his city's health experts were relying on real world scenarios rather than laboratory studies.

On March 11, Mayor de Blasio was recommending that New Yorkers could go on with their lives with only a few life-style changes. Other cities clearly saw the public health threat differently. San Francisco mayor, London Breed issued a shelter in place order and schools had already been closed. At the time, San Francisco had a total of 40 patients infected by COVID-19, while New York City had 463 confirmed cases. Mayor de Blasio's unwillingness to accept the medical authorities or pay attention to the full gravity of the pandemic, would cost the lives of many New Yorkers.

On March 13, Mayor de Blasio resists closing schools, as cases begin to climb in NYC. Teachers and parents seek to close the schools. Mayor de Blasio resists. Calls to shut down the schools reaches a peak and City Council speaker calls for the closing of schools.

On March 14, de Blasio told reporters: Let's not have a city with no bars, no restaurants, no recreation centers, no libraries". It would be Mayor Cuomo not de Blasio that would cancel the St. Patrick's Day parade. Louisiana's outbreak would become linked to the Mardi Gras celebration in New Orleans.

On March 15, Mayor de Blasio finally orders the closing of schools. 35% of the over 1 million students in NYC public schools had already decided not to attend school. Why wasn't Cuomo stepping in to close the schools before this date?

On March 15, de Blasio was still sticking to his 50% capacity for bars and restaurants. His delay in shutting down the bars and restaurants may have significantly contributed to the number of cases and deaths from Coronavirus in NYC.

On March 17, de Blasio for the first time speculates that a stay at home order might be necessary, but Governor Cuomo over-rules him saying no such thing was advisable.

On March 20, Cuomo would reverse himself and a stay at home order is finally issued. Cuomo and de Blasio didn't merely fail to take the necessary steps on a timely basis, they even took their constituents in the wrong direction.

At a March 22, briefing, de Blasio claims that "the jury is still out on asymptomatic transfer of COVID-19", even though Dr. Robert Redfield, director of CDC in Atlanta confirmed that as many as 25% of people infected with COVID-19 may not exhibit symptoms. CDC would eventually suggest that 35% of coronavirus cases are derived from asymptomatic carriers of the virus.

April 3, de Blasio finally acknowledges that asymptomatic transmission of COVID-19 was occurring. He claimed he just learned this in the past two days. This was 63 days after Dr. Fauci declared that asymptomatic transmission of COVID-19 was certainly happening.

May 3, Mayor de Blasio in his televised report to his constituents made some cogent admissions and revelations:

- The city was totally unprepared for the Coronavirus, in complete contradiction of what Governor Cuomo had previously on several occasions told New Yorkers. Mayor de Blasio stated that it had no supplies of swabs, masks or ventilators.
- Nobody was watching Italy, he said. The world depended on facilities in Northern Italy to provide swabs. Suddenly they became unavailable as the production facilities closed down as the cases in Italy mounted. The swabs were needed locally, where exposure to COVID-19 had become the worst in the world. This is hardly a reason for the Mayor not to acknowledge that COVID-19 was asymptomatic until April 3, or that he did not issue an order to stay at home until March 20.
- The Mayor informs his constituents that his city had just developed its own capability to manufacture swabs and that by mid-May the city would be producing 50,000 kits per week. And the kits the City would be making used the old swabs, which are inserted uncomfortably deep up the nostrils. The newer, less invasive swabs were not going to be produced by NYC and the City would still have to rely on the Federal government for it supply of kits. At 50,000

kits a week, it would take the city of 8 million, 160 weeks to test everyone in the city. Why did it take the city until May 4th to even start making kits and then only inferior ones; at a level that would hardly make a dent in the supply of kits needed?

- Mayor de Blasio, as part of his excuses for his mismanagement of the Coronavirus pandemic made it quite clear how difficult it was to get full testing kits made, supplied to hospitals and medical professionals. This involved performing the test itself, properly enclosing in tubes with the required solution, delivering it to a testing lab, obtaining the results from the lab, returning it to the requesting medical facility and ultimately informing the potential victim of COVID-19 as to whether he or she tested positive or negative. Nancy Pelosi and many other left leaning politicians would have everyone believe that this testing could be done over-night to 100's of thousands of people and that somehow President Trump was personally delinquent in his failure to do Pelosi's single, off repeated solution to just do more: "testing, testing, testing". This was the single theme of Pelosi and so many on the left. None of them ever mentioned any specifics as to how they would increase the number of tests, let alone mention the intricacies in performing a test. They would have us believe that all you needed to do was take a swab of a nostril and the test results should be available in under an hour. None of them ever mentioned the steps necessary to complete a complex test for the Coronavirus, until Mayor de Blasio used it as his excuse for his tardiness. Mayor de Blasio had inadvertently made it clear, if one would just stop and think for a minute, that Pelosi and many others on the left, including the media were providing mis-information on how easy testing could be done; falsely discrediting the President for failing to provide adequate and timely testing.

- Once de Blasio saw the error in his ways for not taking positive steps against the Coronavirus for weeks if not months, he apparently reverses himself 180 degrees and overnight seeks to institute practices reminiscent of Hitler's regime and right out of George Orwell's novel "1984". Mayor DeBlasio on a TV broadcast urges his constituents to spy on each other. He tells his New Yorkers that anyone who sees a group of people hanging together; or people standing too close together; or in a line; or a store with "too many" people in it, they should immediately take a photo of those involved and text it to 311. Mayor de Blasio then offers his assurance that the government will immediately step in and deal with the situation. During the Nazi rule in Germany, the Gestapo encouraged people, including children to tell them about anything that their friends, families or even parents were doing that was inappropriate, most specifically harboring Jews. The Gestapo leaders would proclaim that their successful annihilation of so many Jews could not have been achieved without the "snitching" by friends, neighbors and children.

Thanks to the leadership of Mayor de Blasio and Governor Cuomo, it took over a week for New Yorkers to catch up to Seattle residents in enacting social distancing rules. Former head of CDC, Tom Friden estimated that if NYC had moved up its lockdown measures by just 10 days, 50% to 80% of the lives lost could have been saved. A former NYC health commissioner would describe de Blasio's performance: "it was just horrible; maybe it was his arrogance". Not only did Cuomo and de Blasio drag their feet too long in responding to the Coronavirus, they gave advice to their constituents to immediately see a doctor if they had symptoms, exactly the wrong advice and this mis-information along with the delays in acting cost many lives in New York. And if this wasn't enough, Cuomo and de Blasio ordered moving Coronavirus patents out of hospitals to ill-equipped nursing homes, filled with elderly people many with pre-existing conditions; the very people most susceptible to dying from the Coronavirus. The media would suggest that the Trump administration caused the death of many people. They never provide specifics as to how President Trump and his administration failed the public, or specifically what more they should have done? Yet, although the facts surrounding the performance of de Blasio and Cuomo reveal severe ignorance and negligence on their part, the liberal left politicians and the media are silent.

Finally, we should look at Governor Cuomo's and Mayor de Blasio's performance compared to the rest of the United States. Remember, Cuomo kept telling us that his state had the best medical facilities in the world. Here are some basic facts, detailed later in a chart. As of September 20, 2020, New York had 482,821 cases representing 6.9% of our nation's total cases and its 33,170 deaths represented 16.3% of the nation's total deaths. New York experienced 1,705 deaths per one million population. By way of contrast, California, experienced only 379 deaths per million people. Thus, New York, had 4.5 times as many deaths per million people as California. Even though California has twice the population of New York, New York's actual lives lost to COVID-19 exceeded California by 2.2 times. Yet after first praising Trump, Cuomo consistently blamed him for his state's performance, while California Governor Newsom always appreciated the Administration's support.

Three states in the top 5 in terms of casualties were Texas, Florida and Georgia, each run by Republican Governors. Although these states had very high numbers of total cases, they had far lower death rates, even though Florida has an extremely high percentage of senior citizens. New York experienced from 2.7 to 3.3 times the death rates of Texas, Florida and Georgia, yet Cuomo claimed to have the best medical care in the country. Note that California, Texas and Florida have larger populations than New York. (In millions of people: California, 39.6; Texas; 28.7, Florida, 21.2; New York, 19.5)

The 9 Democrat states cited in the following chart represent 33.4% of all the COVID-19 cases and 51.8% of all the COVID-19 deaths in the U.S. And what do the 9 states have in common? They are all run by Democrats. New York, New Jersey, Connecticut and Massachusetts alone account for 31.0% of all the deaths in the United States and in comparison with Texas, Florida and Georgia the death rates of these four states are from 2.0 to 3.5 times higher. These four states accounted for 63,144 deaths. If these states had only matched the average death rate per million in the United States, they would have had only 25,321 deaths; 37,823 less deaths than actually occurred. If these states had matched the average performance of Texas, Florida and Georgia, the four states would have experienced only 24,184 deaths or a total of 38,960 less deaths would have resulted.

New York and New Jersey's exceedingly high death rates were substantially caused by the arbitrary and extremely negligent assignment of COVID-19 patients to nursing homes unequipped to handle COVID patients. These were the elderly with pre-existing conditions and therefore the most susceptible to COVID-19. Many of the residents were infected and died. And yet, the New York leadership would seek to place blame elsewhere.

Finally, we should compare the performance of New York, New Jersey, Massachusetts and Connecticut to the rest of the world. The death rates per million of these four states ranged from 1,260 to 1,822 per million. Compare this to the 10 worst performing countries around the world: Belgium (857); UK (614); Peru (949); Spain (652); Italy (591); Sweden (580), Chile (640), Brazil (647), Mexico (569) and Ecuador(626) . Yet the four states' average death rate per million of 1,534 is 2.3 times the average of the ten countries (672) with the highest death rates in the world.

Coronavirus Experience By State - 9/20/2020

(From Worldometer.Info)

	Cases	% of Total	Deaths	% of Total	% Deaths to cases	Per 1 million Cases	Deaths
Total Country	6,972,163		203,880		2.92%	21,064	616
State							
New York	482,821	6.9%	33,170	16.3%	6.87%	24,819	1,705
New Jersey	202,845	2.9%	16,187	7.9%	7.98%	22,837	1,822
Connecticut	55,527	0.8%	4,492	2.2%	8.09%	15,574	1,260
Massachusetts	127,181	1.8%	9,295	4.6%	7.31%	18,452	1,349
Illinois	275,054	3.9%	8,672	4.3%	3.15%	21,706	684
California	783,957	11.2%	14,987	7.4%	1.91%	19,841	379
Michigan	128,087	1.8%	6,969	3.4%	5.44%	12,826	698
Maryland	119,744	1.7%	3,879	1.9%	3.24%	19,807	641
Pennsylvania	154,261	2.2%	8,014	3.9%	5.20%	12,050	628
Total of 9 states*	2,329,477	33.4%	105,665	51.8%	4.54%		

* All Run by Democrats.

Texas (Repub.)	720,281	10.3%	15,172	7.4%	2.11%	24,841	523
Florida (Repub.)	681,233	9.8%	13,292	6.5%	1.95%	31,718	619
Georgia(Repub.)	305,021	4.4%	6,599	3.2%	2.16%	28,728	622

The Pew Research Center COVID-19 Analysis of May 20, 2020

A Pew Research Center analysis of data on COVID-19 deaths, collected by the Johns Hopkins University Center, found that as of May 20, 2020, nearly one quarter of all deaths in the United States from the COVID-19, have been in just 12 Congressional districts, all located in New York City and all represented by Democrats in Congress.

Of the more than 92,000 Americans who have died of the COVID-19 as of May 25, 2020, nearly 75,000 or 82% were in Democrat Congressional districts. Of the 44 hardest hit Congressional districts (10% of all the districts in the United States), 41 are represented by Democrats and only 3 are represented by Republicans. These hardest hit include: New York City, Boston, Detroit and New Orleans.

The next 100 hardest hit districts, which represent the remainder of the top 1/3 of country-wide districts, are also disproportionately represented by Democrats; (75 Democrats, 25 Republicans. If we then look at the 44 districts least affected by the COVID-19, 68% are represented by Republicans.

Yet the Democrat Congressional leaders not only hide these statistics from their constituents but also shamelessly seek to shift all the blame for their incompetence to the Republican Administration, when the primary responsibility for dealing with the COVID-19, rests with the states. The numbers are so overwhelmingly skewed against the performance of Democrat run states, that we must conclude that the greatest failures in protecting the lives and well-being of our citizens lies with the Democrat Federal and State leaders and they should be held accountable for the poor performance in the states for which they are responsible.

The Health and Economic Recovery Omnibus Emergency Solutions Act – HR6800 also known as the HEROS act.

On May 13, 2020, Nancy Pelosi and fellow Democrats passed the new Coronavirus stimulus package, known as the HEROS Act that would provide $3 trillion new Coronavirus relief. As typical of Pelosi and her fellow Democrats the 1,815-page bill had many items that had nothing to do with Coronavirus relief. Among other things, the HEROS bill would amend the American Vote Act of 2002 and allow a sworn signature as acceptable identification for voters on election days in all states, eliminating the need for voter ID's. What does this have to do with Coronavirus relief? More importantly, why would the Democrats want to open the gates to "vote harvesting" and voter fraud? Imagine blank voter forms being delivered to all prospective voters and a political party hiring "harvesters" to collect the ballots. The harvesters, could persuade voters how to vote; even pay them $50 or less to vote one way or sign blank ballots to be filed in by the harvester. What if, the harvesters would just destroy the ballots that did not back their candidate? Why do only the Democrats want mail-in voting for everyone? Is it because they are prepared to do a better job of harvesting either by fraud or intimidation then the Republicans?

In addition, the HEROS bill would provide $915 billion direct bailouts to state and local governments. These bailouts would be directed solely to the Democrat run states that have been managed irresponsibly for many years and would take hard-earned dollars from taxpayers in well managed states (mostly Republican) that have showed fiscal responsibility and redistribute those dollars to fiscally irresponsible states and local governments. $500 billion would go directly to bailout the poorly managed states and $375 billion to poorly run cities. These funds for state and local bailouts are not related specifically to deficits caused by the Coronavirus, but to all debt existing before the COVID-19 pandemic. The objection that the Republicans offer is simple and straightforward, namely, any bailout of states and cities, should be related directly to the loss of revenues and increased expenses arising from COVID-19 and not to bailout debt existing in states before the COVID-19 The HEROS Act also calls for stimulus payments to illegal immigrants and $25 billion to bailout the U.S. Post Office.

We could just as well be talking about New York, New Jersey, Massachusetts, Connecticut, Illinois, Wisconsin, all states with the highest debt, and high taxes. They cannot fund their liabilities within their state, so they choose to use the Coronavirus Pandemic as the way to get other states to pay for their negligence and mismanagement. This is in contrast to Republican run states like Florida and Texas, with low debt incumbrances. The top 6 states with the highest total tax rates and the top six states with the highest debt per capita are all Democrat run as follows:

		Total Tax Rate			State Debt per capita*
New York	(1)**	13.0%	New York	(1)**	$17,876
Minnesota	(5)	10.3	Massachusetts	(2)	14,132
New Jersey	(7)	9.9	Connecticut	(3)	13,989
Connecticut	(8)	9.7	Illinois	(4)	12,116
Illinois	(9)	9.7	Washington	(5)	11,927
California	(11)	9.5	California	(6)	11,865

*States with over 3.5 million population. ** Represents state ranking highest to lowest.

You will note that 5 states in the top 10 have been left out in the ranking by total tax rate. Except for Iowa, they too are all Democrat states and are as follows: Hawaii (2); Maine (3); Vermont (4); Rhode Island (6) and Iowa (10).

By contrast look at the two major States that are Republican namely Florida and Texas:

	Total Tax Rate	State Debt per capita
Texas	8.18% (33)	$1,759 (ranked 42nd)
Florida	6.56% (47)	$1,646 (ranked 45th)

From Ignorance to Insanity

Isn't it interesting and noteworthy, that all the states with the highest tax rates and the highest state debt/capita are all run by Democrats? These same states are the ones with the highest crime rates, the highest homeless rates and the highest drug addiction rates. And the Democrat Congressional leaders in both the House and Senate, have stood by and done nothing for their states in four years. All they have focused on is to accuse the President of all sorts of wrong doing and seek to impeach him for what turns out to be fraudulent claims of collusion with Russia.

And the programs planned by the Democrats and supported by Presidential candidate Joe Biden, particularly the Green New Deal and National Health Care Plans, will insure the continuance of the misery of massive unemployment that we have experienced from COVID-19 and assure that the lives of senior citizens will be shortened by being triaged out of medical treatment. Recently, Biden pointed out his seriousness of destroying our country through the rapid elimination of all fossil fuels, by telling us that he will appoint Alexandria Ocasio Cortez and John Kerry as the joint Czars of his Climate Change initiative. If the Democrats have their way, there will be long term massive unemployment and those over 65 will be marginalized, as medical services will first be provided to productive workers, not retirees. Do not resuscitate (DNR) and Death Panels will be features of a Democrat National Health Care Plan. The Democrats will claim this is not so, but how else are they going to pay for their National Health Plan? They will have to cut medical treatment and services somewhere and the primary candidates for this are the elderly.

Anecdotally, let's just look at California, Nancy Pelosi's state that she is supposed to be representing. Pelosi has virtually fiddled while California burned. For the past four years, Pelosi has been totally absorbed in the persecution and impeachment of Donald Trump, while the State of California crumbled. Not one day has gone by that Pelosi and her colleagues, Schiff, Nadler and Schumer haven't devoted their efforts to destroying the President of the United States. And all the time the tax burden of Pelosi 'constituents keeps rising; the costs of state and local government get further out of control and state and local government debt keeps soaring. At the same time, the crime rates and homelessness in California are some of the highest in the country.

California has 340,000 employees with paychecks over $100,000, which cost California taxpayers $45 billion a year. California's total debt burden, the highest in the nation, is $152.7 billion (followed closely by New York at $139.2 billion). At the same time, California has unfunded pension liabilities over $1 trillion and growing. Governor Gavin Newsom requested $1 trillion to be added to the HEROS bill to specifically bail out the states (all Democrat run), that have been fiscally irresponsible. What Newsom and other Democrat run states are looking for is to have the well-run, low tax, virtually debt free Republican states bail out the incompetently run Democrat states.

Let's look at some of the incredible excesses of the state of California that help explain why California is a high debt, high tax state. Auditors at Openthebook.com found that state truck drivers in San Francisco make $159,000 a year; 44 lifeguards in LA county make between $200,000 and $365,000 a year and nurses make up to $509,000 per year. 1,420 city employees out earn all 50 state governors at over

$202,000 per year. 11,310 state college and university employees are making over $200,000 per year. San Francisco, Public Works Director, Mohammad Nuru, self-titled "Mr. Clean" best known for his failed efforts in keeping feces and used hypodermic needles off the streets earned a salary of $269,500 in 2018. The San Francisco members of the so-called "poop patrol" were earning up to $184,000 each.

In the community college system, 10,807 employees made six figures and 247 made more than $200,000. K through 12 payrolls show 109,627 teachers and administrators each earning over $100,000 per year and 15,735 are retired with over $100,000 /yr. pensions. Ten educators in California have retired on $300,000/yr. pensions. When El Camino College President, Thomas Fallo was criticized for his supersized salary of $345,000, he simply retired and now receives a pension of $314,021. Administrators of student unions on state college campuses are paid up to $206,000/yr. and they receive pensions up to $136,000/yr. There are 314 six figure administrators of various government associations, with the head of Southern California Association of Governments (SCAG) making $289,109/yr.

In the city of Fremont (population 230,000), there are 700 employees making an average of $130,000 year. Every man woman and child in the city is paying about $400/ yr. to support these 700. The Sanitation District of LA has a history of spiking salaries in the final years of employment to pad pensions. The five highest earners all make over $300,000 and two are retired with pensions of $320,000 and $360,000. In some cases, pensions exceed the current salary of the employee. These outrages are not limited to California. They are indicative of what has happened in many, if not most of the Democrat run states. And now, Pelosi and others see a way out by holding the Federal government Coronavirus assistance programs hostage to demands for money to bail out their states because of their incompetent and outrageous performances.

Obviously, these 340,000 California employees, together with their families and those that expect to eventually attain these lush jobs, will consistently vote Democrat. They are bought and paid for. You don't bite the hand that feeds you. They are dependent on the largesse of the Democrat controlled government, which demands that the hardworking constituents who sacrifice by doing without; live from paycheck to paycheck; do without vacation, a new car or even an occasional dinner out and at the same time are forced to pay exorbitant taxes, so that the state employees can live in luxury, without any fear of being laid off.

A Bit about China

China hid from the world for critical months any information on the nature and extent of the virus; especially about how contagious it was and how lethal. They even hid from the world their own records of cases and deaths. They trivialized the COVID-19 either negligently or fraudulently. We may never know which it is, but we do know that China engaged in a cover-up that would cost many casualties and lives around the world. But the Chinese treachery did not stop there. More than a dozen countries on four continents have disclosed problems with Chinese made test kits and personal protective equipment. The problems have ranged from test kits tainted with Coronavirus to medical garments contaminated with insects. Yet the Chinese government is refusing to take responsibility for the defective supplies it is exporting.

After the pandemic hit Spain, the Spanish government spent $470 million to purchase supplies from China. The Chinese vendors demanded payment up front before making any deliveries. In late March, the Spanish ministry of health reported that 500,000 test kits from a single vendor were inaccurate and defective. The test kits manufactured by Shenzhen Bioeasy Biotechnology, only had an accuracy rate of 32%. Spain, one of the hardest hit countries by the Coronavirus was understandably outraged. The outrage made international headlines forcing Bioeasy to replace the worthless test kits. But the 640,000 replacements were also worthless. Spain demanded a refund. A week later, 350,000 Chinese-made surgical masks were sent to Spain, also defective. They were found to filter out only 71% of aerosols, when they were supposed to filter out 94%.

The Spanish weren't the only ones reporting defective equipment from China. Austria, Canada, India, Australia and the United States were making the same complaints. In the United States, the State of Missouri received defective masks from a Chinese vendor who refused to return the $8.25 million down-payment. Missouri is suing. The BBC reported that thousands of testing kits and medical masks coming from China are defective and useless. Austria reports 500,000 China produced protective masks as useless; Czech Republic reports 300,000 to 400,000 test kits to be defective; Slovak reports 1 million test kits valued at $16 million are worthless; The Netherlands reported 600,000 of 1,300,000 Chinese manufactured face masks were defective. Turkey reports that the test kits they received from China were only 35% accurate.

Where is WHO? Why aren't they protesting the consistent flaws in the supplies of medical equipment provided by China? Not one word out of WHO about the negligence on the part of China that has contributed to more global deaths. The Democrats are not outraged and they call President Trump xenophobic for criticizing the Chinese and claim that the Trump Administration is using China as a diversion from his own blame. Our pro-Democrat media doesn't mention these massive negligent and maybe fraudulent deliveries of medical supplies around the World and to the United States, but vehemently criticizes Trump for holding up WHO funding, pending investigation and for calling China to task for exporting the" Chinese Virus".

Are we prepared to have Joe Biden, pick up on the responsibility for managing our economy and the Coronavirus pandemic, in mid-stream starting in January 2021? There will be a substantial setback to our fight against the Coronavirus for no other reason than the government's actions are postponed during the time of changeover. Can we afford a hiatus of at least two to three months from the election in November to the Inauguration in January and then through the first several months after the inauguration? During that time, new staff is being vetted, replacing the old staff who were well educated and versed in the problems and concerns of our nation. Also, there is the time it will take the new staff to get up to speed on all issues, including the Coronavirus. Such delays could bring us back to square one in our fight against the Coronavirus and we will face more deaths and casualties from the Coronavirus, higher unemployment and a stock market plummeting to even far lower levels. Even if you do not believe this will happen, what about putting your faith and trust in Joe Biden? Will he continue to run our country holed up in the White House, as he has been holed up in the basement of his home since March? Will he continue to refuse to deal with people face to face and continue to hold China blameless? And what about all his miss-statements and "gaffs"? Does this inspire you to feel comfortable with a timid, somewhat senseless old man to run our country at this very difficult time? For three months, Biden holed himself up in his cellar, during the most critical time in recent history for the United States. He was not meeting with any one; nor providing his supporters with any plan that he would implement to fight the Coronavirus if he were president. He was offering no advice, other than to accuse President Trump of poor management. He ridiculed President Trump for criticizing China. Yet this was understandable as the Biden family were firmly entrenched in the Chinese Camp, especially with Hunter Biden obtaining $1.5 billion from the Chinese Government. And Biden was also strongly beholden to Ukraine for paying his son Hunter millions of dollars for doing nothing. If there ever were collusion between a U.S. politician and a foreign country, it was presidential candidate Biden. Yet the Democrats, the media and the entertainment industry continue to ignore Biden's obvious collusion, while continuing to attack President Trump even after an independent counsel found President Trump not guilty of collusion. And we have no idea where Biden stands on any issue, because it is always changing and he stays in hiding. When Biden ventured forth on Memorial Day, May 25, 2020 after 3 months hibernation, he mourned the death of American heroes and ignored the living. Biden was the best that the Democrats could come up with for our country and we are all doomed if he is selected.

The Coronavirus a "Window" into the Future planned by the Liberal Democrats

The Coronavirus has offered us a glimpse into our future if the liberal Democrat Socialists were to gain power over our government. I have previously forecasted in Chapter 12, that the plans the Democrats have for our country would result in the permanent loss of over 17 million jobs and an addition of almost 59 million to our welfare rolls. Our unemployment rate would be 17% and this does not include any losses in our steel or car manufacturing industries. We have already seen our unemployment rate zoom to approximately 20%, due to the Coronavirus. Hardest hit are the restaurant, airline and travel businesses. These industries and the people they employ will become permanently lost under the Democrat plans for us. They want to abolish all use of fossil fuels; do away with airplanes and eliminate cattle as a source of food. What part of the restaurant industry, especially the chain restaurants will survive if you eliminate steak, hamburgers and hotdogs from all menus. How about the restaurants specializing in fish? They soon will be gone, because the harvesting of fish at a rate of three or four times our current rate, to replace the loss of meat, will soon deplete our oceans to an unrecoverable level. Then too, how are patrons to get to restaurants? Are they going to be able to purchase an electric car, when the resale value of their gas fueled car is reduced to scrap value? And how will people go on vacation? There will be no airplanes. Will people drive three days each way to spend one day in Disney World? Or what happens to all the cruise ships, that use fossil fuel? There will be no foreign travel, no domestic travel, no vacations for anyone, if the planned programs of the Socialist Left become a reality. We are living in this hell right now. It started in the U.S. in late January 2020 and will last through the summer of 2020 and maybe even into the fall. It is a reality, but temporary. The plans of the Democrats will make the disruption to our economy permanent. Our way of life will mirror, Venezuela, Cuba, North Korea, China, Somalia, Iran and many other countries that have the hardships of a socialist regime imposed upon them.

The Coronavirus has also shown us, how the Democrats plan to control our lives. We are quarantined in our own homes. All business is shut down that isn't considered essential. We aren't allowed to worship in our churches. What about all the small businesses, which are not allowed to reopen? How many families will be destroyed, by the State governors who refuse to allow small businesses to reopen? And what about the Democrat controlled cities and states, where people are encouraged to spy on each other and drones are used to assure the quarantine mandates of the government are being followed. And what about the Democrat threats of fines and even jail, directed at those who merely seek to provide for themselves and their families. President Trump and the conservative right want to get people back to work; the Democrats want to stall this until everyone can be assured that there is no threat from the Coronavirus. By that time our economy will have been destroyed beyond repair.

We have shown wherever the Democrats have been in control, there has been massive suffering. We have pointed out the major cities of the United States, which under Democrat control have the highest crime and murder rates. We have discussed how the state's worst hit by the Coronavirus are all Democrat run. In many instances the medical facilities have been unavailable or understaffed and the necessary medical supplies have been non-existent. In almost every instance, the state has tried to blame the Trump administration for their own failures. But how do the Democrats intend to address our country's future medical needs? Through a Nationalized Medical Program and eliminating profits of the private pharmaceutical industry. Where is the future medical research to meet the needs of our country going to come from? Are we going to rely on our Federal government to replace private enterprise? Will the State Run Health Care system be the source of all future research; the development of vaccines, new, state of the art medical equipment, hospital facilities and medical staffing for the whole country? Look at how the U.S. government failed in running our Veteran's hospitals, created to serve about 20 million veterans. Now the government under Democrat leadership plans on taking on the responsibility for 320 million Americans. Can we expect our government to successfully nationalize all the hospitals in the United States?

Another example of how poorly a Nationally controlled business fails under Socialism is our U.S. Postal service. The U.S. Post office is over $55 billion in debt and growing. The Democrat proposal, presented by House majority leader Nancy Pelosi called for approximately $25 billion of the emergency funds targeted for use to fight the Coronavirus pandemic, be applied to bailing out the U.S. Post Office.

How many necessary health programs will have to be cut, if the Democrats take control of our government just to meet the staggering costs of the programs they are proposing? I have previously discussed triage and this not only is likely under Democrat control of our government, but will be absolutely necessary. Those of us over 65 will be expendable. Do not resuscitate (DNR) will be the order of the day. Democrat death panels will be created that will determine who will get critical treatment and the elderly, will be placed at the bottom of the list. This is exactly what happens in Canada, a socialist medical system that the Democrats applaud.

Let us take a brief look at socialized medicine in Great Britain and Canada. Forbes issued a report in February, 2018, which described just how bad a nationalized system of health care can be. In the United Kingdom, the starting average salary for a doctor is $32,000 which is 17% below the nation's average income. To put it in prospective, a British Subway operator makes approximately double the income of a junior doctor each year and the junior doctor is often subject to 100-hour work weeks. The salaries do grow, but the average pay of a general practitioner is about ½ that of a primary care doctor. In January, 2018, 68 emergency room physicians in Great Britain reported that it was common to treat patients in hospital corridors and as a result some are dying prematurely. The British National Health service has created a continuing surge in rationing of medical services and has unfairly and unnecessarily expanded the time a patient will spend in pain. Cataract surgery, hip, shoulder, knee replacement, treatment for arthritis are triaged almost out of existence for patients over 65. A 2017 poll of Britain's National Health Doctors found that coupled with inadequate compensation, 40% of general practitioners planned to quit because of the "perilously" low morale existing in their medical profession.

Canada is no better. There the government run health system is so overburdened that the typical patient waits 21.2 weeks for treatment from a specialist after receiving a referral from his general practitioner. In individual provinces, the wait time is even more: New Brunswick 42 weeks; Nova Scotia 38 weeks; Prince Edward Island 32 weeks.

Turning to the United States, it is forecast that we will see a shortage of 122,000 doctors by 2032. This is the forecast before the threat of a Nationalized Health system. Such a shortage will be substantially expanded, as it is the intention of the Democrat national health system to drastically reduce the income of doctors by as much as 40%. Presidential candidate Bernie Sanders constantly bombarded us with the argument that we are the only major country without a national health care system. Did it ever occur to those who thought this was a great reason to have a national health care system, to actually look at how unsuccessful and inadequate they were in other countries? Or even better have they looked at our own Veterans Administration hospital scandal under President Obama which was the nationalized health plan for the limited population of Veterans?

Hypothetical treatment of a Pandemic under a Nationalized Medical System

The Democrats have touted a Nationalized medical system like never before; even greater than during the Obama administration, which succeeded in passing the Affordable Care Act and took our country a long way toward socialized medicine. Now the cries of the Democrats have become more stringent. Bernie Sanders and other leading Democrats wish to dismantle Big Pharma, saying these companies make outrageous profits for their investors and they must be eliminated. In short, the Democrats want to take over control of Big Pharma and the research and development of all drugs and vaccines. There would no longer be any independent research without approval of some politically appointed medical board. They would issue cost plus contracts for pharmaceutical companies and designate specifically what research they can do. A pharmaceutical contractor would have to submit a proposal, which would include an efficacy statement and some statement of cost/ benefit. Pure research will become a thing of the past. There wouldn't be 20 or 30 different companies seeking to find a vaccine for another Pandemic and just the authorization to proceed will take 6 months or more. There will be no private investors willing to take an investment risk, where the only reward is measured in cost plus contracts. Rapid development of new products will disappear.

Speaking from decades of experience contracting with the Federal Government, it is extremely cumbersome, slow moving and heavily skewed in favor of the lowest cost as opposed to the best quality. It is not unusual for Federal contracts to take well over a year for approval; requiring multiple layers of Federal contract reviewers that will review bids from 10 or more companies; require many changes in bid specifications and a number of resubmissions of updated bids. Eventually the number of acceptable bids is reduced to 3 or 4. Then the Federal contracting officers requiring each vendor to make a formal presentation with slides and videos, all leading to a final award. The federal contracting officers, work only from 9 to 5 and will postpone any reviews or actions for holidays and vacations. At 4:45 they wind down the day so they can rush to their car pools to get home. The cost of preparing a proposal can be as much as 5% or 10% of the total contract value. The final vendor bid can count as much as 60% of the Federal Government contractor's evaluation. Capabilities, staffing, facilities and experience can be worth as little as 40%. Why do companies take on Federal government work in competition with others? The contracts cover a lot of direct costs and overhead and hopefully the big profits are made in contracts within the private sector.

Capitalism and socialism just don't work together. It is an either, or proposition and our ability to develop vaccines and cures for new viruses, new diseases and new pandemics will virtually be eliminated. We will be solely dependent on a politically appointed medical panel of so-called "experts" and Federal contract officer technical representatives (COTR's), who will determine what will be developed and how much the government will be willing to spend. And being the best vendor for the research will not be a major criterion.

15 or more of the leading pharmaceutical companies are working to develop a vaccine to combat COVID-19 and they are leading the race to find a safe and effective vaccine. They are all using their own R&D money generated from profits made from the previous development of new products. These are the companies which Bernie Sanders and most on the liberal left want to eliminate. Big Pharma has been constantly condemned by Democrats for making too much money. It is the profits made by Big Pharma that are used for research and development and a small portion of which are returned to

investors, to incentivize them to make investments in these companies. The National Health Plans proposed by Democrats would virtually eliminate Big Pharma and leave us only with the Federal Government as the single source of pharmaceutical R & D. Instead of 15 or more companies doing independent R&D, we will be dependent on the Federal government to determine what vaccines and cures are to be developed, who will develop them and how much will be paid. The developments toward a vaccine for COVID-19 to date (June 2020) have been impressive and it appears that the time to develop a new vaccine will be reduced by more than 50%. The nationalization of health, thereby putting our Federal government in charge of all pharmaceutical R&D will exponentially increase the time to get a vaccine to market, if one can even be produced with one R&D effort instead of 15 or more. Who are some of the Big Pharma companies that Bernie Sanders and other Democrats seek to destroy; seek to cut their profits thereby reducing R&D efforts within all pharmaceutical companies? How many of these companies, which require large profits to sustain the development of new products will survive? These are some of the companies who among others have come up with 41 candidates for a COVID-19 vaccine. Many are not going to work. But we have 41 chances instead of 1 of finding a safe and effective vaccine. These companies include: Pfizer, GlaxoSmithKline, Inovio Pharmaceuticals, Johnson and Johnson, Novavax, Sanofi, Heat Biologies and Gilead Sciences to name a few.

Then too, we cannot forget how private enterprise stepped up to convert production to build ventilators, make masks, produce test kits and provide testing labs. How quickly would the Federal government be able to respond to these needs. A number of independent sources are essential to successfully combat emergencies. The Federal government has shown in the past that it cannot do anything successfully without the assistance of private enterprise. We saw this to be true in WWII and we are seeing it now in our war against COVID-19.

We are already concerned that the $5 trillion already being supplied by our government will create a massive increase in our Federal government debt burden. We also know that the coronavirus will cause some permanent job losses, and that any sustained unemployment will cripple our economy. Our government can only afford so much. Yet, the Democrat plans for a United Health system; free college and university education and the Green New Deal will cost us $13 trillion per year for 10 years and displace over 50 million people. The attending loss of tax revenues; the soaring interest rates, will leave no money for the Federal government to spend on anything other than pay interest on the $10's of trillions it will have to borrow. A Democrat led government will start ordering abortions like China has done, to curtail population growth. Penalties will be imposed for having children and forced abortions will be a reality. Look at Venezuela if you want a clear picture of what the Democrats have in store for you. Maybe the Coronavirus will awaken some to the reality of the impending disaster if Democrats come into power.

And the only weapon that the Democrats have used to convince the public that their programs are the right ones for Americans is to instill over-whelming hatred into the minds of many. Hate is the sole catalyst in the Democrat message. Their plans and programs would not stand the test of reason and reality. Like Hitler, Hirohito, Stalin, Kim Jong un, Saddam Hussein and others have done before, if you can instill enough hate into people all rational behavior disappears. History has repeated itself time and time again that hatred breeds ignorance and ignorance breeds insanity.

My dad told me, when I was young, that hatred was the most useless emotion one can have. It does not motivate anyone to a useful or positive outcome. It is different from anger, because unlike hatred, anger motivates one to do something about the anger. Hatred just festers. Anger motivates one to do something to assuage the anger. And love and caring, much more than anger are the greatest motivators of all.

The Perfect Storm

On June 30, 2000, the movie "The Perfect Storm" was released. The film was based on a true story about an event that occurred at sea off the coast of Gloucester, Massachusetts on Halloween, 1991. Fishing boats and rescue ships are pitted against the forces of nature, when they are confronted by three raging weather fronts, unexpectedly colliding to produce the greatest, fiercest storm in history. A perfect storm is an event in which a rare combination of circumstances come together and drastically aggravates an event. And that is what the COVID -19 pandemic has caused on our planet starting in the first months of 2020 and still continuing as this book is being written. The Coronavirus storm was under-reported; of unexpected magnitude; of proportions never before faced; with an endless cover-up and false information being disseminated by the perpetrator, China; with a level of contagion never experienced in recent memory and a lack of facilities and equipment around the planet to confront the pandemic. This was the perfect storm of 2020. Only this one wasn't limited to a group of fishermen off the coast of Massachusetts.

COVID-19, one of the most contagious viruses in history, spread rapidly around our planet, from Wuhan, China. The exact source in China is not clear, but evidence seems to be a lab in Wuhan, China. The Chinese Government apparently chose not to disclose the virus to the world, nor assist it in curbing the spread. On the contrary, while quarantining the city of Wuhan, the Chinese Government allowed thousands of Chinese to travel out of China to all parts of the world. China continued to under-report the number of cases and deaths from the virus in their country; nor did they even tell the world for several months that it was a new virus strain. China not only provided no assistance to the rest of the world, it sent defective test kits and masks that gravely impacted the effectiveness of the containment efforts of many countries, as I have previously reported. At the same time, many of our states were totally unprepared to combat the virus. They had not inventoried any supplies or equipment essential to combating the virus. It was analogous to our being invaded by a foreign army and we have no weapons or ammunition to stave off the onslaught.

Our country's first line of defense was dependent on China. But they provided us false information and sent us defective equipment. Our next line of defense were other countries for supplies, notably Italy, the major if not only supplier of swabs for testing. But the virus had shut down Italy, and any other country that could provide supplies needed them to confront their own COVID-19 invasion.

The next line of defense were ventilators that each state was supposed to have inventoried, along with masks, gowns, medical gloves, etc. But the states, particularly New York, New Jersey, Massachusetts, Illinois, Pennsylvania and Connecticut were virtually barren of any supplies. The political expediency was to blame not the Federal government for their own failures, but one man, President Donald Trump. He was the perfect scapegoat and it was to the Democrats political advantage to make people believe that the President alone and not the states was solely responsible for any failure of performance in dealing with COVID-19.

Nancy Pelosi was the poster girl for the use of COVID-19 pandemic for political gain. The simple and only suggestion made by Nancy Pelosi again and again as the solution to the COVID-19 pandemic was more: "testing, testing, testing". That's it. That was her plan. And she would imply that the Trump Administration was either doing nothing or not doing enough. Pelosi, either through incredible ignorance or an overt plan to deceive the public for political gain, wanted the public to believe that President Trump was ignoring her simple solution to the COVID-19 virus.

Testing involves having test kits and facilities available. We can't just wave a wand and have enough test kits, testing sites and testing labs available. Testing kits had not been inventoried by the states; the major international manufacturer of swabs, located in Italy had been shut down, kits from China were defective and American manufacturers had to convert their plants to produce kits, masks, ventilators and other necessary supplies. This does not happen overnight. But the biggest problem of all was the logistics of performing the tests. At the outset there was a 48-hour turnaround time from the collection of the sample to it reaching a lab, the sample being tested and the results returned to the testing site. Except for Cuomo and de Blasio, all other states were following the recommendations of the medical authorities that if someone thinks he or she has been infected, they must not go to a doctor's office or medical facility, where they could infect others. Testing had to be done in safe facilities, specifically designed to test for the coronavirus and not in Doctor offices, emergency rooms or clinics. Doctors certainly did not want to infect their other patients so they refused to perform the tests. These special facilities were not available, nor was a rapid testing methodology available. We may recall that the initial tests were extremely uncomfortable involving shoving a swab way up your nostril. Yet Pelosi and other Democrats with knowledge of all these impediments to rapid testing of millions continued to use the lack of testing by the Republican Administration for political gain, desiring only to create divisiveness in the United States, even going as far as to impugn President Trump of "having blood on his hands". The deceit and treachery of the Democrats in the face of "The Perfect Storm" showed no limits.

The Democrat Presidential candidate debates

Many of us watched the Democrat Presidential debates, that began on June 26 and 27, 2019. They started off with 20 candidates, which were split into two groups of 10 and held on successive nights. There would be 12 scheduled; 11 would be held, the last one was cancelled because of the Coronavirus pandemic. The first 10 would be before a live audience in a theater and the 11th and last would be without a live audience.

- June 26 and 27 – The First debate, held in Miami. Florida with Rachel Maddow and Chuck Todd as the key moderators. Like all the debates to come, this would start with a vitriolic bashing of President Trump. That would be the major emphasis of the debate. Unwieldy to say the least, we would learn nothing about the candidates' plans or objectives other than to get rid of the President, their one and only priority. Was this going to be the sole purpose of the debates; just to demonstrate who could hate Trump the most? The apparent victor in this regard was Bernie Sanders, closely followed by Elizabeth Warren.

- July 30-31 - The second debate, held in Detroit Michigan, also a two-night event with 10 candidates each night. This time Jack Trapper was the lead moderator; again, a far-left anti-Trump socialist. Nothing new. The same Trump-bashing.

- September 12 – The third debate, held at Texas Southern University in Houston, Texas, the number of candidates were reduced to 10 as the candidates had to meet polling and fundraising criteria. The candidates were now: Joe Biden, Elizabeth Warren, Cory Booker, Bernie Sanders, Kamala Harris, Peter Buttigieg, Julian Castro, Amy Klobuchar, Beto O'Rourke and Andrew Yang. More focus on bashing of Trump. More expressions of hatred and little if any substance. We come away from the debate concluding that the candidate that can show the most hatred for Trump will win the nomination. In all my years I have voted for a President 16 times and listened to numerous debates among candidates of both parties. Never have I witnessed the vitriol and hatred expressed in the 11 Democrat debates over the past year, all directed at one man and to the exclusion of any meaningful and substantive dialogue between candidates.

- October 15 –The fourth debate was held in Westerville, Ohio. The number of candidates debating has increased by two to include Tom Steyer and Tulsi Gabbard. With the exception of Tulsi Gabbard, all the candidates continued to mainly focus on their hatred of President Trump. However, global warming, getting rid of cattle, free tuition, nationalized medical care became the subject matter of at least part of the debate and even one, Andrew Yang would suggest to pay every American $1,000 per month. That would cost the U.S. government $3.8 trillion a year, slightly less than our total Federal Budget (prior to the Coronavirus pandemic). Couple this with $10 trillion a year for the Democrat Global warming program; $3+ trillion/year for a Nationalized medical program and $1 trillion/year for free college and university tuition for everyone that wants it, the Democrats plan to spend over $17 trillion per year or over 4 times our current pre-corona Virus budget. Yet the moderators don't ask and the candidates don't volunteer how they are going to pay for this lunacy.

- November 20,2019 – The fifth debate held in Atlanta, Georgia, in the Tyler Perry studio. The only thing unique about this debate was that all four moderators were women. We learned nothing from the debate other than the single goal of all the candidates was to get rid of President Trump and that it really wasn't important what they would plan to do if they won the candidacy and ultimately the presidency.

- December 19, 2019 – The sixth debate held at the Loyola Marymount University in Los Angeles is now narrowed down to 7 candidates. The candidates in unison expressed their thrill in the impeachment of the President. The issue of climate change was the second priority, but still no candidate told us how he or she would pay for the massive climate change program that they were proposing.

- January 14, 2020 – The Seventh debate held at Drake University in Des Moines, Iowa. There were now six remaining candidates: Warren, Sanders, Klobachar, Buttigieg, Biden and Steyer. Getting rid of Trump remains the main theme, but the confrontation between Warren and Sanders becomes quite bitter, with Warren refusing to shake Sander's hand at the end of the debate and commenting to Sanders: "I think you called me a liar on National TV". It should not be a shock to anyone that Warren had a proclivity to lie. Remember how throughout her life she claimed to be a native American to allow her to climb the ladder of success by claiming to be a minority? Or that she had been discharged from her job, because she was pregnant; or that her mother physically mistreated her?

- February 7, 2020 – The eighth debate held at Saint Anselm College in Manchester, New Hampshire. Everyone is now aware of the growing Coronavirus pandemic; yet a debate in front of a live audience in an enclosed theater is acceptable to the Democrats, although they would be quick to criticize President Trump for not acting early enough. We would be witness to more hatred and vitriol against Trump. But then there was an attempt at some serious debate. Biden asks Sanders to explain how Sanders would fund Medicare for all? Sanders could not answer. Then the candidates praised Senator Mitt Romney from Utah for being the only Republican voting against Trump's acquittal in the Senate impeachment trial on February 5. The candidates also agreed that abortion rights for women was the only absolute criteria to be a Supreme Court Justice.

- February 19, 2020 - The ninth debate held in the Paris, Las Vegas Hotel, in Las Vegas, Nevada. We are now well into the Coronavirus pandemic, but the Democrats are showing no concern and social distancing is not necessary as far as they are concerned. The candidates are now down to six with Yang and Steyer dropping out and Michael Bloomberg being added. Bloomberg brings with him close to $1 billion to spend on his campaign, many times more than all other candidates combined. Yet this won't even make a small dent in his wealth as he is worth more than $60 billion and the interest alone on that money at even just 3% is $1.8 billon year. Bloomberg, the new boy in town is immediately attacked by the others for his "stop and frisk" policies when he was Mayor of New York and also, he is called out for making derogatory comments about women. Sander's electability was called into question because a poll showed that 2/3's of American voters were not comfortable with a Socialist Democrat. After all, Sanders had previously extolled the virtues of Communism, particularly in the Soviet Union; Fidel Castro was his hero and Sanders even suggested that the United States should seek to emulate the economy of Venezuela. National Health care was heavily debated, but no agreement was reached on facts; on how to pay for it or what should be included.

- February 25, 2020 – The 10th debate, held in the Gailland Center in Charleston, SC. Tom

Steyer returns to the debate and now there are 7 candidates again. We are another week into the Coronavirus pandemic, and the Democrats are still showing no concern for the COVID-19 pandemic or even suggesting social distancing; although they are quick to blame President Trump's lateness in reacting to the pandemic. It is in this debate, that Biden claims that 150 million Americans have been killed by guns in the United States since 2007. That's approximately ½ of our country's total population. Many share my concern with how lucid Biden will be as president. The Democrat leaders are probably ecstatic that they will have a puppet in the White House that they can control. Clashes over foreign policy lasted about 25 minutes with accusations and allegations being fired back and forth between candidates with no apparent winner and no conclusions. The candidates were in disarray on foreign policy as they had been on National Health Care policy in previous debates. The debate moderators were soundly criticized for focusing too much on narrow policy issues; failure to keep control of the candidates' speaking time; allowing candidates to interrupt other candidates; applying debate rules in an inequitable way and permitting the audience to boo and jeer certain candidates without consequences.

- March 15, 220 – The 11th and final debate as the 12th debate, would be finally cancelled because of the Coronavirus. The candidates for this debate were down to three: Sanders, Biden and Gabbard. Warren, Bloomberg. Buttigieg, Klobuchar and Steyer had withdrawn. Bloomberg would spend upwards of $700 million and show nothing for his effort. Just imagine what this money could have done for the homeless, jobless and those in need of medical treatment. The debate had been moved from Phoenix, Arizona to Washington, DC. The debate focused primarily on the COVID-19 pandemic, which was discussed for almost 18 minutes. The major claim coming out of this debate camp from Biden who states that Trump had rejected test kits from the World Health Organization (WHO). Both candidates would compare the COVID-19 pandemic to the Ebola epidemic, a curious display of their ignorance of how much more contagious and deadly the Coronavirus is than Ebola.

- Where are we today in late May, 2020? The Democrat run states are still in shut down. Small businesses, particularly restaurants in those states are being destroyed with no chance of recovery; even though owners are ready, willing and able to more than meet the requirements for a safe environment: i.e. maintaining 6 feet separation; checking temperature of customers at the door; all staff wearing masks and constant sanitizing. People aren't even allowed to attend their churches because the state dictates that they remain closed. This occurs in some Democrat states where bars and restaurants may open, but churches must stay closed because as one Democrat leader stated that singing spreads the Coronavirus more than any other way. The Trump Administration seeks to institute a safe and well-regulated opening for all businesses, but it is up to the state to make the final decision. But in state after state the autocratic Democrat leadership is refusing to allow it. In Michigan, the Governor would not even allow homeowners to cut their own grass or get and plant seeds for their gardens. It is suggested by some Democrats that the 38 million unemployed remain so until there is a vaccine, which may be a year or more from now. In that case, there will be no economic recovery and our unemployment rate will go way beyond the current level to over 20%. This is acceptable to the Democrats, because they already have planned to create 15% to 20% unemployment by the programs they are suggesting if they gain power, namely their Green New Deal, which will eliminate airplanes, gasoline driven cars, the fossil fuel industry, the Health Insurance industry and even the cattle and meat industry. The Coronavirus pandemic is providing us a glimpse of the future; a future which will emulate Venezuela, Cuba, North Korea, Iran, and many other places in the world where meals are found in garbage dumps and starvation is the major cause of death. Socialism is not the answer. The socialist economic system has historically failed in every instance and it fosters dictatorships. We are getting a peek at how socialism operates in our own country at the state level. They dictate that you cannot go to work; that you must stay holed up in your home; that you can't go to church; and that you will be herded into facilities chosen by the state, even if it means higher death rates.

The Murder of George Floyd and the resulting riots.

On May 25, 2020, George Floyd an African-American was killed in Minneapolis, Minnesota, when a white Minneapolis police officer, Derek Chauvin, knelt on Floyd's neck for 8 minutes and 46 seconds. There were three other officers, who stood by and watched, namely Thomas Lane and two Asian-American officers, Tou Thao and Alexander Kiuena. The arrest of Floyd was conducted after Floyd allegedly attempted to use a counterfeit $20 bill in a deli.

Chauvin was not arrested until May 29th and was charged with third-degree murder and second-degree manslaughter. The three other officers were charged with third-degree murder. This understandably appeared to many as an arrest that was late in response and that the charges were lighter than the crime should have received. Officer Chauvin, a 19-year career officer had over his career, 16 complaints filed against him. They were all dismissed with no discipline.

This was a terrible, wrongful act by Officer Chauvin as well as by his fellow officers, who chose to stand by and do nothing. And we can understand that some people will not only see the actions of these four officers as an example of police brutality, but also as an act of racists and white supremacists. The idea of racism and white supremacism are somewhat muted by the fact that two of the four participating in the wrongful taking of George Floyd's life were Asian.

It is appropriate to grieve over the needless, uncalled for loss of life; or the loss of any life for any reason. This year of 2020 has been particularly tragic for so many, not just the loss of over 100,000 deaths from COVID-19, but the loss of so many jobs and sources of income by so many families. I have empathy for all who have experienced the loss of members of their family or loss of friends, especially as the result of a wrongful act of another. My wife and I watched a drunk driver run down our two sons as they were changing a tire, hitting our car at 65 miles an hour and carrying them 120 feet down the road before stopping. The woman was so drunk, that but for her taking some offsetting drugs, she would have been unconscious. My oldest son was killed and my youngest son would be in a coma for 10 days and not expected to live. He survived, with severe injuries and would need a year of rehabilitation.

We are a grieving nation and we are trying to come together, to pray for each other, help each other and care for each other. We seemed to be a nation that was beginning to develop a spirit of caring and unity, despite the ongoing attempts by the Democrats, the liberal media and the entertainment industry, that sought only to criticize and lay blame on the Republican Administration and to sustain hatred, descension and disunity in our country. The terrible, life destroying COVID-19 pandemic was bringing out the best in so many of our American men and women.

But the actions of Derek Chauvin would trigger protests and terrible riots in many cities across our nation. The protests would encompass all the hate, anger, destruction and violence, that our socialist left leaders and their supporters in the media, entertainment industry and our schools have been inundating us with during the past 4 years. Thousands of people across the United States that never even knew the name of George Floyd, have used the wrongful death of George Floyd as a reason to destroy the property, businesses and livelihoods of people both black and white, who are totally innocent of any wrongdoing and had absolutely nothing to do with the murder of George Floyd. We would learn that over 100 businesses in Minneapolis alone, have been totally destroyed by the raging rioters. These tragedies are occurring nation-wide and we are a long way from knowing just how many deaths and how much damage will ultimately be done by these treacherous, rioting mobs.

The chants "black lives matter" once again are raised loudly. It is assumed that the actions of Derek Chauvin as heinous as they were, had to be racist motivated. Whites are often assigned the label by Blacks that they are white supremacists or racists. If Chauvin had murdered a white, there would be no cause for the rioting, the burning, the stealing and the destruction of property throughout the United States. Did any of the rioters seek to determine what were Chauvin's relationships with the black community? Was he considered a racist by his black police colleagues? If we stop to think about it, maybe the acts of the rioters were racist inspired; but not by white racists but rather by black racists. Whether black or white, all in our community must evaluate each other, not on some wrong-thinking basis of the color of our skin, but on the basis of who the individual is. Racism of any kind should not be tolerated, whether white or black. The actions of Derek Chauvin may well have been racially motivated. But the acts of violence, mayhem and destruction across or country were racially motivated as well. This is the "from ignorance to insanity" that is the title of this book.

The response of so many on the liberal left was that we have to let people vent with violence, no matter how many innocent people are hurt. Lawlessness and anarchy are actually condoned by the left. Is that what we want for our country, that any time a group is angered by a wrongful action by the state or local government or wrongful action by a person of authority, that gives the group of people the right to gather not to just protest, but to riot and do violence within their community? In Minneapolis, the police just abandoned their responsibility to the community. They disappeared from the streets; they were nowhere to be seen. They simply faded away and allowed the rioters to beat, injure and even kill innocent people and destroy businesses, burn down buildings and steal property without any fear of being charged or arrested for their crimes.

What justification is it for someone, either individually or within a group in Oakland, Chicago, St. Louis, Washington DC; Los Angeles or many other cities for that matter, destroy businesses, physically confront and attack innocent people and break into stores to loot them or just wantonly destroy, How can this be considered by some leaders to be a person's "right to vent". The message in the ancient Bible, the Torah, tells us that we should not kill or steal and we should honor our parents. These are three of the Bible's Ten Commandments, that the rioters violated constantly, every night for over week, all over our country.

So far, at the time of this writing, more than 20 major cities besides Minneapolis have engaged in violence and turmoil. Buildings are destroyed, fires are set, stores are burglarized, guns are fired, knives and rocks are thrown, all explained away by some Democrats as the rights of people to vent. What are some of the other cities that have witnessed hate, violence and destruction? They are: Atlanta, Chicago, Denver, Los Angeles, Memphis, New York, Oakland, Philadelphia, Portland, Oregon, Salt Lake City and Washington, DC. This is only the beginning. The deaths and injuries to human beings is just beginning. Damage to property and livelihoods is already rampant.

The liberal left has continually demonstrated that it is the right of people to disregard any law that they don't like. For years Democrats and Republicans alike were in agreement about illegal immigrants being restricted from coming into the United States. President Clinton, President Obama, Hilary Clinton, Nancy Pelosi, Chuck Schumer, Jerry Nadler and many others on the left were as vocal in opposition to open borders as the Conservative right. In fact, there were laws prohibiting illegal aliens from coming into, or staying in the United States that are still the law of the land. But they are not enforced in many Democrat run states. Now the liberal left, contrary to the laws they had previously agreed to, want open borders; no walls; amnesty for all illegal aliens and the same benefits for aliens that a citizen has, even the right to vote, free college tuition and free medical. And in violation of Federal law, the Democrat run states have created "sanctuary cities" and "sanctuary states" to protect illegal aliens that break our laws. The hate, violence, destruction proceeding from the death of George Floyd is a natural consequence of the hate, violence and lawlessness that has descended upon us from the liberal Left these past four years.

I turn finally to the New Testament and a quote from Apostle Paul's letter to the Galatians 6:7: "Do not be deceived… A man reaps what he sows". A nation where the leaders from the left along with, their supporting media, the entertainment industry and our educators continue to bombard us with hate and violence; they will only receive more hate and violence in return. The response to the death of George Floyd, is exactly what we should have expected, as so many of us have been trained not only to accept but to participate in the hatred that has become the commonplace of American ideology.

And when we see every night during the last week in May, 2020, the carnage that was being wrought throughout the United States by the most hateful, mean-spirited people in our country, who have no sense of moral purpose and lack any regard for humanity, we think back on "Kristallnacht" Nacht". This was the night of broken glass in Germany, on November 9-10, 1938. It was the night that the Nazis along with German citizens, torched synagogues, vandalized Jewish homes, schools and businesses and killed close to 100 Jews. On those nights, the non-Jewish citizens were encouraged to vent their anger against Jews. This was just the beginning. It would eventually lead to the enslavement, and eventual genocide of 6 million people.

And there cannot be a single true Christian or Jew among the thousands of perpetrators, who randomly and viciously destroyed the property of others and injured and killed innocent people. The Hebrew Bible in Exodus 20: 1-17 and Deuteronomy 5: 4-21 gives us the 10 Commandments, three of which are clearly violated by the rioting throngs, namely: Thou shall not steal; thou shall not kill and thou shall honor thy father and mother. Jesus confirms these commandments in Matthew 16-19 and adds: "Thou shalt love thy neighbor as thyself". The actions of so many rioters even broke the more ancient rule: "An eye for an eye". How can the actions of so many be justified on any basis? Yet many political leaders, many media spokespersons and many in the entertainment industry either outright support the atrocities during the week, or at least believe that people all over the country have the right to vent their anger on the innocent and blameless for a terrible, wrongful act of four policemen in Minneapolis.

Hate, Hubris, Hypocrisy

I have finally come to the end of my book. When I started, I had entitled the book: "From Ignorance to Insanity; Observations of an Old Man". Then, when the Coronavirus pandemic hit America, I was not sure this was the best title. Oh, I did focus on hate right from the beginning, but until the Coronavirus, I wasn't convinced that there was so much hate in America that it would obscure wisdom and the search for truth. I believed that if people just examined the facts and objectively looked at what was happening in our world and more particularly in our country, we would come together as one. The Coronavirus pandemic has showed me that hate is so prevalent in our country, that many on the left offer nothing but criticism of the right, spending all too little time commending the wonderful acts of heroism of the first responders and the people of our country uniting to battle the horrors and hardships brought upon us by the COVID-19 virus.

Whether one believes in God or not, or whether one is Christian, Jew, Islam or any other religion for that matter, there is Wisdom in the Judeo/Christian Bible that many may have never learned and all too many may have forgotten. Here are a few sayings from the Judeo/Christian Bible that are as relevant today as 2000 years ago:

1. Proverbs 10:12 – "Hatred stirs up strife; but love covers all offenses".
2. Leviticus 19:27 – "You shall not hate your brother in your heart, but you shall reason frankly with your neighbors".
3. Proverbs 26: 24-26 – "Whoever hates, disguises himself with his lips and harbors deceit in his heart: though his hatred be covered in deception, his wickedness will be exposed in the assembly."

4. Luke 6: 27-28 – "Love your enemies; do good to those that hate you".

5. John 3: 14-15 – "Anyone who does not love, remains in death. Anyone who hates his brother or sister is a murderer and you know that no murderer has eternal life residing in him".

6. Titus 3:2 – "Speak evil of no one, avoid quarreling; be gentle and show perfect curtesy to all people".

7. 1 Corinthians 13: 4-7 – "Love is patient and kind; love does not envy or boast; it is not angry or rude. It does not insist in its own way; it is not irritable or resentful; it does not rejoice at wrong doing, but rejoices with the truth.

We are now living in a country dominated by **Hate, Hubris** and **Hypocrisy.** Hate is the overwhelming mindset ruling our lives today. Never in my lifetime has hate played such a paramount role in shaping our lives; shaping our future. Our only hope is that people start thinking for themselves; do not blindly accept what politicians say, whether Democrat or Republican; do not accept everything the teachers say, the professors say, the entertainers say or the media say. We see how blind acceptance of the socialist leaders around the world failed the people in Germany, Japan, USSR, Cuba, North Korea, China, Venezuela, Iran, Sudan and many other countries. Hate is the foundation for all that is bad in the world. Hubris, is the excessive self-pride and arrogance that our leaders have used to get us to join in their hatred. Hypocrisy is the attitude of our leaders, that they will say whatever is necessary to achieve their ends without regard to its accuracy and even if it is totally inconsistent with what they have previously said. It is as if there is a special 3-H Club: Hate, Hubris, Hypocrisy Club, consisting of members who seek to gain power, and subordinate all people to their dictates. To be successful, as Nazi Germany, Japan and Russia showed us in the past, you need to bring together all the resources of the politicians, educators, media and entertainment industry. The best catalyst for this is hate. The Democrats have been very successful in doing this. Here are my nominations to the 3-H Club:

Hillary Clinton - Chairwoman emeritus of the 3-H Club. In my mind she has been a woman of hate for most of her adult political career and honed it to a new level since the Presidential campaign. She expressly stated that she hated all Republicans, that they were deplorable and applauded heartily when Madeline Albright said there is a special place in hell for women who didn't vote for her. She ignored the plight of her Ambassador to Libya and allowed him and three others to be murdered. She gleefully called for the destroying of all coal miners and their families and abused and disrespected anyone that didn't agree with her. We came very close to having a woman full of hate as our President.

Nancy Pelosi, Chuck Schumer, Adam Schiff, Jerry Nadler, Bernie Sanders – These are the candidates for President or Chairman of the 3-H Club. I have covered in detail the deceit the hate and dishonor to our country that these five have done and it is all based on their overwhelming hatred of those that oppose them. Along with their hatred, they get high marks for hubris and hypocrisy. They have used their hatred well to divide our country, like it has never been divided before. Kathy Griffin is the poster woman for the entertainers. In 2017, she held up the severed effigy of President Trump's bloodied head on TV and on May 26, 2020, she was suggesting that President Trump be assassinated by emptying a syringe full of air into his body. This even beats the assassination comments of Anthony Bourdrain, Madonna, Snoop Dog and Johnny Depp

Other members of the 3-H Club – There are so many more that deserve to be members of the 3-H Club, but this provides a good sampling

- The Politicians - Maxine Waters, Bernie Sanders, Elizabeth Warren, Alexandria Ocasio Cortez, Keith Ellison, Andre Carlson, Rashida Tlaib, Ilhan Omar, Ayanna Presley, Richard Blumenthal, Chris Murphy, Kamala Harris, Al Green, Robert Menendez, Tom Perez, Dick Durban, Jim Clyburn, Mark Warner, Angus King, Brad Sherman, Tim Kaine, Diane Feinstein, Chris Coons, Cory Booker, Joaquin Castro, Eric Swalwell, Steve Cohen, Bill de Blasio, Mitt Romney, Rohm Emmanuel, Eric Garcetti, James Clapper, James Comey, Peter Strzok, John Brennan.

- The Commentators and Columnists – Rachel Maddow, Bill Maher, Joy Behar, Keith Oberman, Chuck Todd, Brian Williams, Chris Hayes, Joe Scarborough, Mika Brzezinski, Wolf Blitzer, Larry O'Donnell, Steve Colbert, Jim Acosta, Al Sharpton, Louis Farrakhan, Anderson Cooper, Jimmy Kimmel, Max Boot, John Oliver, Paul Krugman, Donald Dutsch, Jennifer Rubin, Michael A. Cohen, Charles Pierce, Jonathan Chalti, Anna Navarro, Adam Davidson.

- The Entertainers – Kathy Griffin, Robert Di Niro, Anthony Bourdain, Barbara Streisand, Deborah Messing, Madonna, Whoopi Goldberg, Snoop Dog, Jennifer Lawrence, Chelsea Handler, Meryl Streep, Miley Cyrus, Susan Sarandon, Johnny Depp, Alec Baldwin, Michael Moore, Jim Carrey, Bette Midler, Rosie O'Donnell, Colin Kaepernick, Megan Rapinoe.

- The Educators –William Ayers, Ward Churchill, Nicholas DiGenova, Preston Mitchum, Mahmoud Ahmadinejad, Ricard Painter, John Eric Williams, Norm Chomsky, Randa Jarrar, Jerry Coyne, Katherine Rettwyler, George Ciccariello, Olga Perez Cox, Albert Ponce, James Fraser, Jennifer Gaboury, Michael Isaacson.

I apologize to all you liberal-socialist hate-mongers that I have left off the list. There are so many more of you that are deserving of membership.

Here Are Some Final Questions for the Reader to Ponder.

1. If the Democratic Party is the party of social justice, why then through the centuries has it been constantly the party of oppression of African-Americans and the party that controls the cities and states today where Black Americans are the most oppressed and victimized? After all, the Democrat party delivered to the Black Community, the Dred Scott case; started the Civil War

to preserve slavery; assassinated President Lincoln; instituted the Ku Klux Klan and the Jim Crow Laws and today allows blacks to be murdered at will in the cities that they control, like Chicago, Baltimore, Detroit, St. Louis, Memphis, Cleveland and Newark.

2. If the Democrats are supposedly the party of social justice, why are the 10 most crime ridden cities in the United States all run by Democrats? Why are the cities with the highest murder rates and the highest homelessness rates all run by Democrats?

3. The Democrats claim that they will provide the best medical care for Americans through a National Health Care Plan. Why then, are all the states controlled by Democrats the worst performers in the containment of the COVID-19 virus and have the worst records in terms of death and casualties per 100,000 population?

4. Why do Democrats keep insisting that global warming is caused by human emissions of CO_2, when CO_2 accounts for only 4 parts per 10,000 of our atmosphere, up from 3.2 parts per 10,000 in the 18th century?

5. Why aren't Democrats at least somewhat suspicious of the claim that global warming is caused by CO_2 emissions when 31,487 scientists including 9,029 PhD's came together and signed the Oregon Petition of 2007, strongly rejecting that global warming is caused by CO_2? Or the Heidelberg Appeal of 1992, where 4,000 scientists including 72 Nobel Prize winners advised that the relevance of CO_2 in causing climate change is based on pseudo-scientific arguments or false non-relevant facts? Or the Leipzig Declaration of 1996, updated in 2005, signed by 80 scientists which opposed the Kyoto Protocol, proclaiming that: "there does not exist a general scientific consensus about the importance of greenhouse warming from rising levels of carbon dioxide? Or the report to the U.S. Senate in 2010 regarding global warming where more than 1,000 dissenting scientists around the globe challenged the claims of the United Nations and former Vice-president Al Gore that CO_2 emissions will cause catastrophic climate change?

6. Even if global warming were caused by human emissions, does it make sense to spend $10 trillion a year for 10 years, increase those on welfare by 50 million; destroy our airline industry, our aeronautical industry, our military, our air force; our cruise line industry; our fossil fuel industry, our restaurant industry, our cattle industry, our meat packing industry and at the same time, create unimaginable inflation and cause our country to become bankrupt? And further, does reducing our CO_2 emissions to 0 within 10 years make any sense when the rest of the world would continue to expand CO_2 emissions on the planet, even if we effectively brought our emissions to a zero level?

7. If socialism is such a desirable socio/economic system, why has it failed everywhere it has ever been adopted? Look at the history of the great socialist regimes, Russia and Germany during WWII; East Germany after WWII, China, Cuba, North Korea, Iran, Syria, and Venezuela to name a few. We even have Democrat Socialist leader Bernie Sanders telling us that he would like to see us emulate Venezuela and Cuba. He was enamored with their regimes. He even sought to meet with Fidel Castro. He called Venezuela the socialist regime he would like America to emulate.

- The Democrats for 4 years claimed that President Trump colluded with Russia to gain victory over Hilary Clinton. This proved to be a false accusation. Yet Russia donated $0 to Trump but gave $145.6 million to the Clinton foundation. Why didn't that massive contribution come under scrutiny? Especially since it was around the same time that Secretary of State Clinton approved the sale of 20% of the U.S. supply of Uranium to Russia.

- Why was President Trump's 30 minute phone call with the Ukraine in which he raised concern about questionable activities of the Biden family sufficient to lead to an impeachment in the House only supported by the Democrats, while Vice President Biden's threat to withhold $1 billion dollars from Ukraine, unless they stopped the investigation of Ukraine Company Burisma was left unchallenged? You may recall, that Joe Biden's son, Hunter had mysteriously obtained a position on the Burisma Board, paying him $1 million per year for doing nothing. Hunter Biden's flight to China along with his father Joe Biden on a government plane would lead to the Chinese government paying Hunter Biden $1.5 billion. Again, no inquiry from Congress. Is the hypocrisy and double standard demonstrated by the Democrat party acceptable to the reader?

- The Democrat party claims that the Republican Party, is the party of white supremacists and white privilege. Hilary Clinton's daughter gets out of college and immediately has a job paying $900,000 per year with NBC. Joe Biden's son, Hunter winds up on the Board of a Ukraine Company and gets paid $1 million a year for doing nothing. He also receives $1.5 billion from China, while on a trip to China with his father. Nancy Pelosi lives in a gated community in a $15 million home in the most expensive neighborhood in the United States, overlooking her San Francisco district, where homelessness, drug addiction, human feces and used drug needles are rampant. She does nothing for her community for the past four years and considers $2,400 of tax savings for a family of four "crumbs". Michael Bloomberg spends $700,000,000 on campaign advertising and this is only pennies from his $60 billion portfolio; Elizabeth Warren is worth millions thanks to pretending to be a minority Native American. Bernie Sanders lives in two mansions and is worth millions. How can Democrats call the Republican Party, the party of white privilege, when their leaders are themselves the privileged white?

- Why do the Democrats say that if you believe in the sanctity of life before birth, you can't be a Democrat?

- Why do the Democrats demonstrate their anti-Jew sentiments by supporting Palestine and criticizing Israel, especially when the goal of most Palestinians is to annihilate all Jews? It was the Democrats that initiated the BDS movement. It was the Democrats who opposed the move of our embassy to Jerusalem. It was the Democrats that abstained in voting in the U.N. allowing Israel to be condemned for acts against humanity in regards to Palestine. It is the Democrat party that welcomes Lois Farrakhan, the radical anti-Jew who calls Jews termites. It is the Democratic party that has anti-Jew members, Tlaib, Omar and Carson.

- Why is a National Health Care Plan costing $3 trillion/year, such a good idea, when the Federal Government cannot effectively run the Veteran's Hospitals or the U.S. Post Office?

- We have learned that Joe Biden will appoint Alexandria Ocasio Cortez and John Kerry as his joint climate change Czars. Cortez wants to ban cars and planes. The Green New Deal insanity is for real. Are you prepared to give up all forms of transportation requiring fossil fuels? Are you ready to give up eating meat? Are you ready to live with unemployment rates in excess of 25% and inflation rates over 1000%?

We are facing the most critical time in the life of our country. The differences between the parties are no longer nuances. They are radical; they are massive. Once the choice is made, there is no turning back. Socialism like cancer is extremely hard to get rid of, if not impossible. The loss of freedom is permanent. The greatest thing we have at stake in this coming election is our freedom. We must not let it be taken from us.

I can only hope that the reader has read this book objectively and with an open mind. I have presented facts and opinions. You may take exception to some or many of them; you may disagree with them and may even develop your own opinions that are contrary to my observations. I understand in some instances I may be wrong in my opinions and observations. I welcome the objective thoughts and ideas of others that may show me where I have gone astray. The most important thing is for you, the reader to examine your own beliefs; for an examined belief is one worth having.

www.ingramcontent.com/pod-product-compliance
Lightning Source LLC
Chambersburg PA
CBHW081144230426
43664CB00018B/2791